Replanting Cultures

SUNY series, Tribal Worlds: Critical Studies in
American Indian Nation Building

Brian Hosmer and Larry Nesper, editors

Replanting Cultures

Community-Engaged Scholarship in Indian Country

Edited by

CHIEF BENJAMIN J. BARNES and
STEPHEN WARREN

Published by State University of New York Press, Albany

For information, contact State University of New York Press, Albany, NY
www.sunypress.edu

Library of Congress Cataloging-in-Publication Data

Names: Barnes, Benjamin J., Chief, editor. | Warren, Stephen, 1970– editor.
Title: Replanting cultures : community-engaged scholarship in Indian
    country / Chief Benjamin J. Barnes & Dr. Stephen Warren, eds.
Description: Albany : State University of New York Press, [2022] | Series:
    SUNY series, Tribal worlds: critical studies in American Indian nation
    building | Includes bibliographical references and index.
Identifiers: LCCN 2022002828 (print) | LCCN 2022002829 (ebook) | ISBN
    9781438489933 (hardcover : alk. paper) | ISBN 9781438489940 (pbk. : alk.
    paper) | ISBN 9781438489957 (ebook)
Subjects: LCSH: Community-based research. | Indians of North America—Research.
Classification: LCC E76.7 .R46 2022 (print) | LCC E76.7 (ebook) | DDC
    970.004/97—dc23/eng/20220201
LC record available at https://lccn.loc.gov/2022002828
LC ebook record available at https://lccn.loc.gov/2022002829

10 9 8 7 6 5 4 3 2 1

Contents

Part I
Community-Engaged Scholarship with
the Three Federally Recognized Shawnee Tribes

Acknowledgments

The editors would like to thank all those Indigenous researchers and centers who have inspired community-engaged scholarship (CES), including the Stó:lō Research and Resource Management Centre and the Myaamia Center. We would also like to thank the many non-Native scholars who have inspired us to think creatively and respectfully about how to go about ethical research. The list is long, and far from comprehensive, but first among them are Julie Cruikshank, Laura Peers, Luke Eric Lassiter, Kathryn Magee Labelle, Carolyn Podruchny, Jon Lutz, Keith Thor Carlson, Christine DeLucia, Jason Baird Jackson, John Bowes, April Sievert, and Alan Burdette.

In 2017, G. Susan Mosley-Howard and Haley Shea delivered portions of "Community-Engaged Scholarship as a Restorative Action," at the 5th International Conference on Language Documentation and Conservation. In that same year, most of the remaining authors delivered versions of these chapters at the Community-Engaged Scholarship in Indian Country Conference, which was held at both the Gilcrease Museum and the headquarters of the Miami Tribe of Oklahoma in Miami, Oklahoma. The presentations made at this conference could never have occurred without the support of the Native nations of the Miami Tribe of Oklahoma, the Shawnee Tribe, and the Stó:lō First Nation, as well as the University of Tulsa, Oklahoma State University, University of Iowa, Miami University, the Myaamia Center, the Oklahoma Indigenous Studies Alliance, the Philbrook Museum of Art, and the Gilcrease Museum.

We could not possibly name all the many shoulders upon which this work stands, and we hope that our efforts will further the conversation about the role of Indigenous nations, scholars, and communities within academia. If we could sum up our feelings in as few words as possible, we offer these words borrowed from our brothers and sisters from around the globe, as well as from Article 11.2 of the United Nations Declaration on the Rights of Indigenous Peoples, which encourages Indigenous peoples to seek

> redress through effective mechanisms, which may include restitution, developed in conjunction with indigenous peoples, with respect to their cultural, intellectual, religious and spiritual property taken without their free, prior and informed consent or in violation of their laws, traditions and customs.

Though we are finally approaching the finish line with this volume, a project that feels to have been a long-awaited great work, it needs to be acknowledged that this particular volume was also produced during a global pandemic. So many beautiful and curious minds are no longer with us. We dedicate this volume to the many Native and non-Native champions of Indigenous sovereignty whose lives were lost to COVID-19. As the world slowly returns to normality, we cannot think of a timelier moment for this volume. We look forward to engaging with you in fellowship, camaraderie, and worshipfulness as a singular, global family.

Introduction

Toward "Hopeful" Research: Community-Engaged Scholarship and New Directions in Native American and Indigenous Studies

CHIEF BENJAMIN J. BARNES AND STEPHEN WARREN

Collected within the pages you now have in your hands are seeds that began to grow at the 2014 annual conference of the American Society for Ethnohistory in Indianapolis, Indiana. For scholars in attendance that work in and with Indigenous communities, the conference proceedings had the feeling of lightning in a bottle: a rare moment when attendees from across "Indian Country" collaborated on equal terms with scholarly experts. The winds of change were blowing, and we could all feel that a power shift was taking place. We hoped that Native nations, citizen-scholars, and academics would leave the meeting committed to the task of inverting the traditional power dynamic. We hoped that Indigenous nations might finally arrest more than a century of ethnological, historical, and economic plunder. Galvanized by the moment, we felt emboldened to demand that the settler-colonial academy—universities, museums, and public institutions—work collaboratively with Native nations and reexamine the cultural riches contained in their archives, seeding a new era of cultural revitalization.

Our hope for a new era of collaboration was premature. We realized that if we wanted to see the changes we desired, we were going to have to work for it. Hundreds of emails, phone calls, personal meetings, and

1

numerous conferences later, you now hold in your hands the fruits of those seeds. It was during the intervening time that some of our cabal traveled to the 2016 meeting of the Canadian Historical Association in Calgary, Alberta, to work more closely with Keith Thor Carlson, then at the University of Saskatchewan. Keith's work with Albert "Sonny" McHalsie and the Stó:lō has been an inspiration for like-minded scholars in the United States and Canada. They didn't need to be proselytized into our movement, as they had for nearly two decades been practicing community-engaged scholarship within the Stó:lō community along the Fraser Valley of British Columbia. It was perhaps seeing these ideas in practice that renewed us, encouraging us that not only could we bring change to our own tribal communities, but change the way that universities see and treat Native Americans and First Nations peoples. Being exposed to the success of the partnership between the Stó:lō and the University of Saskatchewan gave us momentum. We then hosted a 2017 conference on community-engaged scholarship (CES) in Oklahoma, split between the University of Tulsa, the Helmerich Center for American Research, and the Miami Tribe of Oklahoma. We moved between metropolitan Tulsa and Miami, up in the extreme northeastern corner of the state that so many tribes call home. We chose these locations because we wanted to share our work with the communities that are the subject of our research.

The authors included in this volume presented their ideas at our CES conference and have been working with Native nations on collaborative projects directed by Native nations. The seeds of their ideas, like all seeds, have grown out of the efforts of previous "gardeners," choosing the best and strongest crops that will sustain and nourish us. It is from the mistakes and successes of previous forays into Native communities that we have winnowed out selections for your consideration. We feel that despite the missteps of the past, the promise of improved research outcomes for Indigenous peoples and universities alike is long overdue. Together, we need to ask Native peoples, "What do you want to know?" while, at the same time, keeping in mind the mistakes of past efforts.

Most of the authors included in the volume focus their research on some aspect of the Indigenous Midwest. Two Native nations, the Miami and Shawnee, are a focal point of our research. However, these nations have collaborated with universities and institutions far beyond their former homelands, the land between the Wabash and Ohio River valleys. These collaborative partners include the Colonial Williamsburg Foundation, the Newberry Library, the Ohio History Connection, Indiana University, and the University of Iowa. Contributing essays by scholars such as John Bowes, Buck Woodard, Brian Hosmer, April Sievert and Jessie Ryker-Crawford, and Jacki Rand represent the fluorescence of scholarship on Native nations from the Midwest, before and after removal. Thankfully, these scholars, and their allied institutions, have embraced community-engaged scholarship and fostered new and productive lines of inquiry as a result.

Our concentration on the Indigenous Midwest grows out of a long history. Native Americans from the Midwest have long been a focal point of non-Native research, centuries before community-engaged scholarship became part of our scholarly lexicon. In 1824, C. C. Trowbridge, a New Yorker then living in Michigan Territory, traveled to Northeastern Ohio to record the oral traditions of the Miami and Shawnee. It was the eve of Indian removal, and Trowbridge was anxious to collect their histories before they vanished from the earth. Trowbridge arranged interviews with two of the most important men in the tribe. Tenskwatawa, the brother of the Shawnees' most famous warrior, Tecumseh, sat for an interview, as did Black Hoof, Tenskwatawa's rival. In Indiana, Trowbridge interviewed Meehcikilita, or Le Gros, the principal chief of the Miami at the time. Nearly a century later, in December 1909, the ethnologist M. R. Harrington wrote to the US Indian agent for the Sac and Fox Agency. He needed permission to visit the Midwestern tribes living in Oklahoma, including the Miami, Peoria, Shawnee, Kickapoo, and Sac and Fox. Harrington asked the agent to help him acquire "ethnological specimens" for a museum exhibit at the University of Pennsylvania. "If you know anyone who has any old specimens," Harrington explained, "especially in the line of 'sacred bundles' and other 'medicine' articles I would be pleased indeed to hear of them." Harrington was wildly successful. Over several decades of traveling through Indian country he acquired tens of thousands of artifacts. In 1911, near Peru, Indiana, yet another collector of Native American history, Jacob Piatt Dunn met with the Miami elder Gabriel Godfroy to help him explain Indiana's history to Hoosiers in anticipation of the state's centennial celebration. Dunn positioned American Indians, and Godfroy's Miami people, at the beginning of his narrative, *Indiana and Indianans*. Godfroy thus became a human artifact, an embodiment of the state's progress from primitivism.[1]

To Native Americans, ethnologists on quests for their culture—men such as Harrington, Trowbridge, and Dunn—must have seemed relentless. They visited Indiana, Ohio, Ontario, and Oklahoma to collect the cultures and histories of people who had been subject to the successive genocidal campaigns since the eighteenth century.² Confident that Native Americans were doomed, Lewis Cass, the territorial governor of Michigan and ardent Jacksonian, commissioned Trowbridge's oral histories. In contrast, Harrington worked for George Gustav Heye, an engineer and heir to a fortune generated by Standard Oil Company, whose artifacts now make up 85 percent of the collection housed by the National Museum of the American Indian. A contemporary of Harrington's, Dunn traveled back and forth between his Indiana home and Oklahoma in an attempt to save the Miami language from becoming dormant. He argued for the "intrinsic worth" of Native American languages, believing that "any man who wishes to leave a monument more enduring than marble" should consider working to preserve Indigenous languages and local histories. Trowbridge, Harrington, and Dunn had complicated and divergent perspectives on federal Indian policy and the capacity of Native Americans to reconcile themselves to modernity. Sometimes, though not always, they worked in concert with state and federal officials. Historians have been slow to understand how their patrons and their individual beliefs shaped the material, archival, and oral histories they collected. Indigenous studies scholar Linda Tuhiwai Smith explains that "the ways in which knowledge about Indigenous peoples was collected, classified and then represented" became part of the "collective memory of imperialism." Native scholar-activists are now reinterpreting their findings, unpacking how the secondary source literature has been shaped by the first ethnologists and archivists whose work often acts as the foundation for research on Native peoples.³

Unlike Trowbridge, Harrington, and Dunn, the essayists included in this volume answer questions posed by Indigenous communities themselves, and the audience for their work is primarily, though not exclusively, Indigenous. The community-engaged scholars gathered here represent what the Métis-Canadian Indigenous studies scholar Adam Gaudry describes as "insurgent research," because their research "bases itself in Indigenous communities and Indigenous knowledges, both of which are, at their core, relational." Community-engaged scholarship thus marks a significant departure from what Smith describes as the "traveller's tales" of yesteryear.⁴

The people published in these pages understand the long, tumultuous history of scholarly engagement in Indian country. For example, many of us first met through the American Society for Ethnohistory, a society founded by anthropologists and historians funded in part by the Indian Claims Commission, a branch of the US Department of Justice. Before joining the Claims Commission, American Society for Ethnohistory's founder,

Erminie Wheeler Voegelin and her husband, Carl Voegelin, worked for the pharmaceutical magnate Eli Lilly. Lilly defined the aim and scope of their scholarship, and he asked them to adopt a team-based approach to the study of American Indian cultures. The archaeologist Glenn Black and the historian Paul Weer worked with the Voegelin's on a variety of Lilly-funded projects. In their view, "triangulation" promised to unlock the mysteries of Native Americans from the Midwest and beyond. Between 1953 and 1978, many ethnohistorians accustomed to triangulated research hired on to the Indian Claims Commission. Created by the US Department of Justice and intended to settle disputed land claims between the United States and federally recognized tribes, the Indian Claims Commission leaned heavily on scholars affiliated with the American Society for Ethnohistory. Teams of historians, anthropologists, and linguists researched the documentary and, to a lesser extent, oral record of Native Americans. For these scholars and the graduate students they supervised, ICC-funded research created yet another baseline of knowledge about American Indian history.[5]

In the 1950s and 1960s, ethnohistorians thought of themselves as social scientists. They never fully reflected on the moral and ethical problems that grew out of conducting research for the United States on the country's first peoples. They produced knowledge for wealthy industrialists, hobbyists with cash to burn on their obsession. When these funds dried up, the US Department of Justice, and the Indian Claims Commission, put them to work. Hired by a government eager to demonstrate "the utmost good faith" in its treatment of American Indians, ethnohistorians furthered American interests in the context of the Cold War. They privileged the archival record over community knowledge, the scholar over the informant, and the Western legal tradition over Native understandings of diplomacy and land holding. The anthropologist Shannon Speed has shown how these early practitioners are guilty, at minimum, of "collusion with colonial power." Ethnohistorians played a determining role in what the cultural theorist Stuart Hall describes as the ways in which "the West represented itself and its relation to 'the other.' "[6]

Cracks in the facade of objectivity began to emerge almost immediately. Among anthropologists, Sol Tax raised questions about the close allegiance between scholars and the United States government. Tax founded "action anthropology," an essential precursor to the community-engaged scholarship described in this volume. Regarding his colleagues affiliated with the ICC, Tax believed that "people are not rats and ought not to be treated like them. Not only should we not hurt people; we should not use them for our own ends." Tax was a Jewish anthropologist working in the wake of the Holocaust. He understood that scientific research often became a racist tool of the nation state, and he called for ethnology grounded in the needs of vernacular cultures. "Community research," he wrote, is "justifiable only to the degree that the results are imminently useful to the community and easily outweigh the disturbance to it."[7]

Research produced immediately before and after World War II informed Tax's rejection of positivism, or the "notion of research as an objective, value-free, and scientific process for observing and making sense of human realities." Tax understood that intersubjective realities shape how we view and interpret the world, and so he became cautious of Western universalism. He began describing himself as a "clinical" scientist. According to anthropologist Douglas R. Foley, "Tax's notion of a clinical science challenged the positivist notion of social scientists as neutral, emotionally detached, objective recorders of social facts." Linda Tuhiwai Smith argues that positivism is anathema for Indigenous communities, because it lacks an ethical grounding in the host community and confuses means with ends. She writes, "As the ways we try to understand the world are reduced to issues of measurement, the focus of understanding becomes more concerned with procedural problems."[8]

Tax's "action anthropology" was far from a perfect reply to positivism. The Meskwaki Nation in Tama, Iowa, became a central site for Tax's methodology. In all of the years that Tax and his graduate students maintained a research station there, neither he nor his students ever received formal approval from the tribal council for their research. Tax developed his program in conversation with a small number of tribal leaders who he counted as friends. These informal relationships shaped his perspective on the Meskwaki as well as this nascent methodology.[9]

Among historians, Angie Debo was a contemporary of the ethnohistorians and, like Tax, a frequent critic of scholarship conducted on behalf of the settler-colonial state. Just as Wheeler-Voegelin and other first-generation ethnohistorians worked for the Indian Claims Commission, Debo became convinced of "the interrelationship between her country's treatment of people of color and its moral authority in the larger world." For Debo, scholar-activism meant letter writing campaigns on behalf of the world's Indigenous peoples, standing up to peer-reviewers who intended to censor her scholarship, and advocating for African Americans in Oklahoma as the civil rights movement began to flower in the postwar United States. Debo was an independent woman who spoke truth to power. Consequently, she spent most of her career outside of the professorate, as university and state officials tried to suppress her voice.[10]

Today's community-engaged scholars have studied how academic institutions and federal agencies use the specter of objectivity as a cudgel to prevent scholar-activists from applying their research to the world's Indigenous peoples. Tenure and promotion standards emphasize single-authored scholarship and the principle of peer review; criteria that leave Indigenous communities on the outside looking in. Anthropologist Charles R. Hale has challenged scholars working on behalf of Indigenous communities to claim "methodological rigor while rejecting the positivist notion of objectivity" that guided anthropologists and historians for most of the twentieth century. Hale's concern for "rigor" grows out of the frequent canard that activist-oriented research is facile and beneath the standards of most academic disciplines. Still today, few question the ethics of receiving grants designed by the US government or philanthropic institutions; awards created and implemented at a distance from Indigenous communities. The exclusion of Native voices from powerful philanthropic and government institutions has consequences for Indigenous communities and community-engaged scholars alike. Until community partners are treated as intellectual equals—sharing in writing, research, and publication—engaged scholarship will occur at the margins of the professorate.[11]

Triangulated, or team-based research conducted on behalf of Indigenous communities raises alarm bells for scholars accustomed to single-authored, positivist approaches to history and anthropology. Accustomed to third-person omniscient narratives, wherein scholars assume an "objective" perspective on American Indians, these scholars worry that community engagement compromises a fundamental tenet of scholarship: the pose of the disinterested observer. Scholarship written by, and sometimes for, Indigenous communities seems to undermine this basic tenet of historical methods. Community-engaged scholarship and its practitioners are not advocating for the abandonment of single-authored scholarship. Single-authored scholarship is appropriate for a wide array of scholars and circumstances. Rather, we are advocating for the integration of team-based research into the scholarly canon. Single-authored and team-based research are not mutually exclusive.[12]

We also advocate for Indigenous nations to ask their own research questions; questions that academics take seriously and endeavor to answer. When Native communities ask questions in this way, the scholarship produced in response is restorative and inspiring. The fullness and richness of Indigenous cultures comes into view. Community-engaged scholars in Indian country also seek to understand the trauma of settler colonialism. Its practitioners know that painful histories must be recovered and understood if the foundation of cultural recovery is to stand for future generations. Critics of community-engaged scholarship might think that Indigenous people want to recast history with themselves as the heroes. Such hagiographic portrayals lead to foundations made of sand. Scholarship with rigor and integrity is essential to the work of decolonization.

In part 1, "Community-Engaged Scholarship with the Three Federally Recognized Shawnee Tribes," four chapters explain the fruits of ongoing partnerships between Shawnee and non-Native scholars. In chapter 1, Ben Barnes, chief of the Shawnee Tribe, desires to understand the meaning of his long relationship to the White Oak Ceremonial Ground while, at the same time, his Shawnee relatives made very different choices about community and identity. In all of their manifestations, Shawnee individuals and communities refused to conform to the two-dimensional cardboard cutouts of conventional history books. In chapter 2, Sandra Garner, professor of American studies at Miami University, Ohio, describes her career, from working with the Lakota to her subsequent engagement with the Eastern Shawnee Tribe of Oklahoma. Through culture camps for Eastern Shawnee children, Sande has managed to bring Miami University students to Oklahoma, where they work with Eastern Shawnee children and learn while doing, in an immersive field school experience. In chapter 3, Glenna Wallace, the chief of the Eastern Shawnee Tribe, is a force of nature who has worked tirelessly to reverse the legacy of removal in Ohio. In "Earthworks Rising," she collaborates with Christine Ballengee Morris and Marti Chaatsmith (Comanche/Choctaw). Together, they focus their attention on Newark Earthworks, a Hopewell mound complex of great magnitude that was defiled by the Moundbuilders Golf Course for most of the last century and is now a UNESCO World Heritage Site. In chapter 4, "New Paradigms of Integration: Historians and the Need for Community Engagement," historian Stephen Warren challenges readers to consider how the "knowledge claims of the traditional disciples" and the demands of non-Native audiences often ignore or undermine the needs of Native communities. His retrospective analysis of previous efforts at community-engaged scholarship show why it is difficult to reconcile the needs of Indigenous communities and the integrationist demands of the discipline of history.

Part 2, "The Myaamia Center: The History and Practice of Community Engagement," tells the history of this pivotal site of linguistic and cultural revitalization in Oxford, Ohio. In chapter 5, "neepwaantiinki (Partners in Learning): The Miami Tribe of Oklahoma, Miami University, and the Myaamia Center," George Ironstrack (Miami Tribe of Oklahoma) and Bobbe Burke explain the unique history of this interdisciplinary research center, housed at Miami University, Ohio, but staffed and funded by the Miami Tribe of Oklahoma. The remarkable story of this partnership, which grew out of many difficult conversations regarding the university's racist mascot, has not been told before. Once the mascot had been jettisoned, both the Miami Tribe and Miami University built a remarkable partnership out of a long history of painful misrepresentations. The center has become a magnet for language revitalization, historical research, and Miami citizens enrolled at Miami University. In chapter 6, "Community-Engaged Scholarship from the Perspective of an Early Career Academic," non-Native ally and PhD in history Cameron Shriver describes how early career academics can establish meaningful ties to Indigenous communities. Finally, in chapter 7, "Community-Engaged Scholarship as a Restorative Action," G. Susan Mosley-Howard, and three Miami Tribe of Oklahoma citizens and Miami University scholars, Haley Shea, George Ironstrack, and Daryl Baldwin, offer a retrospective analysis of the linguistic and cultural journeys of Miami citizens enrolled at Miami University.

In part 3, "Community Engagement beyond the US Settler Academy," we turn our attention to libraries, laboratories, living history museums, and courtrooms. It must be acknowledged that innovative, community-engaged scholarship has flourished in spaces outside of academic departments. Tenure and promotion standards often ignore CES methodologies or, in some cases, cast it off as service rather than scholarship. Moreover, because academic departments prioritize single-authored scholarship, innovative, collaborative research often takes place outside of university settings.

In chapter 8, "Historians as Expert Witnesses for Tribal Governments," historian John P. Bowes describes his work in the world of litigation, using ethnohistorical work on behalf of the Saginaw Chippewa Indian Tribe of Michigan and the Little Traverse Bay Bands of Odawa Indians. In chapter 9, "Looking Inward from 60 West Walton Street: Reflections on Community-Engaged Scholarship from the Perspective of the Newberry Library," historian Brian Hosmer offers a retrospective on his time as director of the D'Arcy McNickle Center, where he worked to procure grants and created infrastructure that allowed for institutional collaborations with

Indigenous communities. In chapter 10, "The Return of Indian Nations to the Colonial Capital: Civic Engagement and the Production of Native Public History," anthropologist and public historian Buck Woodard gave Native Americans a stage and a platform at Colonial Williamsburg, where they narrated their own histories with colonial America. In chapter 11, "Repatriation as a Catalyst for Building Community-Engaged Curriculum," anthropologists April Sievert and Jessie Ryker-Crawford describe how institutions that hold human remains and associated funerary objects can improve their working relationships with Native nations. Sievert and Ryker-Crawford show how consultations, when done properly and ethically, should recognize Native nations' free, prior, and informed consent under the guidelines of the Native American Graves Protection and Repatriation Act (1990). In chapter 12, "The Collaboration Spectrum: Legendary Stories as Windows into Gendered Change in Stó:lō Understandings of Territoriality," Keith Thor Carlson, Naxaxalhts'i (Albert "Sonny" McHalsie; Stó:lō First Nation), Colin Murray Osmond, and Tsandlia Van Ry (Stó:lō First Nation) take community-engaged scholarship north of the Medicine Line. In Canada, the adage "nothing about us without us" guides the important work of the Stó:lō Research and Resource Management Centre (SRRMC) in Chilliwack, British Columbia.

In the afterword, "Where Do We Go from Here?," historian Jacki Thompson Rand (Choctaw citizen) offers a retrospective on her training in the fields of history and museum studies. Her experience of the disconnect between scholarly methodologies and Indigenous communities underscores the need for community-engaged scholarship. Land acknowledgment statements and overused words such as decolonization require that we take a more thoughtful approach.

Replanting Cultures: Community-Engaged Scholarship in Indian Country offers many different examples of both triangulated and single-authored research. Some chapters chronicle our individual journeys toward community engagement, but the majority offer retrospective analyses of projects designed by and for Indigenous communities in the United States and Canada. Both the Myaamia Center and the Stó:lō Research and Resource Management Centre offer remarkable examples of innovation and Indigenous sovereignty. However, in contrast to the United States, the Canadian government has taken steps to acknowledge and correct its role in funding research that has disadvantaged First Nations. In 2001 the Canadian government created a Panel on Research Ethics, which established rigorous protocols for researchers. Importantly, this panel acknowledged Canada's long history of exploitative research. To chart a new course, national funding agencies require that scholars demonstrate "that research involving aboriginal peoples" is "premised on respectful relationships." These and other guidelines have made community-engaged research the preferred model of the Canadian government. Scholars who fail to embrace research methodologies based on respect and reciprocity are not eligible for national funding.[13]

In the decades before the panel's creation, Julie Cruikshank, Laura Peers, and Alison Brown modeled the kind of research that resulted in this paradigm shift in Canadian scholarship. In *Life Lived Like a Story*, anthropologist Julie Cruikshank describes coming of age as an anthropologist in the late 1960s. She explains that the "ethical dilemmas of anthropological research" convinced her that she had to "do research outside a university framework." Positivism, which in anthropology turns on the "methodological goals of observation and participation," informed her decision to work outside of an academic institution. The Native women in the Yukon with whom Cruikshank worked challenged her to move beyond conventional approaches to anthropological fieldwork. Together, they settled on what we might now describe as "collaborative ethnography." Cruikshank developed a model of "life history investigation" in which the Indigenous women owned the final product. Jointly reviewing and correctingthe life histories became intrinsic to the process. Cruikshank suggests that before the establishment of the Panel on Research Ethics Canadian research institutions might have limited her capacity to conduct this kind of ethical, reciprocal research.[14]

To the south, scholars in the United States have made halting progress toward engagement. The reasons for this are complex, owing in part to the decentralized and diverse nature of higher education in the United States, as well as the limited commitment of federal and private funding agencies to engaged scholarship. As in Canada, scholars of community engagement such as John Saltmarsh and Edward Zlotkowski argue that colleges and universities in the United States are largely to blame. From their perspective, academic institutions founded between the seventeenth to the nineteenth centuries "have remained remarkably stable—or inert." As evidence, they point to antiquated tenure and promotion standards; standards of professionalism that focus on individual achievement rather than inclusive, community-based research that builds capacity in underserved populations. Perhaps because of these conventional standards, the foremost champions of community-engaged scholarship with Indigenous populations typically come from museums, nonprofit organizations, and public-private partnerships beyond university settings. Research centers featured in this volume such as the Myaamia Institute in Oxford, Ohio, the Glenn Black Laboratory of Archaeology at Indiana University, the Newberry Library in Chicago, and the Colonial Williamsburg Foundation cultivate the scholarship of engagement because it is an intrinsic measurement of their success. These institutions recognize that their success depends on outreach with federally recognized Native nations. Some of the best community-engaged scholarship in the United States comes out of the governments of Native nations, or research centers that work closely with Indigenous communities.[15]

However innovative community engagement seems, it is important to recognize that this methodology grows out of an older form of ethnohistorical practice based on team- or "triangulated" research. Today's community-engaged scholars embrace inclusive scholarly practices and honor Indigenous perspectives. "Sharing authority," according to the Anishnaabe archaeologist Sonya Atalay, "builds capacity" in Native communities. The essayists included in this volume model interdisciplinary scholarship that furthers the sovereignty of Indigenous communities.[16]

Collaborative research in Native American and Indigenous studies is a unique strand of the larger movement toward community engagement. Their scholarly products do not always resemble the peer-reviewed publications that many academics have come to expect. Museum exhibits, oral histories, recovered pottery traditions, and Myaamia ribbonwork reflect the diverse outputs that result from engaged scholarship. Unlike mainstream examples of community engagement, allied scholars in Indigenous communities are more circumspect regarding wider publics and the ways in which their work benefits the civic cultures of the United States and Canada. Saltmarsh and Zlotkowski suggest that conventional academic "departments can remain, but only if civic engagement is intrinsic to the curriculum." They call for integrative scholarship whose ultimate end is the creation of life-long learners driven by civic engagement. According to the National Service-Learning Clearinghouse, the notion of the common good, including "community engagement pedagogies . . . combine[s] learning goals and community service in ways that can enhance both student growth and the common good."[17]

Native American and Indigenous communities are justifiably wary of scholars who approach them on universal quests for knowledge and democracy. Concerned with cultural recovery after centuries of genocide, Native peoples search for allies interested in placing the needs of Indigenous communities above those of the American nation-state. Quite literally, institutions such as Indiana University built their reputations on the land of Native peoples, and then compounded their tyranny by exhuming and desecrating the bones of Native peoples' ancestors. At the same time, ethnologists collected the languages and music of the Shawnee and their Midwestern relatives, only to lock them away from the very people who provided their culture, their sound, and their history to non-Natives. These treasures have remained hidden from Native peoples until quite recently. Blocked by paywalls and exorbitant out-of-state tuitions, these colleges and universities have excluded Native peoples from ever enjoying the benefits of the knowledge they possess. Because of this history, it is not surprising that citizens of Native nations often determine that their need for cultural privacy outweighs the scholars' need for publication and other means of disseminating knowledge. Alternatively, Native nations pursue the repatriation of artifacts of culture collected by people such as Harrington. Across the United States, 574 federally recognized Native nations work to return knowledge to their communities; knowledge taken by museums and universities. These goals supersede the needs of the non-Native students and their teachers for whom civic engagement and public service remain their foremost aims. Each in their own way, the authors in this volume argue that Indigenous communities have the right to know, and to respond to, interpretations of their culture and history.[18]

In the essays that follow, we contend that community-engaged scholarship, often written by teams of scholars, yields exciting new discoveries in history, anthropology, and related disciplines. We show how the questions posed by Indigenous communities leads to new discoveries in these disciplines. In our view, new questions, when combined with the expertise of Native scholar-activists and their allies, yields better outcomes than single-authored manuscripts written largely in isolation from the Indigenous community that is the subject of their research.

Community-engaged scholars and teachers frequently work among the most vulnerable populations. Perhaps because of this, leading scholars are now questioning universalist claims for the "common good" that have dominated academic scholarship since John Dewey published *Education and Democracy*. Dwight Giles, a leading scholar on teaching and learning, makes the case for "a practice element to broaden the scholarship to include practitioner voices as co-generators of knowledge." Channeling Giles, the educational theorist Gregory Jay believes that we need to explain both "who we mean when we say 'the public,' and to whom our work is accountable."[19]

Most scholars approach teaching from a problem-solving perspective. We design classes to improve our students' ability to function successfully in the twenty-first century. Alternatively, we worry that our students lack a basic understanding of American democracy. These problem-based approaches to learning, when applied to Indigenous communities, often reflect poorly on academics. We come across as condescending saviors, convinced that we alone can solve a community's problems. When treated this way, Indigenous communities avoid the newcomers, waiting for their departure to return to their normal patterns of life. Engaged teaching and research can avoid these problems. When communities identify the problems they wish to solve, everyone benefits.

Non-Native academics are often the last to challenge the "presumptive universalism of the academic humanities curricula." The Enlightenment quest for truth, for universal understandings of the common good, are baked into these institutional identities. Native Americans know firsthand how these same institutions have stored their ancestors in boxes, conducted tests on their ancestors' remains, patented their seeds, and published their histories of creation, all in pursuit of the common good. These abuses of power give the lie to positivism, to the false idea that "facts exist independently of values and assumptions." Native people know that objective science was never truly objective; that the settler-colonial states that are now sovereign over their lands often use objective science to justify the dispossession of Native people. As evidence, look to the Indian Claims Commission. Settler-colonial benefactors have always played a critical role in our interpretation of human societies, past and present. Federal officials in search of termination got scholars to work for the Indian Claims Commission.[20]

Despite these long histories of working with colonial powers, many scholars continue to subscribe to the false notion that their research, conducted under a smokescreen of positivism, is free of bias. Witness the recent *American Historical Review* AHR Exchange "Historians and Native Americans and Indigenous Studies." In this forum, historian David Silverman worries about the weakening of historical methods, and he suggests that collaborative methodologies undermine the discipline. He accuses community-engaged scholars of both presentism and an unwillingness to tackle difficult histories. CES practitioners, particularly those aligned with the Native American and Indigenous Studies Association, are, in his view, obsessed with "identity politics" to such an extent that our work does not permit "the honest study" of past worlds. Well before the publication of this forum, the authors included in *Replanting Cultures* anticipated Silverman's criticism and explained why scholarly rigor has been so essential to our work. We were heartened by the thoughtful replies of the AHR Exchange respondents, who zeroed in on Silverman's misrepresentation of their, and our, work. For example, historian Christine DeLucia described how her Pequot and Wampanoag interlocutors offered "probing, insightful" comments on her work that improved the quality of her research. Broad-stroke accusations of shallow, presentist research bear little resemblance to our own experience of community-engaged scholarship.[21]

One legacy of settler-colonialism is that non-Native scholars have unparalleled access to, and sometimes control over, a given community's archival record. Historians and archivists in positions of power now seek out collaborative opportunities that democratize their collections. They can bring tribal citizen-scholars into contact with larger networks of scholars and archivists who know the history of the documents in their possession; documents that are often vital to the defense and expansion of tribal sovereignty. For Harry Williams, a citizen of the Owens Valley Paiute, the records of his people housed at the University of California, Berkeley's Bancroft Library "represent an astonishing collection of traditional materials and knowledge now largely lost to the tribe." Archivists, working in tandem with teachers and students, have brought the stories contained in "faded notebooks" back to life, restoring the "lost patrimony of the Paiute people."[22]

Like the Owens Valley Paiute, the Miami and Shawnee communities featured in this volume cultivate scholarly partnerships based in values of reciprocity. They value partnerships with scholars and universities that feature collaboration and repatriation. In the case of the Miami, they have fostered the intellectual growth of their own citizens, people such as the language activist, scholar, and MacArthur fellow Daryl Baldwin. The Miami Tribe of Oklahoma's disciplined focus on linguistic and cultural analysis culminated in the creation of the Myaamia Center, a place where collaboration with tribal partners lives and thrives for students and faculty. For the Shawnee Tribe (one of three Shawnee nations), collaboration was born out of the Native American Graves Protection and Repatriation Act (NAGPRA). Before final disposition of ancestral remains can occur, the Eastern Shawnee Tribe of Oklahoma, the Absentee Shawnee Tribe of Oklahoma, and the Shawnee Tribe need to have discussions to achieve a concurrence. Out of these NAGPRA conversations, relationships have arisen between the tribes and public institutions in the old Shawnee homelands. Unlike the Miami, the Shawnee have a vast area of historical and cultural interest. Shawnee villages and trading posts seem to appear out from under every rock in the historical narrative ranging from Florida up the Atlantic coast into Maryland and New York to as far west and south as Mexico and Texas. Edmond Atkin, the Southern Superintendent for Indian Affairs, described the Shawnees and their travels in his 1755 *Report* as "the greatest Travellers in America." Their historical archive is vast, as their people occupied a prodigious region across more than twenty American states. Borne from consultations in their former homelands, relationships between individuals and institutions have bloomed. The Shawnee Tribe has developed a wide network of collaborative, academic partnerships with community-defined research goals at the American Philosophical Society, the Glenn Black Laboratory of Archaeology at Indiana University, the Kentucky Archaeological Survey, and the Ohio History Connection, as well as other Native nations, universities, and public institution. For both the Miami and the Shawnee, the desire is the same. Language and cultural loss occurs within communities, so it stands to reason that those same communities must be the primary force in restoration. Myaamia citizen-scholar Daryl Baldwin eloquently explains that his people must be the authors of their own destiny:

> Although it is easy to point to the many forces, some delib-
> erate, that served as the impetus for the decline of Myaamia
> language and cultural knowledge, it is clear that the recovery
> process rests largely on the shoulders of the Miami nation
> and its citizens. If Myaamia language and culture survives
> into another century, in whatever form, it will be because the
> people want it to.[23]

Both the Miami and the Shawnee have their national headquarters in Ottawa County, Oklahoma, located in the northeastern-most corner of the state. It is perhaps no accident that nine Native nations are headquartered there. In the aftermath of the Civil War, as non-Native settlement in Kansas accelerated, the Miami, Shawnee, and their Native neighbors were removed yet again, mainly to the northeastern corner of Indian Territory, what is now Oklahoma. It is here in Ottawa County, a peculiar context of multiple removed tribes, that the Shawnee, Eastern Shawnee, Miami, Peoria, Ottawa, Wyandotte, Seneca-Cayuga, Quapaw, and Modoc have learned to value cooperation in this patchwork quilt of allotted lands and jurisdictional areas. Eight of the nine of these nations have connections to eastern states along the Great Lakes, and the Ohio and Mississippi River valleys. The Modoc are the sole exception, being removed by railcar from California, shackled in chains as they arrived in Oklahoma.

For both the Shawnee and Miami nations, dispossession of land deprived them and their neighbors of their living history. The restoration of their archival history is critically important to language revitalization and other aspects of cultural patrimony. Two facts of their respective histories make the repatriation of knowledge critical to their efforts. First, the United States forcibly removed them from their homelands in what is now Ohio and Indiana. Second, even before removal, the chaos of colonialism spread Miami and Shawnee communities over most of the eastern half of North America. Because of this vast diaspora, Miami and Shawnee records are scattered across the United States as well as repositories in Canada, the United Kingdom, France, and Spain.[24]

Repatriating this knowledge through interlinked archives offers a promising means of connecting tribal citizens to what the digital scholar and curator, Kimberly Christen calls "digital heritage." The world's Indigenous people are now working to develop "local cultural protocols" that reflect the unique "intellectual property needs" of their communities. Repatriating knowledge to specific Native nations immediately benefits Indigenous communities seeking to defend their ancestors through the Native American Graves Protection and Repatriation Act. Others value the ability to access information previously hidden behind paywalls and other institutional barriers. Native nations committed to "building the capacity" of their citizens now work to create online content systems that make that possible.[25]

Before the advent of community-engaged scholarship, as the ethnographer Luke Eric Lassiter explains, scholars assumed a "hierarchy of understanding" in which their knowledge superseded that of tribal citizens. In 1993, anthropologist Elaine Lawless called for a new chapter in these quests for cultural information, what she termed "reciprocal ethnography." In *Holy Women, Wholly Women*, Lawless defined a method in which both the interlocutor and the author share authority for the interpretation of culture housed within scholarly books and articles. Lassiter has subsequently taken Lawless's call for "reciprocal ethnography" a step further, toward the collaborative production of ethnographic texts; a process that treats American Indians as co-intellectuals. This new "process of textual production" no longer places the scholar above the needs of the informant or the community they represent.[26]

Native Americans and First Nations' peoples are understandably wary of non-Native scholars and the institutions they represent. It is a mistrust built on generations of exploitative research. Gaudry explains that the "reluctance of communities to engage academic researchers is not, I think, an inherent issue of scholarly research, but rather *the normalization of exploitative and extractive research* as standard scholarly practice." Gaudry makes an important distinction, in that he refers to Indigenous communities in expansive and inclusive ways. Indigenous governments and their elected officials are not the only representatives of Indigeneity. It is with this definition of "community" that the authors in the following pages describe to varying degrees their work. Collectively, we hope that the essays offer useful case studies of engaged, ethical research. Successes and failures are an inherent part of these endeavors. There is really no greater trust that can be shown than by the sharing of sacred seeds of Indigenous knowledge, culture, religion, and traditions. It is our hope that these examples of community-engaged scholarship will help to seed future generations of scholarship predicated on ethical engagement with Native communities.[27]

Notes

1. M. R. Harrington to US Indian agent, December 17, 1909, "Indian History" folder, Sac and Fox Agency Records, Box 189, Oklahoma Historical Society, Oklahoma City, OK; W. Vernon Kinietz and Erminie Wheeler-Voegelin, eds., *Shawnese Traditions: C. C. Trowbridge's Account* (Ann Arbor: University of Michigan Press, 1939); Jacob Piatt Dunn, *Indiana and Indianans: A History of Aboriginal and Territorial Indiana and the Century of Statehood* (Chicago: American Historical Society, 1919).

2. For a recent treatment of the genocidal intentions and actions of the United States in the eastern half of North America, see Jeffrey Ostler, *Surviving Genocide: Native Nations and the United States from the American Revolution to Bleeding Kansas* (New Haven, CT: Yale University Press, 2019).

3. Ann McMullen, "Reinventing George Heye: Nationalizing the Museum of the American Indian and Its Collections," in *Contesting Knowledge: Museums and Indigenous Perspectives*, ed. Susan Sleeper-Smith (Lincoln: University of

Nebraska Press, 2009), 65 105; John Haworth, "100 Years and Counting: Reflections about a Collection, a Collector, and the Museum of the American Indian (before There Was an NMAI)," *American Indian* 17, no. 1 (2016), https://www.americanindianmagazine.org/story/100-years-and-counting-reflections-about-collection-collector-and-museum-american-indian; Jacob Piatt Dunn, "Shall Indian Languages Be Preserved?" *Journal of the Illinois State Historical Society* 10, no. 1 (1917): 96, 95. See also Lana Ruegamer, "History, Politics, and the Active Life: Jacob Piatt Dunn, Progressive Historian," *Indiana Magazine of History* 81, no. 3 (1985): 265–83; Linda Tuhiwai Smith, *Decolonizing Methodologies: Research and Indigenous Peoples*, 2nd ed. (New York: Zed Books, 2012), 1.

4. Adam J. P. Gaudry, "Insurgent Research," *Wicazo Sa Review* 26, no. 1 (2011): 123; Smith, *Decolonizing Methodologies*, 81.

5. Stephen Warren and Ben Barnes, "Salvaging the Salvage Anthropologists: Erminie Wheeler-Voegelin, Carl Voegelin, and the Future of Ethnohistory," *Ethnohistory* 65, no. 2 (2018): 189–214; Keith Thor Carlson, John Sutton Lutz, David M. Schaepe, "Decolonizing Ethnohistory," in *Towards a New Ethnohistory: Community-Engaged Scholarship among the People of the River*, ed. Keith Thor Carlson, John Sutton Lutz, David M. Schaepe, and Naxaxalhts'i (Albert "Sonny" McHalsie) (Winnipeg: University of Manitoba Press, 2018), 7–11; Michael Harkin, "Ethnohistory's Ethnohistory: Creating a Discipline from the Ground Up," *Social Science History* 34, no. 2 (2010): 113–28; Arthur J. Ray, *Aboriginal Rights Claims and the Making and Remaking of History* (Montreal: McGill-Queen's University Press, 2016); Kenneth R. Philp, *Termination Revisited: American Indians on the Trail to Self Determination* (Lincoln: University of Nebraska Press, 1999); Daniel M. Cobb, *Native Activism in Cold War America: The Struggle for Sovereignty* (Lawrence: University Press of Kansas, 2008); Paul C. Rosier, *Serving Their Country: American Indian Politics and Patriotism in the Twentieth Century* (Cambridge, MA: Harvard University Press, 2009).

6. This phrase is drawn from the Northwest Ordinance of 1787, which established the modern states of Ohio, Indiana, Illinois, Michigan, and Wisconsin. For more on the Indian Claims Commission and the larger context of the Cold War, see Rosier, *Serving Their Country*; Shannon Speed, "Forged in Dialogue," in *Engaging Contradictions: Theory, Politics, and Methods of Activist Scholarship*, ed. Charles R. Hale (Berkeley: University of California Press, 2008), 213; Stuart Hall, "The West and the Rest: Discourse and Power," in *Identity and Diaspora*, vol. 2 of *Essential Essays*, ed. David Morley (Durham, NC: Duke University Press, 2019), 225. See also Edward W. Said, *Orientalism* (New York: Vintage, 2003).

7. Sol Tax, "Action Anthropology," *Current Anthropology*, 16, no. 4 (1975): 515. See also Judith M. Daubenmier, *The Meskwaki and Anthropologists: Action Anthropology Reconsidered* (Lincoln: University of Nebraska Press, 2008).

8. Smith, *Decolonizing Methodologies*, 166; Douglas E. Foley, "The Fox Project: A Reappraisal," *Current Anthropology* 40, no. 2 (1999): 172. For more on

Tax's view of action anthropology, see Solomon H. Katz, "Action Anthropology: Its Past, Present, and Future," in *Action Anthropology and Sol Tax in 2012: The Final Word?*, ed. Darcy C. Stapp, JONA memoir 8 (Richland, WA: Journal of Northwest Anthropology, 2012), 198–99; Smith, *Decolonizing Methodologies*, 45.

9. Foley, "The Fox Project," 177.

10. Shirley A. Leckie, *Angie Debo: Pioneering Historian* (Norman: University of Oklahoma Press, 2000), 145.

11. David H. Price, *Cold War Anthropology: the CIA, the Pentagon, and the Growth of Dual Use Anthropology* (Durham, NC: Duke University Press, 2016). See also David H. Price, *Threatening Anthropology: McCarthyism and the FBI's Surveillance of Activist Anthropologists* (Durham, NC: Duke University Press, 2004); Landon R. Y. Storrs, *The Second Red Scare and the Unmaking of the New Deal Left* (Princeton, NJ: Princeton University Press, 2013); Charles R. Hale, ed., *Engaging Contradictions: Theory, Politics, and Methods of Activist Scholarship* (Berkeley: University of California Press, 2008), 4; Carl Rhodes and Peter Bloom, "The Trouble with Charitable Billionaires," *Guardian*, May 24, 2018; Lawrence J. Friedman and Mark D. McGarvie, *Charity, Philanthropy, and Civility in American History* (Cambridge: Cambridge University Press, 2003).

12. Ruth Behar, *The Vulnerable Observer: Anthropology That Breaks Your Heart* (Boston: Beacon, 1996).

13. Social Sciences and Humanities Research Council, home page, accessed March 26, 2022, https://www.sshrc-crsh.gc.ca/society-societe/community-communite/index-eng.aspx.

14. Julie Cruikshank, *Life Lived like a Story: Life Histories of Three Yukon Native Elders* (Lincoln: University of Nebraska Press, 1990), 1, 13. For collaborative ethnography, see Luke Eric Lassiter, "From 'Reading over the Shoulders of Natives' to 'Reading Alongside Natives,' Literally: Toward a Collaborative and Reciprocal Ethnography," *Journal of Anthropological Research* 57, no. 2 (2001): 145.

15. Exceptions to the rule include the Whiting Foundation, https://www.whiting.org/; and the American Philosophical Society, which has created the Andrew W. Mellon Native American Scholars Initiative Fellowships, https://www.amphilsoc.org/grants/andrew-w-mellon-foundation-native-american-scholars-initiative-nasi-fellowships. For recent scholarship promoting engaged research, see Amy Koritz and George J. Sanchez, introduction to *Civic Engagement in the Wake of Katrina*, ed. Amy Koritz and George J. Sanchez (Ann Arbor: University of Michigan Press, 2009), 8. See also John Saltmarsh and Edward Zlotkowski, eds., *Higher Education and Democracy: Essays on Service-Learning and Civic Engagement* (Philadelphia: Temple University Press, 2011), 81. To date, the best examples of integration between academic departments and Indigenous research centers are in Canada. See, for example, Keith Carlson, from the University of Saskatachewan, who holds the Research Chair in Indigenous and Community-Engaged History; the University of Carleton's Great Lakes Research Alliance Aboriginal Arts and Cultures,

https://carleton.ca/grasac/; or the University of British Columbia's First Nations and Endangered Languages Program, http://aboriginal.ubc.ca/programs/#FNLG.

16. Sonya Atalay, *Community-Based Archaeology: Research with, by, and for Indigenous and Local Communities* (Berkeley: University of California Press, 2012).

17. Frank Levy and Richard J. Murnane, *Dancing with Robots: Human Skills for Computerized Work* (Thirdway, 2013); Joe Bandy, "What Is Service Learning or Community Engagement?," Vanderbilt University Center for Teaching, November 6, 2019, https://cft.vanderbilt.edu/guides-sub-pages/teaching-through-community-engagement/.

18. Bureau of Indian Affairs, "Indian Entities Recognized by and Eligible to Receive Services from the United States Bureau of Indian Affairs," *Federal Register* 85, no. 5462 (January 30, 2020): 01707, https://www.govinfo.gov/app/details/FR-2020-01-30/2020-01707/.

19. Dwight E. Giles, Jr., "Understanding an Emerging Field of Scholarship: Toward a Research Agenda for Engaged, Public Scholarship," *Journal of Higher Education Outreach and Engagement* 12, no. 2 (2008): 104; Gregory Jay, "The Engaged Humanities, Principles and Practices for Public Scholarship and Teaching," *Journal of Community Engagement and Scholarship* 3, no. 1 (2015): 52.

20. Jay, "The Engaged Humanities," 52; Edward Zlotkowski, "Service Learning and the Introductory Course: Lessons from across the Disciplines," in *Higher Education and Democracy: Essays on Service-Learning and Civic Engagement*, ed. John Saltmarsh and Edward Zlotkowski (Philadelphia: Temple University Press, 2011), 166–67.

21. David J. Silverman, "Living with the Past: Thoughts on Community Collaboration and Difficult History in Native American and Indigenous Studies," *American Historical Review* 125, no. 2 (2020): 519–27; Christine M. DeLucia, "Continuing the Intervention: Past, Present, and Future Pathways for Native Studies and Early American History," *American Historical Review* 125, no. 2 (2020): 528–32.

22. Patricia Steenland, "Lost Stories and Cultural Patrimony," *Public* 3, no. 1 (2015), https://public.imaginingamerica.org/blog/article/105-2/.

23. Edmond Atkin, *The Appalachian Indian Frontier: The Edmond Atkin Report and Plan of 1755*, ed. Wilbur R. Jacobs (Columbia: University of South Carolina Press, 1954), 65; Daryl Baldwin, personal communication with author Ben Barnes, August 13, 2020.

24. For scholars within and without our communities, interested parties can find the archival resources regarding the Miami, these can be found at the Miami Tribe of Oklahoma Myaamia Heritage Museum and Archive in Miami, Oklahoma; the Myaamia Collection at Miami University's Walter Havighurst Special Collections and University Archives; the Miami-Illinois Indigenous Languages Digital Archive, https://mc.miamioh.edu/ilda-myaamia/; the Myaamia Ethnobotanical Database, https://mc.miamioh.edu/mahkihkiwa/; and the Cranbrook Institute of Science in Bloomfield Hills, Michigan. The Indiana State Museum and the Indiana

Historical Society, in Indianapolis, contain a great deal of Miami-related content. In addition, county archives in Indiana cities such as Peru, Huntington, Marion, Wabash, and Fort Wayne contain valuable archival materials. Archival information on the Shawnee can be found at the Shawnee Tribe Cultural Center in Miami, Oklahoma; the Eastern Shawnee Tribe of Oklahoma's Betty Jane Holden Admussen Tribal Museum in Wyandotte, Oklahoma; and the Erminie Wheeler-Voegelin Papers at the Newberry Library, Chicago, Illinois. More archival resources for both the Miami and the Shawnee reside at the Glenn Black Laboratory of Archaeology's Great Lakes and Ohio Valley Ethnohistory collection at Indiana University Bloomington, the American Philosophical Society in Philadelphia, the National Anthropological Archives, and the National Museum of the American Indian.

 25. Kimberly Christen, "Does Information Really Want to be Free? Indigenous Knowledge Systems and the Question of Openness," *International Journal of Communication* 6 (2012): 2873. Visit the Warumungu archive at Mukurtu-Wampurrarni-kari Archive at http://www.mukurtu.org and the Plateau Peoples' Web Portal at http://plateauportal.wsulibs.wsu.edu; Atalay, *Community-Based Archaeology.*

 26. Lassiter, "From 'Reading over the Shoulders,'" 139, 145; Elaine Lawless, *Holy Women, Wholly Women: Sharing Ministries through Life Stories and Reciprocal Ethnography* (Philadelphia: University of Pennsylvania Press, 1993).

 27. Adam Gaudry, "Next Steps in Indigenous Community-Engaged Research: Supporting Research Self-Sufficiency in Indigenous Communities," in *Towards a New Ethnohistory: Community-Engaged Scholarship among the People of the River,* ed. Keith Thor Carlson, John Sutton Lutz, David M. Schaepe, and Naxaxalhts'i (Albert "Sonny" McHalsie) (Winnipeg: University of Manitoba Press, 2018), 254–55.

Bibliography

Atalay, Sonya. *Community-Based Archaeology: Research with, by, and for Indigenous and Local Communities.* Berkeley: University of California Press, 2012.

Atkin, Edmond. *The Appalachian Indian Frontier: The Edmond Atkin Report and Plan of 1755.* Edited by Wilbur R. Jacobs. Columbia: University of South Carolina Press, 1954.

Bandy, Joe. "What Is Service Learning or Community Engagement?" Vanderbilt University Center for Teaching. Accessed November 6, 2019. https://cft. vanderbilt.edu/guides-sub-pages/teaching-through-community-engagement.

Behar, Ruth. *The Vulnerable Observer: Anthropology That Breaks Your Heart.* Boston: Beacon, 1996.

Bureau of Indian Affairs. "Indian Entities Recognized by and Eligible to Receive Services from the United States Bureau of Indian Affairs." *Federal Register* 85, no. 5462 (January 2020). https://www.govinfo.gov/app/details/ FR-2020-01-30/2020-01707.

Carlson, Keith Thor, John Sutton Lutz, and David M. Schaepe. "Decolonizing Ethnohistory." In *Towards a New Ethnohistory: Community-Engaged Scholarship among the People of the River*, edited by Keith Thor Carlson, John Sutton Lutz, David M. Schaepe, and Naxaxalhts'i (Albert "Sonny" McHalsie), 1–38. Winnipeg: University of Manitoba Press, 2018.

Christen, Kimberly. "Does Information Really Want to be Free? Indigenous Knowledge Systems and the Question of Openness." *International Journal of Communication* 6 (2012): 2870–93.

Cobb, Daniel M. *Native Activism in Cold War America: The Struggle for Sovereignty.* Lawrence: University Press of Kansas, 2008.

Cruikshank, Julie. *Life Lived like a Story: Life Histories of Three Yukon Native Elders.* Lincoln: University of Nebraska Press, 1990.

Daubenmier, Judith M. *The Meskwaki and Anthropologists: Action Anthropology Reconsidered.* Lincoln: University of Nebraska Press, 2008.

DeLucia, Christine M. "Continuing the Intervention: Past, Present, and Future Pathways for Native Studies and Early American History." *American Historical Review* 125, no. 2 (2020): 528–32.

Dunn, Jacob Piatt. *Indiana and Indianans: A History of Aboriginal and Territorial Indiana and the Century of Statehood.* Chicago: American Historical Society, 1919.

———. "Shall Indian Languages Be Preserved?" *Journal of the Illinois State Historical Society* 10, no. 1 (1917): 87–96.

Foley, Douglas E. "The Fox Project: A Reappraisal." *Current Anthropology* 40, no. 2 (1999): 171–92.

Friedman, Lawrence J., and Mark D. McGarvie, *Charity, Philanthropy, and Civility in American History.* Cambridge: Cambridge University Press, 2003.

Gaudry, Adam J. P. "Insurgent Research." *Wicazo Sa Review* 26, no. 1 (2011): 113–36.

———. "Next Steps in Indigenous Community-Engaged Research: Supporting Research Self-Sufficiency in Indigenous Communities." In *Towards a New Ethnohistory: Community-Engaged Scholarship among the People of the River*, edited by Keith Thor Carlson, John Sutton Lutz, David M. Schaepe, and Naxaxalhts'i (Albert "Sonny" McHalsie), 254–58. Winnipeg: University of Manitoba Press, 2018.

Giles, Dwight E., Jr. "Understanding an Emerging Field of Scholarship: Toward a Research Agenda for Engaged, Public Scholarship." *Journal of Higher Education Outreach and Engagement* 12, no. 2 (2008): 97–106.

Hale, Charles R., ed. *Engaging Contradictions: Theory, Politics, and Methods of Activist Scholarship.* Berkeley: University of California Press, 2008.

Hall, Stuart. "The West and the Rest: Discourse and Power." In *Identity and Diaspora*, vol. 2 of *Essential Essays*, edited by David Morley, 185–227. Durham, NC: Duke University Press, 2019.

Harkin, Michael. "Ethnohistory's Ethnohistory: Creating a Discipline from the Ground Up." *Social Science History* 34, no. 2 (2010): 113–28.

Harrington, Mark Raymond. Papers. Sac and Fox Agency Records, Box 189. Oklahoma Historical Society, Oklahoma City, OK.

Haworth, John. "100 Years and Counting: Reflections about a Collection, a Collector, and the Museum of the American Indian (before There Was an NMAI)." *American Indian* 17, no. 1 (2016), https://www.americanindianmagazine.org/story/100-years-and-counting-reflections-about-collection-collector-and-museum-american-indian.

Jay, Gregory. "The Engaged Humanities, Principles and Practices for Public Scholarship and Teaching." *Journal of Community Engagement and Scholarship* 3, no. 1 (2015): 51–63.

Katz, Solomon. "Action Anthropology: Its Past, Present, and Future." In *Action Anthropology and Sol Tax in 2012: The Final Word?*, edited by Darby C. Stapp, 183–224. JONA memoir 8. Richland, WA: Journal of Northwest Anthropology, 2012.

Kinietz, W. Vernon, and Erminie Wheeler-Voegelin, eds. *Shawnese Traditions: C. C. Trowbridge's Account.* Ann Arbor: University of Michigan Press, 1939.

Koritz, Amy, and George J. Sanchez. Introduction to *Civic Engagement in the Wake of Katrina*, ed. Amy Koritz and George J. Sanchez, 1–18. Ann Arbor: University of Michigan Press, 2009.

Lassiter, Luke Eric. "From 'Reading over the Shoulders of Natives' to 'Reading Alongside Natives,' Literally: Toward a Collaborative and Reciprocal Ethnography." *Journal of Anthropological Research* 57, no. 2 (2001): 137–49.

Lawless, Elaine J. *Holy Women, Wholly Women: Sharing Ministries through Life Stories and Reciprocal Ethnography.* Philadelphia: University of Pennsylvania Press, 1993.

Leckie, Shirley A. *Angie Debo: Pioneering Historian.* Norman: University of Oklahoma Press, 2000.

Levy, Frank, and Richard J. Murnane. *Dancing with Robots: Human Skills for Computerized Work.* Third Way, 2013. http://thirdway.imgix.net/pdfs/dancing-with-robots-human-skills-for-computerized-work.pdf.

McMullen, Ann. "Reinventing George Heye: Nationalizing the Museum of the American Indian and Its Collections." In *Contesting Knowledge: Museums and Indigenous Perspectives*, edited by Susan Sleeper-Smith, 65–105. Lincoln: University of Nebraska Press, 2009.

Ostler, Jeffrey. *Surviving Genocide: Native Nations and the United States from the American Revolution to Bleeding Kansas.* New Haven, CT: Yale University Press, 2019.

Philp, Kenneth R. *Termination Revisited: American Indians on the Trail to Self Determination.* Lincoln: University of Nebraska Press, 1999.

Price, David H. *Cold War Anthropology: The CIA, the Pentagon, and the Growth of Dual Use Anthropology.* Durham, NC: Duke University Press, 2016.

————. *Threatening Anthropology: McCarthyism and the FBI's Surveillance of Activist Anthropologists*. Durham, NC: Duke University Press, 2004.

Ray, Arthur J. *Aboriginal Rights Claims and the Making and Remaking of History*. Montreal: McGill-Queen's University Press, 2016.

Rhodes, Carl, and Peter Bloom. "The Trouble with Charitable Billionaires." *Guardian*, May 24, 2018. https://www.theguardian.com/news/2018/may/24/the-trouble-with-charitable-billionaires-philanthrocapitalism.

Rosier, Paul C. *Serving Their Country: American Indian Politics and Patriotism in the Twentieth Century*. Cambridge, MA: Harvard University Press, 2009.

Ruegamer, Lana. "History, Politics, and the Active Life: Jacob Piatt Dunn, Progressive Historian." *Indiana Magazine of History* 81, no. 3 (1985): 265–83.

Said, Edward W. *Orientalism*. New York: Vintage, 2003.

Saltmarsh, John, and Edward Zlotkowski, eds. *Higher Education and Democracy: Essays on Service-Learning and Civic Engagement*. Philadelphia: Temple University Press, 2011.

Silverman, David J. "Living with the Past: Thoughts on Community Collaboration and Difficult History in Native American and Indigenous Studies." *American Historical Review* 125, no. 2 (2020): 519–27.

Smith, Linda Tuhiwai. *Decolonizing Methodologies: Research and Indigenous Peoples*. 2nd ed. New York: Zed Books, 2012.

Social Sciences and Humanities Research Council. Home page. Accessed March 26, 2022. https://www.sshrc-crsh.gc.ca/society-societe/community-communite/index-eng.aspx.

Speed, Shannon. "Forged in Dialogue." In *Engaging Contradictions: Theory, Politics, and Methods of Activist Scholarship*, edited by Charles R. Hale, 213–36. Berkeley: University of California Press, 2008.

Steenland, Patricia. "Lost Stories and Cultural Patrimony." *Public* 3, no. 1 (2015), https://public.imaginingamerica.org/blog/article/105-2/.

Storrs, Landon R. Y. *The Second Red Scare and the Unmaking of the New Deal Left*. Princeton, NJ: Princeton University Press, 2013.

Tax, Sol. "Action Anthropology." *Current Anthropology*. 16, no. 4 (1975): 514–17.

Warren, Stephen, and Ben Barnes. "Salvaging the Salvage Anthropologists: Erminie Wheeler-Voegelin, Carl Voegelin, and the Future of Ethnohistory." *Ethnohistory* 65, no. 2 (2018): 189–214.

Zlotkowski, Edward. "Service Learning and the Introductory Course: Lessons from across the Disciplines." In *Higher Education and Democracy: Essays on Service-Learning and Civic Engagement*, edited by John Saltmarsh and Edward Zlotkowski, 154–68. Philadelphia: Temple University Press, 2011.

Part I

Community-Engaged Scholarship with the Three Federally Recognized Shawnee Tribes

Chapter 1

Fort Ancient/Shawnee Ceramics and the Revival of Shawnee Pottery

CHIEF BENJAMIN J. BARNES

The Shawnee pottery project began with a question. During one of the many springtime workdays at the Shawnee ceremonial ground, one of our elder ladies, Marsha Meyer, shared a newspaper clipping that contained a photo of her mother, Patricia (Secondine) Cox, as well as the famed Cherokee potter Anna Belle (Sixkiller) Mitchell and Wyandotte ceramicist Richard Zane Smith. In the photo, Mitchell, Smith, and Cox were displaying handmade Cherokee-style and Wendat clay pots. Richard and Marsha were discussing the clipping and how he has explored his own Wendat peoples' ceramic traditions. Marsha mentioned how amazing it would be if a group of people would be interested in creating Shawnee traditional pottery. I was within earshot of their conversation and I recall saying, "Whoa, slow your roll. . . . No one really knows for sure what traditional Shawnee pottery looks like."

I joined the conversation between Richard and Marsha, and as we began to discuss the challenges of creating traditional Shawnee pottery, the seed of an idea that had been planted years earlier sprung up. I recalled in Stephen Warren's history, *The Worlds the Shawnee Made*, his discussion of the large body of evidence available from the archaeological sites associated with the Fort Ancient of the Middle Ohio Valley. Decades before, Erminie Wheeler-Voegelin created "element lists" that made subtle distinctions between the Shawnees and their neighbors legible. It is in these mortuary features that archaeologists have found ritually buried ceramics that had been carefully placed by their community to accompany the departed. This troika of mortuary practices, historic records, and Fort Ancient funerary vessels could then be compared to archeological sites in our old homelands, allowing us to travel back in time and see just what Shawnee pottery looked like.[1]

Now more than ever in our history, Shawnee citizen-scholars are reversing the research power structure and are engaging with universities and academic specialists to explore our ancient pottery traditions. By exploring the archival record with critical analysis and deploying a triangulation of disciplines, we hope to discover what links exist between the modern Shawnee nations and the Fort Ancient culture of the pre-contact past. Shawnee people had early contacts with the first Spanish explorers of the American Southeast and the first French colonizers of the Great Lakes. They used the existing trade networks of the Middle Ohio Valley, and European trade goods slowly supplanted the ancient artistic traditions of the Shawnee. It is from this rich legacy of archival material, the tracing of European trade goods in late Fort Ancients locations, and from the ceramics that have been located at sites that have a direct connection to the Shawnee, that our citizen-scholars seek to reclaim our artistic birthright and resurrect a dormant ceramic artform. Through interdisciplinary scholarship, we are using material culture to explore the possibility of tracking Shawnee culture into the precontact past. It is the ambition of our ceramic project that Shawnee people will be able to fill in the missing pages of our own history, but also work as an example of community-engaged scholarship that global Indigenous communities can adopt to write their own histories.

From the start, this project began in our community, and it was important to me that it remain so. Connecting ourselves to the amorphous group that archaeologists named the "Fort Ancient" is intangible and hard to relate to for many Shawnee. But the material culture of our people was different. Our ancient ceramics are beautiful, and Shawnee citizens loved being able to admire the artistry of our ancestors. They could hold the work of ancient hands. To touch and sculpt wet clay, this is what I wanted to see for Shawnee people. On many occasions, I have been asked to describe what recapturing this art means for Shawnee people, and I have always answered, "When you study painting, you study the Dutch masters. Where are our masters? They are in the soil of our homelands."

Figure 1.1. Shawnee Tribe's triangulative interdisciplinary research team exploring and discussing Fort Ancient ceramics within the Shawnee homelands. Shown at the table discussing Fort Ancient ceramics are scholars from the Wyandotte Nation, the Absentee Shawnee Tribe of Oklahoma, Eastern Shawnee Tribe of Oklahoma, Shawnee Tribe, Kentucky Archaeological Survey, the Glenn Black Laboratory of Archaeology, and University of Iowa. (Photo courtesy Ben Barnes)

To connect time and enable our people to study and replicate the ceramic traditions of our ancestors requires careful planning and money. Collecting clay was a free and easy task, as Richard had access to a clay site on land owned by a Cherokee citizen, Rebecca Jim. As he described this clay, it was some of the best he has ever worked with, having a firm and creamy texture even after adding temper to the paste.

Ceramics require a temper material to bind the paste together so that it can withstand the firing process. When you work with Richard Zane Smith, this means building an extremely hot fire on the ground with freshly crafted vessels within the inferno. To work with Richard at his ceramic studio and home, it sometimes requires a summer morning drive at an idyllic, winding pace through the furthest northeastern corner of Oklahoma's oak and hickory forests with springs and streams breaking up green ranches and pastures. The land on all sides of the road was once the sole allotments of Eastern Shawnees that were removed from their Ohio homelands. I have driven the road to Richard's many times over the past few years, as he is more than just our mentor. Richard is a Wyandotte artist and a dedicated cultural preservationist. Behind Richard's dwelling is a spring that he considers sacred, as the water feeds a resurrected ceremonial place for Wyandottes from across the country.

To make pottery with Richard is to witness not just artistry, but also ritual. When he intends to fire the pots, he begins early in the morning making a fire with traditional fire-making tools. Once vessels are placed atop of coals, there is nothing left but to hope they can withstand the heat. It is no wonder that it requires a certain spirituality and prayerfulness when you have the hands of a potter. So much is out of your control as you listen closely, hoping to never hear the tell-tale "ping" of a pot that has spalled in the fire. For Shawnee traditionalists, the patient spirituality of waiting comes naturally, as ceremony is never quick and certainly not easy. Our Fort Ancient ancestors also had this patience, as we discovered that making ceramics is no accident. Clay must be gathered and cleaned. Mussel shells, threatened species in most states, are difficult to acquire, and once obtained must be lightly fired so they will crush easily between two stones. I imagined the industry and artisans of our ancient communities as we processed materials just so that we could begin to fashion lumps of clay into replicas of the relics we have seen only in collections.

It was in one of these collections that I experienced what I like to call a "holy moment." Richard and I had traveled to the Kentucky Archaeological Survey in Lexington, Kentucky. Within a nondescript building, archaeologists David Pollack and Gwynn Henderson had prepared a thousand years of ceramic materials from the Fort Ancient for us to examine. Hours passed as we carefully examined each object, until finally I came upon a small, delicate globular jar that had been found at a protohistoric site that had been occupied by Shawnee people during the historic era. I could still see the impressions of small fingers on the fired clay and the centuries-dead artist had decided to decorate the trapezoidal strap handles of the jar with her (I imagine the artist to be a small girl in my mind) fingernail impressions. Without thought, I stuck my fingernail into the groove of her vessel and it occurred to me that it might very well be that in this singular, sublime moment, she and I had touched, Shawnee to Shawnee. That perhaps, this person could be my own grandmother. When I looked up from my hand, my eyes were wet, and I beheld all of the jars in the entirety of its expansive history and I did not see ceramics. I saw my family.

Unlike many pottery traditions which use "grog," ground up bits of pottery sherds, to temper the clay paste with which vessels are made, Fort Ancient people used the shells of river mussels to temper their vessels. In one of our earliest lessons and failures, we discovered that our fine, shell-tempered vessels self-destructed in mere days after having been fired. It was a brutal lesson in organic chemistry. The calcium carbonate of our mussel shells had transformed under the heat of firing to hygroscopic lime. The vessels were literally sucking the moisture out of the air into the ceramic, causing them to spall and burst. None of our early vessels survived. We did not have the eons of time to become masters of the craft like our ancestors. They had a millennium to refine the technique of firing at a relatively low and fickle temperature range. It seemed to us,

Figure 1.2. Chief Benjamin J. Barnes at the Kentucky Archaeological Survey experiencing the legacy of Fort Ancient pottery firsthand. Shown is a Fort Ancient pottery sherd with thumbnail imprints being held by Chief Barnes and quite possibly bridging centuries of divide between its creator and their descendant. (Photo courtesy Ben Barnes)

that the industry of ceramic production had to have consumed much time and effort, leaving little time for them to fall into the stereotype of a seminomadic, hunter-gatherer people. We did not have the luxury of a community feeding and supporting us, nor the centuries to develop mastery of the art, so we needed to develop a plan and some academic partners.

Our small cabal of Shawnee novice potters discussed the possibility of finding partners, professionals and academics, to aid our efforts. Finding a diverse team of academics would allow us to triangulate an interdisciplinary exploration of Fort Ancient ceramics from careful examination of the archaeological, mortuary, and archival evidence. We found ourselves in a fortunate position of having a very willing mentor in Richard, but now we needed to draw upon more than a decade of acquaintances from academia to assist us in exploring the possibilities of what came to be called by us the ancestral Shawnee ceramics project.[2]

Our community began to organize, first on social media, sharing our thoughts and pictures of our earliest attempts at recreating Fort Ancient pottery. The group began to grow, and it was time to find support for the project. As an elected official of the Shawnee Tribe, I helped find classroom space for our community of potters to grow. The Shawnee Tribe also applied for grants that enabled us to bring together an interdisciplinary research team. The Multicultural Initiative for Community Advancement Group, an NGO that helps connect tribal communities to resources, had a series of grants from their Cultural Resource Fund to which we could apply. We were subsequently notified of our award for our phase-one investigative grant, which would consist of at least two planning meetings, one abroad in our old homelands and one at the Shawnee Tribe's offices in Miami, Oklahoma. Now we needed our academic team.[3]

The federal legislation Native American Graves and Repatriation Act (NAGPRA), passed in 1990, had ironically created networking opportunities between academics and the three modern Shawnee nations: the Eastern Shawnee of Oklahoma, the Absentee Shawnee of Oklahoma, and the Shawnee Tribe. From these dialogues with institutions in our former homelands, mutually beneficial relationships between the Shawnee nations and universities began to grow. Chief Glenna Wallace of the Eastern Shawnee Tribe of Oklahoma has done much to promote Shawnee interests in the state of Ohio, and the Shawnee Tribe has evolved a relationship with Indiana University. Prior to the passage of NAGPRA, Native nations that had experienced removal had little cause to go back to their ancient homelands. The pressures of daily business at home compelled us to spend our time on the immediate and local needs of citizens and nation. NAGPRA created an impetus with the force of federal law, mandating that universities and museums consult with us over the disposition and ultimate repatriation of the human remains housed in their collections. The groundwork of reconnection to the homelands became more frequent in a post-NAGPRA world, and early efforts by people such as Chief Wallace bore relationships with academic institutions that had never had the opportunity to come to know us. Before NAGPRA, these institutions did not know who we were as a people. They did not understand what "coming home" to ancestral soil meant for our leadership and our citizens. Chief Wallace describes one such visit she and a delegation of her nation made to the Shawnee village of Wapatomica in Ohio. For a people like Chief Wallace's Eastern Shawnees, the lack of knowing their own people's history had disconnected them, and a return to "home" gave them a connection to their deep past, leaving them wet with tears.[4]

Out of the Shawnee Tribe's NAGPRA meetings with Indiana University, discussions and subsequent conversations about potential collaborations emerged. I found opportunity while in a "right time, right place" situation when I spent a summer fellowship at Indiana University as part of their Institute for Advanced Study's initiative to immerse community members into the university's collections, archives, and libraries. It was an opportune and fertile ground, where I had many intriguing discussions. I can vividly remember where I was when the idea of how we could conduct research on Shawnee ceramics was born. It was during a late afternoon, sitting in the Glenn Black Laboratory for Archaeology, among the works of the Erminie Wheeler-Voegelin collection of the Great Lakes and Ohio Valley Collection. As I worked, Dr. April Sievert and I discussed the Fort Ancient people. We spoke of Wheeler-Voegelin's "Mortuary Customs of the Shawnee and Other Eastern Tribes" and how we could use the element lists she compiled to locate Fort Ancient sites from the precontact and protohistoric era. We could then compare Fort Ancient ceramics to neighboring cultures as well as other Fort Ancient sites. Armed with a comparative framework, I decided it was finally time for us to form the team of specialists who had spent careers studying the Fort Ancient.

Drawing upon our friendship with historian and community-engaged collaborator, Dr. Stephen Warren of the University of Iowa, we hatched a plan with Steve to draw upon his extended network of acquaintances, such as David Pollack and Gwynn Henderson of the Kentucky Archaeological

Survey, to assist our initial investigations. Henderson and Pollack's experience investigating the archaeological remnants of the Fort Ancient world, combined with their knowledge of the Fort Ancient catalog of publications, pointed our Shawnee efforts to examine the Fort Ancient of the middle Ohio River Valley region. Dr. Penelope Drooker identifies cultural differences between the western and eastern Fort Ancients such as "personal adornment, burial patterns, settlement layouts, subsistence, and exchange networks." It is these Fort Ancient exchange networks that are intriguing to Shawnee people. The trade connections between the Fort Ancient and peoples in northeastern Ohio, Pennsylvania, Kentucky, Tennessee, and West Virginia confirm the long-held oral traditions of ancient relationships between ourselves and the Delaware, Yuchi, Muscogee, and Cherokee. The presence of Spanish trade goods found in Fort Ancient contexts suggests access to the trade of Spanish "La Florida" during the sixteenth and seventeenth centuries.[5]

Fort Ancient influence was not contained to the Middle Ohio Valley. In Aiken County, North Carolina, at the Riverfront Village Site (38AK933) peculiar cord-marked, mussel shell tempered pots resembling Madisonville style pots were discovered. Madisonville ceramic traditions are distinctive when compared to the ceramic traditions in neighboring areas, particularly globular jars with strap-like lugs. The necks of the vessels were occasionally adorned with guilloche scrolls and cord-marked bodies as seen on vessels in the Middle Ohio Valley. Ceramic jars with late Fort Ancient characteristics have also been observed at the Lord Ashley Site in South Carolina and Rae's Creek Site near Augusta, Georgia. The similarity between the mussel shell tempered ceramics at Lord Ashley and Rae's Creek become extremely interesting when you connect the dots of the archival record: in the 1680s, Shawnees traded with the Lord Ashley settlement![6]

The Shawnees first entry into the pages of history is a rather ignominious one. Eric Bowne recounts, in *The Westo Indians: Slave Traders of the Early Colonial South*, Shawnees transacting with the English doctor and slave trader Henry Woodward in 1674. This makes the Lord Ashley ceramics even more intriguing, as it was a slave hub on the Carolina coast.[7]

These connections between the Shawnee and Fort Ancient become more compelling as we examine the texts of archaeologists, such as Drooker's *The View from Madisonville*, where she posits the most likely descendants of the Fort Ancient to be the Shawnee. Given these connections, the Shawnee Tribe and our citizens feel that we need to examine the pottery traditions of the Fort Ancient with a critical eye and that these vessels may indeed prove to be the artistic legacy of our ancestors.[8]

After considerable discussion with professional archaeologists Pollack and Henderson, the Shawnee pottery project began to define limits to what we would investigate. During our conversations, a great many topics of mutual interest arose for future study, but, for the scope of our ancestral ceramics, we had to define the bounds. We decided that we would limit ourselves to the Fort Ancient areas of the Middle Ohio Valley. The Shawnee Tribe is very cognizant that other Native nations likely have Fort Ancient lineages. By limiting ourselves to the Middle Ohio Valley sites that produced large assemblages of pottery, we could mitigate some risk by looking less broadly.

We further reduced our geographic scope to the handful of sites that had occupancies between 1400 and 1700 CE. Locations from southern Ohio, northern Kentucky, and West Virginia were selected. We investigated sites such as Fox Farm, Hardin Village, Bentley, Petersburg, Buffalo, and Madisonville and then compared the data to Savannah Town, near modern Augusta, Georgia. Despite limiting ourselves to a number of sites that fit within these parameters, the assemblages of ceramics are enormous and varied. However, a pattern emerges.

During the period of 1400 to 1750 in these locations, the globular jars become very distinct. The lower, spherical body is either plain or cord marked. All are very thin walled when compared to earlier middle Fort Ancient pots and are mussel shell tempered. The graceful neck of the jar that erupts from the ball-shaped body is either plain or decorated and distinctive, trapezoidal, strappy handles emerging from the body, arching upward and reattaching at the rim. The similarity of jar forms across such a broad region of geography and time, using uniform tempering and construction techniques speaks to us of a standardized artistic expression.[9]

Defining the art form to replicate is just one of the challenges for the Shawnee project. To explore the Fort Ancient connection and make any subsequent conclusions, we needed a team of people to aid us in our endeavors. Our associations with institutions and academics gave us some insight into how these tasks could be approached, as it had been performed by others in a bygone era of research into the Ohio Valley tribes. For example, Eli Lilly's method of triangulation to solve difficult problems, be it pharmacological or chasing the myth of the Walam Olum, was adopted and adapted by Erminie Wheeler-Voegelin during her time as the Great Lakes and Ohio Valley's lead investigator for the Indian Claims Commission.[10]

Taking a cue from Eli Lilly and Erminie Wheeler-Voegelin, we assembled a group of people from within and without the tribe. I was very fortunate to make the acquaintance of a Shawnee citizen and archaeologist, Brian Byrd, and, after discussing our strengths and weaknesses, we put together a short list of professionals who might be willing to assist us with the necessary science, archival, and ethnographic work. We obtained eager collaboration in our tribally led initiative from Stephen Warren, April Sievert, David Pollack, and Gwynn Henderson. We also asked an archaeologist friend from the Ohio History Connection, curator of archaeology Brad Lepper, to serve as an ombudsman of sorts. I have come to know and respect Dr. Lepper over the course of many years, and the reverence he holds for well-conceived science and empirical methods is of great service to us. During our initial discussions, Brian Byrd and I both felt that we needed someone that would hold our feet to the fire and make sure that our research was rigorous and free of "wish fulfillment" thinking. Brad is familiar with the Fort Ancient literature.

From our initial study, our meetings with academics, involvements with institutions, and field trips to examine Fort Ancient ceramics have transformed into gatherings of community members to discuss pottery and create it with their own hands. Elder women from our traditional, religious community expressed interest and support for the project, attending classes and creating vessels of their own. Their enthusiasm was vital to our project as their excitement for additional classes created more opportunities for Shawnee people to create new vessels. I am elated to have witnessed Shawnees from the larger community, outside of the body politic of the Shawnee Tribe, flock to our project when word traveled about the revival of Shawnee pottery. Carrie Lind, a Cherokee citizen as well as a Shawnee descendant, is an artist and potter who quickly adapted her skills to creating Fort Ancient–style vessels. As a father, I am of course proud when my twenty-one-year-old daughter Brianna, my youngest child, takes up one of my interests, but it was witnessing someone else's child that brought about another holy moment. When I witnessed the tiny hands of Mya Blanchard, daughter of Absentee Shawnee and traditionalist Eric Blanchard and his wife Jessica, fashion clay into a globular Fort Ancient jar, I was struck that it had been centuries since one of our children had touched clay in the manner of our ancient ones. We are recapturing our past, retelling our stories in word and deed, and the ancient seed of Fort Ancient is growing in the skilled hands of the next generation.

Seeing these vessels now on display in the inaugural exhibit at our new Shawnee Tribe Cultural Center in Miami, Oklahoma, has inspired our growing community to continue this work. We need to look to our ancestral homelands and examine the art of our masters while working with institutions to recontextualize and repatriate the Shawnee narrative. From these jars of clay, the Shawnee community is growing in our capacity to ask and answer our own research questions.

I have noticed that, whenever I speak to my community or to academics, the questions seem to center on the ceramics, as they are truly impressive and beautiful. However, our ceramic project is not just about making pots. As we dive deeper into our own peoples' past, we are asking new questions. Questions that have never been asked by academics before, as they lack the cultural understandings to know the things that we want to answer. We can now show that Shawnee peoples' history did not begin with Henry Woodward in 1674, and we have the chance to author centuries of our own history. We still have much to learn. We want to know how our ancestors managed to carefully control the firing temperature of the mussel shell temper so as not to ruin the pot. We want to know what they cooked in the pots. Residues such as phytolith traces, the fossilized plant material and pollens from the time of our ancients, on the rim sherds can tell us a great deal about our ancestors' foodways. I want to be able to tell small Shawnee children of the artistry and industry of their ancient ancestors and how extremely difficult it is to create these ceramics. For Shawnee people, the process of unlocking the ceramics is more than just making pots, we are unlocking our own curiosity into our deep past.

For communities, it is vital that we participate in what Sonya Atalay describes as "democratizing knowledge production." For us, the questions we ask are not abstractions, but rather they contextualize our past with our own voices and help define ourselves as we see where we are to continue into a future of our own making. Metis scholar Adam Gaudry is correct when he states that "the long-term survival of Indigenous knowledge ultimately rests in the hands of Indigenous people." We must repatriate knowledge of our past from ancestors long vanished to answer our questions of today. The questions we pose are as diverse as the individuals within our communities. For academics, it may at first glance seem difficult to navigate community-engaged and participatory research. The bounds of community are transparent to those outside of them, yet, for those of us within, we see the boundary plainly. Defining community can be particularly difficult, as I imagine it as a Venn diagram with myself at its center.

Each of us in the community sit within that center, and the boundaries' inclusiveness and exclusiveness might vary in detail, but they all will have the same center. For myself and my community, I contextualize it on my experience of being a citizen and elected official of the Shawnee Tribe, but this is not my identity. I was born into being Shawnee, and as I look back on nearly fifty years of life, I see that I have always been Shawnee and the boundary between the tribal office, our religious and cultural place, and my occupation of a small corner of multitribal Oklahoma is as plain as if there were lines painted upon the ground. Questions from me, and those like me, help us to preserve the boundaries of our identities, rooting us into the soil of our cultures and histories. For Indigenous people and our communities, to continue to thrive, both culturally and politically, we must nourish our roots.[11]

Academics also gain in these relationships. Nearly all the people I have met in universities want to know the full and unabridged truth of a subject. With ever-decreasing resources, Native nations can unlock new sources of funding, from federal grants to direct funding. Also, professors with collaborative relationships with tribes have ready-to-order, boxed projects and theses for their students.

But perhaps most importantly, at least in my opinion, this little ceramic project of ours can show how powerful collaborations between Indigenous peoples can be used to restore the lost history and culture of a people enduring the effects of assimilation and genocidal social policies. In the United States, Native nations first engaged with universities as adversaries, battling the NAGPRA issues of the 1990s. It does not have to be this way any longer. We can still uphold the sacred obligations to our ancestors and ensure their reburial while exploring our ancient past. But now, with the advantages of passing years and some wisdom gained, we can see that Indigenous peoples and academics are both stewards of the truth. It is my sincere hope that our little jars of clay inspire Indigenous people somewhere, everywhere, to start to ask their own questions.

Notes

1. Stephen Warren, *The Worlds the Shawnees Made: Migration and Violence in Early America* (Chapel Hill: University of North Carolina Press, 2014).

2. Warren, *The Worlds the Shawnees Made*; Erminie Wheeler-Voegelin, *Mortuary Customs of the Shawnee and Other Eastern Tribes* (Indianapolis: Indiana Historical Society, 1944).

3. MICA Group, Cultural Resource Fund, accessed February 18, 2019, https://culturalresourcefund.org/.

4. Stephen Warren and Eric Wensman, "An Interview with Glenna Wallace," in *The Eastern Shawnee Tribe of Oklahoma: Resilience through Adversity*, edited by Stephen Warren (Norman: University of Oklahoma Press, 2017), 278–79.

5. Penelope Ballard Drooker, "The Ohio Valley," in *The Transformation of the Southeastern Indians, 1540–1760*, edited by Robbie Etheridge and Charles Hudson (Jackson: University of Mississippi Press, 2002), 115–33. For discussion of Spanish trade goods among the Fort Ancient, see Warren, *The Worlds the Shawnee Made*, 63–64, 66–67, 98. For discussion of European trade goods and the southeastern Shawnee intertribal relations, see Thomas G. Whitley, *Archaeological Data Recovery at Riverfront Village (38AK933): A Mississippian/Contact Period Occupation*, vol. 1 (Atlanta: Brockington and Associates, 2013). For data on ceramics found in southeastern archaeological features with possible Fort Ancient affiliation, please see Jon Bernard Marcoux, "The Savannahs and the Landscape of Indian Slavery at the Turn of the 18th Century," presented at the 73rd Annual Meeting of the Southeastern Archaeological Conference, Athens, GA, October 2016.

6. Whitley, *Archaeological Data Recovery at Riverfront Village (38AK933)*. Information regarding the Lord Ashley and Rae's Creek sites was provided to the author by way of a conference presentation delivered by Jon Bernard Marcoux, "Documenting Southeastern Indian Coalescence during the Early Carolina Indian Trade Period (ca. 1670–1715)," presented at "Connecting Continents: Archaeological Perspectives on Slavery, Trade and Colonialism," Society for American Archaeology and European Association of Archaeologists, Joint Thematic Meeting, November 7, 2015.

7. Eric E. Bowne, *The Westo Indians: Slave Traders of the Early Colonial South* (Tuscaloosa: University of Alabama Press, 2005).

8. Penelope Ballard Drooker, *The View from Madisonville: Protohistoric Wester Fort Ancient Interaction Patterns* (Ann Arbor: Museum of Anthropology, University of Michigan, 1997), 103–5. For one of the earliest mentions of the potential linkage between Shawnees and Fort Ancient, see James Griffin, "Late Prehistory of the Ohio Valley," in *Northeast*, vol. 15 of the *Handbook of North American Indians*, ed. William C. Sturtevant and Bruce G. Trigger (Washington, DC: Smithsonian Institution, 1978), 547–59. More information and an introduction to Fort Ancient protocontact archaelogy can be found by Drooker, "The Ohio Valley, 1550–1750," 115–33.

9. Gwynn Henderson, "Fort Ancient Period," in *The Archaeology of Kentucky: An Update*, ed. David Pollack (Frankfort: Kentucky Heritage Council, 2008), 2:741–42, 797–801.

10. For information on Eli Lilly's triangulation method, refer to James H. Madison, *Eli Lilly: A Life, 1885–1977* (Indianapolis: Indiana Historical Society, 1989). For discussion on Erminie Wheeler-Voegelin's triangulative methodology and her time as a lead investigation for the Indian Claims Commission, please

refer to Warren, *The Worlds the Shawnee Made*, 2014, 248n50. For further discussion on Shawnee usage of triangulation, refer to Stephen Warren and Ben Barnes, "Salvaging the Salvage Anthropologists: Erminie Wheeler-Voegelin, Carl Voegelin, and the Future of Ethnohistory," *Ethnohistory* 65, no. 2 (2018): 189–214.

11. Sonya Atalay, *Community-Based Archaeology: Research with, by, and for Indigenous and Local Communities* (Berkeley: University of California Press, 2012), 3. Adam Gaudry, "Next Steps in Indigenous Community-Engaged Research: Supporting Research Self-Sufficiency in Indigenous Communities," in *Towards a New Ethnohistory: Community-Engaged Scholarship among the People of the River*, ed. Keith Thor Carlson, John Sutton Lutz, David M. Schaepe, and Naxaxalhts'i (Albert "Sonny" McHalsie) (Winnipeg: University of Manitoba Press, 2018), 254–55.

Bibliography

Atalay, Sonya. *Community-Based Archaeology: Research with, by, and for Indigenous and Local Communities,* Berkeley: University of California Press, 2012.

Bowne, Eric E. *The Westo Indians: Slave Traders of the Early Colonial South.* Tuscaloosa: University of Alabama Press, 2005.

Drooker, Penelope Ballard. "The Ohio Valley, 1550–1750: Patterns of Sociopolitical Coalescence and Dispersal." In *The Transformation of the Southeastern Indians, 1540–1760*, edited by Robbie Etheridge and Charles Hudson, 115–33. Jackson: University of Mississippi Press, 2002.

———. *The View from Madisonville: Protohistoric Western Fort Ancient Interaction Patterns.* Ann Arbor: Museum of Anthropology, University of Michigan, 1997.

Gaudry, Adam. "Next Steps in Indigenous Community-Engaged Research: Supporting Research Self-Sufficiency in Indigenous Communities." In *Towards a New Ethnohistory: Community-Engaged Scholarship among the People of the River*, edited by Keith Thor Carlson, John Sutton Lutz, David M. Schaepe, and Naxaxalhts'i (Albert "Sonny" McHalsie), 254–58. Winnipeg: University of Manitoba Press, 2018.

Griffin, James. "Late Prehistory of the Ohio Valley." In *Northeast*, vol. 15 of the *Handbook of North American Indians*, edited by William C. Sturtevant and Bruce G. Trigger, 547–59. Washington, DC: Smithsonian Institution, 1978.

Henderson, Gwynn. "Fort Ancient Period." In *The Archaeology of Kentucky: An Update*, vol. 2, edited by David Pollack, 739–902. Frankfort: Kentucky Heritage Council, 2008.

Madison, James H. *Eli Lilly: A Life, 1885–1977.* Indianapolis: Indiana Historical Society, 1989.

Marcoux, Jon Bernard. "Documenting Southeastern Indian Coalescence during the Early Carolina Indian Trade Period (ca. 1670–1715)." Presented at "Connecting Continents: Archaeological Perspectives on Slavery, Trade and Colonialism," Society for American Archaeology and European Association of Archaeologists, Joint Thematic Meeting, Curaçao, November 7, 2015.

———. "The Savannahs and the Landscape of Indian Slavery at the Turn of the 18th Century." Presented at the 73rd Annual Meeting of the Southeastern Archaeological Conference, Athens, GA, October 2016.

MICA Group. Cultural Resource Fund. February 18, 2019. https://culturalresource fund.org/.

Warren, Stephen. *The Worlds the Shawnees Made: Migration and Violence in Early America*. Chapel Hill: University of North Carolina Press, 2014.

Warren, Stephen, and Ben Barnes. "Salvaging the Salvage Anthropologists: Erminie Wheeler-Voegelin, Carl Voegelin, and the Future of Ethnohistory." *Ethnohistory* 65, no. 2 (2018): 189–214.

Warren, Stephen, and Eric Wensman. "An Interview with Glenna J. Wallace." In *The Eastern Shawnee Tribe of Oklahoma: Resilience through Adversity*, edited by Stephen Warren, 265–79. Norman: University of Oklahoma Press, 2017.

Wheeler-Voegelin, Erminie. *Mortuary Customs of the Shawnee and Other Eastern Tribes*. Indianapolis: Indiana Historical Society, 1944.

Whitley, Thomas G. *Archaeological Data Recovery at Riverfront Village (38AK933): A Mississippian/Contact Period Occupation*. Vol. 1. Atlanta: Brockington and Associates, 2013.

Chapter 2

Community-Driven Research

From Indian Country to Classroom and Back

Sandra L. Garner

"Anthropologists and Other Friends," a chapter in the seminal text *Custer Died for Your Sins*, by Vine Deloria, Jr., offers a scathing manifesto about the production of knowledge in academia and its impact on Native communities. From the first paragraph Deloria resonates with many when he argues, "Indians have been cursed above all other people in history. Indians have anthropologists."[1] While the focus of Deloria's critique was the academic discipline of anthropology, his argument impacted many other scholarly disciplines and Native people. This watershed moment was profound and became a critical turning point. It was a political act, one that triggered a paradigm shift, which encouraged deep reflection about the relationship between scholars and the communities about whom they study, produce knowledge, and teach.

Initial responses to Deloria were often as polemical as his original claim. Conversations focused on insider/outsider (Native and non-Native) perspectives and a historical legacy of inequitable power relationships that served colonial, imperial projects. Initially, Native scholars, such as historian Devon Mihesuah and literary critic Elizabeth Cook-Lynn, suggested that non-Native academics should not engage in the study of Indian people.[2] Cook-Lynn identifies non-Native academic knowledge production as an act of "Anti-Indianism."[3] In response, some non-Native scholars left the field altogether, most notably religious studies scholar Sam Gill, who argued that privileging essentialist perspectives undermined "rational discourse, hypothetic inferences, and the application of scientific method."[4] In the context of the ongoing conversations about the history of knowledge production and the relationships between scholars and the communities that they study, new institutional regulations intended to ensure ethical relations, such as institutional review board (IRB) approval and memorandums of understanding (MOUs), emerged.

In the five decades since Deloria's original critique rocked the academic world, the ways that scholars and Native communities approach their relationships with each other and the production of knowledge has grown more complex, nuanced, and interactive. Today reflexivity, culturally sensitive approaches, and collaborative efforts undergird research in many marginalized communities. Contemporary research on American Indian topics reveals two prominent, recurring, interrelated characteristics. First, regardless of the disciplinary focus of the scholar, attention is paid to the fact that these relationships are shaped by the historical legacy of settler colonialism. In response, today's scholars strive to build relationships that include the voices and are shaped by the local knowledge(s) of communities that were historically silenced.[5] Second, academics and communities are increasingly engaged in collaborative arrangements referred to as community-engaged scholarship (CES) or community-based participatory research (CBPR).[6] These approaches have a great deal in common, but also raise a number of interesting questions. Among the commonalities is the recognition that there are multiple stakeholders in CES/CBPR projects and that a multivocal approach that represents the diversity of voices is required to engage in ethical, reciprocal research relationships. As Native archeologist Sonya Atalay demonstrates in *Community-Based Archaeology: Research with, by, and for Indigenous and Local Communities*, there are a variety of formations available in the "interconnected and overlapping practices within a collaborative continuum."[7] For Atalay, principal organizing features should be attentive to the level of participation and community decision-making in the collaborative continuum as they "signify the level of capacity building and power sharing with the project."[8] Shaping the practices of collaboration and power sharing is a self-conscious effort to engage in reciprocity, a characteristic that has long been identified as central to Native/Indigenous worldviews.

Reciprocity: Community Engaged Scholarship
in Indian Country

For a long time, scholars across disciplines have identified Native/Indige-nous worldviews as oriented toward and grounded in a conceptual under-standing of the universe as interrelated. This ethos privileges the idea of community structured by kin relationships, rather than the individual. For example, more than seven decades ago Boasian-trained ethnographer and linguist Ella Deloria observed and wrote about the centrality of kin-ship in her research on the Dakota/Lakota.[9] Kinship as *the* foundational Dakota/Lakota cultural value and practice was addressed in every piece of work written by Deloria. It is so prominent that scholar Maria Cotera calls it "a veritable leitmotif in Deloria's body of work."[10] In *Speaking of Indians*, Deloria describes the complex kinship network as a dizzying array of blood and social relationships, each relationship carrying its own distinctive conventions of interpersonal engagement. The structure situates individual roles and responsibilities within a complex system of "reciprocal obligations."[11] Deloria suggests that these conventions were deeply encul-turated within the Dakota/Lakota social fabric. She observes that every "term [of address], attitude, behavior, in the correct combinations, were what every member of society must learn and observe undeviatingly."[12] My research on the Medicine Men's Association on the Rosebud Reser-vation concurred. It revealed a worldview that recognized the relatedness of everything and the acknowledgment that a standard of reciprocity in these relationships, through the construct of kinship, brought order. In this ethos, reciprocal obligations, affection, and respect are critical to the well-being of the social fabric.[13]

Religious studies scholar David Delgado Shorter observes a similar focus in his work on the Yoeme of Northwest Mexico. He observes that many Native peoples conceive "of their worlds as a single interrelated net-work of social relations that include other-than-human persons," suggesting that kinship networks are quite complex and include all of creation. This conceptual understanding of the universe gives rise to an important view embraced by Native/Indigenous communities that is structured around the notion of inclusive kinship and an ethos of reciprocity: reciprocal obligations.[14]

Anthropologist Thomas Hall and sociologist James Fenelon observe strikingly similar characteristics among global Indigenous communities.

They argue that a "community" that is inclusive and fosters harmonious relations is a hallmark characteristic of Indigeneity.[15] The Maori are just one of the communities that they study. They find "Maori social values are based on social obligations which always entail a measure of self-sacrifice, a commitment not simply to one's family unit but to extended family, to the tribe, and to one's people."[16]

Recurring themes about a worldview that centers the notion of interrelatedness shaped by reciprocity are found among this wide range of examples. Terms such as reciprocal obligations suggest ideals that privilege (1) an understanding that all things are related and that actions by one impacts others and (2) that each entity has a responsibility or obligation to others engaged in the network of relationships. In CES/CBPR, the frame of reciprocity suggests that identifying the key participants, naming and tracing the structures of the networks of relationships involved, identifying and articulating a shared vision of the projects and their resultant products, and recognizing the "reciprocal obligations" of all stakeholders are critical components of successful projects where all parties mutually benefit. In the remainder of this chapter, I offer a case study of one course with which I am involved as a teacher/scholar working in relationship with Native communities (1) the Eastern Shawnee Tribe of Oklahoma (ESTOO) for six years and (2) the Native American Indian Center of Central Ohio (NAICCO) for two years. I do not suggest this as an exemplary model of best practices in CES/CBPR projects. Rather, this study illuminates critical steps, definitions, and understandings that can expand the way that we think about effective, respectful, responsible community collaborations grounded in the ideal of reciprocal kinship obligations. I begin with a brief description and overview of the project. Then I move to tease out the critical nodes of networks, those intersections that represent various stakeholders and their expressed obligations, to suggest the ways these relationships shape CES/CBPR projects. I conclude with specific examples that can enrich the way that scholars and community members think about what works and what doesn't in collaborative research.

Case Study: An Overview

In 2012 I began teaching a required course (AMS 301) for the American studies major and minor at Miami University (Oxford) that focuses on the methods and practices of American studies. The course, geared toward second- and third-year undergraduate students, highlights collaborative and interactive learning that links students and university faculty with communities and constituencies *outside* the university. Student learning outcomes are described as encouraging critical self-awareness, civic engagement, public service, and social stewardship. Further, the class fulfills both college and university diversity requirements, thus the communities and constituencies engaged outside the university must represent diverse publics. With a background and training in Native American and Indigenous studies, I conceptualized the community as Native and was sensitive to the various conversations, debates, and critiques about the academic study of these groups. I sought pedagogical methods that destabilize the power inequities of the historical academic approaches (discussed previously); what Maori scholar, Linda Tuhiwai Smith calls decolonizing methodologies.[17] Two key characteristics identified by Atalay, drawing on Smith's work in her discussion of CBPR practices, include a focus on research that is driven by the community and produces results that are relevant and useful to the community.[18]

The first offering of the course began in partnership with ESTOO and has since expanded to include NAICCO. As of 2018, this class has been offered seven times and class sizes have grown from an initial twelve to fifteen students to a full enrollment of twenty-five (with a student waiting list to take the course). The success of the on-campus course enabled me to develop a summer study away course, where Miami University students travel to Oklahoma to support ESTOO's summer youth culture camp. AMS 301 and the summer workshop are closely interrelated and involvement in the summer youth culture camp would not be possible without the work accomplished in AMS 301. Since this relationship began, the Tribal Historic Preservation Department at ESTOO regularly identifies materials to be used at camp as projects for AMS 301 student projects. Examples include language workbooks and instructional language PowerPoint lesson plans and involve close interaction with language expert George Blanchard (Absentee Shawnee).

During each fifteen-week-long semester the class is divided into teams that work on specific research projects requested by community partners. At minimum there are two projects being completed during the semester, but there have been as many as six. Ohio is one of a handful of states that is not home to a federally recognized tribe.[19] Most students coming into the class have little to no exposure to Native people or communities and standard K–12 education (in the Midwest region from which the majority of students come) provides only a brief surface level survey of Native American history. Students thus come to the course thinking of Native peoples as inhabitants of past worlds. Most have never met a Native person. As a result, the first task of AMS 301 is to provide students with a necessary toolbox of knowledge about Native Americans broadly and our community partners in particular.

It has taken a number of course offerings to refine a structure that involves four weeks of intensive reading, discussion, and writing. Each class meeting, students are assigned two readings that focus broadly on six interrelated themes relevant to "Indian country": storytelling, history/memory, land, language, spirituality/philosophy, representation, and sovereignty. Each week students submit a paper that synthesizes the interrelated concepts using the readings as evidence. My objective is to provide students with the understanding that there are multiple perspectives within any Native community. Secondly, I train students to identify and describe Native worldviews. My overarching goal is to encourage culturally sensitive research projects. Two additional weeks are dedicated to students learning about the community partner with whom they are working and how to develop and write a research proposal and plan. Eight weeks are dedicated to students' implementation of their research plan, and, during the final week of the semester, students prepare and present their findings to the community partners. All final research projects (and their supporting evidence) are given to the community partner. Throughout this process, from initial conceptualization of projects requested by the community to delivery of the final products there is communication with and participation by the community partners.

This brief description of the case study underpinning this chapter points to a number of issues worthy of closer attention. In the following section I offer a more detailed description of the multiple stakeholders who are involved: tribal communities (ESTOO and NAICCO); teacher/scholars and undergraduate students. These labels do little to reflect the complexities of the subject positions in partnership practice. They oversimplify the networks of relationships that shape CES/CBRP projects and do not adequately address the obligations, constraints, and expectations that shape the capacity of stakeholder reciprocity. I begin with acknowledging the institutional structures that serve as non-named actors in CES/CBRP projects.

Case Study: Stakeholders and Reciprocal Obligations

ESTOO and NAICCO are institutions that are constrained by various federal and state regulations and economic factors. ESTOO is one of three federally recognized Shawnee tribes, whose governmental seats are currently located in Oklahoma after a long history of displacement and migration imposed by settler-colonial projects in the United States. Most notable of the federally imposed displacement strategies was the Indian Removal Act, signed into law in 1830. Many ancestors of today's descendent Shawnee tribal members were removed from Ohio as a result of this legislation in the 1830s. One hundred years later, in the 1930s, ESTOO reorganized under the Oklahoma Indian Welfare Act of 1936. During this reorganization process, ESTOO wrote and ratified a constitution and today the tribe exerts self-determination as it defines citizenship status, elects its own governmental officials, oversees economic development, and serves as an administrative body for multiple human service programs. ESTOO is a governmental institution that has obligations in its relationship to federal and state governments and its citizens.

While NAICCO is not affiliated with or run by a federally recognized Native nation, it is a nonprofit organization that answers to a board of directors. Its funding relies solely on donations and grants. NAICCO is one of many urban Indian centers that emerged post World War II, when Native peoples were recruited by the US government to leave reservation areas. Larger US cities were seen as ideal locations where Indian people could be further assimilated to American culture. According to the government, relocation from rural reservations to urban cities such as San Francisco, Dallas, Denver, Chicago, and Cleveland, promised opportunities in employment, education, and housing. As the government did not provide the support needed to smooth these transitions, urban Indian centers popped up in many major US cities to support the local Native populations. Selma Walker, a Dakota woman, from the Yankton Sioux Reservation, founded NAICCO in 1975. The center has served Indian peoples in Ohio for more than four decades.

The final actor in this complex of institutions is Miami University, a public university in Oxford, Ohio, that is ultimately governed by a state appointed board of trustees. Founded in 1809, Miami promotes its reputation as a "public Ivy" institution of higher education. Miami is focused primarily on offering a high quality, liberal arts education for its nearly seventeen thousand undergraduate students.[20] Graduate education is not a priority for the university and there is only one doctoral program in the humanities. From 2010 until 2019, Miami was ranked as one of the "top ten" universities in the US for faculty commitment to quality undergraduate teaching.[21] Demographically, 75 percent of the student body at Miami identifies as "White," while less than 0.2 percent, of students (thirty-five) identify as American Indian/Alaska Native.[22]

There are no MOUs between these institutions in regard to the case studies examined here, and, in this sense, we might not even identify the institutions as stakeholders. However, as scholars engaged in CES/CBPR projects are nested within and have obligations to the institutions, the institutions exert a tremendous influence on the process. The Myaamia Center at Miami University is one model for tribal and academic cooperative and mutually beneficial relationships. It is a relationship that has been decades in the making and has enjoyed national successes, in particular the removal of Miami's culturally insensitive sports mascot in the late 1990s.

However, as an academic research center rather than an academic department, the Myaamia Center functions outside of many of the constraints of university, college, and departmental obligations, and it is governed by an MOU. The center fully engages self-determination in regard to research agendas, and its language revitalization efforts have gained global recognition. This in turn benefits the university's image as an institution committed to diversity. The center has a home in an academic environment, and a Miami Heritage Scholarship program provides higher educational opportunities at Miami University for Miami tribal citizens. In fact, as of the 2018–19 academic year, 32 of the 35 self-identified American Indian/Alaska Natives at Miami University are Miami tribal citizens.

Nested in these institutions are individual stakeholders who work to put into practice the ideals of CES/CBPR—to contribute research products that, at best, enrich the Native communities engaged in the process. At ESTOO the original point of contact is Chief Glenna J. Wallace. Chief Wallace is the first elected female chief of the tribe and was recently elected to serve her fourth, four-year term. She did not seek the position until she retired from a successful career as an educator and administrator in higher education at Crowder College. Chief Wallace is a dynamic force of personality. She is charismatic, has sharp business, entrepreneurial acumen, and knows people, particularly the citizens of ESTOO. In September 2017, at a community breakfast held during the tribe's annual meeting I watched as she named every member of the tribe sitting in an audience of several hundred. Chief Wallace's primary obligation is to the people that she represents as an elected official.

At NAICCO, the primary contacts are Tyrone and Masami Smith, who are both enrolled citizens of the Confederated Tribes of Warm Springs in Oregon (Wasco, Yakama, Walla Walla, Colville). Masami Smith serves NAICCO as the executive director and Tyrone Smith (who holds a master's in social work from the Ohio State University) is the project manager and provides oversight for grant implementation. These are positions that they have held since 2011. The Smiths arrived in Ohio nearly thirty years ago and, like most Native peoples who come through or settle in the state, gravitated to NAICCO as a site where they could interact with other Native peoples in an area that seemed devoid of American Indians. They became actively involved in the center and, when the previous director stepped down, they were asked to take the helm. As a nonprofit organization, NAICCO's primary obligation is to the community of Native Americans served by the center.

As an associate professor at Miami University, I am expected to conform to a teacher-scholar model, which emphasizes teaching in a liberal arts environment. The Association of American Colleges and Universities (AAC&U) writes that "the key to educational excellences lies not in the memorization of vast amounts of information, but rather in fostering habits of mind that enable students to continue their learning, engage new questions, and reach informed judgments," which the AAC&U refers to as "deep approaches to learning."[23] As a teacher-scholar I work to create an environment for students that promotes "deep learning." Drawing from an active research program in Native American and Indigenous studies, I encourage students to critically examine the impacts of settler colonialism. I ask them to consider solutions to problems that avoid the pitfalls of inequitable power relations in the production of knowledge. Meeting and working alongside these communities is an effective strategy for achieving these goals.

Students comprise the final link in the CES/CBPR projects described here. Each class offering brings a new cohort of students. Less than half of the students are American studies majors. While this makes for a steeper learning curve, it does enrich the range of skills that can be offered to our community partners as the majors range from information management systems (IMS) to strategic communications, and even economics. Rarely do students continue their relationships built with the communities beyond the fifteen-week course. For the student, their primary obligation is to fulfill university requirements for graduation. In 2015, I submitted and received approval for AMS 301 for experiential and service-learning accreditations, both are currently university requirements. Fall term 2016 was the first-time students evaluated this component and in four categories more that 80 percent of the students agreed that their interactive work with the community partners enhanced their learning experience.[24]

From institutions to students to teacher/scholars, we can trace multiple and changing stakeholders. The network of relations and the notion of reciprocity is complicated and never static. In the remainder of this paper, I examine two specific projects: the ESTOO Youth Culture Camp and a fundraising campaign for NAICCO. The two projects cause us to think about what constitutes "community," how we might differentiate between CES and CBPR projects, and the successes and challenges of this type of work.

ESTOO Youth Culture Camp

One of the earliest research requests from ESTOO was assistance in helping them develop and structure their summer youth culture camp. ESTOO had offered a youth culture camp for several years, but the program suffered from inadequate staffing and structure. I suggested this project to an extremely capable senior as her senior honors project. Ms. Smitson began by meeting with George Ironstrack of Miami University's Myaamia Center to learn about that tribe's summer camp. She studied the handbooks, schedules, and activities developed by the Myaamia Center, researched similar youth camp programs as comparative models, and worked closely with Robin Dushane, then director of ESTOO's Tribal Historic Preservation Office (THPO), to develop a model program.

While initially the plan did not involve Miami University students traveling to Oklahoma to take part in the actual camp, it was clear that we needed to be on the ground on Eastern Shawnee lands to assess the efficacy of the program. The first year of the new camp program, the summer of 2014, I traveled with three Miami students to Oklahoma. Smitson was among the group. We arrived several days early and helped ESTOO prepare for the camp. The first year was grueling. Camp lasted for five days and included two overnight stays. ESTOO provided the cultural programming, while Miami students served counselor functions: escorting youth to and from activities, leading short team-building exercises, staying as part of the sleepovers, preparing some meals, and assisting ESTOO youth with their projects. Despite the exhaustion felt by Miami students, all felt that the trip had been worth their time and that engaging with the youth and their families had developed their capacity for intercultural understanding. To be clear, the first-year students participated as volunteers. Smitson had already graduated, one student was working on a summer scholar fellowship, and the other was interested in the tribe as a result of taking the AMS 301 course. They did not receive university credit for their efforts and paid all of their own expenses.

The tribe was pleased with the outcomes from the first culture camp collaboration with Miami University students, and the following year they sought to continue this relationship. On the other hand, because of liability issues, the university frowned on the continuance of the trip unless it became a university activity. I sought and received university approval to offer this opportunity as both a credit and noncredit summer workshop for the summer of 2015. This course became closely tied to the AMS 301 course and is always one of the group projects identified by the tribe. Each year the 301 "camp team" refines the program and works with ESTOO on the actual schedule, and camp runs more smoothly. For example, in 2016 the AMS 301 team assigned to work on camp materials worked closely with Dushane and George Blanchard, one of the few remaining Shawnee speakers. Blanchard is an Absentee Shawnee citizen and the former governor of his nation. During our project, he was employed by ESTOO as a language specialist and instructor. The students developed educational materials for the camp's language programming, including PowerPoint instructional presentations for each day and fun activities and worksheets meant to reinforce the language skills of the youth.

The program was well received by tribal members, and by 2017 the number of Shawnee youth taking part in camp had almost doubled from about twenty to nearly forty. A large number of Shawnee youth are children of tribal employees, but culture camp also draws from the broader diaspora of Shawnee families.[25] Families from a number of states, such as Texas, Oregon, Tennessee, and Washington, travel to Oklahoma and bring their children to camp. We have developed a schedule that works and now requires minimal adjustments each year. ESTOO campers are divided into three groups that work together all week long. Each day starts with a large group activity that serves to build a sense of community among the campers. This is followed by an outdoor sport. Throughout the remainder of the day the three groups rotate between culturally relevant activities. At the end of the day the group comes together as a whole and reflects on the day's activities. The camp runs from Tuesday through Friday, with one overnight, and the structure—that is the timing and rotation of activities—is set and works well. Thus, the schedule and even the meal plans do not need to be reinvented each year.

Programming does change, and it is always determined and instructed by tribal members or employees. Two elements of cultural programming remain the same. Language and an outdoor sport are always a part of camp. In the past the sport has been lacrosse, but in 2016 we began to incorporate "Indian" football. "Indian" football has long been a part of Shawnee tradition and is often played during ceremonies. In the game, the women and men play against each other and the rules governing the ways that each gender can move the football toward the goal differ. In 2018, Blanchard explained to the campers that the game's original purpose was to teach community members about kinship relationships and the proper conventions, the reciprocal obligations, for interacting with each other. The campers enjoy this sport more than the lacrosse, as it requires less skill. It takes more than four days a year to become a good lacrosse player. "Indian" football has the added benefit in introducing the youth to a long-standing cultural practices and values.

On the Miami University side of the relationship, although the number of students who express interest has grown, my goal is to bring six to eight dependable, mature students each year; at least two counselors per group of ESTOO youth and several to serve to provide breaks and float between tasks. In 2015, 2016, and 2017, I took five to six Miami University students. From an institutional perspective this is problematic, as ten students is the minimum for a course to receive university approval for a summer workshop.[26] Through 2017, the university was willing to negotiate this process, to take a loss as long as student fees covered overhead expenses. I closely interview prospective students and have rejected Miami students on several occasions. For example, in 2016, I denied admittance to a number of lacrosse players who had applied because they were under university disciplinary action. I am highly sensitive about the fact that these students will be working with Native youth. To the best of my ability, I want to ensure that they are mature enough to handle the intense atmosphere of working with youth for long periods of time. I want them to be good ambassadors of Miami University and role models for the ESTOO youth. It is quite clear that the ESTOO youth really look up to the college students.

As 2018 culture camp began, there were many changes, particularly in regard to personnel at ESTOO that had been involved with culture camp. Long-time THPO director Robin Dushane had left her position and a new THPO director, Brett Barnes, was hired. This was the first year that Barnes participated in camp. Also, museum specialist Kenny Glass, who had been instrumental in camp for several years, left for another employment opportunity. Communities are not static, which means that the relationships we build and invest in are always subject to change. Due to funding changes by the federal government under the Trump administration, those monies that have, for the most part, sustained cultural programming for ESTOO are in jeopardy, and the future for those ESTOO employees who play critical roles in culture camp is unclear at this time.

Further, in March 2018, I received word from Global Initiatives, the administrative arm of Miami University's study abroad and study away programs, that they were canceling the summer workshop due to low enrollment. My commitment to the program is strong, so I traveled alone to Oklahoma to assist the tribal members with culture camp. We worked with ESTOO summer interns and trained them using the summer culture camp counselor handbook developed by Smitson in 2014. After camp, we reflected and reassessed future collaborations in regard to the sustainability of the ESTOO Youth Culture Camp and Miami University's involvement. I personally feel a deep commitment to the tribe and the program, a sense of obligation, but not a burdensome one. Reciprocal obligations, or the sense of reciprocity provide us with the sense of community, and I do feel kin to the staff at ESTOO, the youth that I've worked with for five years, and their families.

At the end of 2020 and as final revisions to this chapter are completed, we have come full circle on this project. At ESTOO there is not a single employee who began the work on the summer youth culture camp still there. A structural reorganization of the tribe has placed the Cultural Preservation Department under the direction of Ceremonial Chief Shawn King rather than Tribal Administration. Chief King is an adherent of Lakota ceremonial traditions, not Shawnee. While I still maintain what I hope are lifelong relationships with various tribal families and the youth that came through camp, this lesson is indicative that these sorts of reciprocal relationships are not static; they are always in a state of flux.

NAICCO and Social Media

I have been part of the NAICCO community for more than three decades, well before returning to college and earning my degrees or my employment at Miami University. During a conversation at a community event, Tyrone Smith asked me about my work with ESTOO. He was curious about the types of research that my students had done for the tribe and what had been successful and what had not. NAICCO, like ESTOO, is very interested in cultural programming and research, but they do not have the time, staff, or money necessary for the implementation of smaller, practical projects they would like to complete. The classroom, as an arm of scholarship, research, and production, has the potential to be a perfect site for the completion of small projects that a community desires. Our conversation continued for several months, and we decided to work on a project together. NAICCO wanted their website redesigned to provide them with a fresh public and professional look, particularly geared toward future donors and potential grant funding institutions. They also wanted an instruction manual that would tell them how to update and make changes to the web site.

We worked on this project with them during fall semester 2016. NAICCO differed considerably from ESTOO both in the specificity of their requests and in their hands-on participation throughout the project. Fortuitously the student group that worked on the NAICCO project included an IMS (information management systems) major and two journalism and strategic communication majors, who came with skill sets that were critical to the completion of the project. Because NAICCO is located much closer to Miami University, Tyrone and Masami Smith traveled to campus three times throughout the semester. The face-to-face interactions made the students feel more invested in the project. This differs significantly from our work with ESTOO, where, although we communicate via Skype on a regular basis throughout the semester, it is not the same as the personal interactions of the face-to-face meetings.

Despite the frequent communication with NAICCO, at various times the project lagged when NAICCO could not get us the needed materials for the project in a timely fashion. In community-classroom collaborations, an important factor of consideration is that community members have a life, other responsibilities, and duties. Every aspect of the web site went through numerous levels of feedback. NAICCO sent the students text, and students researched and edited the text for web site format (with consideration of the targeted audience in mind). I then edited the text and sent it back to Tyrone and Masami Smith for their input. Oftentimes this process went through two or three feedback loops. NAICCO stumbled on getting pictures to us, so the students mined all of NAICCO's social media outlets, going back a decade, and put them on the site as placeholders. This prompted NAICCO to look critically at the pictures and choose how they wanted their organization represented. It is a collaborative effort.

When the semester was over, the site remained unpublished. NAICCO previously had a bad experience with their original web site. The volunteer who created it fell out of contact, and they didn't have access to change it. As a result, we were not able to update the previous site, but created a new one. Web sites cost money to maintain, and NAICCO wanted to ensure that the previous site was taken down before launching the new site. Although the IMS major graduated that semester, he gave Tyrone his cell phone number and worked with Tyrone through the steps to publish the site.[27] NAICCO was happy with the process and final product, and spring semester the class collaborated with them again on a new social media project. In 2020, the website designed and developed by Miami University students is still in use. NAICCO uses the instruction manual developed by students, and keeps the site up to date with new information.

Concluding Thoughts

The case study examined here makes several contributions to thinking about CES/CBPR projects. First, it enriches the notion of CES/CBPR, as it expands thinking about these projects beyond the dominant model of scholarly expertise on a given community working in collaboration with a Native cultural carrier or what historian Stephen Warren and Shawnee collaborator Ben Barnes call the Native scholar-activist.[28] The studies of ESTOO and NAICCO suggest that short term projects that are carefully defined present another option on the CES/CBPR continuum. In these cases, public scholarship that is identified by the community as a need and where the community collaborates throughout the process until its completion is another model. The undergraduate classroom holds great potential for successful completion of projects that the community may not have the time, funds, or staff to research or implement. Incorporating the teacher/scholar model expands the field of stakeholders to include university students and our ideas about what constitutes scholarship.

Second, as we talk about stakeholders and communities, this case study demonstrates the invisible and often unaccounted for stakeholder—the home institution, governments, higher education, and grant funding institutions that profoundly shape scholars' collaborations (be they academic or Native activists). The notion that communities are nested within institutional structures is rarely considered when CES/CBPR approaches are discussed. Examples such as the ESTOO Youth Culture camp demonstrate that the academic and community relationships are not static; they are always in flux. Who the scholar works with today may not be there tomorrow (and the scholar that a community works with may not be there tomorrow). Lastly, we see that long-term collaborations are not always feasible, no matter the desire.

As a result, the focus on CES/CBPR projects in the classroom must be one that seeks to develop the best practices of cultural sensitivity and community participation on the ground. For me, the Native/Indigenous ideal of reciprocity is the goal to which I aspire in the classroom and in my work with Native communities. I work to ensure that all stakeholders are acknowledged and aware of their obligations to all in the complex web of relationships and that all are benefitted by the relationship. It is a process and practice continually shaped by hard work to keep communication open, the incorporation of continual feedback loops, and the willingness to make mistakes and get up and go back to try again.

Notes

1. Vine Deloria, Jr., *Custer Died for Your Sins* (New York: Macmillan, 1969), 78.

2. See Devon A. Mihesuah, *Natives and Academics: Researching and Writing about American Indians* (Lincoln: University of Nebraska Press, 1998); Elizabeth Cook-Lynn, *Anti-Indianism in Modern America: A Voice from Tatekeya's Earth* (Urbana: University of Illinois Press, 2007).

3. Cook-Lynn, *Anti-Indianism in Modern America*.

4. Sam Gill, "The Academic Study of Religion," *Journal of the American Academy of Religion* 62, no. 4 (1994): 968.

5. Sonya Atalay, *Community-Based Archaeology: Research with, by, and for Indigenous and Local Communities* (Berkeley: University of California Press, 2012).

6. Ibid.

7. Ibid., 48.

8. Ibid.

9. Deloria was one of a large cadre of so-called "Native informants" trained by Franz Boas. While recognition of many of her contributions came posthumously, she is now acknowledged as an accomplished scholar, intellectual, and novelist. She was also the aunt of Vine Deloria, Jr.

10. Maria Cotera, "'All My Relatives Are Noble' Recovering the Feminine in Ella Cara Deloria's Waterlily," *American Indian Quarterly* 28, no. 1/2 (2004), 56.

11. Ella Deloria, *Speaking of Indians* (1944; Lincoln: University of Nebraska Press, 1998), 25.

12. Ibid., 30.

13. Sandra Garner, *To Come to a Better Understanding: Medicine Men and Clergy Meetings on the Rosebud Reservation, 1973–1978* (Lincoln: University of Nebraska Press, 2016).

14. David Delgado Shorter, *We Will Dance Our Truth: Yaqui History in Yoeme Performances* (Lincoln: University of Nebraska Press, 2009), 19.

15. Thomas D. Hall and James V. Fenelon, *Indigenous Peoples and Globalization: Resistance and Revitalization* (Boulder, CO: Paradigm, 2009), 28.

16. Ibid., 42.

17. Linda Tuhiwai Smith, *Decolonizing Methodologies: Research and Indigenous Peoples* (London: Zed Books, 1999).

18. Atalay, *Community-Based Archaeology*, 10.

19. Several intertribal urban Indian centers emerged after the post–World War II relocation efforts.

20. Miami University, "Miami at a Glance," accessed February 6, 2021, http://miamioh.edu/about-miami/quick-facts/.

21. Jan Taylor, "Miami among Best Schools in the Nation for Commitment to Students," Miami University, September 10, 2018, https://miamioh.edu/news/top-stories/2018/09/usnews-teaching.html.

22. We know that thirty-two of the thirty-five students who identify as Native are enrolled in the Miami Tribe. Refer to Miami University Office of Institutional Diversity and Inclusion, "Data, Reports, and Demographics," accessed February 6, 2021, https://miamioh.edu/about-miami/diversity/diversity-snapshot/enrollment.

23. George D. Kuh, Daniel Chen, and Thomas F. Nelson Laird, "Why Teacher-Scholars Matter: Some Insights from FSSE and NSSE," *Liberal Education* 93, no. 4 (2007): 1.

24. Eighty-eight percent of students agreed or strongly agreed that the community participation aspect of the course helped them to see how the subject matter they learned can be useful in everyday life. Eighty-six percent of students agreed or strongly agreed that serving in the community helped them to become aware of their personal strengths and weaknesses. Eighty-four percent of students agreed or strongly agreed that the idea of combining work with the community

and university course work should be practiced in more courses at Miami. Eighty-one percent of students agreed or strongly agreed that their interactions with the community partner enhanced their learning in the course.

25. The Shawnee have a long history of migration. From the colonial period to the present era, the Shawnee have lived in more than twenty states and lived under at least six national flags. See Stephen Warren, *The Worlds the Shawnees Made: Migration and Violence in Early America* (Chapel Hill: University of North Carolina Press, 2014); Sami Lakomaki, *Gathering Together: The Shawnee People through Diaspora and Nationhood, 1600–1870* (New Haven, CT: Yale University Press, 2014). The contemporary diaspora was formed in large part by the 1930s Dust Bowl. See for example, Cathleen Osborn-Gowey, "Eastern Shawnee Migration: Cultural Changes and Disconnection following the Move to the Pacific Northwest," in *The Eastern Shawnee Tribe of Oklahoma: Resilience through Adversity*, ed. Stephen Warren (Norman: University of Oklahoma Press, 2017), 228–36.

26. For an extensive analysis of institutional constraints that shape service-learning projects see: John Saltmarsh and Edward Zlotkowski, *Higher Education and Democracy: Essays on Service-Learning and Civic Engagement* (Philadelphia: Temple University Press, 2011).

27. Native American Indian Center of Central Ohio, NAICCO website, accessed February 6, 2021, http://www.naicco.com/.

28. Stephen Warren and Ben Barnes, "Salvaging the Salvage Anthropologists: Erminie Wheeler-Voegelin, Carl Voegelin, and the Future of Ethnohistory," *Ethnohistory* 65, no. 2 (2018): 190.

Bibliography

Atalay, Sonya. *Community-Based Archaeology: Research with, by, and for Indigenous and Local Communities*. Berkeley: University of California Press, 2012.

Cook-Lynn, Elizabeth. *Anti-Indianism in Modern America: A Voice from Tatekeya's Earth*. Urbana: University of Illinois Press, 2007.

Cotera, Maria. " 'All My Relatives Are Noble': Recovering the Feminine in Ella Cara Deloria's Waterlily." *American Indian Quarterly* 28, no. 1/2 (2004): 52–72.

Deloria, Ella. *Speaking of Indians*. Lincoln: University of Nebraska Press, 1998. Originally published 1944.

Deloria, Vine, Jr. *Custer Died for Your Sins*. New York: Macmillan, 1969.

Garner, Sandra. *To Come to a Better Understanding: Medicine Men and Clergy Meetings on the Rosebud Reservation, 1973–1978*. Lincoln: University of Nebraska Press, 2016.

Gill, Sam. "The Academic Study of Religion." *Journal of the American Academy of Religion* 62, no. 4 (1994): 965–75.

Hall, Thomas D., and James V. Fenelon. *Indigenous Peoples and Globalization: Resistance and Revitalization.* Boulder, CO: Paradigm, 2009.

Kuh, George D., Daniel Chen, and Thomas F. Nelson Laird. "Why Teacher-Scholars Matter: Some Insights from FSSE and NSSE." *Liberal Education* 93, no. 4 (2007).

Lakomaki, Sami. *Gathering Together: The Shawnee People through Diaspora and Nationhood, 1600–1870.* New Haven, CT: Yale University Press, 2014.

Miami University. "Miami at a Glance." Accessed February 6, 2021. http://miamioh.edu/about-miami/quick-facts/.

Miami University Office of Institutional Diversity and Inclusion. "Data, Reports, and Demographics." Accessed February 6, 2021. https://miamioh.edu/about-miami/diversity/diversity-snapshot/enrollment.

Mihesuah, Devon A. *Natives and Academics: Researching and Writing about American Indians.* Lincoln: University of Nebraska Press, 1998.

Native American Indian Center of Central Ohio. NAICCO website. Accessed February 6, 2021. http://www.naicco.com/.

Osborn-Gowey, Cathleen. "Eastern Shawnee Migration: Cultural Changes and Disconnection following the Move to the Pacific Northwest." In *The Eastern Shawnee Tribe of Oklahoma: Resilience through Adversity*, edited by Stephen Warren, 228–36. Norman: University of Oklahoma Press, 2017.

Saltmarsh, John, and Edward Zlotkowski. *Higher Education and Democracy: Essays on Service-Learning and Civic Engagement.* Philadelphia: Temple University Press, 2011.

Shorter, David Delgado. *We Will Dance Our Truth: Yaqui History in Yoeme Performances.* Lincoln: University of Nebraska Press, 2009.

Smith, Linda Tuhiwai. *Decolonizing Methodologies: Research and Indigenous Peoples.* London: Zed Books, 1999.

Taylor, Jan. "Miami among Best Schools in the Nation for Commitment to Students." Miami University. September 10, 2018. https://miamioh.edu/news/top-stories/2018/09/usnews-teaching.html.

Warren, Stephen. *The Worlds the Shawnees Made: Migration and Violence in Early America.* Chapel Hill: University of North Carolina Press, 2014.

Warren, Stephen, and Ben Barnes. "Salvaging the Salvage Anthropologists: Erminie Wheeler-Voegelin, Carl Voegelin, and the Future of Ethnohistory." *Ethnohistory* 65, no. 2 (2018): 189–214.

Chapter 3

Earthworks Rising

Emerging Roles within Collaborations for Indigenous Knowledge

CHRISTINE BALLENGEE MORRIS,
MARTI L. CHAATSMITH, AND GLENNA J. WALLACE

An Introduction to the Earthworks of Ohio

This story begins over 2,000 years ago when the Original People built outdoor structures in a place that is now known as Newark, Ohio. One form of these structures, the Octagon Earthworks, consists of a 50-acre octagon connected to a 20-acre circle by two parallel walls. A rounded rectangular Observatory Mound stands along the outer rim of the circle at a point opposite to the Octagonal enclosure. The earthworks stand as a testament to the architectural and engineering genius of American Indian culture(s) of that time. The builders of these earthworks captured a rhythm of the cosmic and brought its magic down to earth in the form of monumental geometric architecture. The Oxford archaeologist Chris Scarre, in his book *Seventy Wonders of the Ancient World*, lists the Newark Earthworks as one of only three sites in North America that qualify as a "wonder of the world." The other two sites are Cahokia in Illinois and Chaco Canyon in Nageezi, New Mexico.[1]

The Ohio's Hopewell culture earthworks are distinguished by precisely geometric, enormous earthen architecture that held cultural significance and marked cosmic time through astronomical alignments. The Middle to Late Archaic people who began making earthworks and mounds are referred to as Adena. For the convenience of archeologists, this term is used to identify the people, earthworks, mounds, and objects. A large mound called Adena was found on the estate of Thomas Worthington, the Governor of Ohio, elected in 1814. Archeologists viewed the mounds as a "type-site" and applied that name to everything found from that time period. Archeologists who found artifacts on the property of Mordecai Hopewell in 1891 used the term Hopewell culture. Consequently, that misapplied term refers not only to objects but also to the people who build the earthworks. We do not know the names the builders called themselves, but we do know that many of the tribal names of the builders' descendants simply mean the people. Due to the genocide caused by exposure to European disease and warfare from 1492 on, 80 percent of the Native people died. The cord to the past was broken and the dead took with them the accumulated knowledge and memories of thousands of years, leaving present day knowledge quite incomplete.[2]

The earthworks are large structures that connect people to the natural world, where standing inside the earthworks is an awe-inspiring experience. Until quite recently, much of the information about these places and the People who imagined, designed, and built them was characterized by misunderstanding, misinterpretation, and errors. Over the past twenty years, an explosion of research has enlightened researchers, local stakeholders, and Indigenous communities in the Midwest. Because of the consequences of the diaspora of historic era tribes in the Ohio Valley, the American Indian population of today knows little about them. Earthworks Rising, an interactive multiplatform website developed at Ohio State University, was designed with American Indian participation and incorporates Indigenous values. In accessing the website, users can explore four big ideas: Earth, Sovereignty, Connections, and Awe. In addition to the Newark Earthworks, many ancient places, such as the pyramids of Egypt and Stonehenge, were aligned with the cosmos and integrated into the lives of the Indigenous.

The earthworks of the Hopewell culture are unique; their designs and functions represent outstanding human achievements, a criterion for World Heritage recognition. The earthworks are notable for their immense dimensions. The Octagon Earthworks has a combined area encompassing more than 100 acres. To create these places, Indigenous builders used large river cane and bark baskets to gather earth and shape it into precise geometry by making uniform earthen embankments up to 6 feet high supported by 20-foot-wide foundations. The embankments were then made to be perfectly straight or beautifully curved for hundreds of yards. Social and ceremonial life occurred within huge earthen squares with rounded corners, crescents, around two unique, open-cornered octagons and circles, and in polygons consisting of circles and squares pushed together, and others in the shape of the letter "D." Circles were built in various sizes by using a standard unit of measure—some more than 1,000 feet in diameter. All of the earthworks had entrances—rounded breaks in the embankments, many of them facing the northeast. There are interesting mathematical regularities between earthworks in sites, and possibly between sites.[3] Water features were incorporated into many sites by building alongside natural rivers and ponds or constructing them. Water holds special meanings across Indigenous cultures, and, here, the water features reflect the earth and sky, perhaps a physical manifestation of spiritual or religious beliefs—worldviews that are yet to be deciphered.

Earthworks Rising situates the understanding about Ohio's earthworks firmly within Woodlands American Indian cultural ways of knowing. The Earthworks Rising design and content needed to be informed by an American Indian Advisory Committee (Chief Wallace, Sonya Atalay, and Marti Chaatsmith, to name three). Some were able to travel to the Eastern Shawnee Tribe of Oklahoma's tribal office, and lands, hosting tribal heritage tours to the earthworks in Ohio, our accumulated experiences and expertise, and the literature attending to community-engaged research. This project has been a journey of exploration, experiences, and creative work. Multiple disciplines are relevant to the study of the earthworks, and the need for Indigenous-based curriculum is evident.

In their book, *The Native Americans: An Illustrated History*, authors David Hurst Thomas, Jay Miller, Richard White, Peter Nabokov, and Philip Deloria explain that the archaeological history of the Native peoples of the Americas goes back more than thirty thousand years and that by the time Columbus landed in the "New" World, it was an old world that had already seen civilizations rise and fall. They claim that the continents were populated by at least seventy-five million people who spoke two thousand distinct languages and had developed a rich diversity of separate cultures, all linked by a network of trade. Over time, many of these cities became too large and could not be ecologically sustained, resulting in cataclysm, and leading to a breakdown of the social order within the cities.[4]

Evidence from archeological investigations suggest that the people of the Adena and Hopewell cultures (ca. 400 BC and AD 400) lived in small villages scattered along the major tributaries of the Ohio River—especially the Great and Little Miami, the Scioto, and Muskingum Rivers, as reported by the Ohio History Connection. Yet the people of these cultures produced items of high aesthetic quality, spectacular earthen architecture, and complex cultural ideology. They crafted magnificent works of art from materials gleaned from throughout their world: copper from the upper Great Lakes, mica from the Carolinas, shells from the Gulf of Mexico, and obsidian, a black volcanic glass, from the Rocky Mountains. Within oral traditions, stories often reside in objects. These exotic materials may have come to Ohio as valued commodities in a network of trade, but we have little evidence of what items the traders might have given in exchange. Knives and bladelets made from Ohio's beautiful Flint Ridge flint are found scattered throughout eastern North America, but not in the quantities that would suggest a fair trade for the bushels of mica and copper found at Ohio Hopewell sites. Many of these artistic items were created for funerary purposes.[5]

In 1992, archeological research at the Great Circle in Newark, Ohio, found that the outside wall was built with dark earth, while the inside wall was lined with brighter yellow-brown clay. We know that the builders used colored dirt that was not from the immediate area. We do not know the significance of the use of color, but we do know that the dirt was intentionally layered so that each color was evident in its construction. Much of what is known today about the mounds has resulted from connecting contemporary traditions to archeological evidence. As the result of European contact, the establishment of the American government, subsequent colonial settlement, and increasing immigration, the Ohio River Valley became home to many of the American Indian groups of the historic era whose original territories were being usurped by settlers. Most, if not all of these groups were familiar with the Eastern Woodlands. Burial practices varied, but conical mounds, flat top rectangular mounds, and effigy mounds were ubiquitous throughout the region. Two-thousand-year-old ancient earthen constructions, built alongside more recent mounds and earthworks indicate a shared knowledge, maintained over time, across geographical space and cultural changes, likely continuing into the current era before removal and forced migrations. The Hopewell Ceremonial Earthworks, epitomized by the Newark Earthworks, the Fort Ancient hilltop enclosure, and the geometric, rectangular, and conical mounds built along twelve miles of the Scioto River in present-day Chillicothe, Ohio, were intact and complete in the 1840s, and documented for the Smithsonian Institute in their first publication. The identity of the ancient mound builders may not be known, but the historic, multiethnic tribal groups who settled in among the earthworks landscape were the last American Indian stewards of these Indigenous places.[6]

Whether their ancestors or some earlier cultures were said to have built them, many American Indians today view Ohio's earthworks as part of their shared heritage in being the first nations of the Americas. Oral traditions of respect and reverence continue among many American Indian stakeholders, including removed tribes and allies today, and the narrative record is still growing and preserving stories of these mounds. Today many people are reconnecting with these sites, since the removal from Ohio to the central and southern Plains, such as the Eastern Shawnee. Sonya Atalay, Anishinaabe archaeologist, states:

> These sites remind all of us of that connection—that time is not linear, and the past is always with us. In caring for the past, we care for future generations and ourselves. I think these sites have a power in them—by their very nature they move us to reflect and question, to wonder and ponder. These are important lessons for us all to reflect on and I think Newark Earthworks and other powerful places like it have the power to help us do that.[7]

Atalay suggests the idea of decolonization, defined not as a transfer of political power or possession of space from one source to another, but rather a process of becoming oneself.[8] Ohio does not have federally recognized tribes, due to the historic relocation of American Indian groups during the 1800s. In the absence of tribal presence, evidence of American Indians' long history in the Ohio Valley was erased from the land in an ethnic cleansing, and the historical narrative sanitized and romanticized. Until very recently knowledge and cultural authority about the earthworks has been appropriated by non-Native archeologists and historians. In absence of tribal or American Indian participation, they used informants during the historical era until the early 2000s that misrepresented and distorted American Indian responses to the earthworks.

Development within an
Indigenous-Driven Committee

A quasi-state organization, the Ohio Historical Society (OHS), which was later renamed the Ohio History Connection, receives 70 percent of its operational funds from the State of Ohio, and is the deed holder of the Octagon Mound. They lease the land to Moundbuilder's Country Club for $7,000 a year.[9] The country club advertises their colonial hold on the land on their web site: "The golf course at Moundbuilders is unlike any other in the world. It is designed around famous Prehistoric Native American Earthworks that come into play on eleven of the holes."[10] Discovering, documenting, and classifying a culture, object, or space confirms difference and reconfirms a colonialist's agenda.

The idea for the Newark Earthworks Center was initially developed through the advocacy of a group of community stakeholders, the Friends of the Mounds (FOM). Consisting of American Indian citizens and allies, FOM was established to protect the earthworks and promote worldwide recognition in order to preserve them. This ad hoc group formed as a community response to OHS's support of the country club. With continuing community participation, the FOM's goals were successfully implemented through tours, presentations, community educational outreach, such as Newark Earthworks Days, media coverage, and publications. The earthworks have been nominated by the United States government to become a World Heritage site. These sites must represent cultural works that are unique among the most significant in the world and an example of a masterpiece of human creative genius.

Due to a change of leadership of the Ohio History Connection and policies, the nomination for World Heritage recognition began in earnest in 2005. The Newark Earthworks Center and the American Indian studies program at Ohio State University invited American Indian scholars to tour the earthworks. While most participants were learning about the sites for the first time, there was an emerging recognition that knowledge and interpretation about the cultural significance of the Ohio Earthworks needed to be informed, at the least, by tribal histories and Indigenous cultural knowledge.[11] In 2007, Eastern Shawnee chief Glenna J. Wallace traveled to Ohio to meet John Sugden, a guest of

Ohio State's American Indian studies and a historian of the Shawnee nations. The Newark Earthworks Center invited Chief Wallace to tour the Newark Earthworks with Dr. Sugden, an experience she later wrote about:

> Try to imagine the shock and total disbelief I experienced when I stepped out of the car and looked at this intricate array of earthen walls and landscapes where my people, my ancestors had lived more than three hundred years ago. It was surreal. . . . There before me lay an extensive series of hills or walls—in short, earthworks built nearly two thousand years ago, built with earth carried one basket at a time. They appear so simplistic, yet they contain a mathematical complexity that is mindboggling. How these Native Americans who have commonly been depicted as savages could conceive and construct this massive earthen architecture is as phenomenal as Egyptian slaves constructing the Pyramids. . . . The Newark Earthworks are beautiful and massive.[12]

From this chance visit, a relationship developed between the Eastern Shawnee Tribe of Oklahoma and the Newark Earthworks Center that has exemplified respect and reciprocity. Participation by Chief Wallace and her staff and Ohio State University faculty and staff in events spanning both Oklahoma and Ohio continued over the next seven years, leading to mutually beneficial dialogue in both places. Through attendance at a Newark Earthworks Day of activities, Chief Wallace, Christine Ballengee Morris, Marti Chaatsmith, and Michelle Aubrecht met, and seeds of ideas relating to ways to educate audiences about Ohio's earthworks began to sprout.

The American Indian studies program at OSU wanted the world to know about the earthworks in Ohio and their connections to many parts of the world, and with funding from the National Endowment of Humanities, we were able to begin our first phase of the project by developing a digital game about the Octagon Earthworks. Influenced by the work of Deloria, Atalay, and Smith, and with strong motivation to create an inclusive perspective of the earthworks, we knew that a community approach was the only way to proceed. Smith states that there are two distinct ways "through which Indigenous research agenda is being advanced"—community action,

Figure 3.1. Chief Glenna Wallace of the Eastern Shawnee Tribe of Oklahoma leads a delegation of her people on a tour of Ohio's Earthworks. (Photo courtesy of Newark Earthworks Center; photo by Timothy E. Black)

as well as "through the spaces gained within institutions by Indigenous research centers and studies programmes."[13]

In this situation, defining and realizing a community approach was challenging: Who was representative of the American Indian community and how do we become a community? As Smith states:

In North America, the term "Indian Country" defines one sense of community, a named nation such as the Navaho Nation defines another sense of community, a named reserve defines yet another sense. . . . Some writers refer to these multiple layers of belonging as "nested identities."[14]

For that purpose, we (Chief Wallace, Chaatsmith, and Ballengee Morris) began a dialogue through which we created a consulting collaboration approach, to build learning communities with which to maintain ways of communicating with each other that honor traditional ways. Echoing Smith, Ballengee Morris and Stephen Carpenter argue that "consulting collaborative approaches include critical forms of reflective experiences, cultural studies, and research experiences that challenge established ways of thinking and acting by encouraging a reexamination of one's own values and practices."[15] The consulting collaboration approach is based on the meetings protocols of many traditional tribes: each person has the opportunity to talk, and the facilitator's job is to restate the points made while each question or issue is examined. In this process, talking over someone or monopolizing a conversation is eliminated. Thus, in our project, we met either in person or virtually, and took turns in our exchange of ideas, one at a time, with no interruptions. The facilitator of the group, took notes and sent them to the committee for review and revisions. Once notes were reviewed, changes were made and sent to the non-Native project members. One of the first discussions concerned the essence of what should be learned.

Smith states that this process encourages reflective thinking and practice. Consulting collaborative approaches include critical forms of reflective experiences, cultural studies, and research experiences that can challenge established ways of thinking and acting by encouraging a reexamination of one's own values and practices. This process can build learning communities that will support communities' lifelong successes and achievements through practices that question social problems, policies, and ethical dilemmas.[16]

The content team comprised American Indians, including Chief Wallace, and specialists in the areas of Native American studies, earthworks, anthropology and archeology, architectural history, history, art education, astronomy, and science education. The team members discussed the most meaningful topics through the lens of their subject matter and gave advice about how to understand these issues, while the game designers looked for common themes.

To begin our first meeting, Ballengee Morris presented the stages of the project, which included a website with curricula, projects, and games for informal or formal learning experiences that would utilize Indigenous ways of knowing and Western scientific approaches. Indigenous ways of knowing view the cosmos and nature as creative centers from which we and everything else have come and to which we always return. We are "star stuff"; we came from the stars and, the moment we could, we started back again.[17] Aikenhead and Michell explain the distinction between these two ways of knowing: "The noun 'knowledge' does not translate into most Indigenous languages, in part because English is a noun-rich linguistic system while Indigenous languages are verb-rich."[18]

In many Indigenous traditions, it appears that the expansion of such ways of knowing become woven together. Knowledge unfolds in the everyday, and the everyday becomes a story passed down from one generation to the next. Brian Brayboy recommends embracing tribal differences and supporting general approaches such as recognizing the importance of origin stories that help us to understand sovereignty, seeing stories as data, collecting stories as essential for sustainability, and hearing stories as essential to applying native ways of knowing.[19]

During our meetings, we decided to explore four big ideas—Earth, Sovereignty, Connections, and Awe (see examples below)—that encourage exploring the myriad of symbols and layers of meaning incorporated into the earthworks within these unique enormous earth structures that connect people to the sky. Simply standing within the earthworks is awe-inspiring.[20] The Newark Earthworks, such as the pyramids and our earthworks, were aligned with the solar and lunar systems that aided in mapping and measuring time, seasons, and planting. Therefore, topics in our video game include naming, stories and lore, the process of storytelling, night mapping, constellations, and appreciating the magnitude of the sky and its relationship to the earthworks.

The first stage of this project was in creating a video game prototype about the Octagon Earthworks in Newark, *Catch the Moon*, featuring lunar cycles. The earth rotates once a day and revolves around the sun once a year. The moon rotates around the earth once about every twenty-seven days. The moon has an 18.6-year cycle (eighteen years and 219 days) known as the "major lunar standstill" that occurs because of the Sun's gravitational influence on its plane of orbit about Earth. The Octagon Earthworks was designed to track this long lunar cycle. This information was observed, remembered, and passed down through oral and cultural traditions. Our game was designed to help students grasp the concept that the moon has a variable pattern and cycle that is observable and that the people built the Newark Earthworks to observe a particular moment in that cycle. *Catch the Moon* was introduced at two international physics education conferences in the summer of 2013, and because of the way the game teaches the daily, monthly cycle of the moon in addition to demonstrating the major lunar standstill, several physics educators are now using it.[21]

The following text explains the four themes and the possibilities of curricular ideas that the committee discussed at the time, the four big ideas: Earth, Sovereignty, Connections, and Awe.

EARTH: LAND, WATER, AND SKY (MOVEMENT AND DIMENSIONS)

Explanation: The earthworks should be viewed as a part of a dynamic ever-changing eco-system including plants, birds, and animals. Emerging questions included: What did the people eat, what were the natural sounds to the area, what would have inspired the artistic expression used in the icons and used in the carvings? Waterways are clearly important, as mounds are always located near waterways for daily living and travel. But what happens to the earthworks with the development of motor vehicle highways? Discussions today ask what happens to communities and landmarks and buildings with the construction of a new road, within the context of cultural preservation: When memory of the past is destroyed, the identity attached to place is eroded.

Overall Learning Goal: Students will learn that Native issues are current today and can be connected to the past and future. They will understand why identity is important to Native American cultures.

SOVEREIGNTY: MULTIPLE DEFINITIONS OF PAST, PRESENT, AND FUTURE

Explanation: Sovereignty is a process; Sovereignty is the ability to make decisions for oneself or group. This theme covers traditions, origin stories, languages, and histories (pre- and post-contact) that provide tribal identity and a sense of sovereignty on many levels. The survival of American Indian societies depends upon knowing their connections to the homelands. Sovereignty is related to land. At one time, the earthwork builders had the land. Today, sovereignty is about authority, law, ownership, and interpretation—who has the right to make the rules, enforce the rules and set cultural protocols—in the realms of the intellectual and spiritual?

Overall Learning Goal: Students will learn about maps, why people make maps, and see connections to the concept of ownership. The Western idea of ownership will be contrasted to an Indigenous idea of community and use of resources. Students will explore how ownership changes the decision-making process. What is ownership? What is law? What is nationhood? What is authority?

CONNECTIONS: PROTECTING THE EARTHWORKS IS PART OF CARING FOR YOUR ANCESTORS

Explanation: There is a connection between who we are and who our ancestors are and their accomplishments. Learners will come full circle and reflect on their activities to see relationships and connections through the balance of the four aspects of human personality, physical, emotional, mental, and spiritual. Relationships are the center of the human existence; incorporating language, love, family, and exchange of knowledge. This teaches the students a powerful message that we all share these values as humans and citizens of the world.

Overall Learning Goal: Students will learn about concepts of kinship, language, and cultural traditions, such as gifting.

AWE: SOMETHING BIGGER THAN THE INDIVIDUAL

Explanation: Earthworks are large structures; some were used to connect people on earth to the sky. The earthworks and mounds sites are sacred, much like churches are in today's societies. We considered how communities came together to build and maintain the earthworks sites as well as their scale and geometry and the relationship of their shapes and numbers, such as seven and four, to the sacred.

Overall Learning Goal: Students will realize that the people who built earthworks were complex and sophisticated. The Medicine Wheel is one of the most spiritual yet practical approaches to Indigenous education available. The teachings resonate within the individual and beyond to the community, the nation, and the world. Both symbolizing and modeling a holistic education, seeing the learner as a whole person by attending to the learner's body, mind, heart, and spirit. Thus, the learner may achieve a healthy balance and harmony between the self and community. We see this bridge as having potential for a digital feedback cycle. Connecting concepts that are exemplary of holistic and cyclical views, and that incorporate cultural values such as wisdom, humility, and respect, humor, sharing, integrity, strength, noninterference, and reciprocity, was also important to the advisory committee. Native pedagogy is based on the spiral—always moving, yet never going back. It is about the process of the/a journey.

The use of digital media in the classroom incorporates and connects many twenty-first-century skills, helping students understand visual culture and media to communicate complex concepts. Integrating games into the class-room curriculum applies current research to teaching and learning. Technology, in general, can allow a teacher to move into the role of facilitator, partner, and coach and advisor.[22] Teachers can guide students in thoughtful and researched sharing of ideas, recognizing that they themselves do not know all the answers. The role of the student can also be transformed from passive receiver of knowledge to active producer.[23] Video games provide powerful and complex learning tools and environments through their inherent ability to combine such multimedia as video, sound, text (including narrative), visual information (images, tables, graphs), and simulations, including pulling information from databases in real time.

Conclusion

All cultures, including Native American Indian cultures, are always in a transitional process. Political and social constructs and the negotiation of traditions, needs, and contemporary issues create cultural transformation in relation to personal interpretations. Putting forward American Indian voices through utilizing a collaborative consulting approach and teaching approaches, Native pedagogy, offers a unique alternative to mainstream understandings of who we are as human beings. Questions become key to this approach.

During the development of this project, which began around 2005, the management of cultural heritage in the state of Ohio began a trans-formation that continues to the present day. Between 1840 and 2007, the policies about the Hopewell Ceremonial Earthworks and the Octagon Earthworks in particular were set in place without American Indian and tribal involvement. After 2007, after Chief Wallace's historic visit to Newark, Ohio, tribal government participation became a requirement in the management of these ancient sites. To say everything changed in how the sites came to be interpreted and managed is not an understatement. The connection between the earthworks and the tribes who had been the final Indigenous stewards of the earthworks was restored through the Earthworks Rising project and the Newark Earthworks Center's tribal outreach program. These relationships opened new doors of interpretation and exchange of perspectives and priorities, deepening the understanding of Ohio as Indian land and profoundly enriching understanding of Ohio's history.

Most importantly, we can learn to observe, listen, and ask questions. For our students to learn multiple ways of knowing and doing, we must introduce them to sites like the Octagon Earthworks. Most of the earthworks reflect skills and knowledge of scientists, mathematicians, and artists—Indigenous people who observed their environment and collected data to solve problems and communicated their findings effectively. These sites represent integrated ideologies and imagination. We may never know how many generations maintained and accumulated the knowledge required to visualize and design the earthworks before the earthen architecture was built. We can only guess how the leaders traveled the rivers to gain support for the massive effort it took to move tons of earth to construct these monuments through community collaboration and sacrifice. Or what it meant to the people when they gathered at the earthworks to witness the cosmic connections to their lives. We can imagine, and what we do know is amazing and inspires a feeling of awe. And when our children, the next generations, gather at the earthworks to imagine these scenarios, the stories will be told from tribal histories and informed by specific Indigenous cultural knowledge.

The earthwork builders constructed their creations two thousand years ago to express a deeply significant cultural belief system, and today we find they teach and enlighten current and future generations. How wonderful it is that we are still finding ways to share the knowledge associated with these resilient and brilliant Indigenous cultures with relevance to our world today.

Notes

1. For more information, Chris Scarre, *The Seventy Wonders of the Ancient World* (London: Thames and Hudson, 1999).

2. Archaeologists use the term "type-site" when an archaeological site has objects or materials that define a particular cultural time period. For more please refer to Timothy Darvill, in *Concise Oxford Dictionary of Archaeology*, 2nd ed. (Oxford: Oxford University Press, 2008), s.v. "type-site," doi:10.1093/acref/9780199534043.001.0001.

3. "The Ancient Ohio Trail," University of Cincinnati and the Newark Earthworks Center, accessed January 27, 2021, https://ancientohiotrail.org/.

4. David Hurst Thomas et al., *The Native Americans: An Illustrated History* (Nashville: Turner, 1995).

5. Bradley Lepper, "The Newark Earthworks: Monumental Geography and Astronomy at a Hopewellian Pilgrimage Center," in *Hero, Hawk, and Open Hand: American Indian Art of the Ancient Midwest and South*, ed. Richard F. Townsend and Robert V. Sharp (New Haven, CT: Yale University Press, 2004), 77–78.

6. Marti L. Chaatsmith, "Native (Re)investments in Ohio: Evictions, Earthworks Preservation, and Tribal Stewardship," in *The Newark Earthworks: Enduring Monuments, Contested Meanings*, ed. Lindsay Jones and Richard Shiels (Charlottesville: University of Virginia Press, 2016), 217.

7. Atalay, quoted in Christine Ballengee-Morris, "They Came, They Claimed, They Named, and We Blame: Art Education in Negotiation and Conflict," *Studies in Art Education* 51, no. 3 (2010): 279.

8. Atalay, quoted in Ballengee-Morris, "They Came, They Claimed," 279.

9. Moundbuilders Country Club, website accessed February 5, 2021, https://www.moundbuilderscc.com/.

10. Chaatsmith, "Native (Re)investments in Ohio."

11. Ibid.

12. Glenna Wallace, foreword to *The Newark Earthworks: Enduring Monuments, Contested Meanings*, ed. Lindsay Douglas Jones and Richard Shiels (Charlottesville: University of Virginia Press, 2016), x.

13. Linda Tuhiwai Smith, *Decolonizing Methodologies: Research and Indigenous Peoples* (London: Zed Books, 2005), 125.

14. Ibid., 126.

15. Christine Ballengee Morris and B. Stephen Carpenter II, "Shared Reflections and Dialogues: Art Education, Collaboration, and Public Pedagogy," in *Art and Intercultural Dialogue*, ed. Susana Goncalves and Suzanne Majhanovich (Boston: Sense, 2016).

16. Smith, *Decolonizing Methodologies*.

17. Carl Sagan, *Cosmos* (New York: Random House, 1980).

18. Glen Aikenhead and Herman Michell, *Bridging Cultures: Indigenous and Scientific Ways of Knowing* (London: Pearson, 2011), 65.

19. Brian M. Brayboy, "Transformational Resistance and Social Justice: American Indians in Ivy League Universities," *Anthropology and Education Quarterly* 36, no. 3 (2015): 193–211.

20. Glenna Wallace, "Wallace: A Shawnee Perspective on the Newark Earthworks," *Newark Advocate*, July 20, 2019, https://www.newarkadvocate.com/story/news/local/2019/07/20/wallace-shawnee-perspective-newark-earthworks/1759093001.

21. "Earth Works," Ohio State University, accessed January 27, 2021, https://earthworksrising.osu.edu/.

22. Gary Morrison, Deborah Lowther, and Lisa DeMeulle, *Integrating Computer Technology into the Classroom: Skills for the 21st Century* (Upper Saddle River, NJ: Prentice-Hall, 1999); Marc Prensky, *Teaching Digital Natives: Partnering for Real Learning* (Thousand Oaks, CA: Corwin, 2010); Kurt Squire, "Designed Culture," in *Games, Learning, and Society: Learning and Meaning in the Digital Age*, ed. Constance Steinkuehler, Kurt Squire, and Sasha Barab (London: Cambridge University Press, 2011), 10–31.

23. Henry Jenkins, *Convergence Culture: Where Old and New Media Collide* (New York: New York University Press, 2006); James P. Gee and Elisabeth R. Hayes, *Women and Gaming: The Sims and 21st Century Learning* (New York: Palgrave, 2010).

Bibliography

Aikenhead, Glen, and Herman Michell. *Bridging Cultures: Indigenous and Scientific Ways of Knowing.* London: Pearson, 2011.

"The Ancient Ohio Trail." University of Cincinnati and the Newark Earthworks Center. Accessed January 27, 2021. https://ancientohiotrail.org/.

Ballengee-Morris, Christine. "They Came, They Claimed, They Named, and We Blame: Art Education in Negotiation and Conflict." *Studies in Art Education* 51, no. 3 (2010): 275–87.

Brayboy, Brian M. "Transformational Resistance and Social Justice: American Indians in Ivy League Universities." *Anthropology and Education Quarterly* 36, no. 3 (2005): 193–211.

Chaatsmith, Marti L. "Native (Re)investments in Ohio: Evictions, Earthworks Preservation, and Tribal Stewardship." In *The Newark Earthworks: Enduring Monuments, Contested Meanings*, edited by Lindsay Jones and Richard Shiels. Charlottesville: University of Virginia Press, 2016.

Darvill, Timothy. *Concise Oxford Dictionary of Archaeology.* 2nd ed. S.v. "type-site." Oxford: Oxford University Press, 2008.

"Earthworks." Ohio State University. Accessed January 27, 2021. https://earthworksrising.osu.edu/.

Gee, James P., and Elisabeth R. Hayes. *Women and Gaming: The Sims and 21st Century Learning.* New York: Palgrave, 2010.

Jenkins, Henry. *Convergence Culture: Where Old and New Media Collide.* New York: New York University Press, 2006.

Lepper, Bradley. "The Newark Earthworks: Monumental Geometry and Astronomy at a Hopewellian Pilgrimage Center." In *Hero, Hawk, and Open Hand: American Indian Art of the Ancient Midwest and South*, edited by Richard F. Townsend and Robert V. Sharp, 73–82. New Haven, CT: Yale University Press, 2004.

Morris, Christine Ballengee. See Ballengee-Morris, Christine.

Morris, Christine Ballengee, and B. Stephen Carpenter II. "Shared Reflections and Dialogues: Art Education, Collaboration, and Public Pedagogy." In *Art and Intercultural Dialogue*, edited by Susana Goncalves and Suzanne Majhanovich, 233–46. Boston: Sense, 2016.

Morrison, Gary, Deborah Lowther, and Lisa DeMeulle. *Integrating Computer Technology into the Classroom: Skills for the 21st Century.* Upper Saddle River, NJ: Prentice-Hall, 1999.

Moundbuilders Country Club. Website accessed February 5, 2021. https://www.moundbuilderscc.com/.

Prensky, Marc. *Teaching Digital Natives: Partnering for Real Learning.* Thousand Oaks, CA: Corwin, 2010.

Sagan, Carl. *Cosmos.* New York: Random House, 1980.

Scarre, Chris. *The Seventy Wonders of the Ancient World.* London: Thames and Hudson, 1999.

Smith, Linda Tuhiwai. *Decolonizing Methodologies: Research and Indigenous Peoples.* London: Zed Books, 2005.

Squire, Kurt. "Designed Culture." In *Games, Learning, and Society: Learning and Meaning in the Digital Age*, edited by Constance Steinkuehler, Kurt Squire, and Sasha Barab, 10–31. London: Cambridge University Press, 2011.

Thomas, David Hurst, et al. *The Native Americans: An Illustrated History.* Nashville: Turner, 1995.

Wallace, Glenna. "Wallace: A Shawnee Perspective on the Newark Earthworks." *Newark Advocate*, July 20, 2019. https://www.newarkadvocate.com/story/news/local/2019/07/20/wallace-shawnee-perspective-newark-earthworks/1759093001.

Wallace, Glenna. "Foreword to *The Newark Earthworks: Enduring Monuments, Contested Meanings*, edited by Lindsay Douglas Jones and Richard Shiels, x. Charlottesville: University of Virginia Press, 2016.

Chapter 4

New Paradigms of Integration

Historians and the Need for Community Engagement

STEPHEN WARREN

In her 2005 essay "Cultural Studies, Critical Race Theory, and Some Reflections on Methods," Imani Perry, professor of African American studies, argues that we need to devote our energy to the "task of articulating ethical norms around which we can extend a theory and praxis." Since 1969, when Vine Deloria published his landmark book *Custer Died for Your Sins*, Native American and Indigenous studies scholars have been working toward such an ethical methodology. Perry suggests that we have been "called to see how forms of knowing, ideology and dominant epistemologies about race" have adversely affected people of color. In a similar vein, Indigenous studies scholar Linda Tuhiwai Smith describes how the "knowledge claims of disciplines" institutionalized colonial knowledge. In her groundbreaking book *Decolonizing Methodologies*, Smith invites us to pivot away from the objectification of indigencity, toward research that is collaborative, reciprocal, and useful to Indigenous communities.[1]

Indigenous peoples the world over have been the subjects of research in disciplines such as history and anthropology from the beginning. Even so, teaching the histories and cultures of Native peoples has, until recently, been a peripheral component of disciplinary curricula. In 1956, when Erminie Wheeler-Voegelin, the founder of the American Society for

Ethnohistory, proposed a new course on the "history of American Indians in North America," her department chair at Indiana University agreed to offering it "on a temporary basis" while they determined "whether there is a place for it in the history curriculum." Between the 1960s and 1970s, during the Red Power movement and the larger civil rights struggles of the era, many non-Native scholars became committed to the project of integrating Native American histories into the narrative of American history. Progress was slow. In 1969, the University of Wisconsin–Stevens Point advertised the first position in Native American history, and throughout the 1970s most colleges and universities did not offer undergraduate courses in Native American history.[2]

In the wake of Deloria's criticism, numerous academic societies foster new research in their disciplines, signaling ongoing support for the project of integration. But integration did not fundamentally alter the neocolonial relationship between academic institutions and the worlds' Indigenous peoples, and, even when they did, anthropologists and historians often resisted teaching such courses from Indigenous perspectives. Historians remain suspicious of research and teaching that emanates from decolonizing methodologies. For example, historian David J. Silverman's charges that community-engaged scholars have "abandoned basic standards for handling evidence to scrub the historical record and . . . infantilize [their] historical subjects." Historian Philip J. Deloria reminds us that Silverman's misunderstanding of the Native American and Indigenous Studies Association, and community-engaged scholarship more generally, signals "history's deep complicity in the practices of domination" that remain with us to this day.[3]

Since 2007, and the founding of the Native American and Indigenous Studies Association, now the largest academic society devoted to Native American histories and cultures, scholars have engaged in fierce debates surrounding questions of audience, integration, and methodology. At the inaugural NAISA conference, the Mvskoke (Creek) Nation historian K. Tsianina Lomawaima described a blossoming, interdisciplinary field of study whose practitioners support "the health, well-being and vigor of life in Indian country" and research "the central issues and concerns of Native nations."[4] Lomawaima's ambition, widely shared by the current generation of Native American and Indigenous studies scholars, is to prioritize the needs and interests of Native peoples. Community-engaged scholars have found that the older, post-Deloria project of integration often makes it difficult to prioritize Native narratives. In other words, embedding Native

Americans in larger historical narratives often robs Native people of their own perspectives. Practitioners of Native American and Indigenous studies have found that mainstreaming our field has often come at the expense of Native people themselves. The needs of non-Native audiences in print, film, and other mediums often stands in the way of Indigenous peoples. Community-engaged scholars see their research through an ethic of collaboration. By necessity, the needs of Native audiences are paramount.

The field of Native American and Indigenous studies has moved beyond the settler/colonized binary that was customary during Deloria's time. Indigenous individuals and communities have always been complex and multisited. Since the nineteenth century, the allotment of Indian lands, the suppression of Indigenous religions, and the removal of children from Native families has furthered a vast geographic, psychic, and cultural diaspora that has transformed and expanded the location of "Indian country." Urban Indian organizations, in cities ranging from Minneapolis to Columbus, Ohio, are important sites of community engagement. Nevertheless, the historian Coll Thrush remains frustrated by our limited understanding of Native spaces. For Thrush, the geographic and temporal limitations placed on Indigenous people derives from "the notion that indigeneity cannot survive—or even be present in—urban places." This flawed reasoning haunts Native American histories and "is part of a larger binary that estranges indigeneity from modernity."[5]

This essay concerns itself with the geographic, temporal, and methodological frameworks we use when we define research related to Native peoples. For this scholar, community-engaged methodologies offer an important corrective to scholarship that limits the geographic and temporal scope of Native peoples. For example, histories of the Shawnee, and their most famous warrior, Tecumseh, are legion. Scholars and their non-Native audiences have used Tecumseh's life, and death, to carry American national parables ranging from the impossibility of interracial love to what historian James Joseph Buss describes as the Midwestern trope of "Native dispossession and victimless settlement."[6] Returning to Perry, the broad history of the Shawnee in the Ohio Valley has become a "form of knowing" that largely serves the settler-colonial state. Shifting our focus to Shawnee life in post-removal Oklahoma reorients Native American history, from themes of conquest and invisibility to resilience and sovereignty. Following Tecumseh's survivors attunes readers to Indigeneity in the present, challenging mainstream Americans and their tendency to see the world's Indigenous peoples, in the words of the Maori filmmaker Barry Barclay, as existing "outside the national orthodoxy." Barclay wanted filmmakers and scholars alike to tell new stories; to move beyond portrayals describing Indigenous cultures as "ancient remnant cultures persisting within the modern nation-state."[7] For this scholar, community engagement complicates the project of integrating Native American histories into broader narratives of American history. Integrated histories often serve the purposes of the settler-colonial state. In contrast, community-engaged histories, like the "fourth world" cinema Barclay promoted, serves Native audiences, emphasizes resilience, and articulates Indigenous understandings of history and identity.

My own turn toward engaged methodologies began at a moment when I could no longer deny the shortcomings of archival research. It was the summer of 2001, and I had traveled to Oklahoma in the hopes of converting my dissertation into a book. This meant working at archives such as the Western History Collections in Norman. As I sat in the archive, straining to make sense of Shawnee history and culture via a fragmented documentary record, I realized that the OU campus was just a forty-five-minute drive from Shawnee, Oklahoma, and the headquarters of the Absentee Shawnee Tribe of Oklahoma. I was a year out of the PhD program at Indiana University, and I had not met a Shawnee citizen. I decided to drive to Shawnee down Highway 9, a state highway that cuts through the towns of Little Axe, Tecumseh, and thousands of acres of land held in trust by the Citizen Band Potawatomi and the Absentee Shawnee. In the 1930s, what is now the Absentee Shawnee tribal headquarters then served as the Shawnee Sanitarium, a 150-bed facility built by the federal government for the treatment of tuberculosis among Native Americans.[8] To get there today, visitors must ascend a long access road lined by fields of freshly mowed grass dotted with a handful of trees strong enough to withstand the summer heat. The building sits atop a slow rise, giving it a commanding view of the countryside and signaling its separation from the community. To the left, maybe two-hundred yards north of the seat of their tribal government, lies the headquarters of the Citizen Band. Their proximity is revealing, a telling example of how Americans consumed Native lands, forcing sovereign nations from Michigan, Indiana, and Ohio to become next-door neighbors in Oklahoma.

To the people inside the building, the arrival of a wayward white man was an unremarkable event. I distinctly remember a sharply dressed Absentee Shawnee woman who described herself as a member of the White Turkey band. I nodded to hide my ignorance of this subdivision of her people. She quipped, "we're the progressives," before going on with her day. I hadn't made it past the lobby, and my ignorance of Shawnee history had already been made plain. I continued to introduce myself to a half-dozen people before the lieutenant governor, Kenneth Blanchard, rescued me. Ken has an easy stride and a restrained demeanor, but he quickly conveyed his love of tractors, horses, and rural life. Amid his stories of restoring Farmall tractors and bailing hay, Ken described himself as a member of the Big Jim band, a community with a storied history stretching from what is now Kansas to Mexico. Between the lobby and his office, I learned that there were, in fact, two main divisions of his people that had been forced into the Absentee Shawnee Tribe of Oklahoma.

Later that afternoon Ken introduced me to Jennifer Onzahwah, who then worked as the cultural preservation officer for the Absentee Shawnee Tribe. Jennifer's department occupied the southern wing of the first floor, a set of four rooms, one of which was the library and archive of the tribe's history. In another room, Ted Watson, the tribal historic preservation officer at the time, worked through stacks of cell-phone tower construction applications, highway expansion plans, and inventories of human remains and associated funerary objects sent to the Tribe from museums and libraries. Jennifer's office occupied the third room, followed by the tribe's gift shop, a place where tribal citizens could purchase a variety of things, from ribbon shirts and beaded earrings to hats and T-shirts with the tribe's logo. As a historian, I knew something of Shawnee migrations across the continent. Yet here, within these four rooms, the scale and scope of their travels hit home. Jennifer and Ted had to respond to hundreds of projects that might defile the graves of their ancestors; kin left behind as her people traveled across the continent. Oversight of museums and construction projects thus became part of the everyday practice of tribal sovereignty. I could immediately see how my own scholarly knowledge might be of assistance in their fight to defend their ancestors.

In 2001, when I arrived, the Cultural Preservation Office of the Absentee Shawnee Tribe was less than a year old. Jennifer explains, "We were just beginning." Ken Blanchard opened the office and granted Jennifer "a clean slate." The Native American Graves Protection and Repatriation Act (NAGPRA), the federal law designed to protect and repatriate human remains and associated funerary objects, was a little more than a decade old. Then, as now, the applied practice of defending an ancestors' right to eternal rest requires a keen understanding of arcane archaeological and historical records. Anthropologist Kathleen S. Fine-Dare points out that

NAGPRA and other related laws place "the burden of proof for cultural relevance or sacredness on the tribes." Native nations must provide a "preponderance of evidence" from both the sciences and the humanities if they hope to repatriate the remains of their ancestors. Accordingly, the Absentee Shawnee Tribe wanted to create an inventory of Shawnee cemeteries, first in Oklahoma, and then in their ancestral lands. Ken explained, "We put a lot of emphasis on NAGPRA programs to discourage development on possible graves." The legal power struggle over development and repatriation played out at the tribal headquarters. Jennifer had to compel builders, museums, and universities to adhere to federal laws; laws written by Congress rather than Native people themselves. Institutions such as the Smithsonian, a museum one scholar has described as "the largest Indian cemetery in the country," had far more power than Jennifer and her small staff.[9]

For most Shawnees, Oklahoma is the only land they have known. The near total erasure of their collective memories regarding Ohio and the states around it compounds the difficulty of protecting cemeteries and sacred sites in their former homelands. Absentee Shawnees first migrated between the forks of the Canadian River, in what is now Oklahoma, in the 1820s. Pushed west by the scorched earth campaigns of Kentuckians and icons of the Revolutionary War such as George Rogers Clark, most Shawnees abandoned the eastern half of North America well before 1830, when the Indian Removal Act became the official policy of the United States. Jennifer and Ken thought that mapping historic village sites might be an important first step in repatriating their history. We made plans to create a national map of Shawnee locations for a Native nation regarded, in the eighteenth century at least, as "the greatest travelers in America."[10] A couple of years later I collaborated with a geography professor and her students back at Augustana College. Together, we created a map of Shawnee sites in twenty-six states, as well as Canada and Mexico. In 2004, when I presented the map to Shawnee citizens at a community center in Brendle Corner, another small-town west of Shawnee along Highway 9, I will never forget the varying exclamations of shock and surprise at the extent of their ancestors' migrations.

Before I unveiled the map, I became increasingly aware of the fact that scholars such as myself had never bothered to notify or share their work with the Shawnee. We historians may have succeeded in integrating Native Americans into the US history survey. However, in the Shawnee case at least, they remained so far outside the "national orthodoxy" that we had not even bothered to tell them about our published research. Most of the defining histories of my graduate education did not grace the shelves of the Absentee Shawnee tribal library. Jennifer was shocked to learn that a veritable cottage industry of historical scholarship was devoted to her people. I began to share these titles, going through them with the same care and attention that I had in the weeks preceding my qualifying exams. The bare shelves of the tribal library caused me to rethink the project of integration that had defined the life and work of the generation preceding me.

Initially, my scholarly commitment to engagement amounted to sharing my knowledge with the subjects of my research. Thanks in large part to their generosity, our collaborative endeavors have expanded over time. Since 2001, I have spoken at numerous history summits sponsored by the Delaware, Miami, Yuchi, Shawnee, and Eastern Shawnee tribes; attended NAGPRA consultations, and helped to repatriate the documentary record of the Shawnee people. I have worked at teaching-intensive institutions for most of my career. Teaching seven to eight classes per year places a real strain on scholarly productivity, but I kept at it, thanks in part to the encouragement of Native friends and colleagues in Oklahoma. Scholar-activists in Indian country ask original, authentic, penetrating questions about my work. Their questions about primary sources point me toward systematic misrepresentations of Native cultures, and their interest in my research fuels my drive to continue publishing.

Community-engaged scholarship requires a commitment to reflexivity and a willingness to address the long history of exploitative research on Native American and Indigenous peoples. Interlocutors—those Shawnees who shared cultural and linguistic information with ethnologists such as M. R. Harrington and Erminie Wheeler-Voegelin—are often enigmatic. Ken, Jennifer, and the Shawnees with whom I have worked know these familial and communal histories and can help explain what motivated them to share their culture with outsiders.[11] Their insights grant an intimacy that archives rarely afford historical researchers.

Beyond these intimate histories, mainstream America becomes a kind of parallel universe. Popular audiences continue to traffic in mascots that depict Native Americans in derogatory ways. Hollywood continues to make Westerns featuring white saviors who preside over a proud, but ultimately doomed, Native community. Film studies scholar Faye Ginsburg argues that cinematic portrayals of Indigenous people contribute to an "enduring positivist belief that the camera provides a 'window' on reality, a simple expansion of our powers of observation." Christian Bale's performance in *Hostiles* (2018) and Leonardo Di Caprio's reprise of the frontiersman Hugh Glass in *The Revenant* (2015) offer just two examples of America's enduring fascination with frontier violence and the vanishing Indian; essential tropes of American nationalism. Tecumseh, and Shawnee history more generally, has served these tropes of American nationalism for generations.[12]

We have made a lot of progress since *Custer Died for Your Sins*. However, misrepresentations of Native Americans continue to find their way into scholarly arguments. Historian Angela Cavender Wilson (Wahpetunwah Dakota) sees no end to the problem until historians consult with "tribal and family historians" as they write their histories. Until they do, sociologist Duane Champagne (Turtle Mountain Band Chippewa) believes that "knowledge, research, and theory" will continue to "serve the purposes and reflect the interests of Western civilization." He believes that Native American and Indigenous studies scholars have yet to develop "an Indigenous or American Indian approach to theory and research and laying the foundation of a discipline."[13]

Serving the needs of Native audiences and continuing the project of integration remains possible. Native people themselves are renegotiating the terms. Their terms vary widely, because Native North America is complex, dynamic, and multisited, and this reality makes community-engaged research inherently intersectional. Witness the ongoing conflict regarding the place of African American freedmen in the Cherokee and Mvskoke (Creek) Nations. In 1979 and 2007, respectively, the Mvskoke (Creek) Nation and the Cherokee Nation stripped the descendants of African American freedmen of citizenship.[14] They have been fighting to reclaim their citizenship rights ever since. In making their case against the freedmen, both the Creeks and Cherokees invoked their sovereign right to determine citizenship. Contentious debates that often devolved into racist caricatures of African Americans ensued. Importantly, advocates for the expulsion of the freedmen ignored historical evidence about the ongoing contributions of freedmen to the life of the Cherokee Nation, as well as how American racism imposed itself on the identification of Cherokee citizens during the allotment era.[15]

In recent years, tribal governments have passed similar laws restricting the rights of LGBTQI citizens. Journalist and Cherokee citizen Graham Lee Brewer has found that just 35 of the 574 federally recognized tribes in the United States recognize same-sex marriage. The most populous tribes in the United States, the Cherokee and Navajo Nations, enacted gay marriage bans in 2004 and 2005, respectively. Historian and Navajo citizen Jennifer Denetdale argues that these decisions are a direct result of the terrorist attacks of September 11, 2001, a tragedy that has "erased . . . Navajos' historical experiences of injustice and oppression under American colonialism." Echoing Denetdale, Cherokee citizen and literary scholar Daniel Heath Justice argues that the Cherokee effectively surrendered their "sovereignty . . . to the state of Oklahoma" by enacting laws that mimic the hetero-patriarchal norms of the state.[16] Decisions such as these inform literary scholar and Osage citizen Robert Warrior's contention that "tribal governments do not represent the entire Native world." Therefore, Warrior continues, we must always "be looking for leadership across Native communities rather than simply among those elected or appointed."[17] Experts in gender and sexuality or critical race theory might find themselves at odds with sovereign national governments. Their areas of expertise might be best suited for Indigenous communities and service organizations that, for the reasons outlined above, exist apart from tribal governments that suppress their voices.[18]

In Oklahoma, a state with 38 federally recognized tribes within its borders, competition between tribal governments further complicates questions of community and collaboration. To cite one example, the Shawnee Tribe, which regained recognition as a sovereign nation in 2000, has struggled to put land in trust because their lands sit within the jurisdiction of the Cherokee Nation. To the west, in Little Axe and Shawnee, Oklahoma, the Absentee Shawnee face similar opposition from the Citizen Band Potawatomi, which has an exclusive right to their former reservation lands in south-central Oklahoma. For a century, the Citizen Band and Absentee Shawnee possessed equal rights to trust land on their former reservation between the forks of the Canadian River. Then, in 1971, the Indian Claims Commission drastically limited Absentee Shawnee sovereignty when it ruled that the Shawnees were "squatters" on their lands between the forks of the Canadian River. The Absentee Shawnees now operate under the sovereignty of both the governments of the United States and the Citizen Band, a reality that has significantly limited their capacity as a sovereign nation. Erminie Wheeler-Voegelin, founder of the American Society for Ethnohistory, and the foremost expert on the Shawnee at the time, was the government's primary research historian on the case.[19] The Absentee Shawnees were not able to call witnesses of a similar caliber, and, as a result, Wheeler-Voegelin's characterization of their history prevailed. The asymmetry of knowledge production negatively impacts Native nations; community-engaged scholarship might provide an essential corrective.

Indigenous communities face related challenges when they decide to reach out to scholarly experts. Tribal governments and Native scholar-activists often struggle to establish close working relationships with non-Native scholars working on their history. Structural problems account for at least some of these difficulties. Scholars facing the demands of tenure and promotion often have ambitious timetables for research and publication. Mercenary ethnography and short-term, public-facing scholarship sometimes result. Colleges and universities remain ambivalent about engaged scholarship and team-based research, a reality that is readily apparent in antiquated standards for tenure and promotion. These structural problems result in Native communities that often find themselves confronted by scholars hoping for immediate benefits from collaboration. Until these standards change, community-engaged scholars will be working against the grain as they slowly build the kind of lasting relationships, based on trust and shared objectives, that are rare in academe. According to the geographer and ethnic studies scholar Laura Pulido, engaged scholars use their publication record "as a shield of sorts." They are successful because they "understand the objective forces arrayed against" them and have used scholarly production to mitigate the ill-effects of antiquated professional standards.[20]

I will return now to the person of Tecumseh to illustrate why the older paradigm of integration deserves reconsideration. Most histories of the Shawnee are limited to a narrow band of time, from the Revolutionary War through the War of 1812. We know more about the context of Tecumseh's life than any other period in his people's remarkable history.[21] Over the last two decades, citizens of the three federally recognized Shawnee tribes—the Absentee, Eastern, and Shawnee—have both critiqued the aforementioned scholarship and fostered a new and invigorating conversation about their people. They have curated museum exhibits on Shawnee pottery and Shawnee artists, funded research on peacemakers and diplomats, and pushed the focus of scholarship into the late nineteenth and twentieth centuries. New subject matter, and the vast expansion of temporal boundaries, now fuel important new discoveries about their peoples' history. Community-engaged historians hoping for a corrective to the narrow parameters of the Ohio Valley, and the period from 1754 to 1815, now have a way out of the Tecumseh trap. Until recently, historians wrote about the Shawnee without ever consulting with, or notifying, the Shawnee people about their publications. Scholarship from a distance has its place. However, scholars' imperatives have adversely affected the Shawnee people.

Defining both the community we serve and the ethics of our service to those communities is of paramount importance. I learned something about this through hard experience. From 2007 to 2009 I was a subject matter expert for the *American Experience*, five-part documentary, *We Shall Remain: A Native History of America*. Ric Burns and Chris Eyre codirected part 2 of the series: "Tecumseh's Vision." A television station far-removed from Indian country understood the "national orthodoxy," and determined that Tecumseh should remain the defining example of Native American resistance between the American Revolution and the War of 1812. North Ground ceremonial chief Andy Warrior explained that "this documentary has come to us, rather than us coming to the world."[22] In fact, the subject matter of the five films made the title deeply ironic. The *We Shall Remain* series became a kind of elegy for all those Native warriors who had died fighting American expansion. "Tecumseh's Vision" appeared alongside four other films that focused on King Philip's War, Geronimo, the Trail of Tears, and the second battle of Wounded Knee. Native nations might have preferred stories of resilience and cultural renewal, but WGBH opted for historical subjects that were largely familiar to non-Native audiences.

I signed on with the project in spite of these shortcomings. After consulting with elders and scholar-activists who were citizens of the three federally recognized Shawnee tribes, they believed that the film would be better with me in it. They also wanted an advocate, someone who could communicate their desire for the Shawnee language to be heard in the film and for Shawnee actors to appear, however briefly. Beyond these expectations, the Shawnees with whom I spoke wanted "Tecumseh's Vision" to communicate that Tecumseh's people, in fact, remained. A film that ended with his tragic death, at the Battle of Thames, in 1813, would confirm the vanishing Indian thesis and enable non-Native audiences to believe, mistakenly, that Shawnees were historical, rather than contemporary peoples.

During an initial meeting between the film crew and the Shawnee people at their community center, it became clear that they were suspicious of Burns, the historians, and "Tecumseh's Vision" as a whole. Little Axe is a rural community, and the homeland of the Big Jim band. Approximately four hundred Absentee Shawnees live on nearby allotments carved from their former reservation. Non-Indians now make up the vast majority of the population on what used to be tribal lands. The last major project to come through the town, the Lake Thunderbird Dam, expropriated "five square miles of tribal trust land, nearly one-fourth of the tribe's remaining land." In 1962, when construction began, the houses, farms and cemeteries of the Big Jim band lined the banks of the Little River, the source of the lake's water. Holdouts saw the value of their land drop from $450 per acre to $42 per acre. In the end, the Corps of Engineers, backed by the constitutional right of eminent domain, submerged their lands, their homes, and the graves of their ancestors. Today, more than three thousand Absentee Shawnee citizens live well beyond their former reservation.[23]

For those remaining on tribal lands, it is easy to see how the arrival of non-Natives with big ideas might be cause for alarm. Some drew parallels between the film and the creation of Lake Thunderbird. Centuries of experience with colonizers explain why those in attendance responded angrily, but more often fatalistically, to the proposed film. The ongoing reality of dispossession convinced them that "Tecumseh's Vision," like Lake Thunderbird, was going to be made. Non-Natives flooded their lands, and they would place Shawnee history on film, just as they had outlawed their religion and placed their children in boarding schools. Shawnees understood this unbroken history—the logic of settler colonialism—better than the film crew or this historian.

"Tecumseh's Vision" came to the Absentee Shawnee at a sensitive moment in their history. Elders raised speaking Shawnee as their first language were passing on. Younger people now lived in Norman, Oklahoma City, and Dallas, Texas. The demands of work and family made it harder for them to practice communal traditions that were customary for previous generations. Neither this historian nor the film crew fully understood these realities. The rigid timetables of film production exacerbated our collective ignorance and exposed the community to internal discord.

During the community center meeting, an elder named George Blanchard, Ken's brother and one of the last fluent speakers in the tribe, explained how historians, anthropologists, and filmmakers had redefined their people. Andrew Warrior lamented the fact that his people "can only perform these things [dances] on the weekend." Donna Longhorn, an active participant in ceremonial ground life, described how Shawnee culture had become a secondary ingredient in day-to-day survival. According to Longhorn, "Language, culture, tradition . . . is no longer a factor in everyday life."[24] Now wedded to Euro-American notions of time and work, Blanchard, Warrior, and Longhorn described how they and their ceremonial community carried on their traditions in spite of the logics of the non-Native world.

"Tecumseh's Vision" became what anthropologist Raymond D. Fogelson calls an "epitomizing event." Linguists might describe the film as a metaphor, as a means for making sense of cultural loss in a traditional Indian community threatened with language dormancy, rising rates of type 2 diabetes, and the ongoing seizure of tribal lands.[25] Rumors engulfed the making of "Tecumseh's Vision," and, unfortunately, I played an unwitting role in their proliferation. Well before we met in Oklahoma, Burns asked me to describe a coming-of-age ceremony that Tecumseh might have participated in as a child. I chose to describe the game of "Indian football" to him.[26] In broad strokes, the game pits women against men, and it is played from the first planting of corn to mid-June, when the tassels on corn emerge from their husks. Players try to throw or kick a deerskin ball, stuffed with its own fur, between two goal posts made from cut tree saplings. Women can run with the ball, throw it to other women, and hurl it between the goal posts to score. In contrast, men must kick the ball to either pass or score, and they cannot run with the ball. These limitations privilege women, and thus the game reinforces their power and their importance during the spring planting ceremonies. Functionally, then, the game serves two purposes. First, it communicates the power of women and their ability to create life, celebrated during the most fertile time of the year. Second, it is a kinship game. Young people learn "who they can and who they can't catch."[27] Elders demand that close kin cannot be tackled or roughed up. In contrast, players can be rough with distant relatives and members of other tribes.

Burns quickly became fascinated, and he wanted to film a reenactment of the game for "Tecumseh's Vision." We had already let him know that the ceremonial grounds were off limits. Prohibitions against filming or recording there have been in place for as long as anyone can remember. But, in conversations with Chief Warrior, Burns wondered if Absentee Shawnees might reenact the game at an alternative site. Barring that, he wondered if an allied tribe might be willing to help.[28]

Chief Warrior thought that it might be possible for Burns to film a version of Indian football somewhere else, and he guessed that Yuchi reenactors, rather than Absentee Shawnees, might be willing to do it. The Yuchis, like the Shawnees, practice a very similar version of the game, and non-Native viewers would not recognize the differences between them.

Moreover, the Yuchis sometimes record their traditional beliefs and practices, unlike their Absentee Shawnee relatives. As longtime allies of the Shawnees, the Yuchis might be able to offer a close approximation of the game as it might have been played in Tecumseh's time.[29] Unfortunately, these nuances failed to quiet naysayers within the Absentee community. In their view, the filmmakers should have consulted with ceremonial elders. Decades of salvage anthropology, coupled with the ongoing challenge posed by unrecognized "Shawnee" groups in Illinois, Indiana, and Ohio had turned the Absentee toward cultural privacy.

Shawnees worried that reenacting the game would convert their beloved customs into a cultural commodity, now freely accessible to claimant populations who would make a mockery of their ways by copying what appeared in "Tecumseh's Vision." Culturally conservative women who were vital to the Spring Bread Dance, the planting ceremony that effectively transfers power from men to women, did not want their ceremonies to appear in the film. For his part, Burns walked back his request. But for the Absentee Shawnee Tribe of Oklahoma, and the ceremonial community in particular, "Tecumseh's Vision" became yet another source of discord, one that promised to remain with them long after Burns turned his attention to new projects.

Burns, Eyre, and WGBH honored the wishes of the Absentee Shawnee Tribe, and the Big Jim band, in particular. They did not include a staged reenactment of Shawnee football in the film. Some Shawnee actors made cameo appearances in "Tecumseh's Vision," and powerful testimonials about the meaning of Tecumseh's life conclude the program. Absentee Shawnee citizen Kevin Williams quietly asserts that Tecumseh's life tells a story of "hope and freedom" to his descendants. Little Axe resident and Absentee Shawnee citizen Sherman Tiger characterizes him as "a hero for what he attempted to do." Beyond these important elements, the film itself offers a damning portrayal of William Henry Harrison and the treaties he forced upon Native peoples from the Midwest in the name of American land hunger. The scholars who advised in the film's creation, including R. David Edmunds, Colin Calloway, and John Sugden, are Tecumseh's foremost biographers. Even so, a decade after its release, "Tecumseh's Vision" remains a source of contention among the Shawnee.

The very real power inequalities at work in the making of "Tecumseh's Vision" explain much of their discontent. Non-Natives determined to make a film with or without Shawnee input. Editorial decisions were made at WGBH by people who then refused to "share authority" with Tecumseh's descendants. The needs of non-Native audiences largely determined both the choices made by the filmmakers and subsequent editorial decisions. For George Blanchard, the loss of extensive Shawnee language segments was particularly devastating. George lamented that "when they cut out the language" from the film it "lacked the punch" he desired. Finally, the three federally recognized tribes lacked a research board or a related legal mechanism to fairly evaluate participatory research projects that hinged on their contributions. As a result, the Shawnees received very little in return for the knowledge they so freely shared in the making of "Tecumseh's Vision."

To illustrate how community-engaged scholarship might foster a more productive, less discordant conversation with Indigenous communities, I now turn to examples from my own work created in the aftermath of the film. In 2014, I joined a federally funded research grant written by the Eastern Shawnee Tribe. Entitled "A Search for Eastern Shawnee History," the grant addressed a particular void in both Eastern Shawnee and Great Lakes American Indian history more generally: the absence of scholarship on the survivors of Indian removal. The void between the Indian Removal Act and World War II is particularly acute for the Shawnee, a people whose fame revolves around the Indian wars that engulfed them from the Seven Years' War through the War of 1812. Most Shawnees, like most Americans, know very little about Native peoples after the last Indian wars. In the Shawnees' case, this has meant that their formal history often stops with Tecumseh's death, at the Battle of the Thames, in 1813, only to renew with family histories dating back to the Great Depression and World War II. The Eastern Shawnee Tribe of Oklahoma wrote the grant to correct this long period of historical amnesia. We hoped to both recall and repatriate Eastern Shawnee history from 1813 to 1945.

To that end, in June 2015, I accompanied a handful of Eastern Shawnee citizens, including Chief Glenna Wallace, to the Newberry Library, as well as the National Archives in Washington, DC. In my capacity as the lead historian, I worked alongside Eastern Shawnee tribal citizens—Glenna Wallace, Lola Purvis, Robert Miller, Leslie Miller, and Reneé Gokey—as we conducted research at these and other archives. We were amazed by what we found. We marveled over pictures of tribal citizens from the 1930s, detailed descriptions of tribal ceremonies, and interviews with legendary tribal leaders. After just a week of research, we rediscovered tribal histories that had been lost for generations.

Back at the University of Iowa, three PhD students and two under-graduates helped us scan and digitize this research as contract employees of the Eastern Shawnee Tribe. These documents, along with many others, are now in a digital archive of Shawnee history run by the Ohio History Connection (OHC), in collaboration with the Eastern Shawnee Tribe.[30] Both the University of Iowa and the OHC joined forces with the Eastern Shawnee, "sharing authority" in ways that benefitted all of the parties involved.

Over the three years of the grant, the Eastern Shawnee Tribe hosted annual history summits that brought together historians who shared their research with the community. These historians, anthropologists, and legal scholars then contributed their research to an edited volume that combines conventional, single-authored scholarship with oral histories and contributions from Native citizen-scholars. In 2017, the University of Oklahoma Press released *The Eastern Shawnee Tribe of Oklahoma: Resilience through Adversity*.[31] With sixteen chapters, five of which are oral histories, we have engaged in the research of discovery. Importantly, the Eastern Shawnee Tribe continues to host history summits that foster ongoing research on their history and culture.

Simply participating in the life and work of contemporary Native American communities has led to important new discoveries. As a community-engaged historian, I have benefited from listening to the kinds of questions that matter most to my Native friends and allies. For example, more than ten years ago, as I made casual conversation with the Wyandotte ceramic artist Richard Zane Smith, he posed a simple question. "What," he asked, "did Shawnee pottery look like?" Richard is something of a trickster. Tall, lean, and quick to laugh, his comments suggest worlds of possibility beyond the spoken word. Once again, his question revealed another layer of ignorance about a people I thought I knew. When Richard posed the question, I had already published a book and several articles on Shawnee history, so I was embarrassed to reply, as I often do when I am in Oklahoma, that I had no idea. Richard already knew that, so I saw no point in obscuring the obvious subtext of our conversation. His question revealed more than the chasm between scholarly and Indigenous knowledge systems. It spelled out what matters to Native people when they imagine their ancestors' lives. Questions that explain the texture and meaning of their daily lives matter most to people such as Richard.

My search for an answer to his question became the genesis for my second book, *The Worlds the Shawnees Made: Migration and Violence in*

Early America.[32] Thanks to Richard, the book begins in 1400, rather than 1673, the year in which Europeans first laid eyes on people who identified themselves as Shawnee. To answer Richard's question, I would have to read archaeological and archival records amid ongoing ethnographic research in Oklahoma. To move beyond the scholarly record of Shawnee history, which runs from approximately 1673 to 1813, I would have to learn from archival sources and tribal citizens alike.

Scholarly knowledge, and the rigid boundaries between the disciplines, make little sense to Native scholar-activists because Indigenous questions are inherently interdisciplinary, subverting scholarly knowledge systems. Thanks to questions like this I began to investigate why historians carefully mind the gap between archaeology and history. By hewing closely to written, rather than material records of past worlds, historians ignore the *longue durée* of Native American history. When we ignore Native voices, we perpetuate the false notion of prehistory. Native Americans remain victims of modernity, a sharp contrast from Europeans who unleashed, and subsequently manipulate, globalization.[33] The periodization of history offers one illustration of how scholarly training in academic disciplines can lead us away from research that matters to Native audiences. Applied research, conducted in conversation with Indigenous communities, might serve Native audiences and lead to important new discoveries.[34]

Following the release of *The Worlds the Shawnees Made*, Benjamin Barnes, the chief of the Shawnee Tribe, and the coeditor of this volume, took research on late Fort Ancient ceramics to a new level. Ben wrote several grants aimed at bringing together Shawnee citizens, archaeologists, and historians to restore the ceramic traditions of the Shawnee people. His visionary scholarship and leadership has meant that, for the first time in 350 years, Shawnee people are making their own pottery. Richard now regularly hosts events at his ceramic workshop near the Shawnee Tribe's headquarters in northeastern Oklahoma. Guided by extensive collaborations with archaeologists and historians, Shawnee citizens can learn about everything from shell temper ratios to the challenges of open pit firing. They can taste hominy cooked in ceramic pots that closely approximate those of their ancestors, creating an embodied connection to past worlds.[35]

Through a team-based analysis of Fort Ancient pottery, the Shawnees will bring an end to the "culturally unidentifiable" label that museums and universities often use to prevent them from defending sacred sites and the bones of their ancestors. "A Search for Eastern Shawnee History" and the Fort Ancient pottery project brought together teams of researchers who applied their various areas of expertise to complex research problems. This principle of triangulation, so common to medical research and public health initiatives, remains uncommon in the humanities.[36] These forms of cocurricular research might correct the current disconnect between conventional academic practice and the challenges facing Native peoples in Indian country. Research created in partnership with Indigenous communities leads to knowledge production that is socially just and immediately relevant to Native communities.

Community-engaged scholarship is a methodology that seeks to make supporting the needs and ambitions of Indigenous communities an ethical norm in Native American and Indigenous studies. Based in principles of respect and reciprocity, its practitioners research questions generated by the communities they serve. Demographic realities demand that new research protocols govern how non-Native academics conduct their work. Today, citizens of federally recognized tribes make up less than 1 percent of the US population. As of 2010, just 13 percent of American Indians had a bachelor's degree, compared with 28 percent of the overall population. Just 5 percent of American Indians have advanced degrees—the kind of specialized training required to run a tribal government—compared with 10 percent of the overall population.[37] These statistics demonstrate many things, including the responsibility scholars have to share their work with Native audiences.

Even among activist scholars, the needs, concerns, and questions of Native communities are often overlooked. How, then, can scholar-activism be applied to the new, twenty-first century context we inhabit? Indigenous studies scholar Scott Lauria Morgensen contends that "exposing normative knowledge production . . . denaturalize(s) power in settler-colonial societies." Activist-oriented dissertations, theses, and undergraduate research papers are critical to this process.[38] However, it remains true that most scholarship goes unread by the people who are subject to these studies. Even "decolonizing methodologies" can be out-of-step with the needs of Native communities. Returning to Robert Warrior, community-engaged scholarship is motivated by the desire to "come up with an approach that defines people not on what they are, but in what they do in relation to what our communities need."[39]

Engaged scholarship works when tribal citizens identify research problems that are important to their communities and deliverable to their people in ways that are accessible and relevant. Native nations design projects to solve problems that have vexed their communities for years. Interdisciplinary, team-based research under the direction of sovereign nations is a paradigm-shifting methodology that is difficult to accomplish under the best of circumstances. Nevertheless, it is worth pursuing, because engaged scholarship has the potential to yield new discoveries in ways that further the interests of Indigenous communities interested in protecting their cultural and linguistic patrimony.

In our time, partnerships with Native American and Indigenous communities, from federally recognized tribes to urban Indian community centers, are not only possible but ethical and necessary. It takes a skilled hand, because animosities and sites of misunderstanding remain. Nevertheless, today's tribal citizens regularly read what we write. Ben Barnes laments the fact that previous research "reinforced the idea that the Indian has simply vanished from the Ohio Valley." Barnes hopes that a new generation will take the time to "create relationships of mutual collaboration" in which "both sides are willing to listen to each other."[40] In partnership with Native nations, we can help our students avoid the pitfalls of ethnocentric, colonialist understandings of history and culture. Today, ethnographers must relate their interest in field research to tribal citizens who are as engaged with these colonial and neocolonial texts as they are.

Thankfully, there are shining examples of engaged, collaborative scholarship in both the United States and Canada. Justin B. Richland, a non-Native legal scholar working with the Hopi, uses their word *nakwatsvewat*, or "going along together in cooperation," to describe his efforts at engaged scholarship with the Hopi community.[41] Among the Shawnees, the best phrase to define engaged scholarship is *kepiyeelatole*. Roughly translated, it means "I come to you asking to use your knowledge, your power, your strength."[42] My hope is that engaged scholarship, based in principles of respect and reciprocity, will blossom and grow in the years ahead.

Notes

1. Imani Perry, "Cultural Studies, Critical Race Theory, and Some Reflections on Methods," *Villanova Law Review* 50, no. 4 (2005): 915; Linda Tuhiwai Smith, *Decolonizing Methodologies: Research and Indigenous Peoples*, 2nd ed. (London: Zed Books, 2012), x, 9, 64.

2. Harold J. Grimm to Erminie Wheeler-Voegelin, June 22, 1956, Faculty Annual Report and Workload, box 2, GL-OVERP, Indiana University Archives, Bloomington, Indiana; R. David Edmunds, "Blazing New Trails or Burning

Bridges: Native American History Comes of Age," *Western Historical Quarterly* 39, no. 1 (2008): 6.

3. David J. Silverman, "Living with the Past: Thoughts on Community Collaboration and Difficult History in Native American and Indigenous Studies," *American Historical Review* 125, no. 2 (2020): 522.

4. K. Tsianina Lomawaima, Plenary remarks, University of Oklahoma, Norman, May 2007, https://www.naisa.org/wp-content/uploads/2018/01/Lomawaima_Plenary_Remarks_OU_0.pdf.

5. Coll Thrush, "Afterword: How Many Worlds? Place, Power and Incommensurability," in *Beyond Two Worlds: Critical Conversations on Language and Power in Native North America*, ed. James Joseph Buss and C. Joseph Genetin-Pilawa (Albany: State University of New York Press, 2014), 299.

6. For examples of histories that confirm American myths, see William Albert Galloway, *Old Chillicothe: Shawnee and Pioneer History: Conflicts and Romances in the Northwest Territory* (Xenia, OH: Buckeye, 1934), 123–24; Allan W. Eckert, *A Sorrow in Our Heart: The Life of Tecumseh* (New York: Bantam, 1993). For an excellent explanation of how these myths developed, see James Joseph Buss, *Winning the West with Words: Language and Conquest in the Lower Great Lakes* (Norman: University of Oklahoma Press, 2011), 6.

7. Barry Barclay, "Celebrating Fourth Cinema," *Illusions Magazine*, no. 35 (2003), 6–7.

8. John Collier, "Present State of Oklahoma Indians," *Harlow's Weekly*, August 25 1934, 15.

9. Author interview with Jennifer Onzahwah, November 30, 2018, in author's possession; Kathleen S. Fine-Dare, *Grave Injustice: The American Indian Repatriation Movement and NAGPRA* (Lincoln: University of Nebraska Press, 2002), 72; Miami–Absentee Shawnee Field School, June 2004, field notes, in author's possession; Burkhard Bilger, quoted in Chip Colwell, *Plundered Skulls and Stolen Spirits: Inside the Fight to Reclaim Native America's Culture* (Chicago: University of Chicago Press, 2017), 75.

10. Wilbur R. Jacobs, ed., *The Appalachian Indian Frontier: The Edmond Atkin Report and Plan of 1755* (Columbia: University of South Carolina Press, 1954).

11. Stephen Warren and Ben Barnes, "Salvaging the Salvage Anthropologists: Erminie Wheeler-Voegelin, Carl Voegelin, and the Future of Ethnohistory," *Ethnohistory* 65, no. 2 (2018): 194–95. See also Margaret M. Bruchac, *Savage Kin: Indigenous Informants and American Anthropologists* (Tucson: University of Arizona Press, 2018).

12. Faye Ginsburg, "Indigenous Media: Faustian Contract or Global Village?," *Cultural Anthropology* 6, no. 1 (1991): 93; Scott Cooper, *Hostiles* (2017; Santa Fe: Waypoint Entertainment, 2018); Alejandro G. Iñárritu, *The Revenant* (2015; Los Angeles: Regency Enterprises, 2016).

13. Angela Cavender Wilson, "American Indian History or Non-Indian Perceptions of American Indian History," *American Indian Quarterly* 20, no. 1 (1996):

3. Wilson's approach anticipates anthropologist Luke Eric Lassiter's articulation of collaborative ethnography. See Luke Eric Lassiter, "Collaborative Ethnography and Public Anthropology," *Current Anthropology* 46, no. 1 (2005): 83–106; Duane Champagne, "In Search of Theory and Method in American Indian Studies," *American Indian Quarterly* 31, no. 3 (2007): 355.

14. See, for example, Fay A. Yarbrough, *Race and the Cherokee Nation: Sovereignty in the Nineteenth Century* (Philadelphia: University of Pennsylvania Press, 2007); Claudio Saunt, "Telling Stories: The Political Uses of Myth and History in the Cherokee and Creek Nations," *Journal of American History* 93, no. 3 (2006): 673–97.

15. Circe Sturm, "Race, Sovereignty, and Civil Rights: Understanding the Cherokee Freedmen Controversy," *Cultural Anthropology* 29, no. 3 (2014): 582, 593.

16. Graham Lee Brewer, "Why Marriage Equality Is a Matter of Tribal Sovereignty," *High Country News*, March 30, 2018; Jennifer Denetdale, "Carving Navajo National Boundaries: Patriotism, Tradition, and the Diné Marriage Act of 2005," *American Quarterly* 60, no. 2 (2008): 289; Daniel Heath Justice, "Notes toward a Theory of Anomaly," *Journal of Lesbian and Gay Studies* 16, no. 1–2 (2010): 210.

17. Robert Warrior, "The Future in the Past of Native and Indigenous Studies," *American Indian Culture and Research Journal* 35, no. 1 (2011): 55–58.

18. See, for example, Brian Joseph Gilley, "Joyous Discipline: Native Autonomy and Culturally Conservative Two-Spirit People," *American Indian Culture and Research Journal* 38, no. 2 (2014): 17–40.

19. Stephen Warren, *The Shawnees and Their Neighbors, 1795–1870* (Urbana: University of Illinois Press, 2005), 172.

20. Laura Pulido, "FAQs: Frequently (Un)asked Questions about Being a Scholar Activist," in *Engaging Contradictions: Theory, Politics, and Methods of Activist Scholarship*, ed. Charles R. Hale (Berkeley: University of California Press, 2008), 344–45.

21. For more on the historiography of the Shawnee and my own initial attempt at a corrective, see Warren, *The Shawnees and Their Neighbors, 1795–1870*.

22. Author interview with Andrew Warrior, June 11, 2007, in author's possession.

23. Ethnographic field notes, June 18, 2007, Little Axe, Oklahoma, in author's possession; Jessica A. Walker, "Perception and Management of Type II Diabetes: The Narrated Experience of Diabetes in an Absentee Shawnee Community," (MA thesis, University of Oklahoma, 2004), 15–29.

24. Donna Longhorn, quoted in ethnographic field notes, May 29, 2007, Little Axe, Oklahoma, in author's possession.

25. Raymond D. Fogelson, "The Ethnohistory of Events and Non-events," *Ethnohistory* 36, no. 2 (1989): 133–47; George Lakoff and Mark Johnson, *Metaphors We Live By* (Chicago: University of Chicago Press, 1980), 5.

26. Description of the game based on Stephen Warren, ethnographic field notes, June 10, 2007, in author's possession. For a visual depiction of the betting

before the game begins, see Charles Banks Wilson, *Shawnee Ribbon Bets*, oil on canvas, Gilcrease Museum of Art, Tulsa, OK. For a description of the game among the Yuchi, see Jason Baird Jackson, *Yuchi Ceremonial Life: Performance, Meaning, and Tradition in a Contemporary American Indian Community* (Lincoln: University of Nebraska Press, 2005), 117–40.

27. Ethnographic field notes, June 10, 2007, in author's possession.

28. Ethnographic field notes, June 4, 2007, in author's possession.

29. Stephen Warren, "Reconsidering Coalescence: Yuchi and Shawnee Survival Strategies in the Colonial Southeast," in *Yuchi Indian Histories before the Removal Era*, ed. Jason Baird Jackson (Lincoln: University of Nebraska Press, 2012).

30. Ohio History Connection and the State Library of Ohio, Eastern Shawnee Tribe of Oklahoma Digital Collection, https://www.ohiomemory.org/digital/collection/p16007coll27. The author would like to thank the graduate students, Stephanie Grossnickle-Batterton, Jason M. Sprague, Stacey Moultry, and the undergraduates, Thom Johnson and Maxwell Moyer.

31. Stephen Warren, ed., *The Eastern Shawnee Tribe of Oklahoma: Resilience through Adversity* (Norman: University of Oklahoma Press, 2017).

32. Personal communication with Richard Zane Smith, May 2008; Stephen Warren, *The Worlds the Shawnees Made: Migration and Violence in Early America* (Chapel Hill: University of North Carolina Press, 2014).

33. Eric Wolf, *Europe and the People without History*, 2nd ed. (Berkeley: University of California Press, 2010); Claude Lévi-Strauss, *The Raw and the Cooked* (Chicago: University of Chicago Press, 1983).

34. For an important new book on this subject, see Keith Thor Carlson, John Sutton Lutz, David M. Schaepe, and Naxaxalhts'i (Albert "Sonny" McHalsie), eds., *Towards a New Ethnohistory: Community-Engaged Scholarship among the People of the River* (Winnipeg: University of Manitoba Press, 2018); Warren and Barnes, "Salvaging the Salvage Anthropologists."

35. Benjamin J. Barnes, "Becoming Our Own Storytellers: Tribal Nations Engaging with Academia," in *The Eastern Shawnee Tribe of Oklahoma: Resilience through Adversity*, ed. Stephen Warren (Norman: University of Oklahoma Press, 2017), 225.

36. For more on ethnology and triangulation, see Warren and Barnes, "Salvaging the Salvage Anthropologists," 197.

37. "Demographics," National Congress of American Indians, accessed January 13, 2021, https://www.ncai.org/about-tribes/demographics; Tina Norris, Paula L. Vines, and Elizabeth M. Hoeffel, *The American Indian and Alaska Native Population: 2010*, 2010 Census Briefs, United States Census Bureau, 2012, https://www.census.gov/history/pdf/c2010br-10.pdf.

38. Scott Lauria Morgensen, "Destabilizing the Settler Academy: The Decolonial Effects of Indigenous Methodologies," *American Quarterly* 64, no. 4 (2012): 806.

39. Robert Warrior, "Native Critics in the World: Edward Said and Nationalism," in *American Indian Literary Nationalism*, by Jace Weaver, Craig S. Womack, and Robert Warrior (Albuquerque: University of New Mexico Press, 2006), 210.

40. Barnes, "Becoming Our Own Storytellers," 219, 226.

41. Justin B. Richland, "Beyond Listening: Lessons for Native/American Collaborations from the Creation of the Nakwatsvewat Institute," *American Indian Culture and Research Journal* 35, no. 1 (2011): 103.

42. Eric Wensman to Stephen Warren, email communication, May 27, 2016.

Bibliography

Barclay, Barry. "Celebrating Fourth Cinema." *Illusions Magazine*, no. 35 (2003): 6–11.

Barnes, Benjamin J. "Becoming Our Own Storytellers: Tribal Nations Engaging with Academia." In *The Eastern Shawnee Tribe of Oklahoma: Resilience through Adversity*, edited by Stephen Warren, 217–28. Norman: University of Oklahoma Press, 2017.

Colwell, Chip. *Plundered Skulls and Stolen Spirits: Inside the Fight to Reclaim Native America's Culture* (Chicago: University of Chicago Press, 2017).

Brewer, Graham Lee. "Why Marriage Equality Is a Matter of Tribal Sovereignty." *High Country News*, March 30, 2018.

Bruchac, Margaret M. *Savage Kin: Indigenous Informants and American Anthropologists*. Tucson: University of Arizona Press, 2018.

Buss, James Joseph. *Winning the West with Words: Language and Conquest in the Lower Great Lakes*. Norman: University of Oklahoma Press, 2011.

Carlson, Keith Thor, John Sutton Lutz, David M. Schaepe, and Naxaxalhts'i (Albert "Sonny" McHalsie), eds. *Towards a New Ethnohistory: Community-Engaged Scholarship among the People of the River*. Winnipeg: University of Manitoba Press, 2018.

Champagne, Duane. "In Search of Theory and Method in American Indian Studies." *American Indian Quarterly* 31, no. 3 (2007): 353–72.

Collier, John. "Present State of Oklahoma Indians." *Harlow's Weekly*, August 25, 1934, 15.

Cooper, Scott, dir. *Hostiles*. 2017; Santa Fe: Waypoint Entertainment, 2018.

Denetdale, Jennifer. "Carving Navajo National Boundaries: Patriotism, Tradition, and the Diné Marriage Act of 2005." *American Quarterly* 60, no. 2 (2008): 289–94.

Eckert, Allan W. *A Sorrow in Our Heart: The Life of Tecumseh*. New York: Bantam, 1993.

Edmunds, R. David. "Blazing New Trails or Burning Bridges: Native American History Comes of Age." *Western Historical Quarterly* 39, no. 1 (2008): 5–15.

Fine-Dare, Kathleen S. *Grave Injustice: The American Indian Repatriation Movement and NAGPRA*. Lincoln: University of Nebraska Press, 2002.

Fogelson, Raymond D. "The Ethnohistory of Events and Non-events." *Ethnohistory* 36, no. 2 (1989): 133–47.

Galloway, William Albert. *Old Chillicothe: Shawnee and Pioneer History: Conflicts and Romances in the Northwest Territory*. Xenia, OH: Buckeye, 1934.

Gilley, Brian Joseph. "Joyous Discipline: Native Autonomy and Culturally Conservative Two-Spirit People." *American Indian Culture and Research Journal* 38, no. 2 (2014): 17–40.

Ginsburg, Faye. "Indigenous Media: Faustian Contract or Global Village?" *Cultural Anthropology* 6, no. 1 (1991): 92–112.

Grimm, Harold J., to Erminie Wheeler-Voegelin. June 22, 1956. Faculty Annual Report and Workload, box 2, GL-OVERP. Erminie Wheeler-Voegelin Collection. Indiana University Archives, Bloomington, Indiana.

Iñárritu, Alejandro G. *The Revenant*. 2015; Los Angeles: Regency Enterprises, 2016.

Jackson, Jason Baird. *Yuchi Ceremonial Life: Performance, Meaning, and Tradition in a Contemporary American Indian Community*. Lincoln: University of Nebraska Press, 2005.

Jacobs, Wilbur R., ed. *The Appalachian Indian Frontier: The Edmond Atkin Report and Plan of 1755*. Columbia: University of South Carolina Press, 1954.

Justice, Daniel Heath. "Notes toward a Theory of Anomaly." *Journal of Lesbian and Gay Studies* 16, no. 1–2 (2010): 207–42.

Lakoff, George, and Mark Johnson. *Metaphors We Live By*. Chicago: University of Chicago Press, 1980.

Lassiter, Luke Eric. "Collaborative Ethnography and Public Anthropology." *Current Anthropology* 46, no. 1 (2005): 83–106.

Lévi-Strauss, Claude. *The Raw and the Cooked*. Chicago: University of Chicago Press, 1983.

Lomawaima, K. Tsianina. Plenary remarks at NAISA meeting, University of Oklahoma, Norman, May 2007. https://www.naisa.org/wp-content/uploads/2018/01/Lomawaima_Plenary_Remarks_OU_0.pdf.

Morgensen, Scott Lauria. "Destabilizing the Settler Academy: The Decolonial Effects of Indigenous Methodologies." *American Quarterly* 64, no. 4 (2012): 805–8.

National Congress of American Indians. "Demographics." Accessed January 13, 2021. https://www.ncai.org/about-tribes/demographics.

Norris, Tina, Paula L. Vines, and Elizabeth M. Hoeffel. *The American Indian and Alaska Native Population: 2010*. 2010 Census Briefs. United States Census Bureau, 2012. https://www.census.gov/history/pdf/c2010br-10.pdf.

Ohio History Connection and the State Library of Ohio. Eastern Shawnee Tribe of Oklahoma Digital Collection. https://www.ohiomemory.org/digital/collection/p16007coll27.

Perry, Imani. "Cultural Studies, Critical Race Theory, and Some Reflections on Methods." *Villanova Law Review* 50, no. 4 (2005): 915–23.

Pulido, Laura. "FAQs: Frequently (Un)asked Questions about Being a Scholar Activist." In *Engaging Contradictions: Theory, Politics, and Methods of Activist Scholarship*, edited by Charles R. Hale, 341–66. Berkeley: University of California Press, 2008.

Richland, Justin B. "Beyond Listening: Lessons for Native/American Collaborations from the Creation of the Nakwatsvewat Institute." *American Indian Culture and Research Journal* 35, no. 1 (2011): 101–11.

Saunt, Claudio. "Telling Stories: The Political Uses of Myth and History in the Cherokee and Creek Nations." *Journal of American History* 93, no. 3 (2006): 673–97.

Silverman, David J. "Living with the Past: Thoughts on Community Collaboration and Difficult History in Native American and Indigenous Studies." *American Historical Review* 125, no. 2 (2020): 519–27.

Smith, Linda Tuhiwai. *Decolonizing Methodologies: Research and Indigenous Peoples*. 2nd ed. London: Zed Books, 2012.

Sturm, Circe. "Race, Sovereignty, and Civil Rights: Understanding the Cherokee Freedmen Controversy." *Cultural Anthropology* 29, no. 3 (2014): 575–98.

Thrush, Coll. "Afterword: How Many Worlds? Place, Power and Incommensurability." In *Beyond Two Worlds: Critical Conversations on Language and Power in Native North America*, edited by James Joseph Buss and C. Joseph Genetin-Pilawa, 295–318. Albany: State University of New York Press, 2014.

Walker, Jessica A. "Perception and Management of Type II Diabetes: The Narrated Experience of Diabetes in an Absentee Shawnee Community." MA thesis, University of Oklahoma, 2004.

Warren, Stephen, ed. *The Eastern Shawnee Tribe of Oklahoma: Resilience through Adversity*. Norman: University of Oklahoma Press, 2017.

———. "Reconsidering Coalescence: Yuchi and Shawnee Survival Strategies in the Colonial Southeast." In *Yuchi Indian Histories before the Removal Era*, edited by Jason Baird Jackson, 155–88. Lincoln: University of Nebraska Press, 2012.

———. *The Shawnees and Their Neighbors, 1795–1870*. Urbana: University of Illinois Press, 2005.

———. *The Worlds the Shawnees Made: Migration and Violence in Early America*. Chapel Hill: University of North Carolina Press, 2014.

Warren, Stephen, and Ben Barnes. "Salvaging the Salvage Anthropologists: Erminie Wheeler-Voegelin, Carl Voegelin, and the Future of Ethnohistory." *Ethnohistory* 65, no. 2 (2018): 189–214.

Warrior, Robert. "The Future in the Past of Native and Indigenous Studies." *American Indian Culture and Research Journal* 35, no. 1 (2011): 55–58.

———. "Native Critics in the World: Edward Said and Nationalism." In *American Indian Literary Nationalism*, by Jace Weaver, Craig S. Womack, and Robert Warrior, 179–224. Albuquerque: University of New Mexico Press, 2006.

Wilson, Angela Cavender. "American Indian History or Non-Indian Perceptions of American Indian History." *American Indian Quarterly* 20, no. 1 (1996): 3–5.

Wilson, Charles Banks. *Shawnee Ribbon Bets.* 1948. Oil on canvas, 27 1/4 x 35 x 2 1/2 in. (69.2 x 88.9 x 6.4 cm). Gilcrease Museum of Art, Tulsa, OK.

Wolf, Eric. *Europe and the People without History.* 2nd ed. Berkeley: University of California Press, 2010.

Yarbrough, Fay A. *Race and the Cherokee Nation: Sovereignty in the Nineteenth Century.* Philadelphia: University of Pennsylvania Press, 2007.

Part II

The Myaamia Center

The History and Practice of Community Engagement

Chapter 5

neepwaantiinki (Partners in Learning)

The Miami Tribe of Oklahoma, Miami University,
and the Myaamia Center

GEORGE IRONSTRACK AND BOBBE BURKE

George: *aya aya, neewe eempinamaani ooniini wiintaakani neehi ween-*
tamani ooniini aacimooni—myaamia nipwaayonikaani. niila myaamia,
meemeehšhkia weenswiaani, tahkamwa, saakacaahkwa, pinšiwa, palaanswa
ilaapiikasiaani. noošonke siipionki waapankiaakamionki waapaahšiki siipi-
onki eeminooteeciki myaamia eeweemakiki. myaamia nipwaayonikaaninki
myaamia mihši-nipwaantiikaaninki meehkimwiaani.[1]

George: *aya aya.* We appreciate that you are taking an interest in community-engaged scholarship by taking up this volume, and specifically
taking the time to learn more about our story: the history of the Myaamia
Center. I am a citizen of the Miami Tribe of Oklahoma. I descend from
two Myaamia, "Miami Indian," families: that of Tahkamwa and Pinšiwa,
also known as the Richardvilles, and that of Saakacaahkwa and Palaanswa,
also known as the Godfroys. My people's homelands are in northeastern
Oklahoma in the Neosho River Valley, in eastern Kansas in the Marias des
Cygnes River Valley, and in northern Indiana in the Wabash River Valley.
    I was born in *Šikaakonki*, "Chicago," and grew up outside of my tribal
nation. As a child, I had no access to language and culture education, and my

experience was not unique within our nation. The absence of language and culture education in our community was the direct result of actions taken by the United States to forcibly remove our nation from our homelands, diminish reservation and reserve lands controlled by our nation and our citizens after removal, disburse our people into diaspora across the US, and enforce a culturally oppressive educational system on our children. By the time of my birth, the Miami Tribe of Oklahoma was largely landless, and the last speakers of our language had passed away and *Myaamiaatweenki*, our "Myaamia language," entered a sleeping or dormant period.

As a young adult, in the mid-1990s, my father began taking me to some of the first family-centered language camps that took place in *Iihkipihsinonki*, "Peru, Indiana." Daryl Baldwin, current director of the Myaamia Center, was largely responsible for organizing the language learning sessions at these community programs. Working together with the linguist David Costa, Baldwin made use of the extensive written record of *Myaamiaataweeenki* to awaken the language and teach our community to communicate with each other again using it.

Soon after attending these programs, I developed an intrinsic desire to expand my language abilities and walk through the doorways of cultural learning that our language opened for me. When called upon, I served as a volunteer teacher-mentor working with youth learners at these programs. In the 1990s, nearly all of this language and culture work was a labor of love. At that time, no one believed it was possible to create a career or have a paying job that focused on language and culture revitalization.

After a brief but formative period teaching high school social studies in *Šikaakonki*, "Chicago," I entered graduate school at Miami University to pursue an MA in early American history with a focus on Myaamia ethnohistory. I was drawn to Miami for graduate school because Daryl Baldwin had moved there in 2001 to establish the Myaamia Project. This tribally directed research initiative was invested in expanding the reconstruction of our language and creating educational resources for our community to advance our learning of *Myaamiaataweenki*. The Myaamia Project also created supportive space for a young scholar interested in working on research topics that wove together the threads of Myaamia language, culture, and history.

In 2005, at the end of my first year of graduate school, I was hired by the Miami Tribe of Oklahoma to assist the Myaamia Project in the development of the curriculum for the tribe's first week-long youth language and culture educational program called *Eewansaapita*. At the time of this publication, the program continues to operate in two locations: Miami, Oklahoma, and Fort Wayne, Indiana.

The years of revitalization work have transformed the cultural educational opportunities for the next generation of Myaamia youth. As my wife, Tamise, and I welcomed our children into the world, some of the very first words they heard and spoke were in *Myaamiaataweenki*. Throughout their childhood they have been integrated into community cultural events in a manner that was simply not available to me as a child. Their generation has only ever experienced our language as a living means of communication, which is a powerful generational shift. As this generation move towards adulthood in our community, I am inspired by our young people's willingness to take on the work and responsibility of caring for their people.

In 2008, two years after graduation from Miami, I had the opportunity to return to Miami University and take on a position as the assistant director of the Myaamia Project. Currently, I continue that work at what is now called the Myaamia Center at Miami University. The creation and the growth of the center has been a transformative process, personally and collectively, and I am honored to be able to share our story here with you in this volume.

Bobbe: *aya*. Since 1991, I have had the privilege of working with the Miami Tribe, starting when I organized a campus display about the Myaamia and also helped host a group of Myaamia people from Oklahoma for a weekend visit to showcase that display and present a dance demonstration on campus. My work on that project coincided with the arrival of the first Myaamia students at Miami in the fall of 1991.

While gathering items for the display, I had my first interactions with Chief Floyd Leonard and Sharon Burkybile, who made their first trip to campus in 1975. This was shortly after he became chief and she became the Miami Tribe's liaison to the university. A university-wide program in November 1991 included both Miami Tribe and Miami University speakers dedicating the display and introducing the general campus to new educational components focused on the Miami Tribe.

I believe that, due to my new familiarity with the Miami Tribe from the 1991 project, I was assigned a second project in 1992 that afforded the university the opportunity to showcase Woodland Indians' culture with a portrait exhibit of a variety of Woodland tribal leaders. Chief Leonard's portrait was among the many other Oklahoma tribal leaders displayed. I orchestrated this display and planned for a campus event to occur during November, while Chief Leonard arranged for the Eastern Shawnee chief, Buck Captain, to be an additional presenter along with him on the program.

In 1994, I became the student affairs staff member appointed to assist Dr. Myrtis Powell, vice president for student affairs, in building a stronger, more educational, relationship with the Miami Tribe. She created a working committee of faculty to help address the recommendations from the 1994 commission report (the commission is explained in depth below). My main responsibilities were working with this committee's activities and planning campus-wide programming events.

My job assignments came directly from Dr. Powell, who served as the official liaison to the Miami Tribe as the vice president for student affairs. This responsibility was assigned to the VP for student affairs in the early 1980's. Dr. Powell dealt directly with Chief Leonard whenever that was needed or helpful. She encouraged me to communicate about activity or event planning with the Chief and Sharon, but I tried hard not to impose upon their time.

As I look back on this early time, I shudder to think of how unprepared I was. My learning curve was steep, but the work turned out to be intensely educational, addictive, and every bit as personal as it has been professional. Luckily, the Miami Tribe leaders have tolerated my lack of knowledge and allowed me to ask questions without feeling I was inappropriate or being intrusive or insensitive. Additionally, campus networks of faculty and other colleagues helped identify credible resources and eventually moved to hosting additional events sponsored by their respective university departments.

I made my first trip to Oklahoma in September 1994, and during that trip and on every other visit to Miami Tribe events, the welcoming atmosphere and hospitality of the Myaamia community were, and continue to be, amazing. Every group of Miami University guests says exactly the same thing, marveling about the generosity of time shared, the amount of food served, and the kindness of the Myaamia people. It is very nice to have observed during my tenure how "Miami University" has become such a household phrase within the Myaamia community.

Initially, I had limited contact with Myaamia students at Miami University. Over time, my student interaction expanded into the role of a strong resource and advisor for all parts of Myaamia student life on campus. The coordinator of Miami Tribe relations also evolved to be the first line of contact with potential Myaamia students, and to maintain connections with Myaamia alumni.

When Julie Olds, Miami Tribe citizen and current cultural resource officer, became the tribe's university liaison, my interactions with the tribe reached a new level of collaboration. Julie was my go-to person to brainstorm ideas and create new opportunities for programming on campus and find ways for Miami University students to engage with the tribe.

My educational growth would not have happened as successfully without the assistance of Kimberly Wade, a Myaamia student who attended MU from 1996 to 1999. Kim grew up in Miami, Oklahoma, but she struggled with severe health issues in the Ohio Valley weather. While she dealt with numerous hospital stays in Oxford, she and I got to know each other well. On my trips to Oklahoma, Kim helped me meet members of her family, pointed out who people were at meetings and events, and taught me about the fine points of powwow and stomp dancing.

Thank goodness for the arrival in 2001 of Daryl Baldwin who was willing to help me find credible resources for programming ideas and lend his cultural knowledge to provide quick feedback when needed for class projects. My ease with Daryl grew through long distance conversations on drives to Oklahoma, tagging along on his out of town speaking engagements, attending Native conferences, and meeting a wide variety of Native people. One of my best days at Miami was the day that Daryl and I moved into the same office space. The proximity to his, and consequently all the other people who joined the Myaamia Center staff since 2007, allowed me to do my job much more effectively and shaped the position of Miami Tribe relations into what we see today.

George: I hope Bobbe's story makes it clear just how central she is to the story of the development of the relationship between the Miami Tribe and Miami University and the success of the Myaamia Center. Her knowledge of university operations and insights into creation of partnerships were critical to the center's development and our ongoing success. Even after retirement, Bobbe remains an integral voice in the brain trust that guides the Myaamia Center's development.

More importantly, however, Bobbe has had an immeasurable impact on an entire generation of Myaamia students who have attended Miami University between 1991 and her retirement in December 2019. As a mentor and advisor, Bobbe played a seminal role in guiding students toward success in their educational experience and in helping us find ways to connect our educational work to the needs of our Myaamia community. The Miami Tribe of Oklahoma formally recognized Bobbe in 2005 by granting her the status of honorary citizen and we continue to express our gratitude to her at every possible moment. *mihši-neewe*, Bobbe!

George and Bobbe: In the story that follows, we do our best to recount the history of how the relationship between the Miami Tribe of Oklahoma and Miami University evolved and how the Myaamia Center emerged out of that relationship. This story emerges out of our personal experiences, archival research, and hours of interviews with key individuals. In this chapter, we have attempted to be as comprehensive as possible, however, we recognize that we may have missed important events or individuals along the way. We apologize for any errors of omission or fact. Despite any imperfections, we hope that this chapter provides useful insights to those seeking to understand this amazing story and an important record for those who will be tasked with recounting the story of the next twenty years.

In 1972, *Akima Mitehkia*—Chief Forest Olds of the Miami Tribe of Oklahoma, made the first known visit of an elected tribal leader to Miami University in Oxford, Ohio. In the late summer of 1972, Chief Olds was a director of Northeast Oklahoma's Rural Electric Cooperative and, in that capacity, he attended a conference on rural electrification in Cincinnati, about thirty-five miles south of Oxford. Through the facilitation of a Miami alum, Raymond Standafer, Chief Olds made an unexpected visit to Miami's campus.[2] The university president, Dr. Phillip Shriver, was not on campus at the time of Olds's visit, so Chief Olds met with staff from the Division of Student Affairs, and the Division of Alumni and Development Affairs.[3]

School officials organized an interesting impromptu tour. One particularly unusual stop on the tour was to football practice, where he met with one of the coaches.[4] Previously that summer, the university had written to Chief Olds to ask his opinion of the university's then mascot, the Redskins.[5] With the Washington football team's name change in 2020, it is easy to forget that resistance to the use of these race-based names date back to the late 1960s, when campus disturbances pushed schools like Stanford and Dartmouth to change their "Native" mascots and nicknames. During Olds's visit to football practice, university staff asked for his opinion on the use of the Redskins mascot and also if they could send a document to him to consider. Immediately following his visit, the university drafted a resolution of support and sent it to Chief Olds.[6]

Coincidentally, the annual meeting of the general council of the Miami Tribe met a week later and passed the resolution of support.[7]

In the spring of 2016, forty-four years later, *Akima Eecipoonkwia*— Chief Douglas Lankford of the Miami Tribe of Oklahoma—visited campus to attend the Myaamiaki Conference, a biennial community-centered event organized by the Myaamia Center to share the most up-to-date research regarding the revitalization of Myaamia language and culture. Near the end of the morning session that day, Chief Lankford listened as Jarrid Baldwin and Dr. David Costa presented on the Miami-Illinois Digital Archive (MIDA) and *Myaamiaatawaakani*, a new online Myaamia dictionary application.[8] Both resulted from over eight years of collaboration between Miami University computer science faculty and students and center staff. Both tools serve multiple needs. The digital archive software, now known as the Indigenous Languages Digital Archive (ILDA), furthers the development of tribal language revitalization through the creation of web-based means of organizing and processing Miami-Illinois linguistic data preserved in manuscript collections. It also gives tribal educational programmers better access to the documentary record used for developing Myaamia-specific education. In contrast, the online dictionary provides Myaamia community members with a web-based means to aid them in learning their heritage language for use in daily life.

The contrast between the visits of Chiefs Olds and Lankford gives rise to an obvious question: How did a relationship centered around a race-based mascot transition into a meaningful collaboration rooted in mutually beneficial education?

In the forty-four years separating the chiefs' visits, a handful of dedicated individuals, from both the Miami Tribe and Miami University, worked to intentionally foster an educationally centered relationship. Friendships and a deeper mutual understanding grew out of these relationships. Over time, the tribe and the university constructed a system of support for Miami Tribe college students in their education as Myaamia intellectuals and for the employment of fifteen individuals, all dedicated to the furthering of the Miami Tribe's revitalization effort.

By striking a balance between organic growth and carefully planned initiatives, the Miami Tribe and Miami University developed a sense of mutual trust resulting in a willingness to try untested ideas. This sense of trust was critical to the Miami Tribe feeling comfortable locating the research center fueling its language and cultural revitalization over 640 miles from their home in Miami, Oklahoma. This shared connection also helped Miami University successfully find ways to support, and benefit from, a research entity that does not fit easily into a typical university organizational chart. This essay attempts to trace the history of the Myaamia Center and identify the elements that we believe have made the center successful.

Intertwined but Unique Histories

The evolution of this relationship is all the more remarkable given the individual histories of the Miami Tribe of Oklahoma and Miami University. The historic homelands of the Miami Tribe include the lands upon which Miami University sits, and the very same historical forces that enabled the creation and growth of the University encouraged the United States government to forcibly remove and attempt to dissolve the Tribe. These intertwined histories give the Tribe and University a shared connection through place, but their divergent paths have produced unique contemporary needs and outcomes.

The history of the *Myaamiaki*, commonly known as Miami Indians, begins with "*mihtami myaamiaki nipinkonci saakaciweeciki, eehonci saakaciweewaaci, 'saakiiweeyonki' iitamenki.* At first the Myaamia came out of the water, the place where they came out is called the 'Coming Out Place.'"[9] This story describes the *Myaamiaki* emergence into *Myaamionki*, "the Place of the Miami." Historically, *Myaamionki* was centered on the *Waapaahšiki Siipiiwi*, "the Wabash River Valley," located in what is today northern Indiana. *Myaamionki* also included lands that today are a part of the states of Ohio, Illinois, Michigan, and Wisconsin.[10] From the 1780s to the 1840s, *Myaamiaki* became enmeshed in war, treaty making, land loss, oppression, and adaptive resistance. This volatile cauldron shaped, in part, the creation of a centralized Miami Nation.

The lands where Miami University sits were once a part of the traditional aboriginal lands of the Shawnee and the Miami and were utilized as hunting grounds by numerous other tribes with ties to the lower Great Lakes. By the latter half of the 1660s, European colonizers established competing claims for our land north of the Ohio River. In 1763, after the conclusion of the Seven Years War, the French transferred their land claims in North America to the British.[11] In 1783, after the end of the American Revolutionary War, the British ceded their claim to the

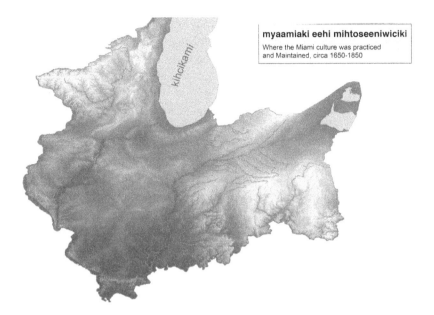

Figure 5.1. Myaamionki: The lands in which the Miami have and continue to live. These areas include our heritage landscape in the states of Ohio, Indiana, Illinois, Wisconsin, and Michigan, as well as our lands in present day Kansas and Oklahoma. The image "River Names in Myaamionki, circa 1650–1850," illustrates the ancestral homeland of the Miami Tribe of Oklahoma. (Map by Brett Governanti and Joshua Sutterfield).

lands east of the Mississippi and south of their Canadian possessions to the newly formed United States.[12] In 1763, just as in 1783, Native nations were not included in treaty negotiations. They fiercely disputed European power to cede their lands. From 1778 until 1794, the Myaamia, Shawnee, Delaware, and many other nations fought against American control of the Ohio River Valley, but, in 1794, this alliance was defeated at the Battle of Fallen Timbers. In 1795, the first Treaty of Greenville brought this war to an end and the Myaamia ceded control of what became Southwest Ohio to the United States.

The war's end, and the land cession treaties that followed, dramatically increased American settlement in the Ohio River Valley, and, in 1803, Ohio became the seventeenth state. The Northwest Ordinance states that Ohio, like other Midwestern states, should "encourage" education by establishing schools. In 1809, the state of Ohio chartered Miami University, one of the oldest public universities in the United States. Its name draws from the Great Miami and Little Miami Rivers, so named because eastern tribes viewed them as pathways via which travelers could reach the large Myaamia villages on the Wabash River. Eventually, the state placed Miami University in Oxford Township. Land sales and quitrents from land within Oxford township funded the construction and operation of the university.[13]

Miami University welcomed its first twenty students in 1824. Most of these young men, aged between twelve and twenty-one, came primarily from farming families. The Presbyterian Church and its old, classical curriculum dominated Miami University's early history and the experiences of these first students, many of whom went off to be ministers, missionaries, teachers, and lawyers.[14]

During the first two decades of operation (1825–45), Miami University built its physical infrastructure and steadily increased the numbers of faculty and students. In this same period, the US government forced the Miami Tribe to cede most of its homelands in the Wabash River Valley and beyond. In 1846, the United States forcibly removed the Miami Tribe from Northern Indiana to a western reservation in what became the state of Kansas. In the first steps of the removal, contractors hired by the US government conducted the Miami Tribe via canal systems in Indiana and Ohio. Five canal boats and over 320 men, women, and children on this forced removal passed through Butler County about twelve miles away from the campus of Miami University, while classes were in session.[15]

After the US Civil War, the Miami Tribe faced incredible pressure to cede their reservation lands in Kansas and move south to Indian Territory. Under the terms of the Treaty of 1867, the United States again forced the Miami Tribe to relocate to a reservation in the northeastern corner of Indian Territory, which became the state of Oklahoma. During both of these forced removals, Myaamia families remained behind in Indiana and Kansas, living on individual allotments or treaty reserve lands.

The latter half of the nineteenth century found Miami University in stressful circumstances due to the US Civil War. Students left to serve on both sides, and Miami's close proximity to the north-south boundary of the Ohio River made it easy for them to join either the Union or Confederate Army.[16]

In 1873, Miami University, like many other colleges and universities across the nation, closed its doors because of financial difficulties. The closing marked the end of the period of "Old Miami," or the university's history between 1809 and 1873. The college buildings were used for other purposes during the closing. However, the university did not have enough money to reopen, and thus begin the New Miami phase, until 1885.[17]

Even before Old Miami ended, changes in administration and faculty brought new ideas about the curriculum and varied expertise allowed new departments, like English language and literature, to evolve and new degrees of bachelor of science and bachelor of literature to emerge. However, not all faculty agreed that moving away from the traditional classical curriculum was best. The same controversy among the faculty existed when New Miami opened and pitted those favoring a traditional curriculum of the classics against those pushing a more modern and scientific course of study. This ongoing split slowed Miami's progress toward updating the curriculum.[18]

After a closure of twelve years, the university needed to make significant adjustments to its curriculum and more completely move away from the classical education that prepared students for careers in law, medicine, and the church. In 1885, when the school reopened, Miami's curriculum began to focus on science, English and modern languages, and new professions such as agriculture, engineering, journalism, social work, and education. With a few exceptions, the university's student body in the late 1800s was white and male. True coeducation did not begin at the university until the passage of a state mandate in 1902. Racial integration was slower still. It was in 1905 that Nellie Craig became the first African American graduate of the university. No Miami Tribe members attended the university in this period. Allotment, land loss, poverty, and continued racism restricted most Myaamia people from accessing higher education in general.[19]

Today, Miami University is a residential college that provides a rich academic and cocurricular student experience. A liberal education core provides the foundation for the specialized studies of 120 undergraduate majors, 15 master's degrees, and 14 PhD programs. Miami consistently ranks among the nation's top public universities for faculty commitment to quality undergraduate teaching.

The main campus is located in Oxford, Ohio, just thirty miles north of Cincinnati, with four regional campuses, including a European Center in Luxembourg. The fall 2020 enrollment totals included 16,502 undergraduates and 2,132 graduate students on the Oxford campus, plus an additional 4,250 at the regional campuses.[20]

During the early twentieth century, the Miami Tribe's land base collapsed following the allotment of the tribe's reservation in Indian Territory

(Oklahoma) and the sale or seizure of allotments and reserves in Indiana and Kansas. These three main population centers fragmented further as land loss and economic collapse forced Myaamia people to emigrate from these areas in order to survive. This fragmentation of land and people had a devastating effect on Myaamia heritage language and culture; by the mid-twentieth century, the last speakers of *Myaamiaataweenki*, "the Miami language," began to pass away.[21] By the 1980s, use of *Myaamiaataweenki* was restricted to memorized forms in prayers, songs, and family use of traditional names. Today, the Myaamia Tribal Nation, the Miami Tribe of Oklahoma, finds itself centered in a new *Myaamionki: Noošonke Siipionki*—the Neosho River Valley in Oklahoma—but 5,800 Myaamia people now live in at least forty-nine states, as well as outside the boundaries of the United States.[22]

Getting to Know Each Other, 1972–89

The 1970s found both Miami University and the Miami Tribe of Oklahoma in moments of transition. Miami University, like all colleges in Ohio, was still managing the aftermath of student unrest over the Vietnam War that resulted in four student deaths at Kent State University in 1970. For the Miami Tribe, the 1970s brought some positive changes as it began to lay the foundation for economic reconstruction and land reacquisition.

In 1939, the tribe reorganized its government and ratified a constitution under the terms of the Oklahoma Indian Welfare Act. This executive governmental body, known as the Business Committee, guided the tribe's efforts to seek compensation for past wrongs committed by the United States and sought new economic opportunities on behalf of its citizens. The Business Committee of the Miami Tribe of Oklahoma consists of a chief, second chief, secretary-treasurer, and two councilpersons. All five positions are elected on a staggered cycle by the general council of the nation, which consists of all adult citizens who assemble on designated days.[23]

Chief Forest Olds's historic visit to Miami University in 1972 marked an important return for the Miami Tribe of Oklahoma to the Great Miami River Valley and a new connection to the university that carried the same name. Unbeknownst to Chief Olds, and the university staff who greeted him, this visit planted seeds that would eventually mature into a collaborative relationship that would bring great pride to both entities.

The Division of Alumni and Development Affairs as well as the Athletic Department worked to help plant and sprout these first seeds.

For decades after this initial meeting, two conflicting university objectives framed the relationship between Miami University and the Miami Tribe of Oklahoma: to maintain their race-based mascot but to base it on criteria that were "authentic, dignified, and in good taste." Controversy around the university's nickname, the Redskins, erupted in 1971–72 due to the efforts of faculty and students to bring about a change away from a race-based moniker. In response to the controversy, President Phillip Shriver appointed an ad hoc committee to investigate the university's identification with the Miami Indians and with the use of the term "Redskins."

The seven-member ad hoc committee was divided on these two main issues, but decided to continue using the term Redskins (5–2). However, they voted to discontinue the use of a person mimicking an Indian on the sidelines (6–1). In addition, they unanimously agreed to "devise a mechanism for continuous evaluation of questions involving Indian sensitivities." Further explanation of that item states that it may be that "a legitimizing agency will be needed," and "one possibility might be to arrange for counsel from an Indian, possibly a Miami." The committee acknowledged, "his reaction will not provide an absolute protection against criticism, especially from other Indian spokesmen, but he would rather effectively reassure most in-house critics that at the least we were trying to be sensitive."[24] In addition to the readily obvious gender bias, the report makes no attempt to obscure the university's desire to utilize an Indian spokesperson, ideally a Miami Indian, to resolve their contradictory quest to authenticate a race-based mascot.

From 1975 until 1996, the Miami Tribe sought to help their new friends at Miami University create and maintain a more authentic and respectful context for the mascot. In 1975, the student body's request to reinstate a "sidelines mascot" led to the development of "Chief Miami," who first appeared in 1977.[25] The tribe created a real fancy dancer outfit and assisted in arranging for the first few male student performers to learn Native dances from experienced powwow dancers in Oklahoma. The first "Chief Miami," Wayne Breakfield, stayed with Chief Leonard and his wife when he received dance training in Oklahoma.[26]

Over time, some issues emerged. It was tedious and costly to maintain the dance outfit, and especially difficult to find people skilled to make repairs outside Oklahoma. It was also challenging to continually train Chief

Miami students in authentic dance steps and techniques. Miami University staff and students viewed the Oklahoma-based training as cumbersome and it was eventually eliminated. As the training ceased, Chief Miami students took creative license in their dance performances on the athletic field, and neither the university nor the tribe had a mechanism to hold students accountable. The mascot remained rooted in stereotypes. In hindsight, it seems clear that attempts to authenticate and educate through the mascot were destined for failure.

Planting Seeds Together, 1990–2001

In the mid-1980s, the relationship between the Miami Tribe and Miami University transitioned away from the care of Alumni and Athletics into the care of the Division of Student Affairs.[27] This administrative transition was critical to the radical changes in the relationship that developed in the 1990s. Chief Floyd Leonard and newly appointed vice president for student affairs, Dr. Myrtis Powell, carefully tended new growth. Chief Leonard was a lifetime educator who retired from the Joplin, Missouri, school district, where he served as assistant superintendent. Chief Leonard had a great interest in securing educational opportunities for the youth of his tribe. Dr. Powell served as the executive assistant to Miami's president from 1981–89 and was already familiar with the tribe-university relationship prior to transitioning to the vice-president position. She was personally committed to enhancing diversity education on campus.

Under the guidance of these two lifelong educators, the focus of the relationship shifted to provide intentional efforts for multicultural education for Miami University students and opportunities for a college education for Miami Tribe youth. In the 1990s, Chief Leonard and other citizens of the Miami Tribe of Oklahoma began to make regular visits to Miami University, where they participated in educational programs focused on tribal histories and the realities of contemporary tribal life. At times, visits included the leaders and members of other tribes who have ties to lands that became Ohio.[28]

In 1991, Miami University admitted the first citizens of the Miami Tribe under the terms of a special tuition and fee waiver called the Miami Heritage Award. The Heritage Award, first established in 1973, shortly after Chief Olds's first campus visit, was designed to recruit Native American students, especially Miami Tribe members.[29] However, no Myaamia stu-

Figure 5.2. Vice president for student affairs Dr. Myrtis Powell and Chief Floyd Leonard in Miami, Oklahoma, 2002.

dents attended Miami University between 1973 and 1991, even though announcements about this opportunity at Miami University were routinely made at the tribe's annual meeting.

In 1990 Travis Hall, a Myaamia parent, heard an annual meeting announcement and contacted Chief Leonard asking for more information about how his daughter could attend Miami University through the scholarship.[30] Chief Leonard, in turn, sent the inquiry along to Vice President Powell and her response to Chief Leonard said, "In the spirit of cooperation which we have enjoyed with the Miami Tribe, Miami University will provide tuition waiver for any member of the Miami Tribe who meets program requirements and is accepted for admission to the University."[31] Chief Leonard recruited two undergraduate students, resulting in three Myaamia students successfully matriculating in the fall semester, 1991. This set the precedent, still in existence today, for the Miami Heritage Award to be a tuition waiver no matter whether the student is an Ohio or an out of state resident.

Shortly after these first Myaamia students arrived on campus, Miami University faced rising conflict over its use of a Native mascot. The national visibility of Native mascots was influenced significantly by increased television coverage of professional sports, and the mascot controversy escalated especially when the Cleveland Indians, Atlanta Braves, and Washington Football Team reached the World Series or Super Bowl. In 1992, when Washington won the Super Bowl, controversy flared related to Miami University's mascot. From 1991 to 1995, the university's struggles became particularly acute, and the Miami Tribe was pulled into the fray.

Between 1972 and 1990, as Miami University continued to garner support for the mascot, people got to know each other and real relationships and friendships developed in the shadows of the mascot controversy. Critically, Floyd Leonard won reelection as tribal chief and Dr. Powell transitioned to the vice president of the Division of Students Affairs just as Myaamia families began to seek out a way for their children to attend the university that shared a name with their tribe.

In April 1994, in the midst of heightened on-campus mascot controversies, the university established the Committee on Relationships between Miami University and the Miami Tribe of Oklahoma, which generated several recommendations.[32] To help implement these recommendations, Myrtis Powell, the official university liaison to the Miami Tribe and the vice president for student affairs, created a part-time coordinator/support staff position and assigned it to Bobbe Burke. Burke worked closely with Powell as they implemented the committee's recommendations. Over the span of the tenures of four vice presidents of student affairs, the part-time coordinator position grew to be the primary hands-on liaison with the tribe, providing consistency by cultivating relationships and managing activities that involve the Miami Tribe. Burke's role expanded to a fulltime position in 2013, and she continued to work as the coordinator of Miami Tribe relations in the Myaamia Center until her retirement in December of 2019.

In the summer of 1996, the Miami Tribe of Oklahoma passed a full resolution, which stated that

> the Miami Tribe of Oklahoma can no longer support the use of the nickname Redskins and suggest that the Board of Trustees discontinue the use of Redskins and other Indian related names in connection with its athletic teams, effective with the end of the 1996–1997 academic school year.[33]

The university agreed to honor that request, and this accelerated the transition to a more mutually beneficial relationship focused on education.

Within the Miami Tribe, the emergence of Julie Olds as both a cultural and political leader had an immeasurable impact on the tribe's early efforts at revitalization as well as on the tribe-university relationship. Olds is a citizen of the Miami Tribe of Oklahoma and a long-time resident of the Miami, Oklahoma, area. Her husband, Dustin, is a great nephew of Chief Forest Olds. From a young age, her family involved her in Miami Tribe events as well as those organized by the broader intertribal cultural community of Northeast Oklahoma. In 1996, Olds was elected secretary-treasurer on the tribe's business committee, and she served in this capacity until 2005. In 1996, Miami Tribe leadership also appointed Olds to serve as the language clerk for an Administration for Native Americans (ANA) language revitalization grant awarded to the tribe.

In 1999, Olds facilitated the creation of the Cultural Preservation Office (CPO). The Tribe created the CPO, now known as the Cultural Resources Office, to respond to the increased interest in Myaamia language and culture, and Olds served as its inaugural officer. At the time of publication, Olds continues to serve her Native nation as cultural resources officer.[34] Olds was uniquely positioned to be aware of the political and cultural needs of her nation, and her skill and experience in both domains has been invaluable to her own people and the partnership between the tribe and university.

Through Julie Olds's leadership, the tribe and university developed more intensive and meaningful collaborative service-learning oriented projects. This engagement focused on Miami University faculty members and students from anthropology, archaeology, journalism, and linguistics in summer field schools that took place in Oklahoma. None of these programs would have been possible or been successful without Olds's hands-on support. She organized logistics and supervised service agendas for the field schools' time in Oklahoma. Throughout the period from the middle 1990s until 2001, Olds provided increased consistency of communication between the tribe and university.[35]

The presence of Miami Tribe students on campus led Olds to assist with the creation of cultural education programs focused on these students. In addition to the field schools, she helped Miami University design events for their general education program that focused on the Miami Tribe. Olds, together with Chief Floyd Leonard, made regular trips to Miami University to help carry out these programs. It was during these visits that they both developed personal relationships with Dr. Powell and Dr. Reed Anderson, the associate dean of the College of Arts and Science at the time. These relationships proved to be centrally important to the growth of the Miami Tribe's language and culture revitalization effort and to the expansion of the tribe-university relationship.

It was through her work with the ANA grant that Olds first met the linguists Daryl Baldwin and David Costa. Daryl Baldwin is a citizen of the Miami Tribe who was born in Northwest Ohio. As an adult, he began to learn *Myaamiaataweenki* from documentation and, together with his wife, Karen, taught what he was learning at home to their children. David Costa fortuitously selected the *Myaamiaataweenki* "the Miami-Illinois language," as the focus of his PhD studies. His dissertation work resulted in the first comprehensive description of *Myaamiaataweenki*. Dr. Costa is not Myaamia by birth but has become an integral part of the Myaamia community through his work.[36]

Word spread quickly about Baldwin's efforts and the community began to call on him to teach and share what he was learning about the language with others. Baldwin and Costa met in the 1990s and both came to Miami, Oklahoma, to help Julie Olds carry out language programming driven by the ANA grant. Together they developed teaching resources for use in community programs and in Myaamia homes, and, by the end of the 1990s, the effort had been astonishingly successful in increasing the number of people using the language on a daily basis. From 1996 to 2000, Myaamia people in Oklahoma and Indiana demonstrated increasing levels of interest in their traditional language. This interest was demonstrated through attendance at language learning events, daily use of the language in homes, requests for the giving of names in the language, the coining of new words for objects like computers and cars, and the creation of new songs in the language. After sixty years of dormancy, the process of learning to speak their heritage language again energized the Myaamia community. Sammye Darling, a Miami Tribe elder, referred to this collective empowerment as an "awakening," often referred to today as *Myaamiaki Eemamwiciki*, "the Miami awaken."[37]

Despite the joy of these early successes, Baldwin and Olds came to realize that advancing the revitalization effort to the next level required research and development capabilities and trained human resources that the Miami Tribe did not possess at the time.[38] Revitalization of a language from documentation was turning out to be an intergenerational endeavor, and collaboration with Miami University offered an opportunity to gain access to research tools that the tribe would take decades to build on its own. Additionally, the Miami Tribe student body presented a unique opportunity to develop tribal human resources through face-to-face mentoring and tribally designed educational programming.[39] Thinking about the need for this "next step," Olds did not hesitate to inquire about what could be established on campus that would help meet the needs of the Myaamia community.[40]

The Garden in Bloom, 2001–20

In 2000, after several discussions between Miami University and the Miami Tribe, an agreement was reached that "the next logical step is to formalize this relationship into a stable program that will create comprehensive cultural enrichment opportunities for both."[41] The initial objective was to open a Miami Tribal research office at Miami University with Daryl Baldwin as its director. Working together, Powell, Anderson, and Olds were able to secure shared funding from Miami University's Office of the Provost, Office of the Dean of Arts and Science, and the Division of Student Affairs for a period of three years in order to test the idea. The Miami Tribe later contributed funding for travel and the production of educational materials. In July 2001, these negotiations resulted in the opening of the Myaamia Project at Miami University. Daryl Baldwin moved to the Oxford area and became its first director.[42]

From its inception, the Myaamia Project was interdisciplinary and focused on the needs of the Miami Tribe. During a visit with Chief Floyd Leonard, Baldwin remembers Leonard instructing him that he was not "there to change the institution," but instead "to do the work of the nation."[43] Strategically, both the tribe and the university chose to place the Myaamia Project within the oversight responsibilities of the Division of Student Affairs. The project/center's location within the university's administrative organizational chart enabled the young office to be truly interdisciplinary and to follow its mandate to advance the Miami Tribe's language and culture research needs. This arrangement continued until 2013, when the Myaamia Project became a full research center, joining other university centers within Miami University's Office of Research and Innovation. These placements kept the initiative at a distance from the established cultures and internal conflicts of the larger departments on campus.

Over time, collaborations between the project/center and Miami faculty members have blossomed. Center staff have had the luxury of developing relationships with faculty who share similar interests and have the skills, knowledge, temperament, and personality to work with the Miami Tribe. Because of this focus on personal relationships, collaborations with particular disciplines tend to have a lifespan tied to a specific faculty member's career on campus. When these collaborations end, academic departments are not obligated to continue a connection to the Miami Tribe.[44]

These open-ended and inclusive relationships have enabled the project/center to develop initiatives with academic fields as wide ranging as architecture, journalism, educational psychology, anthropology, linguistics, history, geography, environmental science, and computer science. Successful initiatives usually start with a trusted friend on campus recommending an individual to the center or with a faculty member reaching out to learn more about the Myaamia Center. Typically, after a few shared lunches or short informal meetings, the interested faculty member invites center staff to visit their undergraduate classes and speak about the center's work. Usually, the Miami Tribe invites the faculty member to Oklahoma to visit during one of the tribe's large gatherings. A year or more often passes before both parties reach a satisfactory comfort level and launch a new initiative. It can take two to three years before the relationship produces results that are mutually beneficial.

The collaboration between the tribe and university is often referred to as *neepwaantiinki*, "learning from each other," or, more officially, as "partners in learning." Through this partnership, a deep bond of trust has been created between the Miami Tribe of Oklahoma and Miami University. Built slowly over decades, this trust created an environment with fruitful soil in which the Myaamia Center could grow organically and develop in form and function to meet the needs of both the tribe and the university.

Remarkably, when the Myaamia Center began, organizers were not aware of community-engaged models that they could follow. Some of the professors conducting service-learning projects drew on the literature describing best practices in that form of engagement. However, to the best of the authors' current knowledge, no one explicitly drew on those resources in planning and organizing the development of the first incarnation of the center. Cofounder Daryl Baldwin describes the existence of the center as akin to being like a tree, with "its roots in Oklahoma," and "its leaves branching out" through Miami's campus.[45] Unlike most of

the examples of community engagement in the literature, the Myaamia
Center is a scholarly community space that mixes Native scholars and
non-Native scholars in its daily operations. In most cases, engagement
bridges a physical and conceptual space between a "community" and a
"scholar." There is a real physical space between Miami, Oklahoma, and
Oxford, Ohio. However, the presence of the Myaamia Center at Miami
University shrinks the physical distance and at times eliminates most of the
conceptual space between the needs of the Myaamia community and the
research being conducted on its behalf on the campus of Miami University.

In 2006, thirty-four years after the beginning of the relationship and
five years after the creation of the Myaamia Project, the Miami Tribe of
Oklahoma and Miami University signed their original memorandum of
understanding. Based on the "common links of geography, educational and
cultural interests" and recognizing the strong, trusting relationship that has
led to working "together informally to support each other's educational
and developmental needs," "these two entities wish to enable cooperation
and exchange in all educational areas of mutual interest, and to expand
the basis for friendship and cooperative educational exchange."[46]

Just two years later, the Miami Tribe of Oklahoma and Miami University signed a memorandum of agreement (MOA) that stated that the
Myaamia Project "has become an important entity for the educational
advancement of members of the Miami Tribe and Miami University communities. The MOA includes several specific articles of operation, such as:

> The research initiatives and educational activities conducted
> through the Myaamia Project must be initiated and approved
> by the Miami Tribe's Cultural Resources Office in order to
> ensure that said research and educational objectives meet the
> needs of the Miami Tribe community.

The agreement is specific to the environment of Miami University. However, the principles of the MOA guide the Myaamia Center's approach
to collaborations beyond the campus of Miami University. Center staff
periodically consult with off-campus researchers. Center staff have found
that consultation is a necessary first step in building collaborations that
meet everyone's expectations for engagement. Usually, there is no expectation that the products of consultation produce the same quality or have
the same degree of impact as the fully engaged projects that follow the
spirit of the MOA.

The agreement explains the specific duties of the center and the obligations of the university, and specifies that "the Miami Tribe, by right of self-determination, has control over its cultural and intellectual property on behalf of the citizens of its nation." Copyright of the center's work remains with the Miami Tribe of Oklahoma and "no reprinting or distribution of materials produced by the Myaamia Project may occur without the express written consent of the Miami Tribe of Oklahoma."[47]

As of October 2020, the Myaamia Center is made up of a dedicated staff of fifteen full and part-time employees. Its internal structure consists of five offices: director, Miami Tribe relations, language research, communications and publications, cultural ecology, and education and outreach. Five of the scholars working at the center are citizens of the Miami Tribe of Oklahoma. Six of the center's employees have earned a PhD and five have earned an MA. Center staff work in an interdisciplinary manner, but each has their core area of expertise. There are three linguists, four education specialists, one historian, two technologists, two psychologists, one transcriptionist, and one expert administrative assistant. The center also has three faculty affiliates, in educational leadership, geology, and informational technology, and four graduate assistants, two from the Department of Computer Science and Software Engineering and two from the Geography Department.[48]

The center and its collaborators have produced a wide array of materials, tools, and research studies that we believe are transformative for the Myaamia community and the Miami University community. To further the shifting of the Myaamia community's language ideology, the center produced the first comprehensive print dictionary of the modern era. The primary purpose behind the dictionary was to further convince the Myaamia community that their language was substantial, complex, worthy of respect, and capable of robust revitalization. The center, together with faculty and students in computer science, developed and continues to maintain a web-based digital dictionary that is the primary reference tool for those learning *Myaamiaataweenki*, "the Miami language," in their homes.[49]

For more than a decade, the Miami Tribe has used these language-learning tools in a wide array of educational programs on and beyond the campus of Miami University. Hundreds of tribal youth have been exposed to Myaamia language and culture.[50] Finally, by collaborating with faculty in educational psychology and educational leadership, the center has facilitated the development of a longitudinal assessment team called the

Nipwaayoni Acquisition and Assessment Team (NAAT). This team consists of educators, a psychologist, a second language acquisition specialist, and cultural specialists that seek to better understand and describe, through quantitative and qualitative measures, the impact of language and culture learning on Myaamia youth and the broader community. The NAAT's work reflects the Miami Tribe's interests in understanding the impact and social value of the ongoing work in community revitalization. Their work is also reflective of the best practices and research agendas of each scholar's area of specialty. The early results of this research demonstrate that these programs are having a positive impact on the identity development of Myaamia youth, which, in turn, fuels their achievements in other domains.[51]

In some fields, scholars have articulated a fear that engagement with Native nations leads professionals to produce work that violates the methods and ethics of their home discipline. Through two decades of collaborative work, the record of the Myaamia Center speaks directly to the illegitimacy of those fears. Moreover, the record of the center stands as a striking example of how a scholarly work is improved and made more meaningful, to both the tribal community and scholarly community, through engagement.

Figure 5.3. For Myaamia, "Miami Indian students," attending Miami University, students will connect with their culture through learning *myaamiataweenki*, Myaamia language. The university and the Myaamia Center have documented better educational outcomes from their tribal citizen-students from participating in Myaamia programs.

The success of the Myaamia Center should not be solely determined by the products and programs it creates. The center has fostered a series of collaborations that have been transformative for everyone involved in the work. The broad and extensive benefits of this partnership have impacted the Myaamia people and Miami University's faculty, staff, and students.

Increasing numbers of Myaamia students enrolled in the Myaamia Heritage Award program at Miami University offer another example of the center's impact. The student numbers have increased significantly over more than twenty-five years. In 1991, three students were enrolled at Miami. By 2018, thirty students were enrolled. High family satisfaction with the program, as demonstrated by the multiple siblings and first cousins who have followed each other to Miami, demonstrate the center's value.

Starting in 2003–4, students in the current program were required to take a series of six 1-credit hour classes that teach them about who they are as Myaamia people. They participate in these classes together, and one central goal, equally important to the course content, is to build a strong Myaamia community on campus whose members care about and support each other. During their senior year, they obtain two additional credits by completing a senior project that is designed to give back to the community in some tangible way. Some of these students arrive with little or no understanding of Myaamia history, language, and culture but graduate after four years with a high level of self-confidence in their identity as Myaamia persons and with a stronger connection to the larger Myaamia community. Students born into families that already participate in community revitalization arrive having been immersed in their language, culture, and history for their entire childhood. The program intentionally blends Myaamia students of different backgrounds into the same learning community. In this way, peer-based learning combines with more traditional, in both the tribal and academic sense, expert instructional techniques to create a vibrant and transformative experience. Together, all of these young adults are a part of the future of the Miami Tribe.

As the Myaamia Heritage Award program evolved and added the heritage series of classes, the graduation rates improved. Between 1991 and 2003 (the years before the heritage classes began), 25 undergraduate Myaamia students entered Miami, 15 graduated (14 graduated in six years), and 10 students left without obtaining degrees. This resulted in a 56 percent six-year retention/graduation rate, and 60 percent overall graduation rate. Between 2003 and 2018, 56 undergraduate students entered Miami, and 48 graduated (43 in four years). The four-year graduation rate for these students was 76.8 percent, and the overall graduation rate for these students was 85.7 percent.[52]

Conclusion: Giving Thanks and Recognizing Obligations

The establishment and continued good work of the Myaamia Center would not have been possible without a small number of dedicated and resourceful individuals building and maintaining the relationships that have become so central to the work of revitalization. These individuals include Forest Olds, Floyd Leonard, Phillip Shriver, Julie Olds, Myrtis Powell, Daryl Baldwin, and David Costa. Other integral players at Miami University have come from Alumni Affairs, University Development, the Division of Student Affairs (including five different vice presidents), the College of Arts and Science, and numerous faculty members from a wide array of academic departments extending over a span of seven different Miami University presidents, from 1972 to present.[53]

Three individuals that the authors would also like to recognize in detail are Cory Foster, Dr. Hugh Morgan, and Dr. Reed Anderson. Alumni affairs director Cory Foster (1988–97) developed a deep friendship with the Miami Tribe and played a significant role in making and encouraging visits to Oklahoma, helping the first Myaamia students adjust to Miami, and managing mascot issues before and during the name change. Journalism faculty member Hugh Morgan provided the first tools for the Miami Tribe to develop a system for producing a useful and aesthetically pleasing newspaper that remains in operation.[54] In addition, the extensive photo record of Miami Tribe activities from 1999–2007 are a result of the generosity of Dr. Morgan's time and funding. Dr. Reed Anderson, while in the position of associate dean in the College of Arts and Science, was critical in leading the discussions and drafting the proposal for the development of a Miami Tribe initiative on the Miami University campus that resulted in today's Myaamia Center.

The development and growth of human relationships lies at the heart of the history of the Myaamia Center. These relationships began at a personal level and evolved into an institutional-national relationship. Ongoing and heartfelt friendships between citizens of the Miami Tribe and the people of Miami University are critically important. Upon reflection of the initial mission of the Myaamia Center, Daryl Baldwin acknowledged:

Even though I was not sent there to change the institution, our long-term presence has over time had an impact on the relationship and has brought about some degree of [institutional] change through continued relationship building.[55]

Sharing the history of this work with those who are not a part of it remains difficult. It is hard to adequately represent the power of the connections that led to these changes, yet everything good that the Myaamia Center does comes from the wellspring of human relationships.

neewe weentamani ooniini myaamia nipwaayonikaani aacimooni. kocimiaanki-nko kati? teepi-hki aacimwaapiiyankwi miinawa eewikawiaanki. kweehsitawiaanki. "Thank you for reading our Myaamia Center story. Do you want to ask us questions? If so, you can talk to us on the phone or write us. With respect."[56]

Notes

1. The authors would like to say *neewe*, "thank you," to the staff of the Myaamia Center and the editors of this volume for taking the time to provide detailed and useful feedback on this essay.

2. Raymond Standafer, "Miami Indians and Redskins," Nickname and Mascot Controversy, 1996, Miami University Special Collections, Oxford, OH.

3. "Chief Olds Visit to Murstein Alumni Center," binder 1 Olds and Leonard, photograph, 1972, Bobbe Burke Collection, Myaamia Center, Miami University.

4. Standafer, "Miami Indians."

5. James Cooley to Chief Olds, July 11, 1972, box 4, folder 4, Chief Forest D. and Lorene Olds Papers, Myaamia Heritage Museum and Archives, Miami, OK.

6. Doug Wilson (director of Alumni Affairs, Miami University) to Chief Olds, September 1, 1972, box 4, folder 4 Olds Papers, Myaamia Heritage Museum and Archives (MHMA), Miami University, Oxford, OH.

7. The university's document was signed by all five business committee members of the Miami Tribe and return dated September 9, 1972. Business Committee of the Miami Tribe of Oklahoma, "1971: Resolutions, 1972 Commission, Chief Miami," Bobbe Burke Collection, Myaamia Center, Miami University.

8. Miami-Illinois is the label that the field of linguistics uses for *Myaamiaataweenki* and *Peewaaliaataweeki*, the language of the Miami Tribe of Oklahoma and the Peoria Tribe of Oklahoma. At the time of the presentation, this software was called the Miami-Illinois Digital Archive (MIDA). In 2020, this software was replaced by the Indigenous Languages Digital Archive (ILDA). ILDA can be found

at https://mc.miamioh.edu/ilda-myaamia/; and the Myaamia online dictionary can be found at https://mc.miamioh.edu/ilda-myaamia/dictionary.

9. David Costa, ed., *myaamia neehi peewaalia aacimoona neehi aalhsooh-kana—Myaamia and Peoria Narratives and Winter Stories* (Miami, OK: Miami Tribe of Oklahoma and the Peoria Tribe of Oklahoma, 2010), 52–53.

10. A more thorough discussion of Miami Tribe homelands can be found on the Myaamia community blog, Aacimotaatiiyankwi (https://aacimotaatiiyankwi.org/2010/12/16/walking-myaamionki/).

11. Fred Anderson, *Crucible of War: The Seven Years' War and the Fate of Empire in British North America, 1754-1766* (New York: Knopf, 2000), 500–506.

12. Richard White, *The Middle Ground: Indians, Empires, and Republics in the Great Lakes Region, 1650-1815*, Cambridge Studies in North American Indian History (Cambridge: Cambridge University Press, 1991), 407–11.

13. Phillip R. Shriver, *Miami University: A Personal History* (Oxford, OH: Miami University Press, 1998), 44–51.

14. Shriver, *Miami University*, 69; Walter Havighurst, *The Miami Years, 1809-1984* (New York: Putnam's, 1984), 74.

15. George Strack, George Ironstrack, Daryl Baldwin, Kristina Fox, Julie Olds, Robbyn Abbitt, and Melissa Rinehart, *myaamiaki aancihsaaciki: A Cultural Exploration of the Myaamia Removal Route* (Miami, OK: Miami Tribe of Oklahoma, 2011), 17–18.

16. Shriver, *Miami University*, 109–13.

17. Havighurst, *The Miami Years*, 134.

18. Havighurst, *The Miami Years*, 140–43. Shriver asserts that the lack of curriculum decisions was another cause of the 1873 closing: "The classical Humanities curriculum was one of the victims of the Civil War, and Miami suffered from holding on to it too long." Shriver, *Miami University*, 117.

19. Elizabeth H. Baer, *The History of the Miami University Libraries* (Oxford, OH: Friends of the Miami University Libraries, 1997), 85; Miami University College of Education, Health, and Society, "Our History," accessed November 6, 2020, https://miamioh.edu/ehs/about/history/index.html.

20. Miami University, *Miami University Report Card 2020-21*, accessed October 23, 2020, https://miamioh.edu/about-miami/recognition/report-card/index.html.

21. Daryl Baldwin and Julie Olds, "Miami Indian Language and Culture Research at Miami University," in *Beyond Red Power: New Perspectives on American Indian Politics and Activism*, ed. Daniel M. Cobb and Loretta Fowler (Santa Fe: School of American Research Press, 2007), 281; Meghan Dorey and George Ironstrack, *keehkaapiišamenki: A History of the Allotment of Miami Lands in Indian Territory* (Miami, OK: Miami Tribe of Oklahoma, 2015), 18–30.

22. Wesley Y. Leonard, "When Is an 'Extinct Language' Not Extinct? Miami, a Formerly Sleeping Language," in *Sustaining Linguistic Diversity: Endangered*

and Minority Languages and Language Varieties, ed. Kendall A. King, Natalie Schilling-Estes, Jia Jackie Lou, Lyn Fogle, and Barbara Soukup (Washington, DC: Georgetown University Press, 2008), 24–25; Teresa L. McCarty, *Language Planning and Policy in Native America: History, Theory, Praxis* (Buffalo, NY: Multilingual Matters, 2013), 94–95. Miami Tribe population data reported from the tribe's enrollment office in October 2020.

23. Bert Anson, *The Miami Indians* (Norman: University of Oklahoma Press, 1970), 260–65.

24. "Report of Ad Hoc Committee to Investigate the University's Identification with the Miami Indians and with the Use of the Term 'Redskins,'" August 29, 1972, Nicknames and Mascot History and Controversy, Miami University Archives and Special Collections, Oxford, OH, p. 5.

25. Phillip R. Shriver, "Growing Concerns on Campus," memorandum, January 6, 1976, Miami University Archives and Special Collections, Oxford, OH; "Miami Indian Symbol Revealed This Weekend," *The Miamian*, January 27, 1977.

26. Correspondence with Wayne Breakfield, February 13, 2006, Chief Miami Binder, Bobbe Burke Collection, Myaamia Center, Miami University, Oxford, OH.

27. R. F. Etheridge, "Chief Miami Memorandum," June 4, 1981. Binder "1971, Resolutions, 1972 Commission, Chief Miami," Bobbe Burke Collection, Myaamia Center, Miami University, Oxford, OH.

28. In November 1992, Chief Leonard's guests were Buck Captain (Eastern Shawnee) and Ray White (Miami Nation of Indiana, Inc.). Vol. 2, Bobbe Burke Collection, Myaamia Center, Miami University, Oxford, OH. In September 1998, guests were Steve Kinder (Peoria), Kevin Dawes (Ottawa), and James Squirrel (Shawnee) who all led a stomp dance on campus. Volume 3, Bobbe Burke Collection. In October 2000, guests were Dee Ketchum (Delaware), Mike Pace (Delaware), James Squirrel (Shawnee) who all provided a lecture along with Chief Leonard and led a stomp dance on campus. Vol. 4, Bobbe Burke Collection.

29. David Lawrence to Mrs. Milton Roll, November 8, 1973, vol. 2, Bobbe Burke Collection, Myaamia Center, Miami University, Oxford, OH.,.

30. Traverse Hall to Chief Floyd Leonard, August 14, 1990, vol. 2, Bobbe Burke Collection, Myaamia Center, Miami University, Oxford, OH.

31. Myrtis Powell to Chief Floyd Leonard, September 11, 1990, vol. 2, Bobbe Burke Collection, Myaamia Center, Miami University, Oxford, OH.

32. "Miami Nicknames" by Committee on the Relationships between Miami University and the Miami Tribe of Oklahoma, April 1994, box 1, folder 17, Student Affairs, Miami Tribe, Materials, 1972–2001, Miami University Archives and Special Collections, Oxford, OH.

33. Business Committee Miami Tribe of Oklahoma, "Resolution 96-34," binder "Miami Tribe of Oklahoma and Miami University Resolutions," July 6, 1996, Bobbe Burke Collection, Myaamia Center, Miami University, Oxford, OH.

34. Daryl Baldwin and David J. Costa, "Myaamiaataweenki: Revitalization of a Sleeping Language," in *The Oxford Handbook of Endangered Languages*, ed.

Kenneth L. Rehg and Lyle Campbell (New York: Oxford University Press, 2018), 561–62.

35. This beginning point mirrors what Giles describes in his 2008 article, which outlines how the earliest examples of the community engagement occurred under the auspices of service-learning. Dwight E. Giles, Jr., "Understanding an Emerging Field of Scholarship: Toward a Research Agenda for Engaged, Public Scholarship," *Journal of Higher Education Outreach and Engagement* 12, no. 2 (2008): 97–98.

36. Baldwin and Costa, "Myaamiaataweenki," 553–74.

37. McCarty, *Language Planning*, 94.

38. Baldwin and Olds, "Miami Indian Language," 282.

39. Ibid., 284–85; Susan Mosley-Howard, Daryl Baldwin, George Ironstrack, Kate Rousmaniere, and Bobbe Burke, "Niila Myaamia (I Am Miami): Identity and Retention of Miami Tribe College Students," *Journal of College Student Retention* 17, no. 4 (2016): 442–43.

40. McCarty, *Language Planning*, 98–99.

41. Reed Anderson, "Proposal to Establish the Myaamia Institute for Miami Indian Culture at Miami University," January 2001, Papers of the Office of Miami Tribe Relations, Myaamia Center, Miami University, Oxford, OH.

42. Reed Anderson and Bobbe Burke, "Report on Progress of Myaamia Center," memorandum, January 2, 2003, papers of the Education and Outreach Office, Myaamia Center, Miami University, Oxford, OH.

43. Daryl Baldwin (Myaamia Center director) personal communication with George Ironstrack, November 30, 2018.

44. Gail Della Piana, Adolph Greenberg, Jason Rech, and Doug Troy, "Faculty Involvement with the Miami Tribe and the Myaamia Project," panel session at 2012 Myaamiaki Conference, March 31, 2012, Myammia Center YouTube video, posted May 1, 2012. https://youtu.be/TJeOS1XI-kE.

45. Daryl Baldwin (Myaamia Center director) in discussion with George Ironstrack, October 30, 2018.

46. Memorandum of understanding, the Miami Tribe of Oklahoma, Miami, Oklahoma, and Miami University, Oxford, Ohio, March 24, 2006, Miami Nickname, Miami University Archives and Special Collections, Oxford, OH, https://miamioh.edu/miami-tribe-relations/history/index.html.

47. Memorandum of agreement, the Miami Tribe of Oklahoma, Miami, Oklahoma and Miami University, Oxford, Ohio, March 19, 2008, Collection of the Office of Miami Tribe Relations, Myaamia Center, Miami University, http://miamioh.edu/miami-tribe-relations/history/index.html.

48. For a complete list of Myaamia Center staff and affiliates, visit https://www.miamioh.edu/myaamia-center/about/staff-faculty-affiliates/index.html.

49. Daryl Baldwin and David J. Costa, *myaamia neehi peewaalia kaloosioni mahsinaakani—a Miami-Peoria Dictionary* (Miami, OK: Miami Nation, 2005), https://mc.miamioh.edu/ilda-myaamia/dictionary.

50. To see more about Myaamia Center research outcomes, visit http://miamioh.edu/myaamia-center/research/index.html; and for more on tribal educational programs see Baldwin and Costa, "Myaamiaataweenki," 566–67.

51. See the Daryl Baldwin, G. Susan Mosley-Howard, George Ironstrack, and Haley Shea essay in this volume for more on the assessment work.

52. Neewe, "thank you," to Kara Strass for providing this data from the records of the Miami Tribe Relations Office at Miami University. Kara Strass (Miami Tribe relations assistant) email to Bobbe Burke, June 13, 2019.

53. Miami University presidents included in this count are Philip R. Shriver (1965–81), Paul G. Pearson (1981–92), Paul G. Risser (1993–95), Anne Hopkins (December 1995–July 1996, acting), James C. Garland (1996–2006); David C. Hodge (2006–16); Gregory P. Crawford (2016–present).

54. Back issues of the Miami Tribe of Oklahoma newspaper *Aatotankiki Myaamiaki* can be found at https://www.miamination.com/newspaper.

55. Daryl Baldwin (Myaamia Center director) in email to George Ironstrack, November 30, 2018.

56. The Myaamia Center can be reached at 513-529-5648. Bobbe Burke's email is burkebi@miamioh.edu and George Ironstrack's is ironstgm@miamioh.edu.

Bibliography

Anderson, Fred. *Crucible of War: The Seven Years' War and the Fate of Empire in British North America, 1754–1766.* New York: Knopf, 2000.

Anderson, Reed, and Bobbe Burke. "Report on Progress of Myaamia Center." Memorandum, January 2, 2003, papers of the Education and Outreach Office, Myaamia Center, Miami University, Oxford, OH.

Anson, Bert. *The Miami Indians.* Norman: University of Oklahoma Press, 1970.

Baer, Elizabeth H. *The History of the Miami University Libraries.* Oxford, OH: Friends of the Miami University Libraries, 1997.

Baldwin, Daryl, and David J. Costa. "Myaamiaataweenki: Revitalization of a Sleeping Language." In *The Oxford Handbook of Endangered Languages,* edited by Kenneth L. Rehg and Lyle Campbell, 553–70. New York: Oxford University Press, 2018.

———. *myaamia neehi peewaalia kaloosioni mahsinaakani—a Miami-Peoria Dictionary.* Miami, OK: Miami Nation, 2005. https://mc.miamioh.edu/ilda-myaamia/dictionary.

Baldwin, Daryl, and Julie Olds. "Miami Indian Language and Culture Research at Miami University," in *Beyond Red Power: New Perspectives on American Indian Politics and Activism,* ed. Daniel M. Cobb and Loretta Fowler, 280–90. Santa Fe: School of American Research Press, 2007.

Business Committee of the Miami Tribe of Oklahoma. Bobbe Burke Collection. Miami Center, Miami University, Oxford, OH.

Business Committee of the Miami Tribe of Oklahoma. "Resolution 96-34." July 6, 1996. Binder "Miami Tribe of Oklahoma and Miami University Resolutions," Bobbe Burke Collection, Myaamia Center, Miami University, Oxford, OH.

Committee on the Relationships between Miami University and the Miami Tribe of Oklahoma. Miami Tribe Collection. Miami University Archives and Special Collections, Oxford, OH.

Cooley, James. Letter to Chief Olds. July 11, 1972. Box 4, folder 4, Chief Forest D. and Lorene Olds Papers, Myaamia Heritage Museum and Archives (MHMA) Miami, OK.

Costa, David, ed. *myaamia neehi peewaalia aacimoona neehi aalhsoohkana— Myaamia and Peoria Narratives and Winter Stories*. Miami, OK: Miami Tribe of Oklahoma and the Peoria Tribe of Oklahoma, 2010.

Dorey, Meghan, and George Ironstrack. *keehkaapiišamenki: A History of the Allotment of Miami Lands in Indian Territory*. Miami, OK: Miami Tribe of Oklahoma, 2015.

Etheridge, R. F. "Chief Miami Memorandum." June 4, 1981. Binder "1971: Resolutions, 1972 Commission, Chief Miami," Bobbe Burke Collection, Myaamia Center, Miami University, Oxford, OH.

Giles, Dwight E., Jr. "Understanding an Emerging Field of Scholarship: Toward a Research Agenda for Engaged, Public Scholarship." *Journal of Higher Education Outreach and Engagement* 12, no. 2 (2008): 97–106.

Hall, Traverse. Letter to Chief Floyd Leonard. August 14, 1990. Vol. 2, Bobbe Burke Collection, Myaamia Center, Miami University, Oxford, OH.

Havighurst, Walter. *The Miami Years, 1809-1984*. New York: Putnam's, 1984.

Indigenous Languages Digital Archives (ILDA). Myaamia Center, Miami University. https://mc.miamioh.edu/ilda-myaamia/.

Lawrence, David. Letter to Mrs. Milton Roll. November 8, 1973. Vol. 2, Bobbe Burke Collection. Miami Center, Miami University, Oxford, OH.

Leonard, Wesley Y. "When Is an 'Extinct Language' Not Extinct? Miami, a Formerly Sleeping Language." In *Sustaining Linguistic Diversity: Endangered and Minority Languages and Language Varieties*, edited by Kendall A. King, Natalie Schilling-Estes, Jia Jackie Lou, Lyn Fogle, and Barbara Soukup, 23–34. Washington, DC: Georgetown University Press, 2008.

McCarty, Teresa L. *Language Planning and Policy in Native America: History, Theory, Praxis*. Buffalo, NY: Multilingual Matters, 2013.

"Miami Indian Symbol Revealed This Weekend." *The Miamian*, January 27, 1977.

Committee on the Relationships between Miami University and the Miami Tribe of Oklahoma. Report and Materials (1994–95), Miami Nicknames, April 1994. Box 1, folder 17, Student Affairs, Miami Tribe, Materials, 1972–2001,

Miami Tribe Collection. Miami University Archives and Special Collections, Oxford, OH.

Miami Tribe of Oklahoma. "*Atotankiki Myaamiaki*, Tribal Newspaper." https://www.miamination.com/newspaper.

———. Memorandum of agreement, the Miami Tribe of Oklahoma, Miami, Oklahoma, and Miami University, Oxford, Ohio. March 19, 2008. In the collection of the Office of Miami Tribe Relations, Myaamia Center, Miami University, Oxford, OH. http://miamioh.edu/miami-tribe-relations/history/index.html.

———. Memorandum of understanding, the Miami Tribe of Oklahoma, Miami, Oklahoma, and Miami University, Oxford, Ohio, March 24, 2006, Miami Nickname. Miami University Archives and Special Collections, Oxford, OH. https://miamioh.edu/miami-tribe-relations/history/index.html.

Miami University. *Miami University Report Card 2020–21.* https://miamioh.edu/about-miami/recognition/report-card/index.html.

Miami University College of Education, Health, and Society. "Our History." https://miamioh.edu/ehs/about/history/index.html.

Mosley-Howard, G. Susan, Daryl Baldwin, George Ironstrack, Kate Rousmaniere, and Bobbe Burke. "Niila Myaamia (I Am Miami): Identity and Retention of Miami Tribe College Students." *Journal of College Student Retention* 17, no. 4. (2016): 437–61.

Piana, Gail Della, Adolph Greenberg, Jason Rech, and Doug Troy. "Faculty Involvement with the Miami Tribe and the Myaamia Project." Panel session at 2012 Myaamiaki Conference, March 31, 2012. Myammia Center YouTube video, posted May 1, 2012. https://youtu.be/TJeOS1XI-kE.

Powell, Myrtis. Letter to Chief Floyd Leonard. September 11, 1990. Vol. 2, Bobbe Burke Collection, Myaamia Center, Miami University, Oxford, OH.

Shriver, Phillip R. "Growing Concerns on Campus." Memorandum, January 6, 1976. Miami University Archives and Special Collections, Oxford, OH.

———. *Miami University: A Personal History.* Oxford, OH: Miami University Press, 1998.

Standafer, Raymond. "Miami Indians and Redskins." Nickname and Mascot Controversy, 1996, Miami University Special Collections, Oxford, OH.

Strack, George, George Ironstrack, Daryl Baldwin, Kristina Fox, Julie Olds, Robbyn Abbitt, and Melissa Rinehart. *myaamiaki aancihsaaciki: A Cultural Exploration of the Myaamia Removal Route.* Miami, OK: Miami Tribe of Oklahoma, 2011.

"Welcome to the Myaamia-Peewaalia Dictionary." ILDA Dictionary. Myaamia Center, Miami University. Accessed February 6, 2021. https://mc.miamioh.edu/ilda-myaamia/dictionary.

White, Richard. *The Middle Ground: Indians, Empires, and Republics in the Great Lakes Region, 1650–1815.* Cambridge Studies in North American Indian History. Cambridge: Cambridge University Press, 1991.

Wilson, Doug. Myaamia Heritage Museum and Archives (MHMA), Miami University, Oxford, OH.

Chapter 6

Community-Engaged Scholarship from the Perspective of an Early Career Academic

CAMERON SHRIVER

Many early career scholars, including graduate students, recognize value in community engagement. This is particularly true for those writing about Indigenous people who are underrepresented in academia while at the same time increasingly important to historical, social, medical, psychological, and other topics of research. Historians, like those in other disciplines, have been attracted to Native history but slow in building engagement with Native communities. Now employed as a professional historian—my position is Myaamia research associate—after earning a PhD in 2016, I here describe my journey into community-engaged scholarship. I seek to explain community-engaged scholarship (CES) from my perspective as an early career academic at the Myaamia Center at Miami University, the research arm of the Miami Tribe of Oklahoma.[1]

This essay's goal is to demystify CES for young-career academics. In many situations, ethics boards, published protocols, and think pieces focus on the *why* more than the *how* of community engagement. This chapter emphasizes how scholars of Native American and Indigenous studies can recognize opportunities to improve their work while addressing the research needs of communities they write about. My experiences will not fit all people, all communities, or all disciplines, because each operates in particular contexts. I work in the realm of Myaamia-engaged scholarship.

There is a core group, and a larger community, with which I am personally engaged through relationships and protocols that are specific. Thus, I cannot provide an authoritative prescription for community-engaged scholarship. Instead, I offer some broad recommendations as part of an ongoing discussion about best practices. I have simplified where possible. Engagement is not an end point, a status to be achieved, but rather constantly negotiated. It is, I think, messy and complicated. That said, most of us need to begin somewhere. Intended both for Native and non-Native researchers, this chapter illustrates how I see CES working. I begin with some personal history, before transitioning to arguments against, and for, community engagement as a scholarly practice. My hope is that airing both ethical and practical concerns may extend this field's conversation about early career academics as community engaged scholars.[2]

While I recall my path toward collaboration as a series of happy accidents, unplanned conversations, and chance opportunities, retrospect offers guideposts that continue to shape my approach and evolving experience of engaged scholarship in teaching, research, and writing.

My story may be instructive for understanding both the beginning and the maintenance of community engagement. All of us will bring unique circumstances to relationships, and mine begins with an unusual privilege. My grandfather was a friend with the much-respected former chief of the Miami Tribe of Oklahoma Floyd Leonard. As president of Miami University and a historian, Phil Shriver (grandpa) found a lot of common ground with Chief Leonard. Both were educators and leaders. Each had served in World War II, a fact that contributed to their friendship. They spent time together at events for both the university and tribal communities: powwows and social dances, gatherings, joint speaking engagements, and athletic games. When I approached citizens of the Miami Tribe for help, this particular history provided a starting point. *Eeweentiiyankwi*, "we are related to each other," is an important concept within the community, and my introduction to many friends and colleagues has been possible through family networks, even though my own family is not Myaamia.

I studied history and anthropology as an undergraduate student at William and Mary in Williamsburg, Virginia, and had the good fortune to learn the basics of NAGPRA, ICWA, gaming, and a history of sovereignty and self-determination. I strongly recommend that all young scholars have a working grasp of these basic issues, which will arise in conversation. (For you historians, it is also useful to know something about the present-tense community rather than relying on knowledge from the deeper past.) In my senior year of undergraduate education, I decided to pursue a thesis on a colorful character named William Wells. Wells continues to fascinate me and other historians—he was an Anglo-Kentuckian, captured by Native men, and grew up in a Miami-speaking community after the American Revolution. My grandfather suggested that I talk to Daryl Baldwin, a Miami citizen and director of the Myaamia Center, and I set up an appointment. I recollect some excitement and nerves. I remember Daryl telling me what Wells's Myaamia name meant: *Eepiihkanita* means "ground nut," and, accordingly, does not connote "carrot top," an apocryphal and oft-cited supposition about his hair color. Here, then, was a fact borne of Myaamia knowledge that remained outside of published scholarship. What other revisions to Wells's biography could I learn through conversation? The final thesis exhibits examples of consulting with Daryl Baldwin but is not an example of engagement. Yet the seed had been planted; there was more work to do combining the knowledge within the Myaamia community with traditional archival research.

Having finished college and still hoping to do history in some form, I asked a favorite anthropology professor, Danielle Moretti-Langholtz, to introduce me to one of her senior doctoral students, Buck Woodard. Dr. Woodard was the director of the American Indian Initiative at Colonial Williamsburg, adjacent to campus. I began an internship soon thereafter, conducting research targeted at building relationships with Ohio Valley tribes such as the Miamis. This scholarship, already underway before I joined Colonial Williamsburg, supported relationships with the three Shawnee tribes. Shawnee language and material culture greatly improved some programming in Colonial Williamsburg, but also required dialogues with multiple stakeholders, bridging political and geographical gaps, and patience. Buck was doing this kind of institutional relationship building with Cherokees and Virginia tribes. I remember loitering on a photography shoot with Buck and some Cherokee actor-interpreters on a local tobacco farm. "We give Indigenous visitors tobacco," he said. "Just like in the eighteenth century." Buck has always been good at that—revealing his process and thinking about it like an anthropologist. He was being a modern intercultural mediator, and he taught me to think in those terms.

Anthropologists would call this type of ethos "reciprocity." Gift-giving *is* important. It establishes or reaffirms a positive relationship. That was true three centuries ago, and I believe it to be true today.

Familiarity with the Myaamia Center and the American Indian Initiative provided a background when I started graduate school at Ohio State University, where I hoped to continue researching the historical experience of Myaamia people. It made sense to email Daryl Baldwin again and pick his brain about language questions. I emailed Daryl *before* I started grad school. As my email record suggests, initial questions about Miami-Illinois language led to a slow but steady drip of questions from me, with Daryl always answering and continuing the conversation by asking, "Is that what you meant?" or "Does that answer the question?" A couple times he finished with "Do you see the common stem in the words?" or something more penetrative about linguistics.

Through email, Daryl also introduced me to George Ironstrack, a historian and Myaamia citizen working in the Myaamia Center. This was a natural alliance, because we were both historians (or, I was in training). My initial email was essentially this: *I'm Cam, I want to understand Miami history, and I'd love to get your feedback on some research ideas.* In hindsight, this was a useful line: "I am currently researching, and I would like to get my bearings with someone who has asked the kind of questions I am asking." We set up a time and we talked in person. This led to more emails, questions, and data sharing. It also inevitably led (at George's instruction) to correspondence with a Miami-Illinois linguist named David Costa, who has always been generous in responding to language questions. This was all in my first year of graduate school. That was a year of seeking opportunities, and the community—in this case, an intellectual community of researchers and educators—responded by offering plenty of them. The result was increased mentorship, an audience with expertise in my subject, and greater confidence in my conclusions.

The correspondence continued. Based on the emails I have, most messages were along the lines of "Have you seen this source?" or "What do you think about that scholarly argument?" I met with George and Daryl several times, and they invited me to come to Miami, Oklahoma, for the Miami Tribe's winter gathering. I asked Christine Ballengee Morris, the American Indian studies coordinator at Ohio State and a scholar working in a collaborative environment, if I could apply for some funds to cover the hotel room from the university's diversity and identity studies, and she approved the request. Traveling to Miami, Oklahoma, the seat of tribal government, was crucial. It allowed me to introduce myself to many people. More importantly, it was an exceptional learning experience. I could see the wider community and sense the place where many of its citizens lived. I gained an appreciation for how folks talked about themselves and their lives and histories, their land and livelihoods. At the same time, I participated in a controlled visit. The tribe knew that I was properly enmeshed in the institutional regulations of Miami University and the Myaamia Center. Introduced into the wider community in such a measured way all but ensured I would behave properly.[3] As this brief personal history illustrates, I was not forging a path myself, but rather (with permission) joining on a path that others were already walking down.

After I finished graduate school and continuing regular conversations with staff in the Myaamia Center, the Miami Tribe offered me a research opportunity. The community identified a need to better understand their reserve lands in the heritage homelands of Indiana and Ohio. Now called the Aacimwahkionkonci, "Stories from the Land," Project, this scholarship is an extension of earlier work by community-engaged scholars on Myaamia allotment experiences in Kansas and in Oklahoma. How did the Miami community as a whole, or Myaamia individuals, gain ownership of or relinquish land in the nineteenth century, a period often characterized by treaties with the US government, massive land loss, and the forced migration of the tribal government from Indiana to eastern Kansas and subsequently Indian Territory (Oklahoma)?

The Aacimwahkionkonci Project has evolved since those fundamental questions but remains focused on collecting data and identifying the best ways to circulate the knowledge it creates. I am the primary archival researcher but not the sole analyst. I frequently share data through conversations, presentations, shared computer network drives. The project team is developing a searchable archive and web-based platform for delivering research results to the tribal community and general public. In turn, the disseminated results will allow tribal members and current landowners access to a rich history and help revitalize the connection between people, places, and the narratives that define their interactions over time. Additionally, the Miami Tribe's and Myaamia Center's effort draws from a wide range of research topics for curricular content used in tribal educational programs. The research into Indiana and Ohio reservations adds significant historical, social, cultural, and ecological knowledge that will enhance ongoing efforts to pass critical information on to the next generation of tribal citizens. To better align the research with stakeholders, I briefed tribal government on my method and results after the first year and presented the project and some interpretations at the biennial Myaamiaki Conference for digestion by a Myaamia public audience. I report progress at regular intervals and meet on a weekly or monthly basis with software engineers, geographers, archive managers, and Cultural Resources Office staff to develop the tools and analysis for the project. Through such dialogues, I can best understand what the community deems useful or interesting (formulate questions), find pertinent data (research), interpret it with a range of perspectives (analyze), and present it respectfully (publish).

Myaamia community needs drive the Aacimwahkionkonci Project, which progresses within a Myaamia research center serving a Myaamia audience. But another community—academic historians—will benefit from this scholarship, because it engages a central problem in American history: How did the continent transition from Native American ownership to predominately non-Native ownership? How did a long-term continental process of land privatization happen in real time and among complicated political, family, and legal dynamics? An extensive case study of one tribe's historical landownership promises to shed new light on a fundamental American process and eventually point to new questions within the field.

Put simply, community-engaged scholarship such as the Aacimwahkionkonci Project can face both tribal and academic audiences at the same time; they are not mutually exclusive. The scholarly processes I am describing—understanding the audience, reviewing public knowledge, and presenting it appropriately—are methods we learn as graduate students in all disciplines. Through engagement, we can apply them to Native American communities and academic communities.

While my primary current research focus is the Aacimwahkionkonci Project, the "community" as a whole pursues a wide range of research avenues. Myaamia Center staff, in conjunction with Miami Tribe and Miami University affiliates, prioritize useful knowledge that advances community education and revitalization. I am one of many people roped into various short- and long-term research conversations. Some recent collaborations include editing policy papers, assisting in developing a digital archive for the tribal public, and gathering source material from untapped historical archives that may benefit researchers in the future. I was recently asked to provide historical sources and symbols that might inform a "veteran's flag" for public ceremonies such as the annual powwow, for example. Because I have access to or have collected many early colonial sources, I am sometimes included in conversations involving the Native American Graves Protection and Repatriation Act (NAGPRA) to support decisions in the Miami Tribe's Cultural Resources Office. Anthropologists call this research "applied" (as opposed to theoretical), and applied scholars carry out their work to solve problems as identified by the communities they study. This application of scholarship is rewarding and enjoyable.[4]

It is an awkward enterprise to draw lessons from one's own experiences, and, because Indian Country—let alone the Indigenous world—is incredibly diverse, there is no single prescription for how to go about this work. Specificity matters, and I do not practice *community*-engaged scholarship as much as *Myaamia*-engaged scholarship, and, even within that, I am not engaged with all 6,000 Miami enrolled citizens, but a group of intellectuals, elected leaders, interested or highly engaged community members, and staff. I am not Myaamia. In the context of scholarship, this is significant. First, there is a history of non-Native people passing themselves as Native, and this seems to be particularly pernicious in the East; therefore, I think it puts some people at ease (rather than the opposite) to have a clear position, whether Myaamia, Native American, or non-Native. Second, I was not raised in a Myaamia household that might have shaped my perspective differently; instead, I was raised in a settler household, an experience I necessarily bring with me. Third, I do not have a thick network of relations among Myaamia people; no built-in permanent connections such as kinship guarantee my obligations to the community, with the caveat that my limited family connections with Myaamia folks did provide an obvious entry point. A researcher who has a circle of relations is best equipped to understand the nature of "community" in context, but also to put those relations in action to find and fruitfully exchange ideas with people with either knowledge or skill related to the research topic at hand.

Despite diverse contexts and the varied paths toward engagement, all engaged scholars need sustainable social capital—durable, reciprocal, and respectful constellations of personal relationships. It is no accident that Buck Woodard exemplified reciprocity, George Ironstrack invited me to Oklahoma, Bobbe Burke (liaison between Miami University and the Miami Tribe) facilitated the trip, and Christine Ballengee Morris approved a funding request at Ohio State University. They are essential contributors to this edited volume. Most graduate students go to academic conferences and will be familiar with acquiring social capital and deepening engagement in their professional communities. Remember the awkward first conference? And how it gets easier as you meet more people, have more conversations, and grow accustomed to the culture of conference-going? Again, these are practical steps that we should recognize and discuss as community-engaged scholars in training. One respectful relationship generates others; one door opens to more.

My experience demonstrates another crucial point: scholars from within and without a community can and do practice CES. "It is not sufficient," Cree scholar Shawn Wilson asserts, "for researchers just to say that they are Aboriginal and are therefore using an Indigenist paradigm." Likewise, the fact of being an enrolled Native person does not in itself make a scholar engaged with a particular community. On the other hand, some assume a different false notion that only non-Native scholars research Indigenous communities. As Madeline Whetung writes, "The protocol on research with Aboriginal peoples is presented as though there are not Indigenous people conducting research. One is either a researcher, or a community member, never both." I have profited a great deal from hearing how Indigenous scholars engage with Indigenous communities. On the other hand, I have read excellent work by Indigenous people who are not necessarily performing community-engaged scholarship.[5]

My story, as well as those in this book, also demonstrates the value of institutionalized engagement that outlasts individuals. Young scholars should consider where those institutions are. The Myaamia Center functions with one foot in the Miami Tribe and another in the Miami University. The "engagement" is based in social (and family) networks more than one-to-one relationships. The easiest way to instigate a scholarly engagement is to find an institution already fostering those relationships. This may be a tribal agency, a nonprofit organization, or a scholarly research center. Perhaps that involves seeking them in your graduate school search, explicitly molding research to use collaborative institutions, or making contacts with higher education centers that participate in long-term partnerships. An increasing number of universities have offices aimed at collaborative scholarship. In my case, for example, I sought the Myaamia Center in order to better understand Myaamia history, although I was enrolled at Ohio State, two hours away. Many Native nations have "resource officers" (such as a cultural resources office, or a tribal historic preservation officer) that are good social network nodes with which to start. As of early 2022, there were 208 THPOs recognized by the National Park Service. Such point-persons probably are busy professionals, but they are also well-connected and knowledgeable, in my experience. Other communities may have designated protectors—gatekeepers—or mouthpieces who can best interface with noncitizens. If you are collaborating with a Native nation, your research will eventually bring you into their orbit. The Navajo Nation, for instance, has a research review board, like many of the larger nations. A pleasant email or phone call is the best way to begin a conversation, but remember that engagement requires time to establish some roots.[6]

In attempting to distill my own experience (and aided by a long email archive stretching back to before I began graduate school!) my path so far can be split into three more or less discernible phases. In my early conversations with Myaamia citizens, I found myself trying to prove that I knew something; that I could contribute. Of course, there is real risk in appearing conceited. I suspect the desire to prove oneself comes from a desire to impress colleagues or new friends. Of course, you want to appear worthy of collaboration. A base level of knowledge is certainly important, and you should take advantage of publications and any tribal web presence early on. Academics gain expertise on the communities they study, but I quickly encountered the limits of my knowledge in Myaamia circles. I searched my email record and did not uncover any egregious messages that put my foot in my mouth, but conversations then and now frequently flow into unfamiliar (to me) ideas. For instance, there is a long string of emails with several scholars about matri- and patrilocality among eighteenth-century Myaamia people. I asked about terms I had seen recorded in colonial Jesuit dictionaries. The conversation clarified those terms in the Miami-Illinois language, but also brought in early ethnographic accounts and traditional stories, showing evidence for matri- and patrilocality respectively. In another case, I had a passing familiarity with a certain *manetoowa*, "manitou," but, over the course of many conversations and storytellings, I learned to appreciate how the manitou is represented in contemporary artistic forms, thus seeing the manitou in many texts that formerly were illegible to me.

This first phase will create some uncomfortable situations—after all, you are learning new community norms of behavior. Community engaged scholarship, for me, is beginning a conversation and remaining invested in learning from members of the community who know more or know differently. For instance, one night in rural Oklahoma I began whistling; I was quickly told to stop. "Don't whistle at night" was not a rule I grew up with, but I know it now. Young scholars should remain moldable when an inevitable rebuke from the community comes; they are opportunities to learn. But as engagement deepens, you will develop the freedom to make mistakes. Phase two conversations evolve into active learning and intellectual growth which occurs in respectful contexts. I find resonance in the experiences of African archaeologists, who are themselves steeped in colonial history, such as George Abungu. Abungu came to dig on Pate Island, Kenya, only to find the residents hostile to his intentions. Decades of top-down, disengaged research teams informed the locals' reactions. Abungu reflected that his team had to "radically reorient our mindset . . . from one who knows to one who wants to learn." Even if a scholar makes a misstep, engaged scholars reflexively discuss the matter further, in a respectful way, because the expectations for relationships have been hammered out. Maori scholar Linda Tuhiwai Smith writes that "the term 'respect' is consistently used by Indigenous peoples to underscore the significance of our relationships and humanity. . . . Respect is a reciprocal, shared, constantly interchanging principle which is expressed through all aspects of social conduct." Respect, negotiated constantly, becomes mutual over time. I recently found an email conversation between George Iron-strack and me, time-stamped a couple of years after we first met. George sent me one of his working papers that used the Myaamia language as evidence for historical change. I saw this as a method that would help my own work and asked if I could—and if I may—use the Miami language as a source base. This catalyzed further conversations about the proper use and citation of Myaamia language sources, offers to help in interpre-tation, and access to digitized materials (such as historical dictionaries). Several years later—and having taken Myaamia language classes with tribal students at Miami University—Myaamia language underpins a great deal of my thinking and analysis of historical currents. This involves taking risks that require back and forth discussion. For example, a couple years ago I attempted to create a word in Myaamia to describe a pattern I had noticed in the historical sources. Historians coin concepts from time to time, but most would agree (and I should emphasize) that suggesting a new word in the Miami-Illinois language itself is precocious. I offered my purpose and rationale for this new word, and through discussions with several people we analyzed the phenomenon itself. I took an intellectual chance and my collaborators made alternative suggestions. I did not use the word in my writing, because it became unnecessary after hashing out its underlying purposes. The conversation led me down some useful linguistic rabbit holes. If I had done this early in the relationship, it likely would have caused damage: *Who is this* Mihši-Maalhsa, *"American"? Why does he think he can use our language in this way?* We continue to discuss methodology using historical language sources and interpreting them accurately and in context.[7]

Phase three involves the proficiency and humility to teach and analyze topics respectfully. After learning the expressed needs of a community, a scholar with time, resources, and a social network can address those needs. In my trajectory this involved meeting an increasing number of Myaamia people, expanding my network within the community, and, as a necessary consequence, increasing the range of perspectives on topics that I hope to understand. Even further, I have learned that one person's opinion is not the same as a community's knowledge.[8]

I am hesitant to assert such a clean narrative, and I am uncomfortable suggesting that I have this level of scholarly sophistication. I am not sure if anyone really reaches a state of universal fluency about any community, but we can at least strive for expertise in our own disciplines and chosen topics. I can assert that engagement has expanded and sharpened my knowledge and development through conversations that are frank and supportive, even when critical. Over time, perhaps you will be asked to work with, and even sometimes on behalf of, a community in limited contexts. You may have the expertise to support (not supplant) community self-determination. And, as you move toward mature engagement, you will avoid the "best friend syndrome" of gaining knowledge and then assuming authority. Teaching a course titled Introduction to the Miami Tribe illustrates the point. I was asked to take on this course, which introduces undergraduates—some of whom are Myaamia—to topics such as tribal law, Myaamia history, language and cultural revitalization, art and appropriation, ecological knowledge, and more. My area of expertise is Myaamia and American history, but the course is best served by emphasizing the narrative that Myaamia culture and politics exists in the present, which means that I must rely on guest speakers to talk about, for example, Myaamia ribbonwork, historical and contemporary foods, Miami language learning in the home, the Tar Creek Superfund Site in Oklahoma, and ethnobotany. I teach it each spring semester, and thus we must discuss the genre of traditional stories called "winter stories" before the frogs wake up with the thunder in the spring, but we have to wait until as late as possible to observe the trees on campus as they begin to leaf out in April. Aside from the clear benefits of community and community-engaged expertise on these topics, the course's entire method and philosophy is shaped by engagement—positioning myself as a facilitator with some (but not all) knowledge; modeling respectful relationships;

avoiding tokenizing Indigenous (Myaamia) perspectives; focusing on the tribal community in the present rather than predominantly in the past; making conscientious requests for in-class guests while recognizing the time and labor it takes to attend; and giving project- and service-based assignments that ask students to consider the benefits of institutional and personal partnerships in Indian Country. Students—both Myaamia and not—are particularly interested in the past and present relationship between the university and tribe. Phase three relationships are stable and respectful when tended. As a process, reciprocal engagement expands our scholarship, builds capacities among communities, involves group research, and increases reciprocity for mutual benefit.[9]

As engagement and (in Indigenous studies) decolonization continue gaining traction as concepts, they still require definition. What follows is an argument for the benefits of community-engaged scholarship as well as an extended discussion of what it really means for those of us early in our careers. Before that, some cautions are in order. First, sustained collaboration—the kind of engagement I am pitching in this essay—takes time. There are less time-consuming interactions a scholar might pursue, but we must not confuse these with the "community-engaged scholarship" being defined in this volume. For example, engagement is not a stamp of approval after the research is done and the conclusions written and published—that is something else. Seeking endorsement for a finished work risks offense, because conclusions have been drawn or arguments published. These requests for late-stage discussions acknowledge that community input is important but simultaneously devalue the time and intellectual significance of the contribution. Engagement is not a fact-checking service and cannot be an afterthought. Additionally, engagement extends beyond its sibling—consultation—which describes a more limited interaction primarily meant to benefit the scholar rather than the consulted community members. In my view, community-engaged scholarship involves collaboration, a sharing of agency. This can include the choosing of research questions, the discovery of data (such as archival sources or participant research), and analysis. It may also privilege community voices over that of the omniscient narrator common in some disciplines. Thus, community-engaged scholarship can look much like community-produced scholarship. CES is a sustained relationship that *informs* research at multiple stages of development. For example, either at my asking or at George Ironstrack's behest, I sent him my first graduate school research paper and he returned comments. When making language-based analysis, I ask several linguists to comment and offer advice. These are things I learned because I was told to do them. I am not alone. Many agencies and individuals successfully collaborate with staff at the Myaamia Center, a result of conversations in which those agencies or individuals come to appreciate the needs of the Myaamia community and vice versa.[10] Successful engagement takes time.

Early career scholars must weigh benefits against other potential costs. Mentors may push you toward engagement without a clear idea of what this means or how to go about it. But, on the other hand, higher education traditionally separates faculty work into three components: research, service, and teaching. These three are not respected equally by administrators, mentors, and hiring committees, who can pigeonhole community engagement as peripheral to scholarship. Typically, disengaged scholars or administrators will lump engagement into outreach as a genre of service. Therefore, despite engagement becoming more fashionable, young scholars are often tasked with proving the benefits of communi-ty-engaged scholarship to skeptical mentors and dissertation committees who are primarily interested in research above teaching or service. Paul Kroskrity declares that "there may be debates about what Native American studies is and should be; all positions confirm the importance of the relationship between Native and academic communities." Explaining this to colleagues outside of Native American studies is still obligatory. As some educational experts have pointed out, "Graduate students may hear that contributing to the public good is important, but they may not see examples of faculty members engaging in this kind of work." Faced with ethical and practical concerns, "the mixed messages within many universities about what work is most highly respected are barriers to the process of preparing faculty members who value and know how to engage in the range of possible work that serves the public good." Indeed, studies suggest that academics face professional obstacles when they perform engaged scholarship, despite the stated ideals of universities and colleges. The uninitiated might find mentors or institutions already engaging in CES, which would provide training, experience, and support in this field. Many institutions profess engagement with communities, although they typically mean local neighborhoods. If your community or institution is disengaged, young scholars can develop those networks. Through it all, whether your department or community collaborates with others or not, the goal is not to check boxes or gain a certificate, but to develop and sustain long-term and reciprocal conversations.[11]

A further potential prejudice to CES is that some believe that collaboration undermines a scholar's objectivity, or that engagement means that some topics must be avoided. It is wise to be aware of this possibility in reality as well as the assumption from mentors, reviewers, or hiring committees. But tackling difficult research questions is precisely what engaged scholars attempt—it is *scholarship*. I have never been told that a topic is off-limits. For example, as a historian engaged with both Myaamia intellectuals and the literature in history, I have had conversations (publicly and privately) about historical Myaamia racial conceptions, human trafficking, and sexual violence, using archival sources, various ethnographies through time, *Myaamiataweenki* (Miami language) and linguistic concepts, and *aacimoona* (histories) and *aahlsookana* (winter stories), as well as the published literature on these important topics. These are subjects valued in Myaamia and non-Myaamia historical literature currently. They are difficult, but they are not forbidden. As with any methodology, we should assess and account for bias. In my own discipline of history, for instance, some may believe that learning about current realities too strongly influences our interpretations of the past. But rather than undermining objectivity, I have found engagement forces me to sharpen my arguments and write in an accessible way. Most importantly, conversations in the present push historians to explain why the past is significant at all. Perhaps the worst review of a scholar's work would be a community response of "who cares?"[12]

As a last cautionary note, it is worth considering the structures of academia.[13] As two practitioners of CES explain, "Scholars who want to collaborate with diverse groups off their campuses are still pressured to defer Community-Based Research and civic collaborations until they receive tenure."[14] Service learning, receiving grants and fellowships, and mentoring undergraduate or graduate research may count toward career advancement, but, while many or most tenure boards or hiring committees value CES as a kind of "service," many or most still privilege traditional disciplinary benchmarks. Administrators interested in institutional rankings, for instance, do not see an implicit link between research output (peer-reviewed research articles, for example) and community engagement. Miami University administrators value the relationship between the college and the Native nation primarily because it (1) provides services such as guest lectures, interviews, and outreach on campus, (2) garners prestigious grants and honors that the university promotes, and (3) enhances diversity through student and staff recruitment, namely, Miami Tribe citizens. I could not say if administrators are aware that Myaamia Center staff and affiliates perform research and publish. Particularly in professional development discussions and on the job market, young scholars should explain how their scholarship impacts multiple beneficiaries or partners, because this may not be obvious to other faculty or administrators. Early career academics practicing engagement must also explain CES methodologies in concrete and personal terms.

Time, methodological questions, a lack of training, and institutional structures all require careful thought, particularly as we embark on research or teaching careers. In light of these significant hurdles, the following argument for community-engaged scholarship takes an *ethical* and a *practical* point of view. There are valid reasons to avoid the time-consuming, sometimes complicated, often misunderstood or underappreciated type of scholarship this book describes. But there are also reasons why early career scholars can or should pursue it.

Community-engaged scholarship is ethical, because it supports community self-determination rather than its colonial opposite. Native communities (both Native nations themselves and other forms of Indigenous communities) have a good sense of their self-interest that deserves engagement. Western research—in its paradigms and methods—has supported colonialism. The growing literature on decolonization, as well as the introduction and other chapters in this volume, makes this clear. Specific and sustained engagement with an Indigenous community or communities is a form of decolonizing research. Much of the philosophy of CES revolves around what Melissa Nelson describes as engagement that is "grounded in Native communities." Some years ago, Duane Champagne argued that American Indian studies (a field related to all engaged scholars working in and around Indian Country) should focus "on the issues, interests, and needs that are of central concern to American Indian nations." Your research might inform policy, build capacity, support sovereignty, or otherwise provide labor with and for a community.[15]

This assertion is neither new nor particular to Native American and Indigenous studies. W. E. B. Du Bois, a founder of community-based research, made a similar point in his seminal *The Souls of Black Folk* at the turn of the last century. Discussing rural African American workers, Du Bois characterized "the car-window sociologist" as one "who seeks to understand and know the South by devoting the few leisure hours of a holiday trip to unraveling the snarl of centuries." Du Bois's evocation of a tourist is, I think, useful. In a separate instance, Du Bois rebuked one commentator on Southern race relations, writing him, "One of the most unfortunate things about the Negro problem is that persons who 'do not for a moment profess to be informed on the subject' insist on informing others." The offender asked for Du Bois's guidance, which earned another stern scolding. Du Bois responded, "That a man of the twentieth century would stand up and indiscriminately vilify one hundred and fifty million or more human beings, and then to ask gently for guidance in a study of these matters in which he has already posed as a guide, is to me astounding." Du Bois's outrage is familiar to practitioners of community engagement and requires both vigilant communities and a venue for reviewing such works. Even among his closer white colleagues, he became fed up with their well-intentioned but fraught attitudes about African Americans. Du Bois later wrote that, "boldly and without flinching, I will face the hard fact that in this, my fatherland, I must expect insult and discrimination from persons who call themselves philanthropists and Christians and gentlemen." As one of his biographers characterized his attitude, "The harder and oftener hit they were, the more likely rich and powerful whites were to learn to couple genuine consideration with formal civility." Du Bois's strategy conjured an image of a hammer pounding steel in a forge. Even when all parties are willing and able, shaping a respectful collaboration requires humility, and sometimes some hammering.[16]

Although many writers have and will continue to illuminate the ethical layers of scholarship, fewer write about its pragmatic dimensions. As Native American studies scholarship trends toward more collaboration, Native and non-Native scholars enter the academy interested in engaging with the Native communities they study and come from a wide range of goals and backgrounds. An ongoing study profiling "publicly engaged scholars" broadly identifies "motivations and identities that contribute to an interest in engaged scholarship." Those of us who develop an interest in community engagement, the study's authors argue, come from communities and academia, from teaching and art, from activism and administration. Some take up engagement due to their individual senses of moral purpose or personal conviction, and others seek community engagement because, as the study's authors have found, the scholar "suspects that publicly engaged scholarship may become prevalent within the academy," a hypothesis that motivates them to get ahead of this particular curve.[17] Despite hurdles, community engagement is (perhaps) becoming more popular.

Community-engaged scholarship is practical, because it enhances the process and results of scholarly activities—engagement can improve your work. There need not be a distinction between scholarship that benefits an Indigenous community and that speaks to an academic literature. Early career academics usually need to keep their discipline's benchmarks in mind. Like the work done in the Myaamia Center, scholarly pursuits are driven by both academic and tribal goals, because those are not mutually exclusive. Spurred primarily by cultural revitalization, the Myaamia Center aims to strengthen the Miami Tribal Nation. To do so, the Myaamia Center "serves the needs of the Myaamia people, Miami University, and partner communities through research, education, and outreach that promote Myaamia language, culture, knowledge, and values." My colleagues know that the academy requires me to publish in peer-reviewed journals and publish books, and respect how different disciplines reward certain types of academic work, such as books, conferences, reviews, or journal articles. These types of scholarship might be considered "CV lines," and, whether we like it or not, they are important to our academic audiences. I have nothing against service, but many of us are going to make our careers through scholarly publications, through grants and projects and the "stuff" that academia values. Young academics cannot ignore them, and so we must be pragmatic in our methods.[18]

What I am proposing is that engagement does not require us to set aside scholarship. Engagement is scholarship and, when developed carefully, improves the quality of those CV lines. That is good news: as young scholars, we are not in a position (yet) to change the standards of the job market, promotion, or tenure. CES can help us meet and exceed those standards by refining our work, even that which is aimed at an academic audience. For example, in my discipline of history, we are still predominantly trained to isolate ourselves in archives, insulate ourselves for "writing," and produce single-authored work. (For the nonhistorians among you, one of the most famous historians of the last century, Fernand Braudel, wrote the first draft of his epic *La Méditerranée* as a German prisoner of war during World War II . . . from memory. This is a story many of us learn in graduate school.) Isolation is poor training for engagement. At the same time, we have all heard of the benefits of conferences, research fellowships, and writing groups, often *because* they provide opportunities for conversations, networking, and the informal feedback that yield intellectual growth and development. Like a group of researchers on a long-term archival fellowship, tribal communities can be a cohort with which to develop, extend, and advance conversations around shared topics of interest. In turn, sharing expertise (and, in some cases, as is the norm in many scientific disciplines, coauthorship) can augment our research by seeking input from diverse disciplines or perspectives while illuminating Indigenous voices. This interdisciplinary and collaborative research frequently happens beyond our departments, because, despite university assertions, collaboration and engagement are devalued. Whether you are Native or not, you can have empathy, obligations, and relationships in a "community," but you will probably need to find it. Those connections can also bolster your research while building a natural audience for the completed project.[19]

Therefore, one practical argument for engagement boils down to increased feedback and review. As scholars professionalizing in academia, we must expect some level of feedback, and this comes in both formal and informal settings. Disengaged scholars may unintentionally evade the best possible interlocutors, undercutting their work. For instance, although Ramón Gutiérrez's book *When Jesus Came, the Corn Mothers Went Away* garnered extensive praise in some academic venues, Pueblo scholars saw fatal flaws in its methodology, application of theory, and conclusions—also in academic venues. The work has become a cautionary tale. Through rounds of feedback and conversations, engaged scholars should understand the vetting process and thus be able to respond appropriately. Gutiérrez wrote that his research described Pueblo sexuality and gave "voice to the mute and silent." Pueblo scholars asserted that Gutiérrez was, in fact, describing Spanish perceptions of Pueblo sexuality, a fundamental difference compounded by Gutiérrez's implication of speaking on behalf of Pueblo ancestors. For those of us who are still building our profiles, it is smart to improve our conclusions through such review as well as receive constructive feedback before journal reviews. In my case, this began through infrequent emails and meetings with some Myaamia people, which has ballooned in recent years to daily interactions—emails, shared documents, research trips, informal chats, and the humdrum of working in a collaborative research center where offices are adjacent and doors are open. Surely it is better to receive and be able to incorporate criticism than ignore or never solicit it from those with key knowledge. It remains up to you or your coauthors to accept or reject community feedback, but it still deserves to be understood on its own terms, a process that in itself requires good faith engagement. Consider from the opposite point of view—if you are reading this, you are probably a member of an academic community with its own norms, networks, specialized language, and ways of communicating knowledge and assessment; this is "professionalization." Someone from a different community would need training or experience to understand those norms, its key players, and to make informed decisions within that community. It is worthwhile for a scholar to professionalize in a community, particularly if they hope that their research will be significant to that community.[20]

In turn, if a young scholar adds value to a community, then academically trained scholars can be a resource. I offer this material motivation *in addition* to the ethical and intellectual arguments for CES. Given that you are collaborating, your colleagues may—you hope!—value your research and writing skills, your expertise, and your intellectual labor. Early career humanities scholars face a collapsing job market in the professorate. "Alt-ac" and non-tenure-track faculty positions are now commonplace. It is worth dwelling on the pragmatic reasons for CES for a young academic—especially in the humanities—because we must think sensibly about the state of the humanities in public, political, and academic life. Tribes are expanding their scholarly and educational capacities, concurrent with cultural revitalization movements and, in some cases, economic self-determination. At the same time, approximately 70 percent of college teachers are contingent, or not on a track toward tenure. I know firsthand the dispiriting effect of these statistics on graduate students in the humanities. In my own discipline (history), the number of new history PhDs conferred each year since 2008 is about twice that of advertised job openings. I also suspect that most graduate students who research tribal histories and cultures do not view the communities they study as potential employers or grant sponsors, even those who are citizens or members of those communities.[21]

But it does happen, and I am one of those hired to produce scholarship for public, academic, educational, and government audiences. I do not forecast that tribes will hire waves of new PhDs. I am also aware that, if a goal of community engagement is reducing the harmful impact of colonialism, the movement will rightly be wary of the "push" of scholars at their doors (that is, in distinction with the "pull" of Native communities). We want to avoid intellectual exploitation. In my admittedly optimistic view, Indigenous communities can harness academically trained scholars as respectful allies and thereby build community resources for nation-building and cultural revitalization or preservation. Scholars may feel that they are walking in the footsteps of early ethnographers who went into the field, gathered knowledge, and published it for their own benefit. I think this should be recognized, but, if both a scholar *and* community want to overcome that barrier, they will, because a reciprocal relationship creates scholarship addressing a community's needs, and not only an academic's professional goals. Further, modern technology allows far more communication from a distance. In the old days of ethnography, a researcher returned "home" and left "the field." That sense of distance is lessened by frequent interactions in web-based spaces, such as email or cloud-based data sharing.[22]

My path toward community engagement was straightened and cleared by relationships before me. Others, including some authors in this volume, undoubtedly have different perspectives, experiences, and advice. From my perspective, as long as relationships are open, respectful, and reciprocal, scholars and tribes may be entering a new era of collaboration. The literature and theory are already available and many voices in and out of academia recognize the benefits of CES. The tools for collaborative scholarship are there for our use. But despite the scholarship extolling its virtues, young scholars must also clarify for themselves a range of purposes for their engagement and be prepared to explain them to academic audiences (hiring committees, colleagues, students, etc.) and potentially the communities with which they seek to collaborate. There are intellectual, ethical, and pragmatic reasons for young academics to adopt CES. After having read the warnings, the histories, the think pieces and state-of-the-fields, you still have to decide whether you want to continue down the path and get to work.

Notes

1. I thank George Ironstrack, Daryl Baldwin, Haley Shea, Susan Mosley-Howard, Bryan Rindfleisch, and the volume's editors for their feedback on this essay.
2. Madeline Whetung and Sarah Wakefield, "Colonial Conventions: Institutionalized Research Relationships and Decolonizing Research Ethics," in *Indigenous and Decolonizing Studies in Education: Mapping the Long View*, ed. Linda Tuhiwai Smith, Eve Tuck, and K. Wayne Yang (New York: Routledge, 2019), 156.

3. For more on institutional checks, see George Ironstrack and Bobbe Burke's chapter this volume; Michelle Sarche, Douglas Novins, and Annie Belcourt-Dittloff, "Engaged Scholarship with Tribal Communities," in *Handbook of Engaged Scholarship: Contemporary Landscapes, Future Directions*, ed. Hiram Fitzgerald, Cathy Burack, Sarena D. Seifer, and James Votruba (East Lansing: Michigan State University Press, 2010), 1:215–28.

4. Edward J. Hedican, *Anthropology in Canada: Understanding Aboriginal Issues*, 2nd ed. (Toronto: University of Toronto Press, 2008), 260; Elizabeth M. Eddy and William L. Partridge, eds., *Applied Anthropology in America* (New York: Columbia University Press, 1978), 4–5.

5. Shawn Wilson, "What Is an Indigenist Research Paradigm?," *Canadian Journal of Native Education* 30, no. 2 (2007): 194; Madeline Whetung, in Whetung and Wakefield, "Colonial Conventions," 147. Here, Whetung is describing Canada's *Tri-Council Policy Statement: Ethical Conduct for Research Regarding Humans*, 2018, or TCPS 2.

6. National Park Service, Tribal Preservation Program, "Tribal Historic Preservation Offices" report, updated February 18, 2022. nps.gov/subjects/historicpreservationfund/tribal-historic-preservation-office-program.htm.

7. George Abungu, "Walking the Long Path to Partnership: Archaeology and Communities in Eastern Africa—Relevance, Access, and Ownership," in *Community Archaeology and Heritage in Africa: Decolonizing Practice*, ed. Peter R. Schmidt and Innocent Pikirayi (New York: Routledge, 2016), 46–69. Also Patricia A. McAnany, "Transforming the Terms of Engagement between Archaeologists and Communities: a View from the Maya Region" in *Transforming Archaeology: Activist Practices and Prospects*, ed. Sonya Atalay, Lee Rains Clauss, Randall H. McGuire, and John R. Welch (Walnut Creek, CA: Left Coast, 2014), 162–63; Sonya Atalay, *Community-Based Archaeology: Research with, by, and for Indigenous and Local Communities* (Berkeley: University of California Press, 2012); Linda Tuhiwai Smith, *Decolonizing Methodologies: Research and Indigenous Peoples* (London: Zed Books, 2012), 120.

8. This relates to a problem arising when some scholars or organizations secure the consent of one Native American individual as a kind of stamp or token of approval or use one individual's knowledge and assume or assert it stands in for communal knowledge.

9. Justin B. Richland, "Beyond Listening: Lessons for Native/American Collaborations from the Creation of the Nakwatsvewat Institute," *American Indian Culture and Research Journal* 35, no. 1 (2011): 107; Vine Deloria, Jr., "Marginal and Submarginal," in *Indigenizing the Academy: Transforming Scholarship and Empowering Communities*, ed. Devon Abbott Mihesuah and Angela Cavender Wilson (Lincoln: University of Nebraska Press, 2004), 24–25. Dr. Alysia Fischer originally organized and taught this course at Miami, and I acknowledge and appreciate her work that directly benefitted my teaching.

10. The W. K. Kellogg Foundation wrote, "Engagement goes well beyond extension, conventional outreach, and even most conceptions of public service . . . by engagement the Commission envisions partnerships, two-way streets defined by mutual respect." Quoted in Ada Demb and Amy Wade, "Reality Check: Faculty Involvement in Outreach and Engagement," *Journal of Higher Education* 83, no. 3 (2012): 338.

11. Andrew Furco, "The Engaged Campus: Toward a Comprehensive Approach to Public Engagement," *British Journal of Educational Studies* 58, no. 4 (2010): 380–81; Paul V. Kroskrity, "Introduction to Productive Paths: Linking Native and Academic Communities," *American Indian Culture and Research Journal* 35, no. 1 (2011): 82; Ann E. Austin and Benita J. Barnes, "Preparing Doctoral Students for Faculty Careers that Contribute to the Public Good," in *Higher Education for the Public Good: Emerging Voices from a National Movement*, ed. Adrianna J. Kezar, Tony C. Chambers, and John C. Burkhardt (San Francisco: Jossey-Bass, 2005), 109; John M. Braxton, William T. Lucky, and Patricia A. Helland, *Institutionalizing a Broader View of Scholarship Through Boyer's Four Domains*, ASHE-ERIC Higher Education Report 29, no. 2 (San Francisco: Jossey-Bass, 2002); John M. Braxton, ed., *Analyzing Faculty Work and Rewards: Using Boyer's Four Domains of Scholarship*, New Directions for Institutional Research 129 (San Francisco: Jossey-Bass, 2006).

12. This perspective was recently enunciated, as part of an exchange with other scholars, by David J. Silverman in, "Living with the Past: Thoughts on Community Collaboration and Difficult History in Native American and Indigenous Studies," *American Historical Review* 125, no. 2 (2020): 519–27. It was debated in this issue by Christine M. DeLucia, Alyssa Mt. Pleasant, Philip J. Deloria, and Jean M. O'Brien.

13. Jerry G. Gaff, "Preparing Future Faculty and Multiple Forms of Scholarship," in *Faculty Priorities Reconsidered: Rewarding Multiple Forms of Scholarship*, ed. KerryAnn O'Meara and Eugene Rice (San Francisco: Jossey-Bass, 2005), 66–71; KerryAnn O'Meara, "Principles of Good Practice: Encouraging Multiple Forms of Scholarship in Policy and Practice," in *Faculty Priorities Reconsidered*, ed. O'Meara and Rice, 296–97; Angela Allen and Tami L. Moore, "Developing Emerging Engagement Scholars in Higher Education," in *Handbook of Engaged Scholarship: Contemporary Landscapes, Future Directions*, vol. 2, *Community-Campus Partnerships*, ed. Hiram Fitzgerald, Cathy Burack, and Sarena D. Seifer (East Lansing: Michigan State University Press, 2010), 447–58.

14. Nancy Cantor and Steven D. Lavine, "Taking Public Scholarship Seriously," *Chronicle of Higher Education*, June 9, 2006.

15. Cantor and Lavine, "Taking Public Scholarship Seriously"; Melissa K. Nelson, "The Future of Native Studies: A Modest Manifesto," *American Indian Culture and Research Journal* 35, no. 1 (2011): 40; Duane Champagne, "In Search of Theory and Method in American Indian Studies," *American Indian Quarterly* 31, no. 3 (2007): 364.

16. W. E. B. Du Bois, *The Souls of Black Folk: Essays and Sketches* (Chicago: McClurg, 1903), 154–55. Du Bois to Charles F. Adams, November 23, 1908; Adams to Du Bois, November 28, 1908; Du Bois to Adams, December 15, 1908, in *The Correspondence of W. E. B. Du Bois*, ed. Herbert Aptheker (Amherst: University of Massachusetts Press, 1973), 1:142–44. Also Stephanie J. Shaw, *W. E. B. Du Bois and "The Souls of Black Folk"* (Chapel Hill: University of North Carolina Press, 2013), 204n11; Du Bois, "A Philosophy for 1913," in *African American Political Thought, 1890–1930: Washington Du Bois, Garvey, and Randolph*, ed. Cary D. Wintz (New York: Routledge, 2015), 108; David Levering Lewis, *W. E. B. Du Bois: A Biography* (New York: Holt, 2009), 308–9.

17. Timothy K. Eastman, "Engaged Scholars Study," Imagining America, accessed March 2, 2018http://imaginingamerica.org/initiatives/engaged-scholars-study/.

18. Myaamia Center, "About" page, accessed October 1, 2020, https://www.miamioh.edu/myaamia-center/about/.

19. John A. Marino, "The Exile and His Kingdom: The Reception of Braudel's Mediterranean," *Journal of Modern History* 76, no. 3 (2004): 626, 645.

20. Devon A. Mihesuah, "Voices, Interpretations, and the 'New Indian History': Comment on the 'American Indian Quarterly's' Special Issue on Writing about American Indians," *American Indian Quarterly* 20, no. 1 (1996): 91–108; commentary on *When Jesus Came, the Corn Mothers Went Away*, by Ramón Gutiérrez, in *American Indian Culture and Research Journal* 17, no. 3 (1993): 141–77.

21. American Association of University Professors, "Trends in Faculty Employment Status, 1975–2011," Research Office, 2013, https://www.aaup.org/sites/default/files/Faculty_Trends_0.pdf; Robert B. Townsend and Julia Brookins, "The Troubled Academic Job Market for History," *Perspectives on History*, February, 2016, https://www.historians.org/publications-and-directories/perspectives-on-history/february-2016/the-troubled-academic-job-market-for-history.

22. My experience agrees with Devon Abbott Mihesuah's assessment that "the crucial issues that Indigenous peoples are concerned about [are] decolonization, Nation building, and how the past impacts the present," in her "Academic Gatekeepers," in *Indigenizing the Academy: Transforming Scholarship and Empowering Communities*, ed. Devon Abbott Mihesuah and Angela Cavender Wilson (Lincoln: University of Nebraska Press, 2004), 42. Another challenging and insightful essay on power and exploitation, this in the context of service learning, is Margaret Himley, "Facing (Up to) 'the Stranger' in Community Service Learning," *College Composition and Communication* 55, no. 3 (2004): 416–38.

Bibliography

Abungu, George. "Walking the Long Path to Partnership: Archaeology and Communities in Eastern Africa—Relevance, Access, and Ownership." In *Community*

    Archaeology and Heritage in Africa: Decolonizing Practice, edited by Peter R. Schmidt and Innocent Pikirayi, 46–69. New York: Routledge, 2016.

Allen, Angela, and Tami L. Moore. "Developing Emerging Engagement Scholars in Higher Education." In *Handbook of Engaged Scholarship: Contemporary Landscapes, Future Directions*, vol. 2, *Community-Campus Partnerships*, edited by Hiram Fitzgerald, Cathy Burack, and Sarena D. Seifer, 447–58. East Lansing: Michigan State University Press, 2010.

American Association of University Professors. "Trends in Faculty Employment Status, 1975–2011." Research Office, 2013. https://www.aaup.org/sites/default/files/Faculty_Trends_0.pdf.

Atalay, Sonya. *Community-Based Archaeology: Research with, by, and for Indigenous and Local Communities*. Berkeley: University of California Press, 2012.

Austin, Ann E., and Benita J. Barnes. "Preparing Doctoral Students for Faculty Careers that Contribute to the Public Good." In *Higher Education for the Public Good: Emerging Voices from a National Movement*, edited by Adrianna J. Kezar, Tony C. Chambers, and John C. Burkhardt, 272–92. San Francisco: Jossey-Bass, 2005.

Braxton, John M., ed. *Analyzing Faculty Work and Rewards: Using Boyer's Four Domains of Scholarship*. New Directions for Institutional Research 129. San Francisco: Jossey-Bass, 2006.

Braxton, John M., William T. Lucky, and Patricia A. Helland. *Institutionalizing a Broader View of Scholarship Through Boyer's Four Domains*. ASHE-ERIC Higher Education Report 29, no. 2 (San Francisco: Jossey-Bass, 2002).

Cantor, Nancy, and Steven D. Lavine. "Taking Public Scholarship Seriously." *Chronicle of Higher Education*, June 9, 2006.

Champagne, Duane. "In Search of Theory and Method in American Indian Studies." *American Indian Quarterly* 31, no. 3 (2007): 353–72.

Commentary on *When Jesus Came, the Corn Mothers Went Away*, by Ramón Gutiérrez. *American Indian Culture and Research Journal* 17, no. 3 (1993): 141–77.

Deloria, Vine, Jr. "Marginal and Submarginal." In *Indigenizing the Academy: Transforming Scholarship and Empowering Communities*, edited by Devon Abbott Mihesuah and Angela Cavender Wilson, 16–30. Lincoln: University of Nebraska Press, 2004.

Demb, Ada, and Amy Wade. "Reality Check: Faculty Involvement in Outreach and Engagement." *Journal of Higher Education* 83, no. 3 (2012): 337–66.

Du Bois, W. E. B. Du Bois to Charles F. Adams, November 23, 1908; Adams to Du Bois, November 28, 1908; Du Bois to Adams, December 15, 1908. In *The Correspondence of W. E. B. Du Bois*, ed. Herbert Aptheker, ed., 1:142–44. Amherst: University of Massachusetts Press, 1973.

———. "A Philosophy for 1913." In *African American Political Thought, 1890–1930: Washington, Du Bois, Garvey, and Randolph*, edited by Cary D. Wintz, 108. New York: Routledge, 2015.

———. *The Souls of Black Folk: Essays and Sketches*. Chicago: McClurg, 1903.

Eastman, Timothy K. "Engaged Scholars Study." Imagining America. http://imaginingamerica.org/initiatives/engaged-scholars-study/.

Eddy, Elizabeth M., and William L. Partridge, eds. *Applied Anthropology in America*. New York: Columbia University Press, 1978.

Furco, Andrew. "The Engaged Campus: Toward a Comprehensive Approach to Public Engagement." *British Journal of Educational Studies* 58, no. 4 (2010): 375–90.

Gaff, Jerry G. "Preparing Future Faculty and Multiple Forms of Scholarship." In *Faculty Priorities Reconsidered: Rewarding Multiple Forms of Scholarship*, edited by KerryAnn O'Meara and Eugene Rice, 66–71. San Francisco: Jossey-Bass, 2005.

Hedican, Edward J. *Anthropology in Canada: Understanding Aboriginal Issues*. 2nd ed. Toronto: University of Toronto Press, 2008.

Himley, Margaret. "Facing (Up to) 'the Stranger' in Community Service Learning." *College Composition and Communication* 55, no. 3. (2004): 416–38.

Kroskrity, Paul V. "Introduction to Productive Paths: Linking Native and Academic Communities." *American Indian Culture and Research Journal* 35, no. 1 (2011): 81–85.

Lewis, David Levering. *W. E. B. Du Bois: A Biography* (New York: Holt, 2009).

Marino, John A. "The Exile and His Kingdom: The Reception of Braudel's *Mediterranean*." *Journal of Modern History* 76, no. 3 (2004): 622–52.

McAnany, Patricia A. "Transforming the Terms of Engagement between Archaeologists and Communities: A View from the Maya Region." In *Transforming Archaeology: Activist Practices and Prospects*, edited by Sonya Atalay, Lee Rains Clauss, Randall H. McGuire, and John R. Welch, 159–78. Walnut Creek, CA: Left Coast, 2014.

Mihesuah, Devon Abbott. "Academic Gatekeepers." In *Indigenizing the Academy: Transforming Scholarship and Empowering Communities*, edited by Devon Abbott Mihesuah and Angela Cavender Wilson, 31–47. Lincoln: University of Nebraska Press, 2004.

———. "Voices, Interpretations, and the 'New Indian History': Comment on the 'American Indian Quarterly's' Special Issue on Writing about American Indians." *American Indian Quarterly* 20, no. 1 (1996): 91–108.

Myaamia Center. "About" page. https://www.miamioh.edu/myaamia-center/about/.

National Park Service, Tribal Preservation Program. "Tribal Historic Preservation Offices" report, 2022. nps.gov/subjects/historicpreservationfund/tribal-historic-preservation-office-program.htm.

Nelson, Melissa K. "The Future of Native Studies: A Modest Manifesto." *American Indian Culture and Research Journal* 35, no. 1 (2011): 39–45.

O'Meara, KerryAnn. "Principles of Good Practice: Encouraging Multiple Forms of Scholarship in Policy and Practice." In *Faculty Priorities Reconsidered: Rewarding Multiple Forms of Scholarship*, edited by KerryAnn O'Meara and Eugene Rice, 290–302. San Francisco: Jossey-Bass, 2005.

Richland, Justin B. "Beyond Listening: Lessons for Native/American Collaborations from the Creation of the Nakwatsvewat Institute." *American Indian Culture and Research Journal* 35, no. 1 (2011): 101–11.

Sarche, Michelle, and Douglas Novins, and Annie Belcourt-Dittloff. "Engaged Scholarship with Tribal Communities." In *Handbook of Engaged Scholarship: Contemporary Landscapes, Future Directions*, edited by Hiram Fitzgerald, Cathy Burack, Sarena D. Seifer, and James Votruba, 1:215–28. East Lansing: Michigan State University Press, 2010.

Shaw, Stephanie J. *W. E. B. Du Bois and "The Souls of Black Folk"* (Chapel Hill: University of North Carolina Press, 2013).

Silverman, David J. "Living with the Past: Thoughts on Community Collaboration and Difficult History in Native American and Indigenous Studies." *American Historical Review* 125, no. 2 (2020): 519–27.

Smith, Linda Tuhiwai. *Decolonizing Methodologies: Research and Indigenous Peoples*. London: Zed Books, 2012.

Townsend, Robert B., and Julia Brookins. "The Troubled Academic Job Market for History." *Perspectives on History*, February 2016. https://www.historians.org/publications-and-directories/perspectives-on-history/february-2016/the-troubled-academic-job-market-for-history.

Whetung, Madeline, and Sarah Wakefield. "Colonial Conventions: Institutionalized Research Relationships and Decolonizing Research Ethics." In *Indigenous and Decolonizing Studies in Education: Mapping the Long View*, edited by Linda Tuhiwai Smith, Eve Tuck, and K. Wayne Yang, 146–58. New York: Routledge, 2019.

Wilson, Shawn. "What Is an Indigenist Research Paradigm?" *Canadian Journal of Native Education* 30, no. 2 (2007): 193–95.

Chapter 7

Community-Engaged Scholarship as a Restorative Action

Daryl Baldwin, G. Susan Mosley-Howard, George Ironstrack, and Haley Shea

The Miami Tribe was the first place [where I found I belonged]. . . . That really made me feel like I was at home in a sense.

—Heritage student, 2017

Community-engaged research (CER) is often framed as inquiry designed to advance research goals of both the scholar and community under study.[1] All too often the research enterprise is dominated by academics who seek minimal community input. In contrast to this approach, the Community-engaged scholarship of the Miami Tribe of Oklahoma in partnership with Miami University in Ohio, is grounded in a relationship defined by *neepwaantiinki*, which means learning from each other or partners in learning. This partnership grew out of the long-standing connection between the university and the tribe (see George Ironstrack and Bobbe Burke chapter, this volume), and involves an interdisciplinary team of faculty along with tribal leadership and tribal students attending Miami University. It is within this context that the community-engaged research of the Miami Tribe of Oklahoma through the Myaamia Center (the research arm of the tribe) is situated.[2]

The Myaamia Center serves the Miami Tribe community as an intellectual source for tribal educational programs that infuse a wide range of content that reflect Myaamia values and the tribes' cultural and historic knowledge system. As a tribally directed interdisciplinary research center, the Myaamia Center assumes the responsibility to work in the best interest of the community. In order to garner community and tribal leadership support, the Myaamia Center had to build trust and respect among all parties concerned and demonstrate continually its ability to serve the people.

The unique roles of many Myaamia Center staff as community members, researchers, cultural practitioners, language speakers, and program developers significantly blur the line between academic interest and community need. On one hand, Myaamia Center staff can be intimately connected with, and concerned for, the general welfare of their community and yet at the same time be committed to producing work that can withstand peer review and community critique. Therefore, as community-centered researchers Myaamia Center staff must be able to approach research and development projects based on work quality and scientific methods and still meet community needs. The humanistic approach embedded in this work ensures that research done serves the community more than it serves academic interests. The Myaamia Center was designed to maintain that focus.

The impact of the tribe's language and culture revitalization on tribal youth, community, and tribal engagement is the focus of this community-engaged scholarship agenda. In this chapter, we present the theoretical framing, ontological context, and empirical work of the Miami Tribe of Oklahoma. This assessment work relies heavily on a community-engaged scholarship approach.

Current Revitalization Efforts of the Miami Tribe of Oklahoma

The Miami Tribe of Oklahoma's cultural revitalization efforts exist on multiple levels, consisting of cultural revitalization (e.g., retrieving artifacts, reviving practices, ribbonwork), language reclamation (e.g., language research, retrieval, and community courses), and cultural education for tribal members and the public (e.g., Miami, Oklahoma, exhibits and Native American Museum exhibits in Washington, DC), among other efforts. Revitalization is defined as a conscious and deliberately orchestrated process of restoring, and in some cases strengthening, cultural experiences that have been lost, disrupted, or diminished.³ We understand language reclamation to mean the complete reconstruction and reintroduction of a dormant language from archival materials. These revitalization and reclamation efforts are valuable, given that the Miami Tribe of Oklahoma (MTO) lives in diaspora while still sharing the bonds of their collective Myaamia heritage. These efforts are also crucial as part of healing from historical trauma. Historical trauma or unresolved grief due to systemic loss is felt by Myaamia people across generations and impacts subsequent generations.⁴

In the 1990s, not too long after this revitalization work began, community leaders noticed positive changes in community behavior and participation levels of tribal citizens. In the words of Julie Olds, one of the founding activists in this movement:

> It's amazing the things that have come back, that have been revitalized and renewed . . . in the sense of community and relations. Prior to the return of language there were maybe 35–40 people at an annual meeting, and now an annual meeting has 150 members who bring their families. We can have 300–350 people in the room, I personally believe because of the return of the language.⁵

These observations encouraged the Myaamia Center and the Miami Tribe's Cultural Resources Office to learn more about the forces driving this revitalization movement. Initial steps in the inquiry process were to affirm an ontological foundation, select a team of qualified researchers to launch the inquiry, and develop a purpose statement for the language and cultural revitalization. Thus, the authors of this chapter, along with two additional faculty colleagues constituted this team. We then had to develop specific research questions that would lead the research team in developing an assessment model. The Myaamia Center and Cultural Resources Office wanted to understand how tribal members (especially youth and young adults) became deeply connected to the tribe as a result of their engagement with language and cultural revitalization. Crafting these purpose statements and affirming the research direction involved extensive conversation between tribal representatives and members of the faculty research team (all but two of whom were non–tribal members). Developed in 2012, each member of this research team had well-developed relationships with tribal members and leadership, a commitment to community-engaged research approaches, and a wealth of experience within their respective fields of study (psychology, education, history, and linguistics).

Team members decided to translate the meaning of the research questions into the Myaamia language. We wrote our working purpose statement and research questions relative to this research, first in standard American English as the team listened to the conversations of Miami tribal members including Myaamia Center staff. Non–tribal members on the research team were conscious of the fact that a purely academic mindset could not do justice to the DNA of this inquiry, nor adequately represent the deep cultural meaning of our collective effort. For example, we all believed that community and cultural context shaped this work in both surface and deep ways. Disciplinary hats, so to speak, in psychology, education, history, and linguistics had to be integrated into Myaamia knowledge and culture to examine this notion. Research documenting the challenges of disciplinary integration are prevalent dating back to Rhoten and Parker's 2004 work on interdisciplinarity and up to Jacobs and Frickel's 2009 critique of the practice.[6] However, according to Aboelela and colleagues in 2007, interdisciplinary research involves a continuum of synthesis among disciplines, a multidimensional inquiry and intended outcomes, and qualitative and quantitative modes of research.[7] Research suggests that interdisciplinary research approaches are optimal for dealing with complex constructs and issues.[8] The process of melding our respective disciplinary hats into an interdisciplinary approach yielded a promising outcome in terms of fostering a shared mental model. It also expanded our own scholarly lenses, and along with a cultural context enhanced our understanding of the research issues at hand, an often-cited benefit of inter-disciplinary research.[9] With this in mind, the team then had the research questions translated into the Myaamia language from the perspective of the culture and ideologies that had emerged through this effort over time. Finally, we retranslated the Myaamia interpretations and questions into English, providing a final Myaamia translation, and English translation of the Myaamia, and thus a free translation for academic research purposes.

We noticed considerable differences between the original English statements and the English translations of Myaamia. For example, the question about the degree to which culture and language education improve academic attainment actually translates in Myaamia as *taaniši milonitee-heeyankwi kineepwaayoneminaani, kati nipwaahkaayankwi*, which means "How does reflecting on our ways of knowing cause us to be wise?" From a "Western perspective," educational attainment may be singularly viewed as GPA or successful graduation in a formal educational setting. While, from a Myaamia ontological perspective, attainment is also aligned with formal and tribal knowledge, learning from elders and others, using that knowledge to benefit both one's community and the world. We provide more details about this translation process later in this chapter. However, we believe that these Myaamia expressions communicate important ideological and cultural attributes about our community (see research questions in "Research Method and Data Exemplar" section).

Over many generations, languages evolve as speakers efficiently and effectively communicate knowledge systems and epistemologies to themselves and others. Grammars, metaphoric expressions, and other ways of speaking reflect an evolving thought process rooted in speakers' experiences and understanding over time. Because the study population is the Myaamia people, we believe it is imperative that their Indigenous knowledge system be reflected in the research process. Myaamia knowledge systems serve as a guide for key concepts embedded in the research questions. This bilingual approach governed our study language and provided an opportunity for important research questions to be framed for both Myaamia people and academic audiences. For example, when we thought about well-being or mental health, we asked what does that construct really mean in the Myaamia way of knowing? For the Myaamia people, mental health may have elements of both Western medicine and Myaamia culture. In measuring that notion, we had to be mindful of both lenses.

The bilingual conversation about the research questions also grounded us in methodology and research implementation procedures. Within the study implementation, we had research tracks (education attainment, wellness and identity, community engagement, tribal continuance-sovereignty) that various members of the research/assessment team pursued. In addition, the institutional research board's (IRB) Human Subjects Office of Miami University, in partnership with the Miami Tribe of Oklahoma, collaborated to ensure that integrity and ethics were fundamental components of our research. Like all IRB approved research, the Myaamia projects adhere to the seminal Belmont Report–driven National Research Act of 1974 guidelines. This act mandates that all research operate within the ethical, legal, and regulatory framework of respect for persons, beneficence, and justice. Therefore, all consents, assents, project disclosures, and best practices guided research methodology and procedures. A formal IRB agreement exists between the two entities and states that both the tribe and university review and approve research work implemented with the tribal community. Even if proposed research adheres to IRB criteria, yet tribal leaders perceive the scholarship as detrimental to the tribe, the proposed research may not be approved in the submitted format.

Myaamia knowledge and value systems are critical to our community-engaged research. The best illustration used by tribal educators to capture the active and sustainable nature of the Myaamia knowledge system is the community web and the *wiikiaami mantepwayi,* "lodge frame," structure used to represent the protective and supportive nature of the Myaamia value system. Collectively, these visuals make up the core for understanding how Myaamia knowledge and values factor into not only the educational process of revitalization but also the design of the assessment tool. The web illustration is made of string and, similar to what one would see in a spider web, symbolizes the various "threads" or aspects of the Myaamia culture and life. The web of interconnected threads is strong, connected, and unique, and, when any one of the web's threads is pulled, dropped, or altered, it reverberates throughout and impacts the entire web (community). Symbolically speaking, when each Myaamia person "picks up a thread," they are engaged in community revitalization. Use of the Myaamia knowledge system to frame the research is consistent with the community-based participatory research approach.[10]

The Myaamia value system as represented by the poles of a *wiikiaami* structure helps us, as researchers, to connect our inquiry to the Myaamia way of knowing. Within the *wiikiaami* structure, there are four vertical poles that are marked with the color black. These poles are associated with the North, with winter, with Myaamia elders, and with a waning physical strength yet a growing wisdom—the strength of mind to know what is the right action (see figure 7.1).

The first pole is *neepwaahkaayankwi,* or "we are wise," and represents elders responsible for the dissemination and passing-down of that knowledge. The second value, or black pole, is *eeyaakwaamisiyankwi,* or "we strive to get/attain something." Striving to attain and to understand is a necessary part of the education of Myaamia youth.

The third value, or pole, is *eeweentiyankwi,* or "we are all related." This value ties back into the notion of the web described previously, as we are all connected in some way. The last black pole of *peekinaakosiyankwi* means "we act in a generous manner." Myaamia people generally live under the notion that we give to others more than we receive.

The next set of poles is marked with red, which is associated with the West, with strength, sacrifice, and vitality. These poles symbolize adults

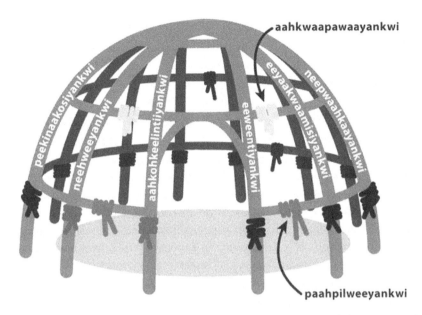

Figure 7.1. *mantepwayi*, "lodge frame," as a representation of the Miami value system. Illustration by Carole Katz, Myaamia Center, Miami University.

who are in the workforce and care for both the elders and the younger generation. The first pole is *aahkohkeelintiiyankwi*, or "we care for each other," and truly represents a sense of mindfulness. The next pole is *neehweeyankwi*, or "we speak well," which means that individuals value speaking properly and with good intentions.

The next set of poles serves as the ribs that run lengthwise on the *wiikiaami* structure. The first pole is blue in color, symbolizing the South and youth or the time when individuals begin to explore the world on their own. This first blue pole is *paapilweeyankwi*, or "we joke," representing the humor Myaamia people use to experience life. Humor is a means for holding everything together, providing a method for diffusing tension, to teach lessons, and to entertain.

The last pole is another horizontal pole that is colored yellow and symbolizes birth. This is the thinnest, topmost pole and is very important to the community. This pole is *aahkwaapawaayankwi*, or "we dream," symbolizing the many possibilities that exist. Historically, Myaamia people used dreams to obtain their life direction.

The Myaamia people use the metaphor of the *wiikiaami* to illustrate their values. Using the Myaamia web and *wiikiaami* framework as a foundation, the research team began to frame an engaged scholarship process.

The Nature of Community Engagement Research

Community engagement research is a framework that seeks and nurtures community involvement, leverages community knowledge, and is led by community need. Community-engaged research is also a process in which researchers work collaboratively with and through groups of people connected via geographic proximity, special interest, or similar situations. Community engagement research can be an effective tool for developing trust within community-academic partnerships, along with community involvement and control.[11] Tina Yuen, an expert in public health and city planning, defines community-engaged research as a continuum with five domains: outreach, consultation, involvement, shared participation and leadership, and community-driven.[12]

Community engagement and participation in research can contribute to a more nuanced understanding of a range of issues, increase the relevance of problems examined for the affected communities, and improve the fit of research activities in community-based settings.[13] In addition, community-engaged research can increase the quality of research, leading to higher participation rates, insightful interpretation of findings, and greater reliability and validity measures in diverse populations.[14] The Myaamia research team wanted to implement an assessment approach that aligned with engaged research practices, particularly at the "shared-leadership/participatory" level. As an aspiration, the team strove for the "community-driven" level. When the team compared the assessment processes and mode of working to the Yuen benchmark, we determined that we had met the community-driven level (e.g., established a mutual relationship, established mutual decision-making, and acquired community grounded research results). We will now outline how the Myaamia study followed this paradigm.

Research Method and Data Exemplars

As previously mentioned, the Myaamia Center research team began the engaged research process by listening to community, crafting a purpose statement, and posing research questions. Our research process is couched

Table 7.1. Continuum of Community-Engagement Research

	Domains of Community-Engaged Research				
Outreach	**Consult**	**Involve**	**Shared Leadership-Participatory**	**Community Driven**
Some community involvement	More community involvement	Community involvement	Strong bidirectional relationship	Strong community leadership
Communication flows from the academic agency research partner to the community to inform or share.	Communication flows from the community to help inform research conducted by academic researchers.	Communication is a two-way path between academic agency, research partner, and community.	Communication is bidirectional; decision-making is equally shared.	Communication is community wide, and final decision-making is at the community level.
Research entity provides community with information.	Entities share information and feedback.	Research involves more participation with community on issues.	Entities have formed strong partnership on each aspect of program from development to solution.	Communities consult with external partners to assist with technical questions regarding project.
Entities coexist.		Entities cooperate with each other.	Entities form bidirectional communication.	
Establish channels for communication and outreach.	Develop connections and obtain information and feedback from the community.	Increased cooperation leads to greater visibility of the partnership.	Partnership building leads to an outcome trust building.	Research reflects the needs and desires of the community or tribal nation leadership.

Note: With each successive level of engagement comes increasing community involvement, impact, trust, and communication.

in the aforementioned Myaamia ontology (knowledge system) and reflects community-engaged research methodologies.

We drafted the following overarching purpose statement to define the tribe's revitalization effort and to assess our outcomes:

Reconnecting the Myaamia People to their Indigenous Knowledge System. Through cultural revitalization, the tribe aspires to help the Miami Nation reconnect to its language, Indigenous practices, and ways of living and knowing for integration into the lives of Myaamia today.

The Myaamia translated version of the statement's opening sentence is as follows:

aalinta eempaapiikinamankwi kineepwaayoneminaani, kati moošaki maamawi ayiileepiyankwi. Translation of Myaamia: "We pick up some of the threads of our knowledge so that we will always remain together."

The nontribal faculty researchers translated the tribe's assessment focus into research questions. Then the Myaamia Center staff translated the research questions into the Myaamia language. The four research questions with Myaamia translations in italics and English retranslations in quotation marks follow:

1. To what degree does language and cultural education improve academic attainment? *taaniši miloniteeheeyankwi kineepwaayoneminaani, kati nipwaahkaayankwi?* "How does reflecting on our ways of knowing cause us to be wise?"

2. Does language and cultural education impact physical and mental health? *taaniši miloniteeheeyankwi kineepwaayonemi-naani, kati nahi- mihtohseeniwiyankwi wiiciilantiiyankwi?* "How does reflecting on our ways of knowing cause us to live properly and help each other?"

3. Does language and cultural education strengthen ties to community resulting in increased community engagement? *taaniši miloniteeheeyankwi kineepwaayoneminaani, kati neenkotiteeheeyankwi neenkoteelintamankwi?* "How does

reflecting on our ways of knowing cause us to be of one mind and one heart?"

4. How does language and cultural education shape beliefs and feelings towards national/tribal growth and its continuance? *taaniši miloniteeheeyankwi kineepwaayoneminaani, kati miihkweelintamankwi weencinaakosiyankwi, neehi aahkohkeelimakiki iineeki mihši-neewaahsiiwankwiki?* "How does reflecting on our ways of knowing cause us to remember where we are from and to care for those we have not yet seen?"

Research Implementation

The primary aspects of the tribe's culture revitalization experience that we examined were Myaamia Heritage program courses taught at Miami University to Myaamia college students, *Eemamwiciki* summer program (*Eewansaapita* and *Saakaciweeta* summer youth camp experiences) in Oklahoma and Indiana, and Tribal gatherings, which include but are not limited to winter storytelling, organized language classes, and the annual business meeting of the MTO.

To assess these events, we used interviews to engage in conversation with tribal members about their experiences, what they were thinking, and how they were engaging with tribal educational experiences consisting of Myaamia Center courses, Miami Tribe youth programs, and Miami Tribe events. For example, twice a year we interview Miami University-Miami Tribe students about their emerging connections with language and tribal activities. We ask them to define what it means to be Myaamia and assess their evolving sense of identity. We also used survey methods and interview data to assess how Miami University tribal students conceptualize identity. We also use observation to examine how tribal events and engagement are unfolding and shaping the way of being or behavior of Myaamia citizens. For example, the chief of the Miami Tribe of Oklahoma began using the Myaamia language and invited citizens to join him in using the language. At a recent annual business meeting, the chief invited Myaamia citizens to share Myaamia words they had learned with him through what has become an annual event called the Chief's Challenge. Numerous citizens lined up before the chief to demonstrate what they had learned. We could never have imagined this happening in previous years.

We have collected four full academic years of data on each successive cohort of Miami tribal students attending Miami University. We have documented their experiences with the tribal classes, looked at their developing identity and expression of what it means to be Myaamia, and chronicled their academic progress and engagement with the tribal community during their university matriculation and postgraduation. We note a growing expression of clarity in their identity as Myaamia individuals as they continue in the Heritage classes. We are beginning to devise longitudinal identity measures for the Myaamia youth who attend the *Eewansaapita* (ages 10–16) and *Saakaciweeta* (ages 5–9) summer youth camps. We will continue to examine ways to measure tribal outcomes under the guidance and direction of the tribe. Below we list the series of studies launched and assessment measures accompanying this tribal-university effort to date.

We launched three studies to examine the impact of cultural revitalization. The first study involved Myaamia college students attending Miami University. In 1991, the tribe created the Myaamia Heritage Award program to financially support Miami Tribal students and facilitate education of tribal youth on their culture, history, and language at Miami University. In 2003, tribal students began taking Myaamia cultural courses called Heritage courses. Tribal students are required to meet with the program coordinator from the Myaamia Center's Tribe Relations Office, meet a minimum GPA requirement, and attend a series of one-credit courses studying various aspects of the Miami Tribe and its knowledge system. Students in the Heritage program take three, one-credit-hour courses beyond the requirements for their major in a three-year rotation of topics ranging from ecological perspectives and history to language, culture, and contemporary tribal issues. In their final year at Miami University, students complete a two-semester senior project that applies their major to community needs. This first study examined Myaamia college student experiences with the language and cultural education courses taken at Miami University and the accompanying changes in identity, academic attainment, and college adjustment.

The second study entailed making community observations to chronicle changes in tribal engagement. As the tribe's revitalization efforts continued to grow, tribal leaders also began to observe increases in attendance and participation at tribal events. This increase has been anecdotally linked with the state of well-being within the community. In 2013, we began formal participant observations at events organized by the Miami Tribe of Oklahoma. Our team has expanded the scope of research

Table 7.2. Current Studies, Myaamia Center Assessment Plan

	Study 1	Study 2	Study 3
Research questions	*To what degree does language and cultural education improve academic attainment? *Does language and cultural education impact physical and mental health? *Does language and cultural education strengthen ties to community, resulting in increased community engagement? *How do language and cultural education shape beliefs and feelings toward national/tribal growth and its continuance?	*Does language and cultural education strengthen ties to community, resulting in increased community engagement? *How do language and cultural education shape beliefs and feelings toward national/tribal growth and its continuance?	*Does language and cultural education strengthen ties to community, resulting in increased community engagement? *How do language and cultural education shape beliefs and feelings toward national/tribal growth and its continuance? Student Outcomes: have fun while learning to . . . . 1. speak language and integrate into daily life 2. practice values 3. learn songs–dance 4. live on the land 5. know kinship bonds 6. know the earth and sky 7. know Myaamia games 8. integrate Myaamia culture into their lives
Measures and longitudinal mixed methods	1. Graduation rates 2. Identity formation 3. Interview about experience 4. Connectedness scale	1. Community observations 2. Participation levels	1. Student survey 2. Student observation 3. Parent survey 4. Teacher reflection 5. Language use
Study Participants	Myaamia college students taking Heritage courses	Myaamia community members participating in tribal events	Myaamia youth ages 9–16 and parents in *Eewansaapita* and *Saakaciweta* camps

from college students to the community as a whole. To examine how the tribe's cultural revitalization efforts have impacted citizens' ability to thrive and recover from historical trauma, our research questions focus on the extent to which language and cultural education strengthens community engagement and feelings about tribal growth and continuance.

The third study examines the impact of language and cultural education camp experiences (*Eewansaapita* and *Saakaciweta*) for tribal youth ages 5–16. We have preliminary data presented here from the summer of 2019 and a COVID-altered data collection approach in 2020.

Method

The project uses a mixed-methods approach (a combination of quantitative and qualitative measures), blending archival institutional data, survey measures, observation, and interview approaches with IRB approval from Miami University and the Miami Tribe of Oklahoma.[15] The human subjects committee examined participant informed consent, ethical practice, and adherence to all tribal and subject protections. Adult participants affirm they are 18, voluntarily participate, are aware of their rights, and know where to seek information about or address concerns about the study. Studies involving youth include a parental consent form and child assent form.

We chose a mixed-methods approach for this assessment for the following reasons: One, tribal cultural revitalization is an emerging area of inquiry and very little groundwork exists to inform its assessment. Two, teaching the Myaamia knowledge system is an emerging effort. Three, qualitative data was needed to inform quantitative data. Four, tribal input and tribal knowledge is respected and serves as a necessary foundation for this work. Five, this is a longitudinal study and mixed methods are best in helping to measure and explain potential results. In searching for quantitative tools, we deemed Angela Snowshoe's Cultural Connectedness scale an appropriate tool to use and assist with exploring identity and tribal engagement outcomes. Mixed methods proved to be most helpful in providing a comprehensive look at study variables. For the participant interviews, we used Rubin and Rubin's responsive interviewing in which the interviewer works *with* interviewees.[16] In this approach, we pose questions to the participants, allow them to respond, then ask further questions based on the content of their responses rather than only asking the predetermined questions. The responsive interviewing approach facilitates more in-depth conversations and a sense of equanimity between researcher and participant.

Results: Data Exemplars

In this section, we have selected data examples to illustrate findings that address each research question.[1]

RESEARCH QUESTION 1: EDUCATIONAL ATTAINMENT AND IMPACT ON YOUTH IDENTITY (BEING WISE)

Three significant factors appear to result from Myaamia youth experiencing their culture via Heritage coursework. The first factor was the impact on students' clarity about identity formation; the second was higher educational attainment; and the third was a commitment to giving back to community. A comparison of a Myaamia student's first-year and senior-year identity statements make this point clear, along with data from the Connectedness survey and interview data. We present first-year and senior-year identity statements below as an example.

Identity Formation

Each year we ask Myaamia college students to write about "What does it mean to be Myaamia?" Here are some of those statements.

Participant 1, freshman year (2005):

> *I am a college student. I am a son. I am an athlete, friend, cousin and somewhere in the mix, I am a Miami Indian. At family reunions, in a survey, on an application: this is where, in the past, I have felt my Native heritage. It is a facet of my life I have been at best, unacquainted with my entire life. Living far from tribal contact has an effect; and in my case its effect was a casual ambivalence. . . . I had no idea what it meant, other than one of my relatives was Chief Little Turtle.*

Participant 1, senior year (2009):

Being Myaamia is an integral part of who I am and I am proud in the face of derision because I know the depth or meaning in that identity and the strength of support from others who are Myaamia. The last four years have been a journey for me as I discover myself and delve into my people's history. I now hope to be able to help other people discover their Myaamia heritage as well so they can have the same experience as me.

Participant 2 (2010; excerpts from a retrospective identity statement):

My freshmen year I answered this question with stating that being Myaamia means being who I am. After four years I still believe that to be true but I understand so much more about that statement. When someone hears that I am a member of the Miami Tribe they say "oh so you are Indian" and often times I simply shake my head in agreement because I don't have the time to explain to them that I am not Indian but I am Myaamia. . . . Being Myaamia is the way I see the world and the way I interact with other people in this world. This year we have taken the time to look around "our world" or at least observe our surroundings on campus. We watch as nature interacts and see how one thing can affect many and how everything is connected to something else. We have also been able to see how our actions can affect things as well. Being observant and using the resources given to us is how our ancestors were able to not only survive but thrive. I try to use that same mindset in my life by being mindful of my surrounds and using my resources to the fullest. . . . But only Miami has the class where I can learn about my culture and heritage. The class not only helps us learn about the Tribal community at large by teaching us the language, telling us the history, and updating us on the current affairs of the tribe but it brings the students together. That gathering is a community of young tribal members who share a past and now share a future together as Myaamia people. Being part of that community and sharing a culture, a history, a language is what being Myaamia means.

Another student provides an integrated reflection of who she is. As a first-year student, in 2013, Participant 3 stated:

Myaamia means being a part of a huge family who takes pride in their heritage and they go even further to teach younger generations the language, their culture and it just . . . I think anyone of the heritage is really proud because we're not letting it go to sleep because we're keeping it alive and we're teaching others about and becoming more knowledgeable about it, living the heritage instead of thinking that it was just part of our past because it's not our past; it's our everyday life.

Then, in 2017, Participant 3 stated:

I can definitely say I am a Miami woman and that is a large part of my identity now, especially just I've learned so much and it's actually a part of me instead of just something that I'm learning about in school. So I identify as that. I also identify as I guess a 22 year old woman and a Christian and all of these things interwove together.

She went on to reflect upon her journey and her ability to "give back" to the Myaamia community. She continues:

Each year I did grow closer with friends in the class and so I think that was a big part of why that class was there, is that we would actually grow in community. But it wasn't till I was actually writing my reflection paper senior year that I realized, looking back, every year building up until senior year we were growing in community. But then senior year [I finally saw] that I'm an individual and how I fit into that community with strengths and weaknesses and that was through the project. I did a summer project of growing the Myaamia miincipi [corn] this past summer. I really got to explore what I had studied with health promotion and sustainability and my own personal interests with the help of tribal members like Daryl and George and Karen. How can I use my strengths to help the Miami Tribe? I think that was pretty amazing as a senior. Looking back, freshman year I had no idea what I was doing. I was just there to learn whatever they were teaching. Then each year I grew more confident with what I was learning and reaching out. I think sophomore year I did—when I was Early Childhood Education—a project with Native American Literacy and reading children's books and how Native Americans were portrayed. That was a personal interest. Then each year I was kind of given the reins to take my personal interest and actually do something with it. Senior year it was pretty cool to see how that came together.

These reflection statements of what it means to be Myaamia demonstrate the evolving sense of identity formation the Miami Tribe college students experienced. Earlier in our research process, we briefly used an identity scale (Gonzalez's Native Identity Scale) in an attempt to measure shifts in identity quantitatively.[17] We later abandoned this scale, because it was an instrument designed for reservation and in-tact tribal experiences. Therefore, it was not appropriate for the diaspora experience of the Miami Tribe of Oklahoma. The NIS measure was appropriate for other Native American experiences but not the Myaamia. Nevertheless, we reported on data derived from the Gonzalez model in a prior publication.[18] In addition to these identity interviews, as stated earlier in this chapter, we are now using an augmented version of the Cultural Connectedness scale to quantitatively measure the identity question along with student identity essays.[19]

Educational Attainment

After 2003, when students began taking Myaamia Heritage courses (those attending Miami University in 2003 and after, n = 73), we saw a significant increase in graduation rates for students who participated in the Myaamia Heritage courses, particularly when compared to Myaamia students who did not have the Miami Heritage experience (those attending Miami University between 1991 to 2002, n = 25, table 7.3). We also compared these graduation rates to the US Department of Education rates for all Native Americans. While this is a flawed comparison, due to varying tribal contexts and experiences, we do not have a perfect control group.

Educational attainment research often suggests that group success derives from prior preparation or ability. In our research, we discovered a significant difference in time to four-year graduation despite ACT scores for the pre-Heritage course group and post-Heritage course group. Further analysis demonstrated that ACT scores did not predict whether or not students graduated, but completion of the Heritage course was a reliable

Table 7.3. Educational Attainment

Years to diploma	Non-Heritage group (n = 25)	Heritage group (n = 76)	National
4 years	40.0%	78.9%	20.4%
5 years	52.0%	90.8%	34.1%
6 years	56.0%	92.1%	39.5%

Note: Comparison of higher education graduation rates of Heritage group composed of Myaamia students entering Miami University between 2003 and 2014, those who were not Heritage participants, and the national Native American graduation rate. Rates as of 2021. Source: National comparison data from public 4-year postsecondary institutions from US Department of Education, National Center for Education Statistics, *Digest of Education Statistics, 2019*, table 326.10 or indicator 21, https://nces.ed.gov/programs/digest/d19/tables/dt19_326.10.asp.

predictor. The data suggest a higher academic attainment rate of Myaamia students after the culture revitalization education courses began.[20]

Youth Camp Impact on Attainment

The youth camps (*Eewansaapita* and *Saakaciweeta*) were created in 2005 for youth ages 5–9 with the goal being for youth to have fun while learning to speak *Myaamiaataweenki* (the Myaamia language) and practice *meesiminaakosiyankwi* (culture) and values and make space for both in their lives. The summer camp curriculum has six revolving themes: *kiikinaana* (our homes), *weecinaakiiyankwi weecikaayankwi* (song and dance), *meehtohseeniwinki asiihkionki* (living on the land), *eeweentiiyankwi* (family), *asiihkiwi neehi kiisikwi* (earth and sky), *weekhikaanki meehkintiinki* (games).

Due to the effects of COVID-19, the programs transitioned to an at-home format for 2020 and 2021, which impacted both participation rates and the method for assessment. As such, here we report the sample sizes and general findings, but the primary data stem from 2018 and 2019 in-person camps.

Using a pre-post child-participant and parent-participant 25-item survey and interviews, data of 81 *Saakaciweeta* campers from 2018 (n = 27), 2019 (n = 31), 2020 (n = 8), and 2021 (n = 15) in Oklahoma and Indiana (where camps are held) suggested that child participants showed evidence of learning language and cultural traditions while at camp. Questions focused on knowledge gained, understanding of values and language, skills learned, and the overall impact of the camp. Parental responses verify this knowledge acquisition. Data of 108 *Eewansaapita* campers from 2018 (n = 39), 2019 (n = 47), 2020 (n = 14), and 2021 (n = 8) suggest that children participating in this experience also gain more knowledge about Myaamia cultural practices and increase their use of Myaamia language. Further, *Eewansaapita* parents reported an "improvement in child behavior and respect for Elders, children seemed happier, and children have an interest in and use more language and cultural knowledge." There were statistically significant differences in pre-camp knowledge and post-camp knowledge on select dimensions.

In both Oklahoma and Indiana, parent and child survey responses signal that learning goals are being met through camp participation. Although Oklahoma youth may seem to have more knowledge prior to the camp experience than Indiana youth (singing a Myaamia song; $t_{(23)}$ = 2.59, p < .05); the tribe's goal for youth to have fun while learning Myaamia language and culture is being accomplished. A longitudinal study will need to be completed with former camp attendees to determine if the tribe's final goal of *cultural practices being implemented in campers' lives outside of the program* is being reached. However, the following comment by a camper suggests this goal is within the realm of possibility. A 2019 camper stated, "Knowing our land and how to use it helps us to know each other. It brings us together by food, medicine, and knowledge." Participants in 2020 and 2021 reported feeling happy to stay connected despite COVID-19, but some prefer to connect in-person and others prefer online because they live far away from the in-person programs.

Saakaciweeta campers reported an increase in knowledge gained as well. At pretest 48% (n = 58) of campers said they knew a Myaamia song, versus 74% after camp. Further, 77% of campers know how to say "aya" before camp and 87% after camp.

The following charts show observational data or quantitative differences on select survey questions supporting the inference that the camp experience is effective. Of note, 98.33% of campers in 2018 and 100% of campers in 2019, 2020, and 2021 reported having fun at *Saakaciweeta* and *Eewansaapita*.

Research Question 2: Physical and Mental Health (Living Properly)

Often research about Native American health focuses on alcohol, diabetes, and other physiological or psychological pathologies. We recognize the need to understand these conditions. However, we wanted to adhere to the Myaamia notion of "living well" or "living properly." Toward that end, we used the Connectedness scale, which measures levels of connection with one's Indigenous culture/heritage along with patterns of living and adhering to tribal practices.[21] It also contains a few questions about how tribal members cope with life stressors and adhere to Indigenous practices when dealing with health-related issues.

Through our observations and student self-reports, we see Myaamia young adults choosing to live in accordance with the Myaamia knowledge system, subsequently impacting their health practices (e.g., use of teas and food), wedding ceremonies, and heritage activities (e.g. storytelling).

In addition, Connectedness scale scores provide empirical validation for the observed shifts in students' connection to the tribe. Two cohorts of seniors responded to the scale using a retrospective approach. Seniors compared their freshman-year perspective (before Heritage courses) with their senior-year perspective (after Heritage courses). The reflective comparisons focused on three domains: "time spent with tribe," "sense of belonging," and "when overwhelmed, using Myaamia culture to cope." Seniors' responses demonstrate that they experienced a significant shift in levels of connection with the tribe by the end of their fourth year.

Data on 28 seniors who completed the Connectedness scale show an increased level of connection from first year to senior year, through "time spent trying to learn," "sense of belonging," and "when overwhelmed look to culture." A paired t-test results show increases that are significant.

RESEARCH QUESTION 3: STRENGTHENING COMMUNITY
(ONE MIND AND HEART)

Similar to the differences noted with the Miami Tribe students, we have observed shifts in the level of engagement among other tribal members. As participant-observers, we have attended winter gatherings and annual meetings over the past eight years. Per our tracking, there has been an increase in attendance, participation, and seeking to learn cultural ways through numerous events. There has been an increase in attendance at tribal annual meetings and winter gatherings in which storytelling is a key experience. There is also an intergenerational team of storytellers, a growing number of young tribal adults who include Myaamia traditions in their wedding ceremonies, and tribal leaders and youth who offer prayers in the Myaamia language. In addition, lacrosse has become a strong anchor of youth activity, along with an annual intertribal lacrosse game with gift giving. Both

Table 7.4. Paired *t*-Tests on Select Pre and Post Survey Questions from *Eewansaapita*, 2018

Pre-post item pair	n	Pre		Post		$t_{(29)}$	p	d
		M	SD	M	SD			
Learned about Myaamia heritage	29	1.71	.46	1.93	.26	2.27	< .05	.59
Can sing Myaamia song	29	1.73	.45	2.00	.00	3.24	< .05	.85

Eewansaapita Parent Responses

Year Survey question	2018 N = 13	2019 N = 11	2020 N = 7	2021 N = 4
My child can understand some of Myaamia language.	100%	80%	NA	75%
My child knows the Myaamia values.	76.92%	80%	NA	50%
My child knows how to play a Myaamia game.	100%	80%	NA	50%
My child has sung me a song in Myaamia.	100%	80%	NA	50%

Note: Not all survey questions included in this chart. Not all questions were asked in 2020, due to COVID-19 changes.

Saakaciweta Parent Responses

Year Survey question	2018 N = 9	2019 N =10	2020 N = 9	2021 N = 6
What has your child told you about his/her experiences in *Saakaciweeta?*	Had fun Lacrosse Cook Art	Songs Language Lacrosse Moons Games	N/A	N/A
What did your child learn about Myaamia culture while at camp?	Language Games Songs Dances Art	Lunar calendar Myaamia words Games	N/A	N/A
Did your child meet your goals for sending them to camp?	100% Yes	100% Yes	75% Yes	100% Yes

Note: Not all survey questions included in this chart. Not all questions were asked in 2020 and 2021, due to COVID-19 changes.

Table 7.5. Paired *t*-Tests for Select Pre and Post Connectedness Scale Scores

| Pre-post item pair | n | Pre | | Post | | | |
		M	SD	M	SD	t	p
Spent time trying to learn	27	2.07	1.24	4.56	0.89	-10.85	.00
Strong sense of belonging	28	2.14	1.11	4.36	0.95	-11.36	.00
When overwhelmed, look to culture	28	2.00	0.82	3.25	1.27	-5.49	.00

Note: Select Connectedness scale questions from the 2017 through 2021 senior cohorts of Myaamia students. Items scored on a 1 to 5 Likert scale. Retrospective scores of freshman-year responses (pre-Heritage course) were compared to senior-year responses (post-Heritage course). Item's full text: (1) I have spent time trying to find out more about being Myaamia, such as its history, traditions, and customs. (2) I have a strong sense of belonging to my Myaamia community/nation. (3) When I am overwhelmed with my emotions, I look to my Myaamia culture for help (e.g., using humor).

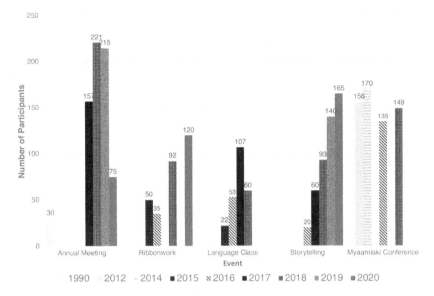

Figure 7.2. Continuum of community engagement research.

workshops on ribbonwork, a traditional Myaamia art form, and language classes draw strong attendance. Finally, cultural displays in Washington, DC, and in Oklahoma, along with the biennial Myaamiaki conference, designed for the purpose of communicating research findings and culture knowledge to the tribe and public, has seen success. All of these experiences hold great significance in the Myaamia tradition. Their reemergence is symbolic of the growing reclamation and affinity for all that is culturally Myaamia.

RESEARCH QUESTION 4: TRIBAL/NATION GROWTH AND
CONTINUANCE (CARE FOR THOSE UNSEEN)

Each year we chronicle how our Miami students find ways to contribute to the tribe whether through formal means of career choice, volunteering or by being intentional with their tribal engagement. Below we outline some ways in which our students are "giving back" to the tribe.

Discussion

In this chapter, we presented a process by which a community-engaged approach to research was used to assess the Miami Tribe of Oklahoma's

Table 7.6. Giving Back to Support Tribal Growth and Continuance

Number of former Miami Tribe Heritage program students	Mode of giving back to tribe
5	Working on Myaamia research while pursuing graduate studies
1	Working as a Myaamia graduate assistant while pursuing graduate studies
1	Teaching Myaamia language to the tribe
6	Doing storytelling at tribal gatherings
4	Engaging in ecology and environmental research
65	Completing senior research projects that focus on a tribal need
7	Serving as *Eewansaapita* and *Saakaciweeta* program coordinators
53	Students serving as *Eewansaapita* and *Saakaciweeta* camp counselors
1	Starting career as a professor doing Myaamia research

revitalization efforts. These revitalization efforts were needed due to stemming from forced removals and historical trauma. Literature has been fairly clear about the impact of historical trauma among Native Americans.[22] Experts suggest that there are three aspects to this historical trauma concept. The first is the domination and assault of the dominant culture on the masses. The second aspect is that the generation receiving the trauma exhibits biological, societal, and psychological symptoms of the trauma. Finally, the recipients of the trauma transfer symptom responses to successive generations.[23] Within this context, community-engaged research can be seen as a proactive approach of a people attempting to restore their cultural selves and begin a healing process from this kind of trauma. When a people reclaim their cultural context, an awakening occurs. This is not to say that the Myaamia people were ever completely detached from their cultural selves, but one might suggest that a strengthening of cultural ties refreshed the self and the community. Revitalization became the channel for healing.[24]

Community-engaged research became the vehicle through which the Miami people launched the validation of their restorative action. The process of restoration involves reconciliation, empowerment, and returning what may have been lost at some level. The Myaamia people were purposeful in their commitments to restore the cultural core of the community through education and strengthening the web of connection. There is power and empowerment in this process. Equipped with this type of renewed spirit, intentional inquiry, and research information, the tribe not only further enhanced knowledge about tribal heritage among the Myaamia community, but also for those outside of the tribe.

On the community-engagement research continuum, the Miami Tribe of Oklahoma inquiry process reflected elements of the "community driven" dimension by grounding this research inquiry in a fifty-year relationship between the tribe and Miami University. Over the years, university and tribal leaders have maintained a level of communication, familiarity, and mutual respect. When it comes to issues that relate to the tribe, the decision rests with the tribe, and the university shows respect for tribal sovereignty and their self-determination efforts. This is not to say that this relationship is flawless. There have been instances where some level of insensitivity has emerged (e.g., inappropriate use of symbols or terms like "redskins" or an Indian head). However, these conflicts have been largely addressed within the context of this valued long-standing relationship. University researchers were keenly aware of and educated about the university-tribal relationship. The researchers also consciously adopted the community-engaged research approach. As an extension of this, it was natural for the assessment team to adopt the notion that the community representatives were driving the assessment agenda and the results were for the benefit of the tribe's ongoing educational developments. Our collective reliance on the community-engaged research model enhanced both the inquiry process and the successful completion of projects designed according to this model. The assessment team is now named *Nipwaayoni* Acquisition and Assessment Team (NAAT; *nipwaayoni* means knowledge), which illustrates the full adoption of the community-engaged approach.

In summary, the Miami Tribe of Oklahoma has a better understanding of the impact of its revitalization work because of the data collected on the four research questions. In terms of educational attainment, data suggest that tribal college students who complete the Heritage classes graduate at higher levels than those who do not. Further, these students show through their identity statements (and connectedness measures) that their sense of Myaamia identity develops over time. In addition, these same data points suggest that Myaamia college students begin to see their cultural knowledge and community as a support that is able to help them with life challenges and help them understand how to "give back" to the tribal community. Data also suggest that tribal youth attain cultural and language knowledge through the youth camps and leave with an emerging sense of community and identity as well.

The Miami Tribe has benefitted from the Miami Heritage students' desire to "give back." Before and after graduation, current and former Miami Heritage students attend and participate in community events at a much higher level. Their engagement with our communities in Oklahoma and Indiana enhances the culture and sovereignty of the tribe. In addition, data on tribal engagement and language acquisition also shows an increase among noncollege tribal members, and this increased engagement emanates through the community.

Former and current Myaamia students enhance intertribal relations and improve the Miami Tribe's capacity to work with local, state, and federal governments. Some former students write community-based grants that advance the sovereignty of the Miami Tribe. Internally, *nipwaayoni*, or knowledge, lends itself to an added sense of Myaamia identity; an awakening and strength that resurrects intergenerational cultural transmission. The restoration of *nipwaayoni* to the community increases community outreach, connection, and action, and positions future generations to establish what it means to be Myaamia. In this case, the youth have demonstrated that they hold a key to the dawning of a new era for the Miami Tribe of Oklahoma.

Notes

Acknowledgments to Myaamia Center staff Kara Strass and David Costa. For information about the Myaamia Center and its research/assessment agenda, see its website at http://myaamiacenter.org/. For information about the Miami Tribe of Oklahoma, see http://www.miaminuation.com. Portions of this paper were presented at the 5th International Conference on Language Documentation and Conservation, "Vital Voices: Linking Language and Wellbeing," March, 2017, Honolulu, Hawaii, and the "Community-Engaged Scholarship in Indian Country" conference, University of Tulsa and Miami, Oklahoma, April, 2017. Correspondence concerning this manuscript should be addressed to Daryl Baldwin, Myaamia

Center, 200 Bonham House, 351 E. Spring Street, Miami University, Oxford, OH 45056. Email: baldwidw@miamioh.edu 513-529-5648.

1. Meredith Minkler and Nina Wallerstein, eds., *Community-Based Participatory Research for Health: From Process to Outcomes* (New York: Jossey-Bass, 2008), 5–19.

2. More extensive study results can be found in the following publications: Shea et al., "Revitalization as a Restorative Process to Combat Cultural Trauma and Promote Living Well," *Cultural Diversity and Ethnic Minority Psychology* 25, no. 4 (2019): 553–65; G. Susan Mosley-Howard, Daryl Baldwin, George Ironstrack, Kate Rousmaniere, and Bobbe Burke, "Niila Myaamia (I Am Miami): Identity and Retention of Miami Tribe College Students," *Journal of College Student Retention* 17, no. 4 (2016): 437–61. 3. Robert K. Merton, "Social Structure and Anomie," in *Social Theory and Social Structure*, ed. Robert K. Merton, rev. and enl. ed. (Glencoe, IL: Free Press, 1957), 131–60.

4. Lisa Grayshield, Jeremy Rutherford, Sibella Salazar, Anita Milhecoby, and Laura Luna, "Understanding and Healing Historical Trauma: The Perspectives of Native American Elders," *Journal of Mental Health Counseling* 37, no. 4 (2015): 295–307.

5. Julie Olds, personal communication with Daryl Baldwin, 2000.

6. Diana Rhoten and Andrew Parker, "Risks and Rewards of an Interdisciplinary Research Path," *Science* 306, no. 5704 (2004): 2046; Jerry A. Jacobs and Scott Frickel, "Interdisciplinarity: A Critical Assessment," *Annual Review of Sociology* 35 (2009): 43–65.

7. Sally W. Aboelela, Elaine Larson, Suzanne Bakken, Olveen Carrasquillo, Allan Formicola, Sherry A. Glied, Janet Haas, and Kristine M. Gebbie, "Defining Interdisciplinary Research: Conclusions from a Critical Review of the Literature," *Health Services Research* 42 (2007): 329–46.

8. Rebekah Brown, Lara Werbeloff, and Rob Raven, "Interdisciplinary Research and Impact," *Global Challenges* 3, no. 4 (2019), https://doi.org/10.1002/gch2.201900020. David Budtz Pedersen, "Integrating Social Sciences and Humanities in Interdisciplinary Research," *Palgrave Communications* 2, no. 1 (2016): 1–7, https://doi.org/10.1057/palcomms.2016.36.

9. R. Dean Hardy, "A Sharing Meanings Approach for Interdisciplinary Hazards Research," *Risk Analysis* 41, no. 7 (2018): 1162–70.

10. Nina Wallerstein and Bonnie Duran, "Community Based Participatory Research Contributions to Intervention Research: The Interaction of Science and Practice to Improve Health Inquiry," *American Journal of Public Health* 100, no. S1 (2010): S40–S46.

11. Frances D. Butterfoss and Vincent T. Francisco, "Evaluating Community Partnerships and Coalitions with Practitioners in Mind," *Health Promotion Practice* 5, no. 2 (2004): 108–14; Stephen B. Fawcett et al., "Evaluating Community Initia-

tives for Health and Development," in *Evaluating Health Promotion Approaches*, ed. Irving Rootman et al. (Copenhagen: World Health Organization, 2001), 241–77; Barbara Israel et al., "Critical Issues in Developing and Following Community Based Participatory Research Principles," in Minkler and Wallerstein, *Community-Based Participatory Research for Health*, 46–66; Minkler and Wallerstein, eds., *Community-Based Participatory Research for health*, 5–19.

12. Tina Yuen, Alice N. Park, Serena D. Seifer, and Devon Payne-Sturges, "A Systematic Review of Community Engagement in the US Environmental Protection Agency's Extramural Research Solicitations: Implications for Research Funders," *American Journal of Public Health* 105, no. 12 (2015): e44–e52.

13. Margaret Cargo and Shawna L. Mercer, "The Value and Challenges of Participatory Research: Strengthening Its Practice," *Annual Review of Public Health* 29 (2008): 325–50; Justin Jagosh et al., "Uncovering the Benefits of Participatory Research: Implication of a Realist Review of Health Research and Practice," *Milbank Quarterly* 90, no. 2 (2012): 311–46; Robin L. Miller and Mary Beth M. Shinn, "Learning from Communities: Overcoming Difficulties in Dissemination of Prevention and Promotion Efforts," *American Journal of Community Psychology* 35, no. 3–4 (2005): 169–83; Wallerstein and Duran, "Community-Based Participatory Research Contributions," S40.

14. Cargo and Mercer, "The Value and Challenges of Participatory Research," 325–50; Justin Jagosh et al., "Assessing the Outcomes of Participatory Research: Protocol for Identifying, Selecting, Appraising and Synthesizing the Literature for Realist Review," *Implementation Science* 6 (2011): 24–32; Denise De Las Nueces, Karen Hacker, Ann DiGirolamo, and LeRoi S. Hicks, "A Systematic Review of Community-Based Participatory Research to Enhance Clinical Trials in Racial and Ethnic Minority Groups," *Health Services Research* 47, no. 3, pt. 2 (2012): 1363–86.

15. John W. Creswell and Vicki Plano Clark. *Designing and Conducting Mixed Methods Research*, 2nd ed. (Thousand Oaks, CA: Sage, 2011).

16. Herbert J. Rubin and Irene S. Rubin, *Qualitative Interviewing: The Art of Hearing Data* (Los Angeles: Sage, 2012), 25–41.

17. John Gonzalez and Russell Bennett, "American Indian and Alaska Native Mental Health Research," *Journal of the National Center* 17, no. 2 (2011): 22–42.

18. Mosley-Howard et al., "Niila Myaamia (I Am Miami)," 437–61.

19. Angela Snowshoe et al., "Development of a Cultural Connectedness Scale for First Nations Youth." *Psychological Assessment* 27, no. 1 (2015): 249–59.

20. A logistic regression analysis was conducted to predict graduation for Myaamia students using ACT score and heritage versus non-Heritage course groups as predictors. A test of the full model against a constant only model was statistically significant, indicating that the predictors as a set reliably distinguished between those who graduated and those who did not (χ^2 = 11.30, p < .01, df = 2). Nagelkerke's R^2 of .194 indicates a moderate relationship between prediction and grouping. Prediction success overall was 80.5% (100% for those that graduated and 0% for those who did not). The Wald criterion demonstrated that only

completion of the heritage course predicted whether or not students graduated (p = .001). ACT scores, however, did not predict whether or not students graduated.

21. Snowshoe et al., "Development of a Cultural Connectedness Scale"; Angela Snowshoe, "The Cultural Connectedness Scale and Its Relation to Positive Mental Health among First Nations Youth" (PhD diss., University of Western Ontario, 2015), http://ir.lib.uwo.ca/etd/3107.

22. Maria Brave Heart, Josephine Chase, Jennifer Elkins, and Deborah B. Altschul, "Historical Trauma among Indigenous Peoples of the Americas: Concepts, Research, and Clinical Considerations," *Journal of Psychoactive Drugs* 43, no. 4 (2011): 282–90.

23. Kathleen Brown-Rice, "Examining the Theory of Historical Trauma among Native Americans," *Professional Counselor* 3, no. 3 (2013): 117–30; Michelle Sotero, "A Conceptual Model of Historical Trauma: Implications for Public Health Practice and Research," *Journal of Health Disparities Research and Practice* 1, no. 1 (2006): 93–108.

24. Anthony F. C. Wallace, "Revitalization Movements," *American Anthropologist* 58, no. 2 (1956): 264–81.

Bibliography

Aboelela, Sally W., Elaine Larson, Suzanne Bakken, Olveen Carrasquillo, Allan Formicola, Sherry A. Glied, Janet Haas, and Kristine M. Gebbie. "Defining Interdisciplinary Research: Conclusions from a Critical Review of the Literature." *Health Services Research* 42 (2007): 329–46.

Brave Heart, Maria Yellow Horse, Josephine Chase, Jennifer Elkins, and Deborah B. Altschul. "Historical Trauma among Indigenous Peoples of the Americas: Concepts, Research, and Clinical Considerations." *Journal of Psychoactive Drugs* 43, no. 4 (2011): 282–90.

Brown, Rebekah, Lara Werbeloff, and Rob Raven. "Interdisciplinary Research and Impact." *Global Challenges* 3, no. 4 (2019). https://doi.org/10.1002/gch2.201900020.

Brown-Rice, Kathleen. "Examining the Theory of Historical Trauma among Native Americans." *Professional Counselor* 3 no. 3 (2013): 117–30.

Butterfoss, Frances D., and Vincent T. Francisco. "Evaluating Community Partnerships and Coalitions with Practitioners in Mind." *Health Promotion Practice* 5, no. 2 (2004): 108–14.

Cargo, Margaret, and Shawna L. Mercer. "The Value and Challenges of Participatory Research: Strengthening Its Practice." *Annual Review of Public Health* 29 (2008): 325–50.

Creswell, John W., and Vicki Plano Clark. *Designing and Conducting Mixed Methods Research*. 2nd ed. Thousand Oaks, CA: Sage, 2011.

Fawcett, Stephen B., Adrienne Paine-Andrews, Vincent T. Francisco, Jerry A. Schultz, Kimberly P. Richter, Jannette Berkley-Patton, Jacqueline L. Fisher, et al. "Evaluating Community Initiatives for Health and Development." In *Evaluating Health Promotion Approaches*, edited by Irving Rootman, Michael Goodstadt, Brian Hyndman, David V. Mcqueen, Louise Potvin, Jane Springett, and Erio Ziglio, 241–77. Copenhagen: World Health Organization, 2001.

Gonzalez, John, and Russell Bennett. "American Indian and Alaska Native Mental Health Research." *Journal of the National Center* 17, no. 2 (2011): 22–42.

Grayshield, Lisa, Jeremy J. Rutherford, Sibella B. Salazar, Anita L. Mihecoby, and Laura L. Luna. "Understanding and Healing Historical Trauma: The Perspectives of Native American Elders." *Journal of Mental Health Counseling* 37, no. 4 (2015): 295–307.

Hardy, R. Dean. "A Sharing Meanings Approach for Interdisciplinary Hazards Research." *Risk Analysis* 41, no. 7 (2018): 1162–70.

Israel, Barbara, Amy Schulz, Edith Parker, Adam Becker, Alex Allen, and J. Ricardo Guzman. "Critical Issues in Developing and Following Community Based Participatory Research Principles." In Minkler and Wallerstein, *Community-Based Participatory Research for Health*, 46–66.

Jacobs, Jerry A., and Scott Frickel. "Interdisciplinarity: A Critical Assessment." *Annual Review of Sociology* 35 (2009): 43–65.

Jagosh, Justin, Ann C. Macaulay, Pierre Pluye, Jon Salsberg, Paula L. Bush, Jim Henderson, Erin Sirett, et al. "Uncovering the Benefits of Participatory Research: Implication of a Realist Review of Health Research and Practice." *Milbank Quarterly* 90, no. 2 (2012): 311–46.

Jagosh, Justin, Pierre Pluye, Ann C. Macaulay, Jon Salsberg, Jim Henderson, Erin Sirett, Paula L. Bush, et al. "Assessing the Outcomes of Participatory Research: Protocol for Identifying, Selecting, Appraising and Synthesizing the Literature for Realist Review." *Implementation Science* 6 (2011): 24–32.

Merton, Robert K. "Social Structure and Anomie." In *Social Theory and Social Structure*, edited by Robert K. Merton, 131–60. Rev. and enl. ed. Glencoe, IL: Free Press, 1957.

Miami Tribe of Oklahoma. "Kiiloona Myaamiaki Miami Tribe of Oklahoma." https://www.miaminto.com/.

Miller, Robin L., and Mary Beth M. Shinn. "Learning from Communities: Overcoming Difficulties in Dissemination of Prevention and Promotion Efforts." *American Journal of Community Psychology* 35, no. 3–4 (2005): 169–83.

Minkler, Meredith, and Nina Wallerstein, eds. *Community-Based Participatory Research for Health: From Process to Outcomes*. New York: Jossey-Bass 2008.

Mosley-Howard, G. Susan, Daryl Baldwin, George Ironstrack, Kate Rousmaniere, and Bobbe Burke. "Niila Myaamia (I Am Miami): Identity and Retention of Miami Tribe College Students." *Journal of College Student Retention* 17, no. 4 (2016): 437–61.

Myaamia Center. Home page. https://miamioh.edu/myaamia-center/.

Nueces, Denise De Las, Karen Hacker, Ann DiGirolamo, and LeRoi S. Hicks. "A Systematic Review of Community-Based Participatory Research to Enhance Clinical Trials in Racial and Ethnic Minority Groups." *Health Services Research* 47, no. 3, pt. 2 (2012): 1363–86.

Pedersen, David Budtz. "Integrating Social Sciences and Humanities in Interdisciplinary Research." *Palgrave Communications* 2, no. 1 (2016): 1–7. https://doi.org/10.1057/palcomms.2016.36.

Rhoten, Diana, and Andrew Parker. "Risks and Rewards of an Interdisciplinary Research Path." *Science* 306, no. 5704 (2004): 2046.

Rubin, Herbert J., and Irene S. Rubin. *Qualitative Interviewing: The Art of Hearing Data*. Los Angeles: Sage, 2012.

Shea, Haley, G. Susan Mosley-Howard, Daryl Baldwin, George Ironstrack, Kate Rousmaniere, and Joseph E. Schroer. "Cultural Revitalization as a Restorative Process to Combat Racial and Cultural Trauma and Promote Living Well." *Cultural Diversity and Ethnic Minority Psychology* 25, no. 4 (2019): 553–65.

Snowshoe, Angela. "The Cultural Connectedness Scale and Its Relation to Positive Mental Health among First Nations Youth." PhD diss., University of Western Ontario, 2015. http://ir.lib.uwo.ca/etd/3107.

Snowshoe, Angela, Claire V. Crooks, Paul F. Tremblay, Wendy M. Craig, and Riley E. Hinson. "Development of a Cultural Connectedness Scale for First Nations Youth." *Psychological Assessment* 27, no. 11 (2015): 249–59.

Sotero, Michelle. "A Conceptual Model of Historical Trauma: Implications for Public Health Practice and Research." *Journal of Health Disparities Research and Practice* 1, no. 1 (2006): 93–108.

Wallace, Anthony F. C. "Revitalization Movements." *American Anthropologist* 58, no. 2 (1956): 264–81.

Wallerstein, Nina, and Bonnie Duran. "Community Based Participatory Research Contributions to Intervention Research: The Interaction of Science and Practice to Improve Health Inquiry." *American Journal of Public Health* 100, no. S1 (2010): S40–S46.

Yuen, Tina, Alice N. Park, Serena D. Seifer, and Devon Payne-Sturges. "A Systematic Review of Community Engagement in the US Environmental Protection Agency's Extramural Research Solicitations: Implications for Research Funders." *American Journal of Public Health* 105, no. 12 (2015): e44–e52.

Part III

Community Engagement beyond the US Settler Academy

Courts, Libraries, Laboratories, and Living History Museums

Chapter 8

Historians as Expert Witnesses
for Tribal Governments

JOHN P. BOWES

At the annual conference of the Organization of American Historians
held in New Orleans in April 2017, Professor Richard White spoke as
part of a plenary session titled "Historians in Court." Since the late 1970s,
White has served as an expert witness in at least four different court
cases dealing with federal recognition and treaty rights for various Native
American tribes. White noted in his remarks that treaty lawyers and historians "want different things from the past, and in a treaty case we need
to find a place where our concerns converge."[1] While true, his statement
is only one strand in the larger tapestry of ideas encompassing the work
historians perform as experts in legal proceedings. In my experience as
an expert witness, the challenges of the work are greater than narrowing
the gulf between legal and historical perspectives on the past. If retained
by a tribe or tribes, expert witnesses also represent Native nations and,
in this sense, we must endeavor to be collaborative. Should such expert
witnesses double as advocates? Should we simply label it work for hire?

In the following pages, I seek to address those questions within
both the broad context of expert witness employment and my personal
experiences in the world of litigation. The legal realm has been a critical
arena of ethnohistorical production and analysis since 1946, when Congress
passed legislation creating the Indian Claims Commission (ICC). The ICC

established a process intended to resolve tribal claims of treaty fraud. The founding legislation for the ICC granted tribes a five-year window to file claims against the United States. Tribes now had a defined process through which they could seek financial remuneration from the United States for underpayment on lands ceded through treaties from 1789 to 1871 or for outright fraud in the negotiation and ratification of treaties. This initial time frame of five years proved vastly insufficient to address the claims filed, however, and the commission did not conclude its work until 1978.

Congress authorized the ICC to compensate defrauded tribes monetarily, but it did not allow the ICC to change title to or otherwise restore lands to tribes, no matter how egregious the swindle. Although perhaps not initially envisioned as such, the process became adversarial. Claims activities quickly resembled court cases in which tribal attorneys and expert witnesses faced off against their federal counterparts. Both the commission and the claimant tribes called upon the expertise of anthropologists, archaeologists, and historians to sort through the histories of land claims and transfers of territories. The ICC relied on these scholarly experts to determine the claims of tribes to the regions affected by the treaties in question. Their work not only led to the development of the methodology known as ethnohistory, but also connected this ethnohistorical scholarship to litigation involving Native American tribes from that point forward.[2]

The participation of academics in litigation did not end with the dissolution of the commission in the late 1970s. Indeed, scholars continued to enter the legal realm, and everything I have experienced in my own career indicates that the nature of litigation involving Indian tribes ensures the ongoing participation of academics for decades to come. As more tribes obtain the financial resources and more law firms acquire expertise in American Indian law, the cases filed in the federal court system proliferate. The number of scholars involved in such cases, whether hired by the defendants or the plaintiffs, has increased accordingly.

My introduction to this work came in the late summer of 2007 when I received a call from a Minneapolis-based attorney who wanted to discuss possible employment related to my particular areas of research and writing. This lawyer requested my assistance as an expert witness on a case in which the Saginaw Chippewa Indian Tribe of Michigan sought to resolve a reservation boundary dispute with the state of Michigan. In the years since that first call, I have completed research and written affidavits or reports in five different cases. Most recently, in addition to ongoing litigation involving the Saginaw Chippewas, I have submitted an expert witness report and endured a deposition in a case filed by the Little Traverse Bay Bands of Odawa in

Michigan. Endured is a word I choose purposefully, for the deposition experience requires focused stamina as opposing attorneys probe your assessment of the events and concepts involved in the case. Sentences and paragraphs I wrote as part of past book projects became fodder for legal dissection. In my case the deposition lasted a total of ten and a half hours over two days. At the conference table with me were a stenographer, two attorneys representing the state of Michigan, and the two attorneys representing the Little Traverse Bay Bands. Their past, present, and future were the reason for this gathering at a Hampton Inn in Lexington, Kentucky, but the Odawas themselves were not in the room.

Although scholars have written about the role of an expert witness in general, the purpose of this essay is to assess expert witness work within the context of community engagement or collaboration with Native American tribes.[3] I will specifically address the work of scholars hired either by a particular tribe or by the attorneys representing that Native nation. It is an assessment of collaboration within a legal context, and not simply an examination of expert witness work on a comprehensive level.

We must start, then, with the principle of collaboration and the ways in which it has been defined or described. At the annual meeting of the American Anthropological Association in 1999, Professor Glenn Hinson stated that "true collaboration entails a sharing of authority and a sharing of visions. . . . Sharing authority and visions means inviting consultants to shape form, text, and intended audience."[4] Hinson's description fits much of what we understand about community-engaged scholarship. Yet Hinson's definition is not the only one worth considering. Amy E. Den Ouden writes of "histories with communities" as a term that "evokes engagement, collaboration, advocacy, even political activism." In this way, she emphasizes "history-making, or historical production, as a political and social—as well as intellectual or academic—project." In addition, Den Ouden asserts, "To be a student of how community-based histories and knowledge are sustained over many decades and centuries, means that there will be many occasions when you must listen only." Information provided in any collaborative process is not always meant for distribution or publication beyond a community or personal relationship. Outside academics must not assume that a shared story equals permission to publish the same. Sometimes the story is intended for the listener alone.[5]

Collaboration can occur with communities and with individuals. The power and importance of relationships and engagement on an individual level is displayed effectively by the Canadian anthropologist Julie Cruikshank in the collaborative book *Life Lived like a Story*. Cruikshank discusses in detail the process in which she engaged to make sure the words recorded and published were those that properly reflected the narratives crafted by the Athapaskan and Tlingit elders Angela Sidney, Kitty Smith, and Annie Ned through their stories. One challenge Cruikshank noted regarding her work with Kitty Smith was "to pull together various narrative elements to reflect minimal Western expectations about life history while showing how, in her [Kitty's] view, traditional stories provide a precise, reflective way of accounting for a life well lived."[6] In Cruikshank's telling, it took time for her to understand the frameworks built by the three women with whom she worked. They knew the stories and the structure that would best reflect their lives, and Cruikshank eventually recognized the necessity of surrendering her preconceived notions about matters like the sequence of events to the narratives they created.

The learned wisdom and perspectives of Hinson, Den Ouden, and Cruikshank reveal common principles, and two deserve particular emphasis. It is necessary to understand where authority rests in the collaborative process. Following Cruikshank's lead, academics seeking to engage with an individual or a community should surrender the reins of whatever agenda sparked the project to achieve true collaboration. Respect and responsibility must be at the heart of such collaborations. "From the start," Rodney Frey remembers from his relationships with a Crow and Schitsu'umsh elder respectively, "they asked what I intended to do with that which was entrusted to me."[7] The information provided and developed over the course of collaboration is not always for public consumption. Collaborative researchers build trust with their interlocutors by respecting a community's desire for cultural privacy.

Nor does a community's right to cultural privacy have a statute of limitations, a point made clear by the Acoma Pueblo in its dispute with scholar Peter Nabokov. In 2015, Penguin Books and its subsidiary Viking Press published two books—*How the World Moves: The Odyssey of an American Indian Family* and *The Origin Myth of Acoma Pueblo*—and a controversy erupted over both the manner in which they were released and their content.[8] In *The Origin Myth of Acoma Pueblo*, Nabokov presented an updated edition of a volume first published by the Bureau of American Ethnology in 1946 and whose foundation was stories provided by two Acoma men who had been banished from their community.[9] The governor of Acoma in 2015, Hon. Fred S. Vallo, Sr., took specific aim at the fact that Nabokov had not followed through on his apparent promise to submit the manuscript for review to the tribal council. In addition, according to Vallo, the initial Pueblo source for the BAE volume "never

had the permission of the pueblo to impart any Acoma sacred information to anyone, much less to the Bureau of Ethnology for publication."[10]
From the Acoma perspective, then, Nabokov's actions compounded a
preexisting breach of trust.

Matters of authority and respect must be at the heart of any kind of
collaboration, regardless of timing. Yet, while those two critical points may
shape our understanding of collaboration, the principles are not so easily
applied within the context of litigation and the rules of a courtroom. Native
needs and narratives do not have the same power in encounters with the
legal world and within the structures established by the Western legal system.
Noted ethnohistorian and frequent expert witness Helen Hornbeck Tanner
once commented that her experience "has taught me that the law is opposed
to history; that history and law are in a state of perpetual warfare in the
courts of law."[11] Tanner first entered a courtroom in the early 1960s as an
expert witness in ICC cases, and while some particulars changed over the
course of her nearly four decades of work, at first glance her observations
of the tension between history and law resonate in the present.

Yet, the relationship between history and the law is more entangled
than Tanner's words imply. It is more accurate to say that Native histories
and the law are at odds while the histories of colonizers have shaped and
reinforced the legal frameworks of the American system. Federal Indian
law is grounded in rulings like the 1823 *Johnson v. M'Intosh* decision that
embedded the doctrine of discovery into Supreme Court precedent. Before
an Indian tribe has entered a courtroom, then, the established law states
that they and their ancestors only had the right to occupy the land, not
to own it.[12] The legal framework created by the Supreme Court decisions
of the 1800s also reflects the racial prejudices that shaped those same
rulings. "While the Supreme Court no longer openly describes Native
Americans in pejorative terms in modern opinions," Walter Echo-Hawk
observes, "it commonly relies upon and gives effect to older cases that
turn on such descriptions."[13] Contrary to Tanner's assertion, therefore, not
all history is in conflict with the law. Instead, some of the most enduring
precedents owe their existence to histories of conquest and colonization
and, just as important, have yet to be overturned. The American legal
system is built on rules, processes, and precedents made by the colonizer,
not by the colonized.

The precise language and rules of legal practice and its demands were
never so clear to me as when I sat through my first deposition as an expert
witness. To prepare me for the questioning, the attorneys with whom I

work hammered into my head a constant refrain to deploy during depositions: "I am answering as a historian and not as a lawyer." Tribal attorneys assured me that they would object to any question that appeared to require a legal conclusion. As a result, I framed all of my answers with the caveat that I had trained as a historian and not a lawyer. I did not purport to use words like diminish or candor in ways that opposing counsel might argue indicated I was speaking beyond my expertise. I am not qualified to testify as an attorney. To the degree that my words have weight within a legal setting, their weight is relative to my expertise as a historian.

Even so, courtroom obstacles do not arise simply from the gulf between legal and historical perspectives. Conflict also exists due to more unique characteristics of tribal litigation. "I really believe," Helen Tanner argued, "that Anglo-Saxon law, because of its imbedded value system, is fundamentally incapable of reaching decisions that achieve justice in Indian terms." She even advocated for what she described as an Indian Law Center that might help "put the 'Indian' back into Indian law."[14] Jack Campisi similarly illustrated the disconnect between Western law and a Native perspective within his account of the 1970s court case *Mashpee Tribe v. New Seabury, et al.* In that case the Mashpee sued to recover land on Cape Cod in Massachusetts that they argued had been taken in contradiction of federal law. However, a decision on that issue also centered on whether or not the Mashpee constituted a tribe, and therefore the case and court hearings included discussions of the Mashpee's historical and contemporary status. Vine Deloria, Jr., called as an expert witness in the case, was asked to define the meaning of "tribe" for the court. He found it difficult to respond to this request, explaining that, Native people "don't make the distinctions you do in the Anglican [Anglo] world, religious, political, and everything else."[15]

Knowing what collaboration can and should mean, and recognizing the broader tensions at play between Native histories and the legal world, the central question remains—To what extent do expert witnesses fit into the range of what we term collaboration or community engagement? The remainder of my essay focuses on three main points. First, I discuss the manner in which Richard White and Helen Tanner's similar assessments that treaty lawyers and historians "want different things from the past" fits my own experience. Second, I assess the opportunities for community engagement that do exist during the course of a historian's participation in tribal litigation. Finally, I examine the impact of the material produced within the context of casework for the larger tribal community.

Lawyers want clarity from the past. They want simple and definitive lines drawn in historical narratives that can be used to connect the past to the present. Historians famously revel in complicating these familiar narratives. This is not a new issue, nor is it limited to the interactions between scholars and treaty lawyers. In the course of my work for the Little Traverse Bay Bands, I came across a letter written in 1948 by an Odawa man from Petoskey, Michigan, named Robert Dominic. Dominic was writing to another Odawa man named Cornelius Bailey regarding their efforts to petition the recently created Indian Claims Commission on behalf of the Odawas of northern Michigan. This particular ICC claim had been filed by an organization called the Northern Michigan Ottawa Association, which Robert Dominic helped found in 1948 and led until his death in 1976. Dominic and his wife Waunetta used the ICC process as well as the federal courts to relitigate treaties signed by their ancestors between 1795 and 1836. For most of their adult lives, then, Robert and Waunetta fought not only for treaty rights but also for the broader acknowledgment that federal government efforts to remove, assimilate, and dispossess the Odawas of Michigan had failed. At the early stages of their ICC claims process their efforts included procuring the oral histories of Odawas throughout northern Michigan. In the fall of 1948, Robert Dominic had some advice for Cornelius Bailey, based largely on observations of the early experiences of the Sault Ste. Marie Ojibwes with the ICC. "Waunetta Dominic and John Ance attended the first day of the hearings," Robert wrote, "and from their report our Ottawa witnesses had better know something about those old treaties when the Ottawa hearings are held. Their stories have to be definite, you can't say maybe, I think so, etc."[16]

At the first reading of those words, I was struck by the manner in which Dominic expressed the need to coach his peers to be precise in their interactions with the commission. The ICC, in some of its early responses to the petitions filed in its office requested revisions to the written claims that would make things more "certain and definite," whether the information was related to the treaties consulted or the people involved in filing the petition. Not surprisingly, at least to anyone familiar with such dealings, this congressional commission gave priority to written documents, material objects, and the authoritative opinions of non-Indian academic experts. As Dominic noted, the commission did not want to hear "maybe" or "I think," especially when its members were already disinclined to grant credibility to oral histories. In the 1940s, the Odawas of northern Michigan, like tribal communities throughout the United States, were adjusting to yet another Western legal context where lawyers and judges did their best to draw clear lines in and around what was and is a more complicated history of land use and tribal relations.

Yet it is not merely an issue of clarity. Helen Tanner observed in the process of providing testimony in a treaty rights case in 1978, "I'm always worried about the legal mind handling historical data. Strange things seem to happen." As she discussed the manner in which archaeological evidence indicated the continuities of Indigenous cultures in the Great Lakes region into the nineteenth century, she apparently lectured the assistant state attorney of Michigan "as if he were an unruly student who refused to accept what she considered logical conclusions."[17]

Helen Tanner was right. In my experience, litigation involving treaty rights and tribal sovereignty often diminishes the complex nature of the historical past. To meet the standards of the imposed Western legal frameworks, attorneys desire unambiguous statements as part of a process that tends to undermine sophisticated analysis. And, as discussed earlier, that desire is shaped by the demands of the legal realm within which they operate. The courtroom's distaste for the gray areas in which historians thrive—its declared need for objectivity—deepens the barrier between history and law.[18] Ignorance compounds that barrier between the disciplines. For example, judges who seek to frame treaty discussions within a context more familiar to them may approach the issue within a framework of contract law that is a foundation of their legal education.

A December 2011 hearing involving the National Labor Relations Board (NLRB) and an adjudication of its authority on Indian reservations illustrated well the obstacles presented by unfamiliarity with Indian law and history. Jurisdictional issues related to employee and employers have become increasingly prominent in the past twenty years. Casinos that operate on trust lands employ more and more non-Natives. Consequently, the NLRB has sought to extend its authority first granted under the National Labor Relations Act of 1935. In this instance, then, a federal agency was asserting its perceived right to enforce its rules on Indian lands. Native nations have pushed back, arguing that the NLRB actions compromised their sovereignty. They ground their argument in treaties signed in the nineteenth century. The case with which I was involved concerned the Saginaw Chippewa Indian Tribe of Michigan. During the course of that experience, I was particularly struck by how the expression and explanation of treaty rights was hindered by the lack of knowledge as much as by a faulty system. The implementation of treaty rights is impeded by a legal system that not only seeks a clear-cut explanation, but also at times demonstrates a remarkable degree of ignorance of Native American law. At one point, for example, the judge overseeing that December 2011 hearing made clear what shaped his perception of the issues at stake. When the topics of nineteenth-century treaties arose, he stated that "agreements are generally construed from an objective standpoint." A contract is a contract, and, as long as its terms are clearly stated, the interpretation of that contract should be limited.[19]

The judge's statement demonstrated that he was not familiar with what are known as the canons of treaty construction. Neither was the NLRB attorney, who had objected to witness testimony describing how the Saginaw Chippewas would have understood the treaty they signed in 1855. The canons of treaty construction are particular to Indian law and thus distinct from the contract law more familiar to the presiding judge and opposing counsel. The canons are the critical principles federal courts are supposed to utilize when interpreting Indian treaties. Among these canons are "Courts interpret Indian treaties to achieve the intent of the parties; they read them broadly in favor of the tribe; they resolve ambiguous expressions in favor of the tribe; they interpret treaties as the Indians would have understood the treaty and negotiations; and they consider the history and circumstances behind a treaty."[20] Because of her ignorance of those canons, the NLRB attorney was at a bit of a loss to grasp the testimony provided by the linguist with particular expertise in Ojibwe. To be more specific, she stated, "I just have not heard what the tribes were thinking of in terms of in 1855, how that is any way relevant to trying to decide the jurisdictional issue."[21] However, because of the canons of construction, the thoughts of the Ojibwes and their interpretation of the treaty at the time of its negotiation was crucial to the case.

This scene indicates that in the production of information for litigation—affidavits, depositions, expert witness reports, and testimony—the standard set by the system remains one based on a Western legal framework and thought process. That standard existed for testimony provided for ICC dockets in the 1950s, and it has not dramatically changed in the present day. Advances in ethnohistorical scholarship are not typically reflected in courtroom interpretations and legal decisions. As discussed earlier, this Western legal framework is not just an expression of documentation or standards of testimony. The principles embedded in the workings of American courtrooms most often have been plucked from a historical narrative that has elevated European discovery over Indigenous inhabitation and Western "civilization" over Native "savagery." Officers of the court are not aware of the canons of treaty construction because that knowledge is not prioritized in the practice of their craft.

The knowledge and standards privileged by the legal system have consequences for the points of community engagement arising from a historian's participation in tribal litigation. My experience thus far has been mixed. In the first cases for which I was hired, I met infrequently, if at all, with members of the Native nation whose interests I had been asked to represent. Instead, my interactions were limited primarily to one or two tribal attorneys and the lawyers hired by the tribe who subsequently retained my services. That initial experience made me see working in a legal context as a heavily mediated collaboration at best. It appeared that scholars like me would more often than not work on behalf of tribal interests without interacting on more personal or even professional terms with members of the affected community.

I am a historian by training and my knowledge of treaties signed in the nineteenth century often defines my role in these cases. My directives and the scope of my research are more limited, perhaps, than that of an anthropologist hired as an expert witness. Indeed, as I was searching for various perspectives on this topic, I found a piece of advice from Douglas Mertz, an Alaskan attorney whose practice includes American Indian legal matters. "Keep a little distance from your clients," Mertz stated in a paper he delivered at the annual conference of the Alaska Anthropological Association in 1994. That distance matters, because "the impressive expert witness is the one who projects objectivity even while supporting the views of the client." In part, Mertz is focused on advising experts to maintain their intellectual integrity when dealing with attorneys who may or may not want the scholar to manipulate their report to serve the client's interests. But he is also warning anthropologists specifically that a close relationship with the people they serve may be something that can give the appearance of compromising the conclusions they bring to the courtroom.[22]

This notion of distance in the cause of principled objectivity initially framed my understanding of the work I was asked to do. As an expert witness, I am contacted by attorneys, but my employer is technically the tribe. Typically, I am asked to conduct research and provide analysis in response to a specific question or set of questions. More recent litigation experiences have provided more opportunities for contact and communication with the tribe bringing the case on which I am working and its citizens. The research phase provides the most opportunities to engage with individuals, and at various times I have obtained information from tribal archives, met with tribal councils, and toured reservation lands with tribal members.

Despite the heartening shift in this direction, however, even these interactions and communications do not alter the overarching dynamic at play within a legal framework. At its core this remains a mediated relationship, and no number of visits or interviews will change that fact. The association between the expert witness and the tribe is never free from the legal framework within which it operates. The question I have been asked to research will not change based on what the community or an individual might want to know. My research and analysis support one piece of a larger legal proceeding, and the purpose of my report fits the contours of a legal strategy. Information I obtain from tribal members affects the conclusions I am able to draw but the particular desires of any tribal member will not eliminate procedures established by the Western legal process. As a historian, I am obligated to adhere to the principles of my discipline. This means that I should follow the accumulated evidence where it leads me, and I should not ignore or omit evidence that does not support or appears to contradict my interpretation.[23] I make the arguments that the information I gather allows me to make, and I do not shape my conclusions based on what the tribe or the attorneys want me to say. Nevertheless, my report exists because of a court case, and thus its existence is shaped by the legal world it is made to inhabit.

However, the law is not all-powerful. Like any expert witness, I have the obligation to behave respectfully and act with integrity. Though this work may not represent what we defined earlier as true collaboration, I still have an obligation to do what I can to engage with the tribe on whose case I am working. This is the responsibility we have as scholars and as people. I need to initiate contact with members of the communities I am serving and not surrender to the idea that my relationship must be mediated. Nothing in any of my contracts prohibits communication, and I am granted a certain measure of allowable expenses for research and travel. In short, there is room for engagement within the process, and I can utilize that space to be a more respectful, responsible, and effective expert witness.

Community engagement must be appropriate and purposeful, which brings this essay to its concluding point—namely, the impact of the information and analysis produced by expert witnesses. Court cases produce an extraordinary amount of material, from motions to affidavits to depositions. Each expert witness collects documents and writes reports. All of this material in some way becomes part of the court record. Yet is the information and analysis produced within the context of a court case helpful to the Native nation it is intended to serve? Does the information go anywhere other than the files of the court and the attorneys who are parties to the case? Who benefits from the documentation that is retrieved in the course of the process, and to what extent do expert reports end up in the hands of those who might benefit from them outside of the legal context? And, perhaps most importantly, how helpful is such information when it is simply one more example of material produced by an outsider like me, for a specific legal context, and without the benefits of any real collaborative process?

The supporting structures for tribal litigation have meaning beyond the legal process, and therefore my reports and testimony have value. The courtroom has been a critical forum for the defense and assertion of tribal sovereignty for two centuries, and the work produced in that context has weight beyond any single case. The research performed within the process of litigation can also prove helpful to communities seeking to gather information about particular aspects of their history. Both the documents collected and the reports written can support that goal and are not the exclusive property of the expert witness. In that respect, the work done for litigation can and should have life beyond the four walls of the courtroom.

If, once the litigation has finally ended, the terms of the contract allow the expert witness to publish based on the work produced, he or she should use that opportunity to engage more fully the tribe and its members. The responsibility of that relationship does not expire when the court renders its ruling or the terms of a contract come to an end. Among other concerns, information provided for a court case may not be information a tribe or a tribal member wants disseminated to the larger public.

When all is said and done, unless dramatic changes occur within the American legal system, the work performed by expert witnesses will continue to be far more mediated than collaborative. Or, perhaps, as is the case for academia in general, more change will come when attorneys move away from the reliance on non-Indian academics as experts in tribal litigation and promote the expertise that exists within Native communities.

Notes

1. "Historians in Court," *American History TV*, April 6, 2017, C-SPAN, https://www.c-span.org/video/?425540-4/historians-court.

2. Wilcomb E. Washburn, "Land Claims in the Mainstream of Indian/ White Land History," in *Irredeemable America: The Indians' Estate and Land Claims*, ed. Imre Sutton (Albuquerque: University of New Mexico Press, 1985), 21–33; Harvey D. Rosenthal, "Indian Claims and the American Conscience: A

Brief History of the Indian Claims Commission," in *Irredeemable America: The Indians' Estate and Land Claims*, ed. Imre Sutton (Albuquerque: University of New Mexico Press, 1985), 35–70; Stephen Warren and Ben Barnes, "Salvaging the Salvage Anthropologists: Erminie Wheeler-Voegelin, Carl Voegelin, and the Future of Ethnohistory," *Ethnohistory* 65, no. 2 (2018): 189–214.

3. Examples include Donald C. Gormley, "The Role of the Expert Witness," *Ethnohistory* 2, no. 4 (1955): 326–46; David J. Rothman, "Serving Clio and Client: The Historian as Expert Witness," *Bulletin of the History of Medicine* 77, no. 1 (2003): 25–44; S. Charles Bolton, "The Historian as Expert Witness: Creationism in Arkansas," *Public Historian* 4, no. 3 (1982): 59–67.

4. Quoted in Luke Eric Lassiter, "Authoritative Texts, Collaborative Ethnography, and Native American Studies," *American Indian Quarterly* 24, no. 4 (2000): 606.

5. Amy E. Den Ouden, "Histories with Communities: Struggles, Collaborations, Transformations," in *Sources and Methods in Indigenous Studies*, ed. Chris Andersen and Jean M. O'Brien (New York: Routledge, 2017), 143, 145.

6. Julie Cruikshank, in collaboration with Angela Sidney, Kitty Smith, and Annie Ned, *Life Lived like a Story: Life Stories of Three Yukon Native Elders* (Lincoln: University of Nebraska Press, 1990), 165.

7. Rodney Frey, *Carry Forth the Stories: An Ethnographer's Journey into Native Oral Tradition* (Pullman: Washington State University Press, 2017), 85.

8. Alex Jacobs, "Don't Buy This Book! Acoma Pueblo vs. Peter Nabokov: When the Sacred Is Made Profane," *Indian Country Today*, February 11, 2016; Peter Nabokov, *How the World Moves: The Odyssey of an American Indian Family* (New York: Viking, 2015); Edward Proctor Hunt, *The Origin Myth of Acoma Pueblo*, ed. Peter Nabokov (New York: Penguin, 2015).

9. Khristaan D. Villela, "Controversy Erupts over Peter Nabokov's Publication of *The Origin Myth of Acoma Pueblo*," *Pasatiempo*, January 15, 2016.

10. Fred S. Vallo, Sr., "New 'Origin' Publication Is an Affront to Acoma," *Santa Fe New Mexican*, September 23, 2015. The situation is not unique to Acoma Pueblo and is not limited to the publication of stories. A list of publications regarding cultural authority, repatriation, and the struggle to reacquire sacred objects would be too long for inclusion here, but for starters, see Michael F. Brown, *Who Owns Native Culture?* (Cambridge, MA: Harvard University Press, 2003); Chip Colwell, *Plundered Skulls and Stolen Spirits: Inside the Fight to Reclaim Native America's Culture* (Chicago: University of Chicago Press, 2019); Karen Coody Cooper, *Spirited Encounters: American Indians Protest Museum Policies and Practices* (Lanham, MD: AltaMira, 2008).

11. Helen Hornbeck Tanner, "History vs. the Law: Processing Indians in the American Legal System," *University of Detroit Mercy Law Review* 76 (1998–1999): 694.

12. Lindsay G. Robertson, *Conquest by Law: How the Discovery of America Dispossessed Indigenous Peoples of Their Lands* (New York: Oxford University Press, 2007).

13. Walter R. Echo-Hawk, *In the Courts of the Conqueror: The 10 Worst Indian Law Cases Ever Decided* (Golden, CO: Fulcrum, 2010), 42.

14. Tanner, "History vs. the Law," 706, 708.

15. Jack Campisi, *The Mashpee Indians: Tribe on Trial* (Syracuse, NY: Syracuse University Press, 1991), 32.

16. Robert Dominic to Cornelius Bailey, September 11, 1948, Collection of Cornelius Bailey, Little Traverse Bay Bands of Odawa Tribal Archives, Harbor Springs, Michigan; James M. McClurken, *Gah-Baeh-Jhagwah-Buk, The Way It Happened: A Visual Culture History of the Little Traverse Bay Bands of Odawa* (East Lansing: Michigan State University Museum, 2009), 106–8.

17. "Fed Witness Says Indians Fished 1,000 Years Ago," *Petoskey News-Review*, March 2, 1978.

18. The differences between American Indian law and the frameworks of American law originating in Western European frameworks are discussed in Sidney L. Harring, "Indian Law, Sovereignty, and State Law: Native People and the Law," in *A Companion to American Indian History*, ed. Philip J. Deloria and Neal Salisbury (Malden, MA: Blackwell, 2004), 441–59; Robert B. Porter, "Strengthening Tribal Sovereignty through Peacemaking: How the Anglo-American Legal Tradition Destroys Indigenous Societies," *Columbia Human Rights Law Review* 28 (1997): 235–96.

19. National Labor Relations Board hearing, *In the Matter of: Soaring Eagle Casino and Resort, an Enterprise of the Saginaw Chippewa Indian Tribe of Michigan, Respondent, and International Union, United Automobile, Aerospace and Agricultural Implement Workers of America, Charging Party*, case no. 07-CA-053586, transcript of December 14, 2011.

20. Robert Miller, "American Indian Treaty Glossary," *Oregon Historical Quarterly* 106, no. 3 (2005), 490–91; Jacob Schuman, "Indian Canon Originalism," *Harvard Law Review* 126, no. 4 (2013): 1100–21.

21. National Labor Relations Board hearing, *Soaring Eagle Casino and Resort*, transcript of December 14, 2011.

22. Douglas K. Mertz, "The Role of the Anthropologist as an Expert Witness in Litigation," accessed May 30, 2018, http://www.mertzlaw.com/Anthropologist_as_Witness.html.

23. American Historical Association, *Statement on Standards of Professional Conduct*, June 2019, https://www.historians.org/jobs-and-professional-development/statements-standards-and-guidelines-of-the-discipline/statement-on-standards-of-professional-conduct#Scholarship.

Bibliography

American Historical Association. *Statement on Standards of Professional Conduct*. June 2019. https://www.historians.org/jobs-and-professional-development/

statements-standards-and-guidelines-of-the-discipline/statement-on-standards-of-professional-conduct#Scholarship.

Bolton, S. Charles. "The Historian as Expert Witness: Creationism in Arkansas." *Public Historian* 4, no. 3 (1982): 59–67.

Brown, Michael F. *Who Owns Native Culture?* Cambridge, MA: Harvard University Press, 2003.

Campisi, Jack. *The Mashpee Indians: Tribe on Trial*. Syracuse, NY: Syracuse University Press, 1991.

Colwell, Chip. *Plundered Skulls and Stolen Spirits: Inside the Fight to Reclaim Native America's Culture*. Chicago: University of Chicago Press, 2019.

Cooper, Karen Coody. *Spirited Encounters: American Indians Protest Museum Policies and Practices*. Lanham, MD: AltaMira, 2008.

Cruikshank, Julie, in collaboration with Angela Sidney, Kitty Smith, and Annie Ned. *Life Lived like a Story: Life Stories of Three Yukon Native Elders*. Lincoln: University of Nebraska Press, 1990.

Dominic, Robert. Letter to Cornelius Bailey. September 11, 1948. Collection of Cornelius Bailey, Little Traverse Bay Bands of Odawa Tribal Archives, Harbor Springs, Michigan.

Echo-Hawk, Walter R. *In the Courts of the Conqueror: The 10 Worst Indian Law Cases Ever Decided*. Golden, CO: Fulcrum, 2010.

Frey, Rodney. *Carry Forth the Stories: An Ethnographer's Journey into Native Oral Tradition*. Pullman: Washington State University Press, 2017.

Gormley, Donald C. "The Role of the Expert Witness." *Ethnohistory* 2, no. 4 (1955): 326–46.

Harring, Sidney L. "Indian Law, Sovereignty, and State Law: Native People and the Law." In *A Companion to American Indian History*, edited by Philip J. Deloria and Neal Salisbury, 441–59. Malden, MA: Blackwell, 2004.

"Historians in Court." *American History TV*, April 6, 2017, C-SPAN. https://www.c-span.org/video/?425540-4/historians-court.

Hunt, Edward Proctor. *The Origin Myth of Acoma Pueblo*. Edited by Peter Nabokov. New York: Penguin, 2015.

Jacobs, Alex. "Don't Buy This Book! Acoma Pueblo vs. Peter Nabokov: When the Sacred Is Made Profane." *Indian Country Today*, February 11, 2016.

Lassiter, Luke Eric. "Authoritative Texts, Collaborative Ethnography, and Native American Studies." *American Indian Quarterly* 24, no. 4 (2000): 601–14.

McClurken, James M. *Gah-Baeh-Jhagwah-Buk, The Way It Happened: A Visual Culture History of the Little Traverse Bay Bands of Odawa*. East Lansing: Michigan State University Museum, 2009.

Mertz, Douglas K. "The Role of the Anthropologist as an Expert Witness in Litigation." Accessed May 30, 2018. http://www.mertzlaw.com/Anthropologist_as_Witness.html.

Miller, Robert. "American Indian Treaty Glossary." *Oregon Historical Quarterly* 106, no. 3 (2005): 490–91.

Nabokov, Peter. *How the World Moves: The Odyssey of an American Indian Family.* New York: Viking, 2015.

National Labor Relations Board, Region 7. *In the Matter of: Soaring Eagle Casino and Resort, an Enterprise of the Saginaw Chippewa Indian Tribe of Michigan, Respondent, and International Union, United Automobile, Aerospace and Agricultural Implement Workers of America, Charging Party.* Case no. 07-CA-053586. Transcript of December 14, 2011.

Ouden, Amy E. Den. "Histories with Communities: Struggles, Collaborations, Transformations." In *Sources and Methods in Indigenous Studies,* edited by Chris Andersen and Jean M. O'Brien, 143–51. New York: Routledge, 2017.

Petoskey News-Review. "Fed Witness Says Indians Fished 1,000 Years Ago." March 2, 1978.

Porter, Robert B. "Strengthening Tribal Sovereignty through Peacemaking: How the Anglo-American Legal Tradition Destroys Indigenous Societies." *Columbia Human Rights Law Review* 28 (1997): 235–305.

Robertson, Lindsay G. *Conquest by Law: How the Discovery of America Dispossessed Indigenous Peoples of Their Lands.* New York: Oxford University Press, 2007.

Rosenthal, Harvey D. "Indian Claims and the American Conscience: A Brief History of the Indian Claims Commission." In *Irredeemable America: The Indians' Estate and Land Claims,* edited by Imre Sutton, 35–70. Albuquerque: University of New Mexico Press, 1985.

Rothman, David J. "Serving Clio and Client: The Historian as Expert Witness." *Bulletin of the History of Medicine* 77, no. 1 (2003): 25–44.

Schuman, Jacob. "Indian Canon Originalism." *Harvard Law Review* 126, no. 4 (2013): 1100–21.

Tanner, Helen Hornbeck. "History vs. the Law: Processing Indians in the American Legal System." *University of Detroit Mercy Law Review* 76 (1998–1999): 693–708.

Vallo, Fred S., Sr. "New 'Origin' Publication Is an Affront to Acoma." *Santa Fe New Mexican,* September 23, 2015.

Villela, Khristaan D. "Controversy Erupts over Peter Nabokov's Publication of 'The Origin Myth of Acoma Pueblo.'" *Pasatiempo.* January 15, 2016.

Warren, Stephen, and Ben Barnes. "Salvaging the Salvage Anthropologists: Erminie Wheeler-Voegelin, Carl Voegelin, and the Future of Ethnohistory." *Ethnohistory* 65, no. 2 (2018): 189–214.

Washburn, Wilcomb E. "Land Claims in the Mainstream of Indian/White Land History." In *Irredeemable America: The Indians' Estate and Land Claims,* edited by Imre Sutton, 21–33. Albuquerque: University of New Mexico Press, 1985.

Chapter 9

Looking Inward from 60 West Walton Street

Reflections on Community-Engaged Scholarship
from the Perspective of the Newberry Library

BRIAN HOSMER

The Newberry Library's D'Arcy McNickle Center for Native American and Indigenous Studies enjoys a well-deserved reputation for nurturing scholarship in American Indian studies, broadly defined. In fact, it is no stretch to claim that the DMC, fueled by a rich admixture of highly regarded conferences and symposia, workshops and seminars, fellowship programs and informal conversation, regularly fulfills its desire to function as a "meeting ground" for diverse ideas and persons, and an incubator for scholarship and careers. Indeed, the Newberry and the center, profoundly shaped my own intellectual development. I utilized library collections to craft my dissertation, which became my first book. I met key center staff and, like so many, did my best to absorb the inestimable wisdom and experience of John Aubrey, longtime Ayer Librarian, the quiet force behind hundreds of publications, many central to the development of ethnohistory and other American Indian studies methodologies. Years later I had the honor to return as DMC director, fulfilling a professional dream, a personal desire (I wanted to live in Chicago), and Fred Hoxie's observation that the Newberry can be likened to the "Hotel California" ("you can check out any time you like—but you can never leave").

I did leave in 2009 after half a dozen years at the helm, and many enriching relationships and experiences. I draw upon those days regularly as I attempt to respond to changing scholarly and ethical landscapes in and around Indigenous studies. That Tulsa, my home, is located at the confluence of three Indian nations, inside a state profoundly shaped by the "Indian experience," and home to thirty-eight federally recognized tribes that exercise their sovereignty, means Oklahoma can credibly claim (as our vehicle license plates once did) to be "Indian Country." At the same time, the Supreme Court's ruling in *McGirt v. Oklahoma* potentially raises the stakes by introducing the prospect of concrete assertions of nationhood in and among competing sovereignties. My own home sits on a Creek allotment. Neither historical depth nor physical proximity presuppose cordial, or productive, relationships between Indigenous peoples and the academy, mine or others, much less truly reciprocal relationships based upon mutual respect. What I understand as the guiding principles of community-engaged scholarship hold great promise for restructuring relationships between Oklahoma universities and Indigenous communities. And perhaps what I learned at the Newberry, largely through trial and error and marked by missteps, contributes in some fashion to developing understandings of community-engaged scholarship in Tulsa, and Stillwater, where I now work. Indeed, if our shortcomings and mistakes guide better actions for the future, then my story may hold some value.[1]

One narrative begins at a moment of fiscal and perhaps "reputational" crisis. Just months into my tenure as McNickle Center director, and before I had even hosted my first major event, I learned that our second most important source of funding had decided against renewing our series of well-regarded summer institutes for university instructors. If that wasn't enough, the Rockefeller Foundation also elected to redirect funding away from fellowship programs for scholars in favor of humanitarian assistance. Of course, we endorsed that direction even as we considered its potential cost to our programming, and our bottom line. Good news was the Rockefeller grant still ran for two more years, allowing us some time to plan. Still, this combination confronted us with a fairly significant challenge. Though rich in books and collections and prestige, the Newberry is famously impoverished, and relies upon external funding to a sustain its programs. Most of what we did (including salaries) was on "soft money," as the phrase has it.[2]

Lesson 1

Fortunately, the Newberry's abundant human intellectual resources *mostly* balance limited fiscal capacity. Drawing upon their advice and my own experiences in Wyoming and elsewhere (which I will consider below), we pitched a revised program to the Lannan Foundation. Founded in 1960 by entrepreneur and financier J. Patrick Lannan to support "innovative and controversial forms of visual and literary art," the Lannan Foundation gradually broadened its scope to include mounting exhibitions, hosting annual literary awards, sponsoring a residency program for writers, and a program of direct grants. In 1994, and just a few years before relocating from Los Angeles to Santa Fe, the foundation inaugurated its Indigenous Communities Program for initiatives in language preservation, legal rights, environmental preservation, and education.[3] An invitation to submit a proposal followed a personal conversation with a foundation board member and led to a formal letter of inquiry[4] (Lannan does not accept unsolicited proposals). Our idea drew upon existing summer institutes, summer workshops dating from the 1990s,[5] and our Rockefeller fellowships for "community" rather than university-based scholars.[6] My letter specifically referenced "feedback" from the 2001–3 summer institutes, showing "that, had we decided simply to renew our current model, we would continue to offer a valuable service to our profession, and to American Indian communities more generally."[7] Of course renewing "our current model" was *not* an option, but never mind!

Lannan II, as I came to describe it, redirected focus to faculty and staff at tribally controlled community colleges. Though identified as "intention" of the existing program, we had to acknowledge, "if our goal is substantial impact on humanities education in Indian communities, we need to focus even more directly on the needs and experiences of those who actually work in those locations." Drawing upon available studies, some commissioned by *Tribal College Journal* (which became a key partner in publicizing "Lannan II"), we argued, "Those American Indian students who attend tribal colleges before transferring to four-year institutions are many times more likely to graduate than those who enter universities directly from reservation high schools."[8]

But even more critically, we asked for help, and in our proposal highlighted "recent and systematic communications with tribal college faculty and administrators" supporting the "proposed reorientation" of our activities. In presentation to the foundation, I noted, "Virtually all responded enthusiastically to our ideas, and several remarked that curriculum development and professional development ranked at or near the top of a list of unmet needs at their institutions."[9]

We knew this line of argument should appeal to the foundation, as they listed a desire to fund community initiatives as a reason for *dis*continuing support for the original Lannan institutes. And so, we emphasized "studies and communications" that emphasized the importance of tribal colleges. Beyond "providing educational and cultural services," they "often act as engines for cultural revitalization and economic development," dual and multiple roles that placed tremendous demands upon instructors and impacted their capacity to participate in summer programs the Newberry might offer. Since "tribal college faculty typically have demanding teaching loads, are responsible for advising, and in many cases take on administrative tasks that are essential to the functioning of the college itself," we observed, faculty lack time to "conduct research, develop new classes, or produce classroom materials." Moreover, time constraints faced by tribal college faculty rendered "our present model—four-week summer sessions oriented around personal research projects"—unworkable. "Summers are extraordinarily busy in most Native communities," we argued, and research told us "those most likely to find our institutes useful tend to be those with the greatest claims upon their time. Put more directly, tribal college faculty simply cannot be away from home for a month during summer, no matter the evident benefits provided by scholarly programs."[10]

So, what did we do? Many things, as it turns out. First, we requested support for five two-week institutes spread over a three-year period, each based upon a series of interlocking goals that coupled studying important issues under the direction of field specialists with producing "document-based lesson and curriculum materials" utilizing Newberry collections, and disseminating curricular materials electronically. As importantly—to *us* anyway—institutes would become a vehicle for "repatriating, in the form of digital or photographic reproduction, primary source documents" (more in this below) and "creating in effect a 'community of scholars' for tribal college faculty."[11] Upon reflection, this idea of digital repatriation as capacity building for tribal colleges, faculty, and the communities they serve emerged out of several more or less independent conversations. I recall using this term when promoting the institutes to my colleagues and superiors at the Newberry, but I cannot claim authorship. Rather, I drew inspiration from a suite of conversations prompted by the passage of NAGPRA and the uncertainty surrounding plans for implementation, in Wyoming, where I worked. Later, the emergence of the Smithsonian's National Museum of the American Indian intersected with NAGPRA in a material sense but also in my mind and led me to consider the implications, and opportunities, for diverse repatriations of printed, documentary, materials for tribal communities and their educational institutions. By this time, I had already donated my book notes to the College of Menominee Nation, in Wisconsin, and the Tsimshian Tribal Council in British Columbia. So, to the extent I am able to recreate the sequence of events, I had already had this idea in my mind, had named it, but also understand I drew from multiple sources.[12]

Our reasoning offered a bit more detail on presumed purposes and benefits. The center would encourage, but not require, tribal colleges to send a team of faculty members to an institute or institutes. This, we argued, "would offer the opportunity for collaborative work and thus enhance prospects for the production of quality classroom materials." Even more significantly, we proposed to "tailor lesson plans to the needs of particular tribal colleges—and the communities they serve"—by asking participants to utilize Newberry holdings to "build lessons around documents touching upon the history, culture, and experiences of home communities." To accomplish this objective, we promised the "repatriation" of materials that may, in one or many settings, advance the mission of tribal colleges by helping to develop library holdings and serving the needs of community members beyond students enrolled in classes" and committed center staff to "research in Library collections, identifying, and preparing for use primary source documents relevant to each participant's project. These materials would be available for use on the first day of the institute and thus minimize (though probably not eliminate entirely) the need for participants to devote scarce time to individual research." In the end, we again emphasized that "revisions to the Lannan Summer Institutes . . . did not originate in the Newberry Library or D'Arcy McNickle Center." Rather, "tribal college personnel drove their scope, content, and purposes," out of a shared desire to model "concrete, measurable, and beneficial collaboration between Native communities and cultural institutions like the Newberry Library." To our team, this endorsement of the central importance of ongoing and meaningful consultation with tribal colleges was central to this project, and others we began imagining.[13]

We succeeded. The Lannan Foundation agreed to fund the institutes in full, and off we were. Results were promising indeed. Out of twenty-two applications for the inaugural institute, one led by Professor David Wilkins of the University of Minnesota, we accepted twelve. Our annual report highlighted "appreciation for the summer institute and its director, David Wilkins," and, through anonymous surveys, participants shared perspectives on experiences, and results. One participant reported, "I am teaching a survey course on contemporary American Indian issues and will assign many of the readings from our seminars." Another "planned to write an article with sample lessons for high school and undergraduate classes," and a third planned to "create a fall seminar course on sovereignty." To our delight, others predicted, "the resources in the library will find their way into *all* my classes, not just sovereignty," and expressed an eagerness to "incorporate their institute experience within their tribal-specific courses," with one observing the institute "galvanized and focused my thinking on what to teach in [my] Crow Indian Law course," and another commenting that the experience "help[ed] me to beef up course content in discussions of Supreme Court decisions and my approach to the impact of local cases on my tribe."[14]

The remaining institutes functioned similarly. Topics varied, applications rolled in, and responses remained positive, for the most part, to the extent that I was invited to visit foundation headquarters and propose an extension. Here again, we found in Lannan an energetic and creative partner eager to explore its own interests in community engagement. Through the relationships we built, program representatives were not satisfied to simply replicate existing programs. They encouraged still deeper engagement with community partners (perhaps resembling what we now call community-engaged scholarship). We expected this, and arrived with yet another elaboration, this one even more ambitious. So, at the close of the third year, we coupled a comprehensive assessment of the institutes with a request to submit a new proposal. This new idea was largely mine (which may have been a problem, as I will explain) and pivoted around a desire to link tribal colleges with an existing program focused on graduate training and faculty development with and for Big Ten universities. Beginning in 2002, the Newberry hosted and ran an American Indian Studies Consortium. The brainchild of an incredible collection of faculty working in conjunction with the Newberry, the Committee on Institutional Cooperation, American Indian Studies (CIC AIS), offered an annual series of seminars, workshops, and conferences. Largely funded by deans of liberal arts colleges, the CIC AIS enjoyed a successful run and was, in truth, the initiative that drew me to the Newberry and the University of

Illinois at Chicago, where I held a tenured position in the history department, from whom the Newberry and partners purchased half my time to manage center programming. It also was the McNickle Center's single largest source of program and administrative support. Like the Lannan institutes, it ran on a three-year cycle and had been renewed in 2005. In my desire to broaden its impact, and convince the various partners of its value, I requested permission to host a "summit" for tribal college faculty and CIC AIS faculty as a way to consider new initiatives. That event, which took place in 2005, generated results sufficiently encouraging to propose what I came to call "Lannan III."

My letter to the Lannan Foundation requesting planning grant described this "big idea." "The diverse strengths of several Newberry based partnerships offer a framework for considering broader partnerships. We propose beginning with a small step that will enable three very different types of institutions to share their resources: tribal colleges, 'mainstream' universities, and a research library with extraordinary collections in American Indian studies. We have in mind a set of paired fellowships that would constitute an *exchange* of tribal college faculty members and CIC American Indian Studies graduate students. This program would promote professional development, service learning, research, curriculum building, recruitment into graduate programs, and perhaps much more."[15]

Lannan awarded a planning grant, but this is where the story becomes complicated. I had misinterpreted, even exaggerated, the level of interest among our various stakeholders. Concerns ranged from the logistical (How would this be administered?) and the financial (it looked expensive) to fears that this new approach would dilute, even damage, the very successful CIC AIS program. As tellingly, questions emerged about whether this truly served the needs of tribal colleges or Big Ten universities. Was it simply a recruitment tool for universities? Did it replicate unequal power relationships? All were valid concerns and dovetailed with a reassessment of the CIC AIS program that my objectives ultimately precipitated. Lannan declined to pursue the initiative, and it died a mostly quiet death (even as I attempted to resurrect it through a grant proposal to Fund for the Improvement of Post-Secondary Education, or FIPSE). In the end, Lannan III stands as a cautionary tale about the limitations of partnerships and the hazards of single leaders pursuing their own objectives.

Here it should be noted that at the time I contemplated and designed programs for the McNickle Center, I had little to no familiarity with community-engaged scholarship as a discrete methodology, and next to no familiarity with its corpus of academic literature.[16] To be frank, I was generally cognizant of emerging discussions and tensions surrounding the ethics and responsibilities of conducting research touching upon Indigenous communities, and had witnessed some tensions at several of my postings, including the State University of New York, Oswego, my very first academic posting, but was generally ignorant when it came to scholarship and specific practice. Yet I did arrive at the Newberry with a general interest in reorienting at least one corner of our initiatives to more closely align with tribal needs and expertise, and as determined by community scholars themselves. Several experiences drove this impulse. Shortly after my arrival in Chicago, I came to know members of the Chicago American Indian community, and particularly leadership associated with the American Indian Center, the nation's oldest continuously operating urban Native organization. In this capacity, I particularly benefited from working with AIC executive director Joe Podlasek, and Susan Kelly Power, a truly legendary figure in the city's Indian community. Both Podlasek and Kelly attended McNickle Center events. And we often included one or both in our public forums, frequently by having the local drum group, Crickethill, open proceedings. That was fine, as far as it went, but it was also clear that academic programming and activities hosted by AIC were rather different, leaving me with the uncomfortable feeling that the Chicago Indian community conferred a kind of legitimacy upon our programming without receiving equivalent value in return. Collaborations with Native American Educational Services (NAES) College revealed similar institutional and conceptual limitations, as McNickle staff periodically offered classes at Chicago's only independent, private, American Indian–operated college, but we tended not to codesign programming, much less offer initiatives designed by NAES. This partly had to do with the NAES's curriculum and institutional focus, which differed substantially from the library's more traditionally academic mission.[17]

A second influence followed trends in American Indian studies scholarship. I arrived at the Newberry just as we began thinking seriously about "decolonizing" American Indian studies, and the academy more generally. I was marginally conversant in the area, having read, if not fully absorbed, groundbreaking work by Devon Mihesuah and Waziyatawin (Angela Cavender Wilson).[18] My sense of this movement's importance changed with the publication of Linda Tuhiwai Smith's blockbuster *Decolonizing Methodologies*. The ideas Smith articulated so powerfully deeply influenced the scholarly community gathered around the McNickle Center.

So much that "Decolonizing American Indian Studies" became the second symposium organized through the CIC initiative. Like many, I found Smith's observation that "research is probably one of the dirtiest words in the Indigenous world's vocabulary," both challenging and even unsettling, as it identified the institutional and professional power disparities that perpetuated the marginalization of Indigenous communities, peoples, and indeed scholarship.[19] It also struck a chord partly because it recalled Vine Deloria's critiques of academic research, concerns that evidently remained unaddressed decades after the publication of *Custer Died for Your Sins*, and challenged me to consider my role, and the Newberry's role, in perpetuating those power disparities.

A final influence was less direct, but perhaps more relevant to subsequent initiatives. In the late 1990s, the American Indian studies program at the University of Wyoming began developing an infrastructure for collaborative research, mostly with the Northern Arapaho and Eastern Shoshone tribes on the Wind River Reservation. The High Plains American Indian Research Institute (HPAIRI) was the brainchild of Judith Antell (White Earth Ojibwe), a sociologist by academic training, cultural geographer William Gribb, and cultural anthropologist Michael Harkin. These days, HPAIRI describes itself as "an entity that tribes and scholars can access and utilize for both tribally-driven research and for research initiated by UW scholars that pertains to Native American people, their lands, and resources," and emphasizes "many ways for the University of Wyoming and the Northern Arapaho and Eastern Shoshone people to work together in ways that empower tribes, nurture innovation for American Indian sustainability, and demonstrate respect for Native peoples' cultures, traditions, laws, and diverse expressions of sovereignty."[20] HPAIRI's website archives the many projects pursued subsequent to its founding and archives a variety of resources, potentially of some use to tribes and academic researchers.[21]

My involvement with HPAIRI was direct, in the sense that I was an affiliated faculty member with American Indian studies, but also indirect in that I had very little background organizing or carrying out collaborative research. But my research at Wind River, an oral history project documenting work and attitudes toward labor and economic change during the middle decades of the twentieth century entitled "Working and Belonging," dovetailed with HPAIRI's mission.[22] Through "Working and Belonging," I became aware of Julie Cruikshank's discussions of orality and storytelling, and the importance of collaborative research, along with *When They Read What We Write*, Carolyn Brittell's examination of the politics of ethnography.[23] More to the point, spending time on Wind River alerted me to the groundbreaking work of community-based scholars like Sara Wiles, an anthropologist turned photographer who honored the people with whom she interacted, and who, in a real sense, drove her scholarly production.[24] More importantly, through HPAIRI, Judith Antell intended to manage research projects at Wind River as a way of promoting collaboration and ending the unidirectional approach to research that benefitted academic scholars but not necessarily tribal members. This last impulse was less evident to me at the time, and only became apparent after I left Wyoming for Chicago in 2002 and began thinking more deeply about relationships between academic institutions and Native Nations. This is to say that, while I rarely, if at all, referenced HPAIRI in grant proposals or reports, its example always lived in the background, no more so then as we developed a series of collaborations with the College of Menominee Nation.

Lesson 2

Since the time I became DMC director, I had a desire to work more closely with the Menominee Nation. That relationship began in the context of my first book, which considered the history of logging and lumbering on the Menominee Reservation. Over time, that relationship deepened. I donated my entire research collection to the College of the Menominee Nation, a tribally controlled community college, and made several visits to the reservation, and college, after relocating to Chicago. In the middle 2000s, the college invited me to deliver their commencement address, which was and remains a highlight of my professional career and an honor I will never forget. Those visits ultimately generated ideas to link the college with the Newberry and drew upon our desires for the Lannan summer institutes and other similar projects. The Newberry had its objectives, and the college saw funding opportunities through NEH. Certain NEH initiatives prioritized interinstitutional partnerships, which faculty and administrators at the college sought to exploit. So, in the spring of 2003, while we were developing the Lannan institutes, our collaboration yielded "Sustaining the Spirit: Partnership in Fostering a Menominee Centered Historical Inquiry and Interpretation."[25]

Again, I quote from the proposal:

This project seeks to create a learning environment and repository of knowledge that builds upon and sustains the Menominee community experience. It proceeds from the conviction that communities and their members can be empowered through a dynamic interchange between the historic record and lived experiences of community members. This also represents the initial stage of a longer-term collaboration between the College and the Newberry Library's D'Arcy McNickle Center for American Indian History that will be dedicated toward enhancing humanities offerings at CMN and engaging community members in the creation and dissemination of Native-centered modes of historical inquiry. These objectives are consistent with the mission of both institutions and research supported by this grant will directly enhance curricular offerings in the humanities, and provide professional development experience for College of the Menominee Nation faculty, staff and students.[26]

Program design followed this overall concept and reveals some familiar themes. We oriented the project around research in Newberry collections, *led* by college faculty, with the assistance of center staff. This research, we argued, "would advance the College's institutional and pedagogical goals and would include the historical record of Menominee family life, community economic activities (such as the fur trade, regional exchange, and labor activities), human interactions with natural environment, and the arts and material culture as documented in the historical record." Those initial visits were to commence in spring and summer of 2004, and included space reserved in upcoming Lannan summer institutes. A second phase, scheduled for that fall, looked toward identifying specifically "materials to be included in College humanities course offerings" *and* "as the foundation for community exhibits."[27]

Discrete project goals emphasized our determination, as we stated in our proposal, to "*create a learning environment and repository of knowledge that builds upon and sustains the Menominee community experience*" (emphasis in the original), by

1. provid[ing] for the opportunity for exploration of historical materials held in the Newberry Library. The historical material will be inventoried and described with the aim being

to foster access to materials documenting the historical experiences of Menominee people.

2. provid[ing] professional development opportunities for CMN faculty and staff, who will conduct research and benefit from participation in the Newberry Library's intellectual community. CMN faculty and staff will be able to take part in the Newberry Library's Summer Institute for Tribal Colleges. CMN faculty and staff will have access to Newberry Library fellowship opportunities.

3. provid[ing] for venues for interpretative aspects of the Menominee experiences. Opportunities will be provided to engage the faculty and staff in dialog with community historians and actors. This will be to encourage a dynamic interchange between the historical record and lived experiences of community members.[28]

We assessed the first phase of "Sustaining the Spirit" as sufficiently promising to warrant drafting a proposal for an implementation grant. Phase 2, also "Sustaining the Spirit,"[29] anticipated "concrete action toward addressing a strategic initiative of the College of Menominee Nation," identified as enhancing "its humanities education by serving as an active agent in the collection, preservation, dissemination, and production Menominee culture and history." Building on the first phase, the inventory of library holdings, this project also identified a series of tasks:

1. Producing an exhibit on Menominee History and Culture at the Newberry Library for the summer of 2006. This exhibit will draw upon an already-planned exhibition of reproductions of Menominee-related materials housed at the Newberry Library, to be held at the College in the fall-winter of 2005. Significantly, the Newberry exhibit will incorporate materials belonging to Menominee community members, who will be encouraged to donate reproductions of family photographs, letters, and other keepsakes. College-based programming also will include demonstrations of preservation techniques and discussion of CMN's potential role as a repository of community history. By incorporating donated materials, the Newberry exhibit will advance this

partnership in a unique direction, serving as evidence of a dynamic, reciprocal, and ongoing collaboration between the College and the Library.

2. Initiate a survey of Menominee related materials housed in other regional archives and museums. The inventory of resources held by the Newberry Library also helped identify repositories with complimentary collections. Working jointly, Newberry Library personnel and College faculty will extend our survey to include Menominee related materials at the Wisconsin Historical Society, Marquette University, the Milwaukee Public Museum, and the National Archives, Great Lakes Regional Branch (located in Chicago).

3. Research, design and develop additional exhibits of Menominee history and culture, all with the aim of elaborating further the central goal of creating a learning environment and repository of knowledge that affirms the Menominee community experience.

4. Develop curriculum and course materials utilizing Newberry and complimentary collections. Working jointly, College faculty and Library staff will organize and categorize materials and begin producing resources to support College teaching in the humanities. This work will take place at the Newberry and College, and in the form of four two-day working sessions (two at each location). Where appropriate, and in conformance with Library digitization protocol, Newberry materials will be digitized and delivered to College of Menominee Nation faculty for use in courses or public exhibits.

5. More fully elaborate the developing partnership between the College of Menominee Nation and the Newberry Library's D'Arcy McNickle Center for American Indian History. Already, this partnership has yielded significant results. As importantly, it has demonstrated, to both parties, that they have complimentary goals. This project will allow both partners to explore those goals and continue producing concrete results.

Phase 2 met with differing results. Collaborative research into New-berry collections continued and with more focused attention to curriculum materials and support for exhibits. We extended our reach to other archives. But the proposed exhibits never really materialized. The college hosted at least one, but it was largely a local event. That made a great deal of sense, but staffing and time issues prevented a more coherent set of shared exhibitions. What is more, college priorities gradually moved toward supporting STEM projects, moving away from humanities. But, still, as an example of community-driven research "Sustaining the Spirit" ranks as a success and demonstrated possibilities that might be applied elsewhere.

Discussion

Upon reflection, it is clear that our attempts at community-engaged research yielded mixed results. As an aspect of our commitment to reorient Newberry programming toward tribal colleges, the Lannan summer institutes altered the way we looked at library collections, our purposes, and what we could do to attract teachers and researchers. This fulfilled our desire to begin rethinking the role and purposes of the McNickle Center in light of developments across Indian Country and evolving notions of American Indian studies. Our idea to reorient library resources toward curricula and professional development enacted our determination to assist tribal colleges and think of "practical" applications for humanities research. In those areas, we were successful. On the other hand, the idea of "virtual repatriation" now strikes me as naive at the least, and paternalistic at worst. While I understood the potential for digitization to bridge relationships between Indigenous communities, and build local capacity for archiving, research, and dissemination of knowledge, my vision was constrained by what I considered possible given competing notions of stewardship and the still nascent capacity at some communities. While I ruminated about a future where the relationship might reverse, with tribes holding the originals and places like the Newberry having stewardship over digital copies, I felt that moment was out of reach, for many reasons. More directly, challenges associated with holding, and stewardship, of the elements of tribal history and identity are far more complex, and fraught, than I understood at the time. I also failed to appreciate how expressions of sovereignty might prompt a more rapid change to the dynamics between tribes and archives.[30] Moreover, even as we consulted tribal college partners in advance of applying for funding, the idea—at the end of the day—was ours. We still drove the process.

"Sustaining the Spirit" was far more community driven than the Lannan institutes. The idea originated at the college and with their faculty. I followed and did my best to promote the program. It worked at the level of collaborative research, but did it really deepen interinstitutional engagement? Partially. We did recognize, as Keith Thor Carlson argues, "a truly community-engaged scholarship must be not only of benefit for communities and of high academic quality, but it must also be genuinely collaborative and cooperative. Such relationships are built upon a web of cultural expectations and social obligations that ultimately transcend the actions and the personalities of any one researcher."[31] Moreover, had we pulled off exhibits (for which we discussed some really creative ideas!), the impact would have been greater, in my estimation. To our credit, personal relationships drove and sustained the entire initiative. But we fell short in that we failed to "institutionalize" those relationships and so the initiative, and the relationships, expired when I left the Newberry. Yet even as we acknowledge its limitations, I regard "Sustaining the Spirit" as a hopeful model for other similar projects.

As I reflect upon these experiences, I am heartened by the degree to which the ideas driving our programming reflected the general spirit of CES. What is more, we understood, even if our words and actions sometimes fell short, what Adam Gaudry identifies as an even more robust community-engaged scholarship. "I think researchers also must push themselves to a deeper form of engagement with community," he writes, "one that further empowers Indigenous research practice and supports Indigenous peoples in creating research self-sufficiency in our communities." The goal must be to "support research capacity building in Indigenous communities to ensure that community members are fully engaged in conducting research of their own."[32]

From my perspective in Tulsa a decade removed from those initiatives, what have I learned? First, that institutional power matters. As Carlson observes, faculty, staff, administrators, and (perhaps particularly) fundraisers must understand fundamental distinctions between "outreach," "service learning," and CES. To that list, I'd add capacity building. Administrators love service learning and outreach, and for many good reasons. But they need to understand that embracing community-engaged scholarship means ceding power. And we scholars need to educate them. As a related point, ceding power is easy to describe, and endorse, but considerably more difficult to actually practice. I know this from my own work, and the deep sense of ownership I hold over my research, writing, teaching, and even the programs I build (and I use "I build" intentionally for it too speaks to notions of power and ownership). Like many, I try to complicate relations of power by turning over classes to community leaders, artists, and entrepreneurs. This represents a good beginning. Finally, and perhaps paradoxically, given my observations about "Sustaining the Spirit," collaborations not only are complex, but often have lifespans. Several years ago, I worked with colleagues from two other institutions to create the Oklahoma Indigenous Studies Alliance. OISA was designed as a platform for collaborative programming and a way to highlight Native-produced scholarship, arts, music, and associated creative activity. It worked well; we hosted a wide variety of events that, I think, served a vital role in opening Tulsa's arts community to Indigenous peoples and their creative work. OISA emerged through, and always relied upon, personal and professional relationships. But, over time, our several home institutions seemed to lose interest. In fact, we encountered barriers to institutional buy-in, partly, I think, because those entities resisted sharing credit, much less resources. Ceding power is difficult.

But perhaps the better lesson is that OISA outlived its usefulness. It planted a seed and started things, but the artistic communities outgrew us, and don't need us anymore. So perhaps CES also requires getting out of the way.

Notes

1. Jack Healy and Adam Liptak, "Landmark Supreme Court Ruling Affirms Native American Rights in Oklahoma," *New York Times*, July 11, 2020, https://www.nytimes.com/2020/07/09/us/supreme-court-oklahoma-mcgirt-creek-nation.html.

2. I discuss the Newberry's fiscal constraints and their effects upon programming in Brian Hosmer, "The Research Library and Native American Collections: A View from the D'Arcy McNickle Center," *Western Historical Quarterly* 38, no. 3 (2007): 363–70.

3. Lannan Foundation, "History," accessed February 7, 2021, https://lannan.org/about/history.

4. Brian Hosmer, D'Arcy McNickle Center director to John Lannan, May 5, 2003. Personal copy of author; original in the Newberry Library archives.

5. This was a program of Newberry-NEH institutes for tribal high school and community college teachers, which ran at various times in the 1980s and 1990s.

6. "Newberry Library Wants Scholars for D'Arcy McNickle Center in Chicago," *Indian Country Today*, December 23, 2002, https://newsmaven.io/indiancountrytoday/news/education-newberry-library-wants-scholars-for-dar-cy-mcnickle-center-in-chicago/.

7. D'Arcy McNickle Center for American Indian History, Newberry Library, "Proposal to the Lannan Foundation for Summer Institutes for Teachers in Tribal Colleges," September 29, 2003. Personal copy of author; original in the Newberry Library archives.

8. Ibid.

9. Ibid.

10. Ibid.

11. Ibid.

12. "S. Verna Fowler Academic Library/ Menominee Public Library," S. Verna Fowler Academic Library/ Menominee Public Library, accessed February 5, 2021, https://cmn.booksys.net/opac/svfa/index.html?mode=main#search:Expert Search?ST0=Z&mat_filter=&SortDescend=0&SF0=hosmer.

13. D'Arcy McNickle Center, "Proposal to the Lannan Foundation for Summer Institutes for Teachers in Tribal Colleges."

14. "Annual Report for the Lannan Foundation Summer Institutes for Teachers in Tribal Colleges," October 15, 2004.

15. D'Arcy McNickle Center for American Indian History, Newberry Library, "Proposal to the Lannan Foundation for a Planning Grant to Explore a Fellowship and Service Learning Initiative for Tribal College Faculty and CIC AIS Graduate Students."

16. Here, I am influenced by Keith Thor Carlson, John Sutton Lutz, and David Schaepe, "Decolonizing Ethnohistory," in *Towards a New Ethnohistory: Community-Engaged Scholarship among the People of the River*, ed. Keith Thor Carlson, John Sutton Lutz, David M. Schaepe, and Naxaxalhts'i (Albert "Sonny" McHalsie) (Winnipeg: University of Manitoba Press, 2018), 1–38; Stephen Warren and Benjamin Barnes, "Salvaging the Salvage Anthropologists: Erminie Wheel-er-Voegelin, Carl Voegelin, and the Future of Ethnohistory," *Ethnohistory* 65, no. 2 (2018): 189–214.

17. With the possible exception of the Chicago American Indian Oral History Pilot Project, which served the community and NAES. Chicago American Indian Oral History Pilot Project, Newberry Library, Ayer Modern MS Oral History, https://mms.newberry.org/detail.asp?recordid=247.

18. See, in particular, Devon A. Mihesuah, ed., *Natives and Academics: Researching and Writing about American Indians* (Lincoln: University of Nebraska Press, 1998).

19. Linda Tuhiwai Smith, *Decolonizing Methodologies: Research and Indigenous Peoples* (London. Zed Books, 1999), 1.

20. High Plains American Indian Research Institute (HPAIRI) / University of Wyoming, HPAIRI home page, accessed February 7, 2021, http://www.uwyo.edu/hpairi/.

21. Ibid.

22. Brian Hosmer, " 'Dollar a Day and Glad to Have It': Work Relief on the Wind River Indian Reservation as Memory," in *Native Pathways: American Indian Culture and Economic Development in the Twentieth Century*, ed. Brian Hosmer and Colleen O'Neill (Boulder: University Press of Colorado, 2004), 283–307.

23. Julie Cruikshank, *Life Lived like a Story: Life Histories of Three Yukon Native Elders* (Lincoln: University of Nebraska Press, 1992); *The Social Life of Stories: Narrative and Knowledge in the Yukon Territory* (Vancouver: University of British Columbia Press, 1998); Carolyn Brittell, *When They Read What We Write: The Politics of Ethnography* (New York: Praeger, 1996).

24. Sara Wiles, *Arapaho Journeys: Photographs and Stories from the Wind River Indian Reservation* (Norman: University of Oklahoma Press, 2011).

25. "Sustaining the Spirit: Partnership in Fostering a Menominee Centered Historical Inquiry and Interpretation," proposal submitted to the National Endowment for the Humanities, January 2004. Author's personal files.

26. Ibid.

27. Ibid.

28. Ibid.

29. "Sustaining the Spirit: Partnership in Fostering a Menominee Centered Historical Inquiry and Interpretation," implementation grant proposal submitted to the National Endowment for the Humanities, January 2005.

30. A recent experience regarding actual repatriation of a document collection, held for decades by the Gilcrease Museum, to its home nation, underscores the complexities inherent in this issue. The museum digitized this collection and provided a full set of images to the tribal community. But that action, consistent as it was with museum and archival understandings of "stewardship," also replicated, even entrenched, notions of ownership and structural power inequities. Ultimately, the City of Tulsa (which holds the deed to Gilcrease collections) agreed to repatriate the originals, and keep for itself the digital copies. [NB: The story is more complex than I've represented here, and involves some privileged conversations and negotiations, but this summary captures its essence.]

31. Carlson, Lutz, and Schaepe, "Decolonizing Ethnohistory," 26.

32. Adam Gaudry, "Next Steps in Indigenous Community-Engaged Research: Supporting Research Self-Sufficiency in Indigenous Communities," in *Towards a New Ethnohistory: Community-Engaged Scholarship among the People of the River*, ed. Keith Thor Carlson, John Sutton Lutz, David M. Schaepe, and Naxaxalhts'i (Albert "Sonny" McHalsie) (Winnipeg: University of Manitoba Press, 2018), 254, 256.

Bibliography

Brittell, Carolyn. *When They Read What We Write: The Politics of Ethnography.* New York: Praeger, 1996.

Carlson, Keith Thor, and John Sutton Lutz, and David Schaepe. "Decolonizing Ethnohistory." In *Towards a New Ethnohistory: Community-Engaged Scholarship among the People of the River*, Keith Thor Carlson, John Sutton Lutz, David M. Schaepe, and Naxaxalhts'i (Albert "Sonny" McHalsie), 1–38. Winnipeg: University of Manitoba Press, 2018.

Chicago American Indian Oral History Pilot Project. Newberry Library, Ayer Modern MS Oral History. https://mms.newberry.org/detail.asp?recordid=247.

College of Menominee Nation and the Newberry Library. "Sustaining the Spirit: Partnership in Fostering a Menominee Centered Historical Inquiry and Interpretation." Implementation grant proposal submitted to the National Endowment for the Humanities, January 2005. https://securegrants.neh.gov/publicquery/main.aspx?f=1&gn=AD-50003-06.

Cruikshank, Julie. *Life Lived like a Story: Life Histories of Three Yukon Native Elders.* Lincoln: University of Nebraska Press, 1992.

———. *The Social Life of Stories: Narrative and Knowledge in the Yukon Territory.* Vancouver: University of British Columbia Press, 1998.

D'Arcy McNickle Center for American Indian History, Newberry Library. "Proposal to the Lannan Foundation for a Planning Grant to Explore a Fellowship and Service Learning Initiative for Tribal College Faculty and CIC AIS Graduate Students."

———. "Proposal to the Lannan Foundation for Summer Institutes for Teachers in Tribal Colleges." September 29, 2003. Personal copy of author; original in the Newberry Library archives.

Indian Country Today. "Newberry Library Wants Scholars for D'Arcy McNickle Center in Chicago." December 23, 2002. https://newsmaven.io/indiancountry-today/news/education-newberry-library-wants-scholars-for-darcy-mcnickle-center-in-chicago/.

Gaudry, David. "Next Steps in Indigenous Community-Engaged Research: Supporting Research Self-Sufficiency in Indigenous Communities." In *Towards a New Ethnohistory: Community-Engaged Scholarship among the People of the River*, edited by Keith Thor Carlson, John Sutton Lutz, David M. Schaepe, and Naxaxalhts'i (Albert "Sonny" McHalsie), 254–58. Winnipeg: University of Manitoba Press, 2018.

Healy, Jack, and Adam Liptak. "Landmark Supreme Court Ruling Affirms Native American Rights in Oklahoma." *New York Times*, July 11, 2020. https://www.nytimes.com/2020/07/09/us/supreme-court-oklahoma-mcgirt-creek-nation.html.

High Plains American Indian Research Institute (HPAIRI)/ University of Wyoming. HPAIRI home page. Accessed February 7, 2021. http://www.uwyo.edu/hpairi/.

Hosmer, Brian. D'Arcy McNickle Center director to John Lannan. May 5, 2003. Personal copy of author; original in the Newberry Library archives.

———. " 'Dollar a Day and Glad to Have It': Work Relief on the Wind River Indian Reservation as Memory." In *Native Pathways: American Indian Culture and Economic Development in the Twentieth Century*, edited by Brian Hosmer and Colleen O'Neill, 283–307. Boulder: University Press of Colorado, 2004.

———. "The Research Library and Native American Collections: A View from the D'Arcy McNickle Center." *Western Historical Quarterly* 38, no. 3 (2007): 363–70.

Lannan Foundation. "Annual Report for the Lannan Foundation Summer Institutes for Teachers in Tribal Colleges." October 15, 2004.

———. "History." Accessed February 7, 2021. https://lannan.org/about/history.

Mihesuah, Devon A., ed., *Natives and Academics: Researching and Writing about American Indians*. Lincoln: University of Nebraska Press, 1998.

"S. Verna Fowler Academic Library—Menominee Public Library." S. Verna Fowler Academic Library/ Menominee Public Library, accessed February 5, 2021. https://cmn.booksys.net/opac/svfa/index.html?mode=main#search:ExpertSearch?ST0=Z&mat_filter=&SortDescend=0&SF0=hosmer.

Smith, Linda Tuhiwai. *Decolonizing Methodologies: Research and Indigenous Peoples*. London. Zed Books, 1999.

Warren, Stephen, and Benjamin Barnes. "Salvaging the Salvage Anthropologists: Erminie Wheeler-Voegelin, Carl Voegelin, and the Future of Ethnohistory." *Ethnohistory* 65, no. 2 (2018): 189–214.

Wiles, Sara. *Arapaho Journeys: Photographs and Stories from the Wind River Indian Reservation*. Norman: University of Oklahoma Press, 2011.

Chapter 10

The Return of Indian Nations
to the Colonial Capital

Civic Engagement and the Production
of Native Public History

Buck Woodard

During the 2000s the Colonial Williamsburg Foundation, a public history
institution and museum in Virginia, established an American Indian
program to interpret the experiences of Native Americans during the
eighteenth century. Until the formation of that project, Native peoples
were not well represented in public interpretations in Williamsburg,
despite their significant presence during the colonial period. Over fifteen
years after the founding of the American Indian Initiative, Native peoples
are now part of the interpretive staff and multiple Native communities
have participated in public history programs at Colonial Williamsburg.
However, the return of Indian nations to the public spaces of the colonial
past was a journey of conflict, success, and irony for both the museum
and tribal communities.[1]

Through the lens of applied anthropology, this chapter examines
civic engagement with Native peoples in Williamsburg and explores the
successes and challenges of Native partnerships in public history production. The discussion highlights the difficulties in establishing Native

historical interpretive programs at heritage sites and museums associated with the founding of English colonies and the American nation-state, and identifies antagonisms present at these locales, particularly with regard to historical memory and narratives about Indigenous peoples. At Colonial Williamsburg, museum professionals and Native interlocutors held divergent understandings about history, authenticity, and culture change. The foundation's staff needed an education on the contemporary political landscape facing Native peoples. These issues slowed our ability to come to an agreement on Native representations in the museum's public spaces. Ultimately, I argue that civic engagement and collaborative projects require significant infrastructure and funding in order to facilitate long-term relationships between institutions and tribes. Organizers need specific skill sets and experience both in Native communities and at the museum to be able to traverse the pathways of culture and history for the mutual benefit of partners.

Public History and Native Narratives

Public history takes place in formerly Native spaces throughout the United States, in places transformed by settler colonialism. While these places are of historical significance to the colonial encounter, the narratives of settler peoples overlay society's memory of the Indigenous. Thus, for Native people, the public history of colonization ignores Indigenous perspectives on places that were epicenters for culture contact and exchange—locations formerly on the frontier or connected in substantive ways to a frontier dynamic. In Virginia, the venues for public history production are museums, historical sites, and heritage destinations linked to the founding of American society, not remote borderlands or marginalized spaces. Examples include sites of significance to the nation's historical memory, such as Jamestown, Williamsburg, and Yorktown.

Finding ways to interpret Native history within these locales is difficult, because it requires the simultaneous production of colonization narratives (culture contact, resistance, and marginalization) while embracing the historical outcome (defeat, massive culture change, and strategies of accommodation). This asymmetry is burdensome, even to the most resilient of colonized populations. In the case of American Indians, to access the historical imagination of the general public, who today are a global audience and consumer, Native peoples must demonstrate *continuity*—"who we were / who we are"—and *relevance*—that acculturation occurred in both directions and that Indian peoples made contributions to the development of contemporary society. In places such as coastal Virginia—the colonial beachhead of English plantation in North America—Native descendant communities remind the immigrant populations that "we helped the first settlers survive" and that "we're still here."[2]

The emotional response of non-Native museumgoers to such sentiments has currency, perennially reviving politically laden majority-minority relationships for heritage events and commemorative cycles in Virginia. These activities typically memorialize the anniversary of colonial benchmarks, such as the founding of Jamestown (1607–2007), the marriage of Pocahontas to John Rolfe (1614–2014), or the first representative English government (1619–2019). One Virginia tribal leader, Chief Stephen Adkins of the Chickahominy, is often publicly quoted in response to these romantic ideas about pastness, in order to access colonialist tropes for tribal political purposes: "My tribe . . . welcomed English settlers to Virginia"; "the nation owes a debt of gratitude to the native peoples, who provided the environment that helped sustain the settlers"; "it was through the beneficence of these tribes that the first permanent English settlement at Jamestown survived."[3]

Adkins's statements remind the contemporary populace of earlier relationships from the colonial encounter but speak to a broader issue and challenge for Native peoples within the nation's memory.[4] In order to be more inclusive of Native history, the public presentation of Native peoples needs to (but typically doesn't) extend beyond the expected cameo appearances in the national narrative of American exploration, settlement, and the westward movement of Manifest Destiny. The historical imagination of the American past should recognize that Indigenous peoples have histories beyond initial contact or select events that conveniently dovetail with national narratives. The forgetting of specific historical events and ethnic peoples is not particular to the United States nor colonialism in America; societies choose what they remember as much as what they choose to forget. Historical amnesia is a result of produced national narratives, the consumption of settler population histories, and the essentializing of identities within the nation-state.[5]

Moreover, the historical narratives of the colonial population are overlaid by other multiple waves of American immigration histories, which overshadow longer histories of Indigenous people stretching to the present day. American Indians also consume the colonial narrative of events, which they often counter with storylines of resistance. Many times, however, Native peoples are unable to articulate the historical points between opposition and surrender. Hegemony occurs through a process, and ruptures in Native historical memory are characteristic of trauma, loss, and domination. Native histories of earlier times tend to be organized as timeless traditions that have deep connections to kinship, language, and ritual life, and tend to be less concerned with the specifics of the event level.[6] But it is the very Indigenous narratives that do survive—of resistance, defeat, removal, and annihilation—that may obscure earlier historical processes of culture change, accommodation, and agency.[7] For example, among the Seneca-Cayuga and Shawnee, nineteenth-century histories of coalescence and forced removal from the Ohio to west of the Mississippi dominate contemporary discussions about the Native past. As an outcome, these Native histories point to the Seneca-Cayuga and Shawnee removal era, connect them to their contemporary environment in Oklahoma, and situate their "traditional" cultures within the postcolonial period. However, these important oral histories and traditions unintentionally obfuscate intense seventeenth- and eighteenth-century narratives of engagement with British and French diplomacy and trade in Virginia, Maryland, and Pennsylvania.[8]

In my over twenty years of work in Mid-Atlantic archaeology, ethnohistory, and community engagement, I have observed that, to be effective and explanatory, Native public history must address the majority narrative, while allowing Native voices to be empowered and continue an adversarial position. For instance, during the 1607–2007 Jamestown four hundredth anniversary events, a major Native counterpoint to the commemoration of English colonization was the civic engagement and archaeological investigation of the deeper history of the Algonquian village of Werowocomoco, "A Powhatan Place of Power." Seventeenth-century residents of the town, such as Chief Powhatan and Pocahontas, are well known to the American public, but the Powhatan chiefdom and its capital of Werowocomoco, less so. Virginia Indians' participation in the high-profile collaborative research at Werowocomoco reoriented the public discussion away from a solely English version of history. In practice, Native public history rewinds the forgone conclusion of colonization and displacement and provides evidence of continuity and resilience. Overcoming the difficulties of bringing two opposing worlds of the past together for a commemoration in the present was facilitated, in part, by the scholarly partnerships that encouraged and supported a Native-centered challenge to the dominant historical perspective. Scholars, anthropology students, and Native community members excavated and interpreted alongside one another, utilizing an "applied" model of research focused on community engagement.[9]

There are indeed challenges with interpreting Native history in spaces that access America's historical consciousness and national narrative, such as the Historic Triangle of Jamestown, Yorktown, and Williamsburg, Virginia. These locales are the places where colonialism is the most complete. By the very nature of the colonial process, Indian peoples have been eradicated from the landscape, removed from historical memory, and Native spaces completely transformed. Until recently, the heritage sites and museums of Jamestown and Colonial Williamsburg either ignored or grossly underplayed Native Americans' importance at these interpretive spaces. These foundational sites thus perpetuated an American narrative that eradicates Native peoples from public memory. Native peoples' absence from historical museums has been noted for multiple generations, and truly, if the solution were an easy task, many living museums would have adequate Native representation. In order to restore Native narratives to these locales, priority must be given to reestablishing linkages with Native peoples and returning some measure of indigeneity to colonized spaces.[10] How practical or reasonable this proposal may be speaks to the heart of reconciliation and repatriation discussions, and whether the ideology of decolonization is realistic or even feasible at non-Native institutions.[11] Colonial Williamsburg would seem to be a perfect place for these unexpected Native narratives; the colonial capital was the historical arena of much Euro-Indian interaction, and indeed the historic town has significant cache in the American consciousness.

The American Indian Initiative at Colonial Williamsburg

Virginia was Great Britain's oldest, largest, and wealthiest colony in North America. As the first place of permanent English plantation in the New World, Virginia was the geography in which Native peoples engaged, traded, warred against, and made peace with European settler populations. During the eighteenth century, Virginia's colonial capital at Williamsburg was the seat of government for a territory that stretched, at least in British minds, from the Chesapeake to the Mississippi, and north to the Great Lakes. Thus, for Indigenous peoples living within this geography, Williamsburg was one focal point for colonial-era formal exchanges—a location in which the relationships of the Euro-Indian trade could be brokered, Indian diplomatic envoys could ally for peace or war, and territorial claims between the colony and Indian nations could be negotiated. Multiple treaties were signed in the Virginia capital, hundreds of warriors rallied in the city as allies of the British crown against the French, and the Brafferton Indian School received dozens of Native students at the College of William & Mary. However, with the outbreak of the American Revolution, and the 1780 move of Virginia's capital to Richmond, Indian peoples' relationship with Williamsburg waned. As the United States emerged as a nation-state and the frontier moved westward, the center for American Indian political policy and diplomacy shifted to new spaces. Williamsburg became a parochial town within the sleepy backwaters of the Virginia tidewater.[12]

Founded in 1926, the Colonial Williamsburg Foundation (CW or CWF) operates the world's largest "living history" museum, dedicated to the preservation and restoration of Virginia's eighteenth-century capital city. While the institution's educational mission aspires to represent "diverse peoples who helped shape" America, CWF struggled with the inclusion of Indigenous peoples and developing a sustainable Native public history. During the 2000s, CW launched an American Indian "initiative" to counter the lack of Native program development, and to find ways to attract tribal representation in Williamsburg. This change in CW programmatic focus reflected wider national trends of "diversity" and "multiculturalism" in museum settings, often with ethical considerations and community collaborations at the forefront of institutional reorientation.[13]

My work with CWF began as a consulting anthropologist in 2007, and, from 2008 to 2016, directing their tribal relationships and developing their American Indian Initiative. While I formally worked with the institution during that time, I had a peripheral awareness of the museum's prior Native programs and first efforts during the early 2000s, through intermittent training contracts and ad hoc advice to museum staff. From 2008 forward, I produced the initiative's strategic plan, directed the overall research agenda, and managed the museum's Native programming. Operationalizing the project for CWF necessitated a civic engagement with Native partners in Oklahoma, New York, North Carolina, and Virginia. I was also tasked with working with the foundation's development office to attract external funding and donor support. Thus, based on my external and internal observations of the institution over more than a decade, I offer an insider's view of the return of Native nations to the colonial capital and CW as a public history museum. My perspective is informed by my training as an historical anthropologist, but also my lifelong cultural, personal, and social experience living and working in multiple Native communities.

In my initial 2007 analysis, Williamsburg's deficits for Native collaboration and recruitment were twofold. First, the institution had little mastery of, or expertise in, minority historical narratives. Even from within the sphere of academia, Black representation in Colonial Williamsburg (with limited exceptions) was a fourth-quarter of the twentieth century development.[14] In the Mid-Atlantic social history of that late-century era, "constructionist" narratives shifted focus toward the "middling sorts" and the "other half" of common Whites and free and enslaved African Americans. Thus, the histories of colonial-era women, Blacks, and the lower class preceded attention given to Native peoples.[15] Broadly in the Chesapeake region, postcontact era American Indian communities remain comparatively understudied, their postcolonial histories little known, and mostly unaddressed in ethnohistory and archaeology beyond the seventeenth century.[16] Due to the lack of existing research and knowledge, the American Indian presence in Williamsburg was only superficially included in the institution's master narrative and program plan.

Substantive anthropological and historical research completed between 1980 and the 2000s mostly addressed the contact-era Chesapeake and the first century of the colonial encounter, with additional work focusing on the region's contemporary Native "descendant communities."[17] However, between colonization and the recent Native past there remains much needed research on the last epoch of British colonialism, what some scholars call the "long nineteenth century."[18] As one anthropologist describes the research situation, "There have been too few cultural anthropologists, linguists, human geographers, and folklorists available and interested to participate in the broader project of writing the social and cultural history of the region."[19] Recognizing this deficit, historical and cultural research became the primary focus of the American Indian Initiative at Colonial Williamsburg. We hoped to identify tribal groups connected to the colonial capital and consider how we might weave their histories into programming at Colonial Williamsburg.

The second deficit for the proposed return of Native peoples to Williamsburg was that CW officials had little or no knowledge of contemporary Indian communities—those stakeholders with historical connections to the very museum spaces CW wished to interpret. Moreover, museum officials had little sensitivity to long processes of historical culture change and community transformations, nor familiarity with issues of contemporary Native politics. Although there were recently successful "high profile" collaborations with local Native communities that had public-facing agendas and historical representations, CW officials remained insecure and hesitant through the mid-2000s.[20] The diversity of the Native constituents—their numbers and the complexity of individual communities' histories—contributed to the foundation's confusion and initial difficulties in navigating tribal relations.[21]

Despite hesitancy about whom to invite and in what way to engage American Indians, initial museum outreach in the late 1990s and early 2000s to local Native community members proved positive. Virginia Indians recognized the prominence of Colonial Williamsburg and saw the potential for personal or tribal opportunities. The CW staff were particularly excited about the prospect of Chickahominy and Pamunkey interpreters who might make public history representations of eighteenth-century Native peoples available to museumgoers. However, misunderstandings by both parties about the shared past created challenges for the desired outcome.

Museum requests for visiting American Indians to produce "historical" representations were met with Native peoples offering "traditional" demonstrations in nonhistorical dress, many times with a time-flattened synchronic voice, or what may be termed renditions of the "mythic present."[22] In one presentation, Native interpreters flint knapped Archaic spear points (1200 BCE) alongside contact-era (1587 CE) cook pots, the latter based on Roanoke paintings by English watercolorist John White. Tribal members dressed in Plains-inspired fringed elk skins and furs similar to contemporary powwow attire. Discussions included precontact technologies, more recent plant and animal lore, contemporary relationships with the Commonwealth of Virginia, and community affiliations with the Baptist church.

Thus, Native contractors rejected portraying specific periods in time, mostly because their relationship to the deeper event-level narrative was not developed and they were unwilling to accept the "colonial" version of past happenings as explanations of their history and culture change over time. Similarly, they resisted interpreting historical figures, and, rather, preferred to blend aspects of the past (such as material culture) with personal reflections on the outcomes of the colonial encounter. As Laura Peers notes in her review of Native interpretations at historical parks, "Native interpreters have first-hand knowledge of the effects of colonialism on Native lives. 'Playing ourselves,' gives a whole new meaning to the idea of 'living history.' "[23] However, the merging of what constituted "historical culture," as measured by the museum, with what was valued as "traditional culture" by the community, created an unsatisfying result and both parties were displeased. The museum was confounded by the perceived absence of the "historical" and the Indian participants' mostly divergent view of history.[24] This dismay occurred alongside tribal members' indignation over the museum's lack of cultural understanding and recognition of the visiting tribes' political status.[25] Compounding the disagreements, neither the museum nor the Native participants were able to adequately articulate or explain the transformative processes of colonialism on Indigenous communities, circa 1700–1900, and thus sufficiently provide some middle ground for exploring the cultural representations of the present and historical materials from the past.[26]

Disheartened by the museum's rejection of contemporary "traditional" presentations and the institution's lack of knowledge about tribal identities, the visiting Virginia Indian participants retreated and spread a sentiment of distrust and displeasure. There was an unmistakable outcome for these first 1990s–2000s forays into Native public history with Colonial Williamsburg. The interaction produced a level of discomfort among the Native participants—what I term *recognition anxiety*—a self-deprecating perspective that asks, "Are we or am I legitimate?" which may be translated at the public level as, "Are you a real Indian?" In response, Native community members also essentialized the museums of the Historic Triangle into one entity, conflating three Jamestown museums (private, federal, and state), two Yorktown sites (federal and state), and Colonial Williamsburg as being "all you White people at Jamestown."[27] By collapsing the museums into a race-based perspective, symbolically aligned with the colonial encounter, tribal communities in Virginia distanced themselves from public history and saw their rejection of the "colonial" museums as an act of resistance.

From the museum side of the aisle, there were recognizable barriers to long-term projects and collaborations with "the Indians."[28] The institution was discouraged by the unwillingness of the Native population to whole cloth accept the majority historical narrative, and to "play" supporting roles in an otherwise predetermined retelling of the past. Without alternative storylines, either from academia or tribal sources, the lack of postcontact Native narratives in Virginia remained a major impasse. The result of these failed or muddled-through museum attempts at inclusion and collaboration was a hiatus from Native program development. Colonial

Williamsburg, steeped in the archaeology, architectural preservation, and curation of objects and artifacts of the eighteenth century, needed more than a little assistance in working with human subjects. Until this conservative institution was confident in their perspectives, had the "right" approach and personnel, Colonial Williamsburg would forgo American Indian public history.

Enter anthropology. North American anthropology has its origins in the museum setting, so it is often puzzling to those of us who specialize in applied research when institutions that require cultural understanding for education outreach, exhibitions, or programming do not recognize the role of the anthropologist. Historical anthropology is well suited to address the museum issues outlined above. Applied anthropologists are accustomed to devising solutions and strategies for best collaborative practices with communities or groups they study. As a discipline, anthropology has an admittedly checkered past when considering the ethical practices of earlier researchers. However, anthropology is a discipline of critique and reflexivity, and has made great strides in addressing and correcting the criticisms of the midcentury.[29] For the museum, anthropology's continued work with tribal communities allows for an interrogation of past and present Native cultures and lifeways, and, due to our position within academia, a measure of control of both the majority and minority historical narratives. Long periods of time spent in Native communities, combined with our theoretical models, allows for an interpretation and explanation of culture and the historical processes of culture change. Our applied approach merges advocacy with fieldwork, utilizing comparative, multidisciplinary methodologies with ethnographic and documentary research. Practicing anthropologists working within museums and Indigenous communities bring an understanding of Native cultural practices and social politics alongside a familiarity with the museum culture and the needs of academia. As cultural mediators between the museum and tribal communities, we encourage building trust and reciprocity among collaborators through establishing working relationships that seek to meet identified mutual needs.[30]

At the beginning of my time with Colonial Williamsburg in 2007, more than five years had passed since their earlier attempts to develop an ongoing Native American program. In the interim, CWF had consulted the American Indian Resource Center in the department of anthropology at William & Mary, where I worked as a graduate student. The center provided support to CWF in reformulating their approach to Native collaboration and outreach, directing the institution to reestablish communication through the Virginia Council on Indians, to conduct staff training on Native topics, and to organize a symposium on Native public history. We also encouraged CWF to open a dialogue with the Eastern Band of Cherokee Indians (EBCI) through the Museum of the Cherokee Indian (MCI). Renewed conversations with Virginia tribal representatives were again initially successful, as was the public forum on museum representations of Native peoples. In December 2004, the Museum of the Cherokee Indian presented the first full-scale Native event within Colonial Williamsburg's Historic Area, interpreting a war dance on the Palace Green that the Cherokee last offered the residents of Williamsburg in 1777. Through to 2006, the MCI troupe known as the "Warriors of AniKituhwa" returned several times. However, funding shortages and staff turnover at CWF again interrupted these fledgling Native programs.

As I was one of few historical anthropologists working on Native topics in the Chesapeake, CW recruited me to lead training modules on colonial-era Virginia Indian cultures and history. Through their recent years of Native outreach, the institution's leadership not only learned how difficult civically engaged projects could be, but also became aware how few specialists there were working with contemporary Mid-Atlantic Native communities. When I accepted the offer to manage the American Indian Initiative, all Native programmatic activities had ceased, tribal communication was silent, and there was no sustainable funding. Fortunately, the failures of the late 1990s and the deliberate, targeted Native outreaches of CWF in the early 2000s helped improve the overall receptiveness to Native program development and collaboration. An important difference in my approach from those of the earliest CWF attempts was that I broadened the museum's perspective on Native partnerships to include communities historically related to Williamsburg but whose tribes resided beyond the borders of Virginia. These groups are federally recognized by the United States, and per their treaty status, have government-to-government relations. This distinction is important, because the contemporary federal status tribes are the successors of their colonial and federal treaties, some with direct linkages to historical Native diplomacy in Williamsburg. Accordingly, I led CWF to approach tribes now resident in Oklahoma, North Carolina, New York, and elsewhere. Tribal leaders and museum officials alike began to recognize the hemispheric interactions of colonial Virginia with the distant Native communities, such as the Cherokee, Delaware, Haudenosaunee, Shawnee, and Wyandot.

During the next phase of the "renewed" American Indian Initiative, the museum staff provided much flexibility because of their desire for a "solution" and positive corrective to an otherwise stunted program launch. Based on the ethics and methodology of anthropological fieldwork, I established a philosophy and protocol for CWF outreach to Native communities and interlocutors. I provided avenues for Native artisans, leaders, material culture experts, and scholars to discuss their area of expertise, contribute to preproduction development and critique, and suggest potential program ideas. Following an historical anthropological approach, my team accumulated original research on tribal interactions in eighteenth-century Williamsburg, as well as conducted ethnological studies of period collections associated with the historical cultural groups. To match the museum standard for authenticity, and to overcome the lack of public awareness of eighteenth-century Eastern Woodland cultural milieu, Native and non-Native experts on period wardrobe and accoutrements were contracted to design appropriate material culture, based on primary sources and ethnographic collections. These alternative roles for Native and expert collaborators assisted with bridging the gap between frontline historical representations for public history and contemporary community interests and resources. The applied work in material culture became critical for shared institutional and Native community education, dispelling stereotypes and misconceptions, and providing an accurate visual representation for public consumption. These research-based activities occurred alongside renewed and new dialogues with Native communities—a period of relationship building and reciprocity development. American Indian Initiative staff engaged with tribal museums, representatives, and experts well before any frontline interpretations of public history occurred at Colonial Williamsburg.

To the museum's credit, noteworthy resources were identified and allocated to affect the desired outcome of tribal collaboration—despite somewhat of an institutional blind faith that success was forthcoming. Relations with the EBCI "cultural partners"—the Cherokee Historical Association, the Cherokee Cooperative, and the Museum of the Cherokee Indian—were reestablished, bringing Cherokee programming, training, and Native-made products to Williamsburg. By the end of 2010, annual public-facing Cherokee interpretive programs included visiting delegations to the Historic Area, guest lectures, evening programs, storytelling, and participatory activities such as games and dances. Cherokee interpreters, performers, and their families, sometimes upwards of forty individuals, produced historically themed programs such as "Our Bond of Peace," "A Public Dance," and "The Camp of the Cherokee." Each of these semiannual events was well attended by the general public in Williamsburg, with "A Public Dance" by the Warriors of AniKituhwa regularly attracting 750–1100 spectators and crowd participants. The attention the Native programming received from the media and museum guests increased CWF's recognition of the importance and productivity of the collaborative work. From these forays, the CWF development office worked toward finding appropriate private donors and institutional financial support, in order to continue and expand the American Indian Initiative toward year-round programing.

With increased funding and institutional support, I recommended CWF expand their Native engagement to include other nations who were historically linked to the capital city. In 2009 and 2010, we opened discussions with scholars and representatives of the three federal-status Shawnee tribes: the Absentee Shawnee Tribe, Eastern Shawnee Tribe of Oklahoma, and the Shawnee Tribe. Chiefs, tribal leaders, and scholars convened in Williamsburg on multiple occasions to discuss the Shawnee presence in Virginia and to explore an historical narrative involving four Shawnee headmen who lived in Williamsburg as diplomatic hostages during the fall 1774, into the summer 1775. CWF proposed developing a series of scripted theatrical scenes that would tell the story of these Shawnee men and their people in the aftermath of Dunmore's War on the eve of the American Revolution. For the preliminary meetings, I invited Cherokee collaborators from ECBI to share their experience of working with CWF, in order to facilitate these potential new Shawnee partnerships.

As of the 2000s, the Eastern Band of Cherokee Indians were the geographically closest federal tribe to Colonial Williamsburg. When tribal members came to Virginia for special events and programs, CWF covered travel expenses, lodging, and contractual fees for Cherokee artisans, dancers, interpreters, singers, and storytellers. Collaboration between the Museum of the Cherokee Indian and CW allowed resources to be shared and information disseminated, including research about material culture and wardrobe, which Cherokee people incorporated into their historical representations. In contrast to the Cherokee model, whereby tribal members portrayed themselves, our CWF proposal to the Shawnee was to collaborate on historical research and language—but to hire an all-Native cast of professional actors to portray the eighteenth-century Shawnee in Williamsburg. It would be preferable to have Shawnee actors, but, like television and film, Native actors come from multiple tribal backgrounds; the skillset needed for scripted theatrical scenes was acting experience. The Shawnee partnerships were crucial to accessing cultural content, in particular Shawnee language consultants and the leaderships' perspectives about script development. During the meetings of Shawnee leaders with CWF executives, it became clear that the united Shawnee return to Virginia was the first since the American Revolution, and that the opportunity to showcase Shawnee peoples' historical place in the East could be productive for all involved.

Between 2009 and 2014, the CWF-Shawnee partnership produced multiple scripted programs, utilizing historical research, linguistics, and civic engagement as the vehicles for collaboration. The Shawnee scenes of Williamsburg's "Revolutionary City" were titled "So Far from Scioto," "The War Party," and, an electronic fieldtrip broadcast on PBS, "The American Revolution on the Frontier." Follow-up meetings were convened at the Fort Pitt Museum in Pittsburgh, Pennsylvania, tribal offices in Wyandotte and Miami, Oklahoma, and back in Williamsburg. Success from these collaborative projects led to further tribal participation in Williamsburg whereby Delaware, Mohawk, Pamunkey, Tuscarora, Oneida, and Wyandot representations, among others, appeared in programs such as "The American Revolution in Indian Country" and "Beyond the Ohio: Native Peoples of Virginia's Old Northwest."

Between 2009 and 2016, multiple tribal groups returned to Williamsburg.[31] An annual pilgrimage of dozens of American Indian academics, actors, chiefs, interpreters, and tribal representatives followed, to the great satisfaction of everyone involved in the American Indian Initiative. As the projects unfolded, the museum staff (like the public) was excited. They were impressed and captivated by the productions. Charmed by the authenticity, albeit which initially drew upon expected visages of chiefs and warriors, the emotional response of the public and staff were similar. Using research from museum collections and utilizing the real materials to reproduce Native garments and accoutrements provided a level of authenticity to their wearers. Specific cultural content used throughout the Native projects (including Native languages) conveyed the reality of cultural difference, despite the shallowness of interpretation. The projects were visually similar to the realism of film. When Native participants cloaked themselves in the materials and approximate behaviors of the eighteenth century, the "look," the "voice," and the "action" were front stage Goffmanesque. The Native interpretations imitated life so well, they were convincing to the masses, to the semi-initiated, and even to associ-

Figure 10.1. Experts of art history, material culture, and historical anthropology contributed to the construction of accurate wardrobe and accoutrements for Native interpretations. At left, Kody Grant portrays the Cherokee headman Woye (photo courtesy of Jürgen Vsych). Grant's 2014 impression was based on a 1761 illustration from the *Military Commission Granted to Chief Okana-Stoté of the Cherokee by Governor Louis Billouart, Chevalier de Kerlérec* (middle image, courtesy of the National Archives), and Francis Parson's 1762 painting of *Cunne Shote*, Cherokee Chief (at right, courtesy of the Gilcrease Museum, Tulsa, Oklahoma).

ate disciplines in the humanities. For example, a retired linguist wrote to inquire about our use of Indigenous language: "The actors appear to be speaking a full-fledged language. . . . It sounds very authentic." So too, the general public often remarked about the "realness" of the portrayals: "Now we're talking! That's a real Indian." "It's finally nice to hear the true history." "It was so authentic." "They look so beautiful." "1 am so glad we came to see this. They looked amazing."[32] The museum and public were satisfied with the impressions of historical Native peoples, which was no doubt augmented by the realism of Williamsburg's stage for public history.

For sure, the Native projects in Williamsburg impacted the way the museum's staff and visiting general public perceived the colonial world. Majoritarian perspectives about vanishing Indians, their forced removal, and the foregone conclusion of Manifest Destiny were destabilized. The portrayal of an eighteenth-century Black-White Chesapeake "suddenly" became complicated by the regular presence and highly visible "new" demographic. The restoration of Native peoples to the interpretation of the eighteenth century changed the way in which the museum staff conceptualized multiple historical topics, from land tenure to slavery to alliance in warfare; new training materials and extensive reeducation were required. The museumgoers were unprepared to encounter Native peoples in Williamsburg, which underscored the importance and meaningfulness of our collaborative work. We found that the general public were eager to learn more about each tribe's eighteenth-century historical experience, but also were very much interested in the present-day world of the Native actors and interpreters. To assist, I developed a companion moderated program for all of our scripted Native productions, whereby the twenty-first-century cast and tribal representatives could discuss issues important to them and the visiting public could ask questions about contemporary Native communities.

Of the portrayals in Williamsburg, Native participants representing their own tribal communities reflected on the unfettered access to the general public, and the opportunity to be spokespersons for their tribal histories:

And you feel it [American history] is important, so we come to Williamsburg. We [Shawnee] want to be part of that. We want to be part of that history, part of telling our story as well as conveying how it connects into the American story—because we are part of the American story.

It's a great opportunity for me personally simply because, well, I'm Cherokee and this is a story very much concerning the lifestyle of that time and is regrettably lost to some extent in the modern day.

I feel very good about it. It is my tribe's story. I'm Pamunkey. It's just a really good opportunity to come out here and portray—tell our own story—the way we believe it should be.

It's a great honor for us to come out here and represent ourselves to the folks that live in this area—since our tribes [Delaware,

Figure 10.2. During the eighteenth century, "great numbers" of Cherokee regularly came to Williamsburg. Pictured here, a 2010 delegation from the Eastern Band of Cherokee recreates meeting with the governor's executive council in the Capitol Building. As in 1777, the contemporary Cherokee delegations included extended families and "upwards of forty gentlemen and ladies of the Cherokee nation" (courtesy of the Colonial Williamsburg Foundation, #D2010-DMD-0605-2179).

Shawnee, Seneca-Cayuga, Wyandot] were removed from here and are now in Oklahoma—*we* just do not get the opportunity to come out here in the East and tell our story.[33]

The Native actors hired by CWF, who many times were not from the tribes they portrayed, tended to focus on the broad strokes of educating the public about Indigenous peoples. They remarked more often about dispelling stereotypes and making connections to contemporary Native communities:

I'd like to try to be an example of what Indian people are today. Not so much what Hollywood has created, "what the Indians should look like," or in some cases, what society *has thought* "what the Indians are like." So hopefully we're breaking a lot of those stereotypes and educating people and that's one of the benefits of being here [in Williamsburg]. A lot of the guests that come here, you know, they want to learn and that's why they're coming to a historical place like this rather than just going to an amusement park.

There's a lot more Native American culture than people realize. Whereas a lot of people just consider the majority of Indians are all Plains Indians with the teepees and war bonnets . . . there are broader aspects. . . . It's just not talked about in today's society.

We were, you know, human beings. I mean we, we had feelings and emotions, as [did] the Europeans. We went through hardships . . . the humanity of the Native American people back then. You know, we weren't just bloodthirsty savages.

I think it's very important that American history be rediscovered by our youth. I think it's important that we all get from this [scene], and from the different series of [scenes in the] street theater that we have here at Williamsburg, that we are all human beings and that we all need to coexist together.[34]

Despite positive remarks during the 2009–2016 productions, museum faculty and their public audiences engaged with our Native interlocutors at a surface level, in terms of both content and analysis. Some specialists understood the entire project, and obviously those of us who worked together closely to manage, develop, and produce the projects had an intimate relationship with the successes and challenges. But, generally speaking, the majority of the players were unable to control all of the information or see how it fit together, whether because of their short duration of engagement or a narrow area of focus. Examples include material-culture researchers' focus on Native period dress without attention to an historical Indigenous voice; or the lack of knowledge about linguistics and specific cultural patterns; or the required behind-the-scenes diplomacy and management of heritage relationships that allow for the emergence of community-engaged public history. Based on these observations, I have come to believe that the long-term success of these collaborative projects requires institutional investment in infrastructure and management—a deliberate and strategic shift in financial and human resources. To increase Native peoples' presence in critical roles—from the public-facing frontline to research and planning—institutions will have to continue building and maintaining relationships that center Native communities' abilities, interests, and needs. However, to overcome the decades, if not centuries, of nonengagement with Native peoples, both the institution and the tribal communities need ethical facilitation from those few that work closely in both cultural spheres. If properly developed, this tripartite model situates the institution, the Native community, and activist scholars in an "ethical clientage" relationship for "public engagement."[35]

For Native people, access to the resources of the museum and the general public's attention is desirable. However, Native agendas were often not the same as those of the museum. My observation is that there is an extension of tribal historical experience to CWF as a physical representation of the colonial past, another form of the "mythic present" or experienced history, which plays out in unexpected ways. For example, Native interlocutors maintained multiple forms of resistance to settler society through modifying public programs in Williamsburg, changing the time allotment or format—despite the agreed upon plan—or the participation in some activities, but not all.

Those interlocutors with perennial visits to Williamsburg demonstrated an increased historical cultural competency through participation in activities associated with the past, such as using diplomatic language and accessories in dramatized treaty negotiations, learning new skills associated with historical archery or woven textiles, and the construction and wearing of period clothing. Thinking about the past, and narrating the same for public consumption, creates critical thinking about the processes of change and what aspects of culture mean in the present, and what they meant in the past. Questioning the location of knowledge, and the production of knowledge about the past, has led to more than one Native interpreter to consider the lens of anthropology. The museum collaboration has provided some Native people a different window through which to view knowledge of the past. An illustration may be made of one Cherokee man who has worked for the last decade in the public history sphere of Williamsburg and Cherokee, North Carolina. This Cherokee public historian now compares traditional knowledge learned from tribal relations—stories, cosmological beliefs, and practices of daily life—with written historical accounts of eighteenth-century Cherokee, twentieth-century ethnographic data, and archaeological evidence. In essence, he explores Cherokee historical culture and knowledge from comparative sources, forming interpretations of Cherokee life. This configuration of knowledge is no less valid or authentic than "traditional" knowledge, in that "knowledge" is derived from experience, examination, and exchange, but its source no longer emanates exclusively from oral tradition. Few aspects of contemporary life do.[36]

The entrée into multiple modalities of knowledge does impact present-day Native cultural representations at home and abroad, and I have noted some factionalism among tribal members and groups as a result of access to the museum's resources.[37] As well, there is some anxiety from a few tribal members who observe the cultural presentations in Williamsburg, whether as guests or via social media, but cannot decipher their ancestral historical culture or specific historical content; their culture has understandably changed over the last two hundred years, and many histories have been forgotten. There is pride among community members for their tribesmen who "represent" in Williamsburg, but some confusion about the origins of the knowledge presented. As should be expected, Native peoples are agents, borrowing content and articulating it in traditional ways, but, at times, without historical context, and thus sometimes creating syncretic productions and blurring the lines between

Figure 10.3. Haudenosaunee emissaries with their French interpreter reenacting the 1781 march to the Battle of Yorktown during the 2012 public history program "Prelude to Victory" (photo courtesy of Robert Hunter).

the historical museum interpretation and contemporary perspectives about "traditional" culture.

Conclusion

The American Indian Initiative at the Colonial Williamsburg Foundation is a cautionary tale about success. The "direction" of the overall CWF American Indian project became contested once the product was successfully, and repeatedly, delivered. Agents within multiple museums mobilized to capitalize on the "new" Native product. Based on the CWF success, Historic Jamestowne (HJ) soon implemented the "Indigenous Chesapeake" and "The World of Pocahontas" programmatic initiatives, drawing resources and personnel away from the CW Initiative to supplement new Native programs at another historical museum. As a consequence, there again was a blurring of lines between institutions and a conflation of Native peoples and agendas. The museum staffs' overall lack of familiarity with Native communities, and to some degree the methodology of public anthropology, had the consequence of museum officials having little understanding of *how* the CW project was designed and produced. Direct *access* to Native America was mistakenly identified as the source of success for the American Indian Initiative. In this way, museum officials perceived Native public history only relied upon *introductions* to Indians, rather than historical anthropological constructions and long-term collaborative relationships based in the dialogic of civic engagement.

With the recognition of museumgoers' dollars spent on Native programming, the CW public history of Indigenous peoples became commodified. Thereafter was a contest of highly placed executives and individual museums for the Native American product. This competition was based on the desire to have everyday Native American public history in colonized spaces. The institutions were happy with the outcome of the CWF and HJ Native initiatives, but there was little comprehension as to *how* the projects were produced or *how* they might be maintained.

Ultimately, the museums' personnel conflated the "authenticity" of the Native public history product with the source of its origin. The enchanted museum officials, spurred by public comment and financial incentive, were unable to identify that the Native "realness" and "authenticity" they coveted was a construction. The disparate parts of the project were assembled—Native actors, researchers of wardrobe and accoutrements,

Figure 10.4. Special programs and staged performances: 2015 production of "The Beloved Women of Chota: War Women of the Cherokee," with an all-Native cast, including Tonantzin Carmelo (left, photo courtesy of Robert Hunter); Kody Grant and Michael Crowe interpret 1774 Shawnee diplomatic hostages at the "Governor's Palace Ball," 2009 (top right, photo courtesy of the Colonial Williamsburg Foundation, #D2010-DMD-1210-9259); producer Larry Pourier and actors Zahn McClarnon and Michael Spears provide contemporary Native perspectives in "Behind the Scenes," 2013 (bottom right, photo courtesy of Lucie Kyrova).

Native language speakers and linguists, cultural brokers on the reservation, and activists at the museums—these parts worked in tandem with one another for the final product. The "authentic" Native interpretation was not the source material, but the outcome of the production. Due to the confusion about the *process* of producing the "historical" deliverable, there was a misidentification and collusion of the event-level representation for a "true" or "real" access to the deeper structure and conjuncture of culture. Notably, the same misguided strategy of only needing "access" to Native communities was applied during the earlier failed 1990s CWF outreach. The difference rests in infrastructural development; long-term relationship building between institutions and tribes, adequate funding for Native-focused management and researchers, and an applied approach that utilizes field methodologies to the mutual benefit of partners.

As of my 2016 departure from CWF, there were multiple partnerships with state- and federal-status tribes, and established collaborations with tribal museums and dozens of Native contractors. In 2015–16, CWF hired six full-time Native interpreters and hosted annual diplomatic and programmatic visits from Native nations from 500 to 1,500 miles away. Native peoples' public endorsement of the American Indian Initiative project allowed CW to produce highly visible Native programs with positive reviews from majority and minority populations. The program's growth included multiple Native voices within the museum setting, and multiple projects emerged: from theatrical dramatizations, to academic lectures and tribal roundtables, to Native-focused media products, to publications. As a result of showcasing the project's successes, the foundation also developed significant financial resources, in the form of Native-specific donations, grants, and endowments. In 2012, the late Douglas Morton, and his wife, Marilyn Brown, created the Morton-Brown American Indian Endowment Fund at CWF, with a contribution of $2.5 million by 2015. However, with the hiring of full-time Native staff in 2016, the income from this endowment was shifted to support the new employees. Tribal programming and civic engagement were thereafter suspended. Absent genuine engagement with tribal communities, the viability of the program is now in jeopardy.

As a twenty-first-century collaborative project, Native public history at non-Native institutions is a fundamentally negotiated and contractual product. American Indians may continue to return to the old capital at Colonial Williamsburg, in my view, as part of a wider phenomenon of displaced or disenfranchised Native peoples turning their gaze "back east" to old homelands and former centers of tribal diplomacy and commerce. However, the articulation of so many aspects of historical Native culture for the purposes of producing a "believable" or "authentic" public history may only serve *interpretations* within the museum setting. When disarticulated, linguistics, reproductions of material culture, theatrics, and historical contexts established by the museum and tribesmen to be a specific *people*, in a specific *time* and specific *place*, do not allow elaboration on their own. Public history representations are fundamentally interpretative. They do not emanate from the original culture, but rather are themselves constructions, based on forms of triangulated knowledge with relationships to the past and present. Moving forward we will have to disentangle the event level from the conjuncture and be more transparent about the process of public history production. The long-term success of collaborative and community-engaged applied projects will require a fuller understanding by stakeholders, from both sides of the aisle, of the methodologies employed to navigate contemporary heritage relationships. In the interim, the American Indian Initiative model demonstrates that anthropology has a role in shaping this future and helping translate the human condition of the past and present for a new generation.

Notes

1. Throughout the chapter, I use the terms or phrases "American Indian," "Indian," "Indigenous," "Native," "Native American," and "Native peoples" interchangeably, as well as specific tribal names such as "Cherokee" and "Shawnee" where appropriate. There is no consensus among tribal nations about these identifications, except that Indigenous community names are preferred where possible. Colonial-period documents most often use "Indian," "Nation," and tribal names. More recent federal laws and institutions demonstrate the myriad of nomenclatures, each with historical and cultural reasons for their usage: the Indian Child Welfare Act (1978), the American Indian Religious Freedom Act (1978), and the Native American Graves Protection and Repatriation Act (1990) are just a few of the better-known legal examples; the Smithsonian's National Museum of the American Indian, the US Department of the Interior's Bureau of Indian Affairs, and the Native American and Indigenous Studies Association are examples of museum, government, and academic usage. The Colonial Williamsburg Foundation selected "American Indian Initiative" for its institutional effort, in part because of the Smithsonian example and due to the preference of Native communities in the Chesapeake who refer to themselves as "Virginia Indians."

2. Sandra Waugaman and Danielle Moretti-Langholtz, *We're Still Here: Contemporary Virginia Indians Tell Their Stories* (Richmond, VA: Palari, 2006).

3. Stephen Adkins, "U.S. Is Overdue for More Inclusive History," *Virginian-Pilot*, October 10, 2017; Michael Miller, " '400 years Is Long Enough': Virginia's 'First Contact' Indian Tribes Demand Federal Recognition," *Washington Post*, May 26, 2017; US Congress, S1074 Senate Committee on Indian Affairs Testimony, October 30, 2013.

4. For a discussion of contemporary Virginia Indians' use of history for political alliances, see Buck Woodard, "An Alternative to Red Power: Political Alliance as Tribal Activism in Virginia," *Comparative American Studies* 17, no. 2 (2020): 142–66. On Native strategic essentialism in the Chesapeake, see Martin D. Gallivan, Danielle Moretti-Langholtz, and Buck Woodard, "Collaborative Archaeology and Strategic Essentialism: Native Empowerment in Tidewater Virginia," *Historical Archaeology* 45 (2011): 10–23.

5. Paul Connerton, *How Societies Remember* (Cambridge: Cambridge University Press, 1989); *How Modernity Forgets* (Cambridge: Cambridge University Press, 2009). And see Russell Thornton, ed., *Studying Native America: Problems and Prospects* (Madison: University of Wisconsin Press, 1998).

6. For an overview of Native historicity, ways of knowing and communicating about the past, see Peter Nabakov, *A Forest of Time: American Indian Ways of History* (Cambridge: Cambridge University Press, 2002).

7. An example of Native peoples' historical ruptures and strategic narratives of accommodation and resistance can be found in Gerald Sider, *Living Indian Histories: Lumbee and Tuscarora People in North Carolina* (Chapel Hill: University of North Carolina Press, 2003).

8. Buck Woodard, Eastern Shawnee, Seneca-Cayuga, and Shawnee correspondence and field notes (Missouri, Oklahoma, Pennsylvania, and Virginia, 2013–20). Methodological considerations from anthropology, history, Native studies, and oral traditions specific to the Seneca-Cayuga past can be found in Brian Joseph Gilley, *A Longhouse Fragmented: Ohio Iroquois Autonomy in the Nineteenth Century* (Albany: State University of New York Press, 2014), 1–14. For discussions about Shawnee histories and approaches to the past, see Stephen Warren, *The Worlds the Shawnees Made: Migration and Violence in Early America* (Chapel Hill: University of North Carolina Press), 1–24; *The Shawnee and Their Neighbors, 1795–1870* (Urbana: University of Illinois Press), 1–11.

9. I was fortunate to be part of the public-facing aspect of the Werowocomoco research project, contributing to early media interpretations and education outreach (2004–7); Buck Woodard, Danielle Moretti-Langholtz, and Angela Daniel, "Werowocomoco: A Powhatan Place of Power," poster session, annual meeting of the Society for Applied Anthropology, Vancouver, BC, March 2006); "Pocahontas Revealed," dir. Kirk Wolfinger and Lisa Quijano Wolfinger, *Nova*, season 34, episode 7 (Boston: NOVA/WGBH Educational Foundation, 2007), television [contributing as line producer]; *The New World*, dir. Terrence Malick (Hollywood, CA: New Line Cinemas, 2005), DVD [contributing as animateur]. And see Martin D. Gallivan, *The Powhatan Landscape: An Archaeological History of the Algonquian Chesapeake* (Gainesville: University Press of Florida, 2016), 141–78; Martin D. Gallivan, and Danielle Moretti-Langholtz, "Civic Engagement at Werowocomoco: Reasserting Native Narratives from a Powhatan Place of Power," in *Archaeology as a Tool of Civic Engagement*, ed. Barbara J. Little and Paul A. Shackel (Lantham: AltaMira, 2007), 47–66; Gallivan, Moretti-Langholtz, and Woodard, "Collaborative Archaeology."

10. For views about decolonization agendas and praxis, see J. Kēhaulani Kauanui and Patrick Wolfe, "Settler Colonialism Then and Now," *Politica & Società*, no. 2 (2012): 235–58; Devon Abbott Mihesuah and Angela Cavender Wilson, eds., *Indigenizing the Academy: Transforming Scholarship and Empowering*

Communities (Lincoln: University of Nebraska Press, 2004); Corey Snelgrove, Rita Kaur Dhamoon, and Jeff Corntassel, "Unsettling Settler Colonialism: The Discourse and Politics of Settlers, and Solidarity with Indigenous Nations," *Decolonization* 3, no. 2 (2014): 1–32; Eve Tuck and K. Wayne Yang, "Decolonization Is Not a Metaphor," *Decolonization* 1, no. 1 (2012): 1–40.

    11. Amy Lonetree, *Decolonizing Museums: Representing Native America in National and Tribal Museums* (Chapel Hill: University of North Carolina Press, 2012), 108–9, 119–22. For further indigenous/museum contexts see James Clifford, "Four Northwest Coast Museums: Travel Reflections," in *Exhibiting Cultures: The Poetics and Politics of Ethnography*, ed. Ivan Karp and Steven D. Lavine (Washington, DC: Smithsonian Institution, 1991), 212–54; Susan Sleeper-Smith, ed., *Contesting Knowledge: Museums and Indigenous Perspectives* (Lincoln: University of Nebraska Press, 2009).

    12. Historian Daniel Richter may have been the first to recognize that the War for Independence forever changed the new nation's memory of Williamsburg and the city's relationship to Native peoples: "In its heyday, Williamsburg had frequently been the scene of treaty conferences, a powerful reminder of Indian and Euro-American coexistence in the colonial world that the American Revolution erased from historical memory." Daniel Richter, *Facing East from Indian Country: A Native History of Early America* (Cambridge, MA: Harvard University Press, 2001), 153–54. The intersection of British colonial policy, territory, Indian trade and alliances, and Williamsburg's Brafferton Indian School are examined and detailed in Danielle Moretti-Langholtz and Buck Woodard, eds., *Building the Brafferton: The Founding, Funding, and Legacy of America's Indian School* (Williamsburg, VA: Muscarelle Museum of Art, 2019).

    13. For North American examples, see Miranda J. Brady, "A Dialogic Response to the Problematized Past: The National Museum of the American Indian," in *Contesting Knowledge: Museums and Indigenous Perspectives*, ed. Susan Sleeper-Smith (Lincoln: University of Nebraska Press, 2009), 133–55; Jason Baird Jackson, "Ethnography and Ethnographers in Museum-Community Partnerships," *Practicing Anthropology* 22, no. 4 (2000): 29–32; Lonetree, *Decolonizing Museums*; Gwendolyn Saul and Ruth Jolie, "Inspiration from Museum Collections: An Exhibit as a Case Study in Building Relationships between Museums and Indigenous Artists," *American Indian Quarterly* 42, no. 2 (2018): 246–70; Ruth B. Phillips, "Disrupting Past Paradigms: The National Museum of the American Indian and the First Peoples Hall at the Canadian Museum of Civilization," *Public Historian* 28, no. 2 (2006): 75–80; Jennifer Shannon, "The Construction of Native Voice at the National Museum of the American Indian," in *Contesting Knowledge: Museums and Indigenous Perspectives*, ed. Susan Sleeper-Smith (Lincoln: University of Nebraska Press, 2009), 218–50. And, in a global context, see Alison K. Brown and Laura Peers, eds., *Museums and Source Communities* (London: Routledge, 2003); James Clifford, *Returns: Becoming Indigenous in the Twenty-First Century* (Cam-

bridge, MA: Harvard University Press, 2013); Ivan Karp and Steven D. Lavine, eds., *Exhibiting Cultures: The Poetics and Politics of Museum Display* (Washington, DC: Smithsonian Institution, 1991).

14. Ywone Edwards-Ingram, "Before 1979: African American Coachmen, Visibility, and Representation at Colonial Williamsburg," *Public Historian* 36, no. 1 (2014): 9–35; Eric Gable and Richard Handler, "Deep Dirt: Messing Up the Past at Colonial Williamsburg," *Social Analysis*, no. 34 (1993): 3–16; Christopher D. Geist, "African-American History at Colonial Williamsburg," *Cultural Resource Management* 20, no. 2 (1997): 47–49; Richard Handler and Eric Gable, *The New History in an Old Museum: Creating the Past at Colonial Williamsburg* (Durham, NC: Duke University Press, 1997).

15. Handler and Gable, *The New History*, 60–70; James H. Merrell, "Some Thoughts on Colonial Historians and American Indians," *William and Mary Quarterly* 46, no. 1 (1989): 94–119; "Second Thoughts on Colonial Historians and American Indians," *William and Mary Quarterly* 69, no. 3 (2012): 451–512.

16. Anthropologist and Yuchi folklorist Jason Baird Jackson and Catawba historian James Merrell have independently discussed research inequities of Native communities, particularly in the Southeast and Mid-Atlantic. Jason Baird Jackson, *Yuchi Folklore: Cultural Expression in a Southeastern Native American Community* (Norman: University of Oklahoma Press, 2012), xvi–xxiii; Merrell, "Some Thoughts" and "Second Thoughts." Researchers have attempted to address gaps in scholarly understanding of the eighteenth- and nineteenth-century reservation communities in Virginia-Carolina. For the Chowan, see Bradley J. Dixon, "'His One Netev Ples': The Chowans and the Politics of Native Petitions in the Colonial South," *William and Mary Quarterly* 76, no. 1 (2019): 41–74; Forest Hazel, "Looking for Indian Town: The Dispersal of the Chowan Indian Tribe in Eastern North Carolina, 1780–1915," *North Carolina Archaeology* 63 (2014): 34–64; Michelle LeMaster, "In the 'Scolding Houses': Indians and the Law in Eastern North Carolina, 1684–1760," *North Carolina Historical Review* 83, no. 2 (2006): 193–232. For the Meherrin, see Lewis R. Binford, "The Ethnohistory of the Nottoway, Meherrin and Weanock Indians of Southeastern Virginia," *Ethnohistory* 14, no. 3/4 (1967): 103–218; Shanon Lee Dawdy, "The Meherrin's Secret History of the Dividing Line," *North Carolina Historical Review* 72, no. 4 (1995): 387–415. For the Mattaponi, see Buck Woodard, Danielle Moretti-Langholtz, and Martha McCartney, *Heritage Properties of Indian Town: The Mattaponi Indian Baptist Church, School, and Homes of Chiefly Lineages* (Richmond: Virginia Department of Historic Resources, 2017). For the Nottoway, see Helen C. Rountree, "The Termination and Dispersal of the Nottoway Indians of Virginia," *Virginia Magazine of History and Biography* 95, no. 2 (1987): 193–214; Buck Woodard, "Indian Land Sales and Allotment in Antebellum Virginia: Trustees, Tribal Agency, and the Nottoway Reservation," *American Nineteenth Century History* 17, no. 2 (2016): 161–80. For the Pamunkey, see Helen C. Rountree, *Pocahontas's People: The Powhatan Indians of Virginia through Four*

Centuries (Norman: University of Oklahoma Press, 1990); Ashley Atkins Spivey, "Knowing the River, Working the Land, and Digging for Clay: Pamunkey Indian Subsistence Practices and the Market Economy, 1800–1900" (PhD diss., William & Mary, 2017); Woodard "An Alternative to Red Power." For the Tuscarora, see Anthony F. C. Wallace, *Tuscarora: A History* (Albany: State University of New York Press, 2012). Book-length treatments about the sixteenth- and seventeenth-century Native peoples of the Albemarle and Chesapeake regions include Martin D. Gallivan, *James River Chiefdoms: The Rise of Social Inequality in the Chesapeake* (Lincoln: University of Nebraska Press, 2003); *The Powhatan Landscape*; Frederic Gleach, *Powhatan's World and Colonial Virginia: A Conflict of Cultures* (Lincoln: University of Nebraska Press, 1997); Margaret Holmes Williamson, *Powhatan Lords of Life and Death: Command and Consent in Seventeenth-Century Virginia* (Lincoln: University of Nebraska Press, 2003); Seth Mallios, *The Deadly Politics of Giving: Exchange and Violence at Ajacan, Roanoke and Jamestown* (Tuscaloosa: University of Alabama Press, 2006); Michael Leroy Oberg, *The Head in Edward Nugent's Hand: Roanoke's Forgotten Indians* (Philadelphia: University of Pennsylvania Press, 2013); Stephen Potter, *Commoners, Tribute, and Chiefs: The Development of Algonquian Culture and History in the Potomac Valley* (Charlottesville: University Press of Virginia, 1994); Helen C. Rountree and E. Randolph Turner III, *Before and after Jamestown: Virginia's Powhatans and Their Predecessors* (Gainesville: University of Florida Press, 2002).

17. A phrase first coined by Michael L. Blakey and colleagues to describe contemporary Black stakeholders of the biological, cultural, and historical resources associated with the African American Burial Ground in New York City. Howard University and John Milner Associates, Inc., *Research Design for Archaeological, Historical, and Bioanthropological Investigations of the African Burial Ground (Broadway Block) New York, NY* (Washington, DC: Howard University, 1993); Cheryl J. LaRoche and Michael L. Blakey, "Seizing Intellectual Power: The Dialogue at the New York African Burial Ground," *Historical Archaeology* 31 (1997): 84–106. For contemporary Native descendant communities in Virginia-Carolina east of the Blue Ridge, see Elaine Adkins and Ray Adkins, *Chickahominy Indians-Eastern Division: A Brief Ethnohistory* (Bloomington, IN: Xlibris, 2007); Karen I. Blu, *The Lumbee Problem: The Making of an American Indian People* (Lincoln: University of Nebraska Press, 2001); Arica L. Coleman, *That the Blood Stay Pure: African Americans, Native Americans, and the Predicament of Race and Identity in Virginia* (Indianapolis: Indiana University Press, 2013); Samuel R. Cook, *Monacans and Miners: Native American and Coal Mining Communities in Appalachia* (Lincoln: University of Nebraska Press, 2000); Forest Hazel, "Occaneechi-Saponi Descendants in the North Carolina Piedmont: The Texas Community," *Southern Indian Studies* 40 (1991): 3–30; Patricia Barker Lerch, *Waccamaw Legacy: Contemporary Indians Fight for Survival* (Tuscaloosa: University of Alabama Press, 2004); Malinda Maynor Lowery, *Lumbee Indians in the Jim Crow South: Race, Identity, and the Making*

of a Nation (Chapel Hill: University of North Carolina Press, 2010); Christopher Arris Oakley, *Keeping the Circle: American Indian Identity in Eastern North Carolina, 1885–2004* (Lincoln: University of Nebraska Press, 2005); Theda Perdue and Christopher Arris Oakley, *Native Carolinians: The Indians of North Carolina* (Chapel Hill: University of North Carolina Press, 2010); Marvin D. Richardson, "Racial Choices: The Emergence of the Haliwa-Saponi Indian Tribe, 1835–1971" (PhD diss., University of North Carolina at Chapel Hill, 2016); Rountree, *Pocahontas's People*; Sider, *Living Indian Histories*; Waugaman and Moretti-Langholtz, *We're Still Here*; Woodard, "An Alternative to Red Power"; Buck Woodard, Danielle Moretti-Langholtz, and Stephanie Hasselbacher, *Sites of Significance in the Sappony Indian Settlement: High Plains Churches, Schools, and Christie General Store* (Richmond: Virginia Department of Historic Resource, 2017).

18. Eric Hobsbawm, *The Age of Revolution: Europe, 1789–1848* (London: Weidenfeld and Nicolson, 1962); *The Age of Capital, 1848–1875* (London: Weidenfeld and Nicolson, 1975); *The Age of Empire, 1875–1914* (London: Weidenfeld and Nicolson, 1987). Following Braudel's "long sixteenth century," Fernand Braudel, *Civilization and Capitalism, 15th–18th Century*, 3 vols. (Berkeley: University of California Press, 1979). For a recent examination of the long nineteenth century in the Native American South, see Gregory D. Smithers, ed., *Indigenous Histories of the American South during the Long Nineteenth Century* (London: Routledge, 2018).

19. Jackson, *Yuchi Folklore*, xvii. Here, I am using Jackson's quote to describe the Upper South, including the "Southern" Mid-Atlantic states of the Chesapeake watershed.

20. Gallivan and Moretti-Langholtz, "Civic Engagement at Werowocomoco"; Gallivan, Moretti-Langholtz, and Woodard, "Collaborative Archaeology."

21. In the early 2000s there were eight state-recognized tribes in Virginia and seven state-recognized tribes in North Carolina, and further supratribal entities included the Governor's Virginia Council on Indians, the North Carolina Commission of Indian Affairs, and at least six urban Indian organizations between Carolina and Washington, DC. The Commonwealth of Virginia recognized three additional tribes in 2010. At the federal level, the Eastern Band of Cherokee and Catawba Nation bordered the Carolinas. By 2016, the Bureau of Indian Affairs acknowledged the Pamunkey in Virginia as a federally recognized tribe, which was followed by US congressional recognition of six more of the Virginia tribes in 2018.

22. Claire Farrer's work among the Western Apache argues that tribal members oscillate between the lived experience of the present and retelling events of the deeper past, merged to navigate and understand contemporary reservation life. Claire R. Farrer, *Thunder Rides a Black Horse: Mescalero Apaches and the Mythic Present* (Long Grove, IL: Waveland, 1996). In my observation, Mid-Atlantic Native communities regularly reflect on the broad strokes of colonialism and more recent state-enforced racial segregation, using a form of *experienced history* to interpret the past, present, and future. While less specific in time and place, it is a similar

phenomenon as observed by Farrer, whereby historical figures such as Pocahontas, places like Jamestown, and community experiences under Jim Crow continue to resonate and discursively inform local Native worldview. For a fuller discussion, see Woodard, "An Alternative to Red Power."

23. Laura Peers, *Playing Ourselves: Interpreting Native Histories at Historic Reconstructions* (London: Rowman and Littlefield, 2007), 67.

24. Nabakov, *A Forest of Time*; Richard White, "Indian Peoples and the Natural World: Asking the Right Questions," in *Rethinking American Indian History*, ed. Donald L. Fixico (Albuquerque: University of New Mexico Press, 1998), 87–100.

25. Tribal members who engaged Colonial Williamsburg's early attempts to explore Native American history were all members of Virginia state-recognized tribes, several with reservations whose origins predate the United States and were outcomes of treaties signed with England. State tribes' plight to achieve federal acknowledgment and the stratified relationship that exists among federally recognized and state-level groups has remained a complex and difficult subject for museums and other non-Native institutions to thoroughly comprehend.

26. Peers, *Playing Ourselves*; White, "Indian Peoples and the Natural World."

27. Comment of a Nansemond representative on the Governor's Virginia Council on Indians in 2004 during a presentation by CWF officials attempting to reconcile the failed launch of the American Indian Initiative.

28. CWF personnel often collapsed Native tribal affiliations into the category of "the Indians," through their own race-based perspective of society, despite recognizing the lack of Native political unity. CWF officials struggled with tribalism—that is, an understanding that "Indian" was not always the essential category in relationship to tribal affiliation and politics—and that competition and animosity existed among tribal groups.

29. The Native critique of anthropology was most famously articulated in Vine Deloria, Jr., *Custer Died for Your Sins* (New York: Macmillan, 1969). The 1960–70s divorce of Native America from anthropology has been the subject of limited, but noteworthy discussions. James Clifford, *The Predicament of Culture: Twentieth Century Ethnography, Literature, and Art* (Cambridge, MA: Harvard University Press, 1988). For the outcomes of those critiques and the more recent rapprochement of anthropology and Native America, see Thomas Biolsi and Larry J. Zimmerman, *Indians and Anthropologists: Vine Deloria Jr. and the Critique of Anthropology* (Tucson: University of Arizona Press, 1997); Orin Starn, "Here Come the Anthros (Again): The Strange Marriage of Anthropology and Native America," *Cultural Anthropology* 26, no. 2 (2011): 179–204; Pauline Turner Strong, "Recent Ethnographic Research on North American Indigenous Peoples," *Annual Review of Anthropology* 34 (2005): 253–68.

30. For a fuller review of the ethics and principals of professional responsibility in the discipline of anthropology, see the American Anthropological

Association statement on ethics, "Principles of Professional Responsibility," posted November 1, 2012, http://ethics.americananthro.org/category/statement/.

31. Here, I am making a distinction between the extensive list of tribal affiliations of American Indian Initiative participants and groups who had tribal leadership (government) representation. Federal status Nations with representatives or leadership visits to Williamsburg included the Absentee Shawnee Tribe, Chickasaw Nation, Eastern Band of Cherokee Indians, Eastern Shawnee Tribe of Oklahoma, Pamunkey Indian Tribe, Seneca-Cayuga Nation, Shawnee Tribe, and Tuscarora Nation. At the state-recognition level, the chiefs of the Chickahominy Tribe (now federal), Meherrin Indian Tribe, Nottoway Indian Tribe of Virginia, Patawomeck Indian Tribe of Virginia, and Upper Mattaponi Indian Tribe (now federal) also came for meetings or program participation.

32. Communications received via social media and CWF visitor response cards.

33. Interviews conducted with Native participants during CWF programming, 2012, 2014, and 2016.

34. Interviews conducted with Native actors during 2009 CWF public history productions.

35. Michael Blakey, "Archaeology under the Blinding Light of Race," *Current Anthropology* 61, no. S22 (2020): S190–93.

36. For a review of ethnographic authority and authenticity, juxtaposed against literacy and globalization, see James Clifford, "On Ethnographic Allegory," in *Writing Culture: The Poetics and Politics of Ethnography*, ed. James Clifford and George E. Marcus (Berkeley: University of California Press, 1986), particularly 116–17, "An Account of a True Parable from Gabon."

37. An example of the ways in which the CWF public history experience has played out in Cherokee representations of their past and present may be found in Barbara Duncan, *Cherokee Clothing in the 1700s* (Cherokee, NC: Museum of the Cherokee Indian Press, 2016); and from an earlier, pre-CWF era, cf. Barbara Duncan and Brett Riggs, *Cherokee Heritage Trails Guidebook* (Chapel Hill: University of North Carolina Press, 2003).

Bibliography

Adkins, Elaine, and Ray Adkins, *Chickahominy Indians-Eastern Division: A Brief Ethnohistory.* Bloomington, IN: Xlibris, 2007.

Adkins, Stephen. "U.S. Is Overdue for More Inclusive History." *Virginian-Pilot*, October 10, 2017.

Binford, Lewis R. "The Ethnohistory of the Nottoway, Meherrin and Weanock Indians of Southeastern Virginia." *Ethnohistory* 14, no. 3/4 (1967): 103–218.

Biolsi, Thomas, and Larry J. Zimmerman, eds. *Indians and Anthropologists: Vine Deloria Jr. and the Critique of Anthropology.* Tucson: University of Arizona Press, 1997.

Blakey, Michael. "Archaeology under the Blinding Light of Race." *Current Anthropology* 61, no. S22 (2020): S183–97.

Blu, Karen I. *The Lumbee Problem: The Making of an American Indian People.* Lincoln: University of Nebraska Press, 2001.

Brady, Miranda J. "A Dialogic Response to the Problematized Past: The National Museum of the American Indian." In *Contesting Knowledge: Museums and Indigenous Perspectives*, edited by Susan Sleeper-Smith, 133–55. Lincoln: University of Nebraska Press, 2009.

Braudel, Fernand. *Civilization and Capitalism, 15th–18th Century.* 3 vols. Berkeley: University of California Press, 1979.

Brown, Alison K., and Laura Peers, eds. *Museums and Source Communities.* London: Routledge, 2003.

Clifford, James. "Four Northwest Coast Museums: Travel Reflections." In *Exhibiting Cultures: The Poetics and Politics of Ethnography*, edited by Ivan Karp and Steven D. Lavine, 212–54. Washington, DC: Smithsonian Institution, 1991.

———. "On Ethnographic Allegory." In *Writing Culture: the Poetics and Politics of Ethnography*, edited by James Clifford and George E. Marcus, 98–121. Berkeley: University of California Press, 1986.

———. *The Predicament of Culture: Twentieth Century Ethnography, Literature, and Art.* Cambridge, MA: Harvard University Press, 1988.

———. *Returns: Becoming Indigenous in the Twenty-First Century.* Cambridge, MA: Harvard University Press, 2013.

Coleman, Arica L. *That the Blood Stay Pure: African Americans, Native Americans, and the Predicament of Race and Identity in Virginia.* Indianapolis: Indiana University Press, 2013.

Connerton, Paul. *How Modernity Forgets.* Cambridge: Cambridge University Press, 2009.

———. *How Societies Remember.* Cambridge: Cambridge University Press, 1989.

Cook, Samuel R. *Monacans and Miners: Native American and Coal Mining Communities in Appalachia.* Lincoln: University of Nebraska Press, 2000.

Dawdy, Shannon Lee. "The Meherrin's Secret History of the Dividing Line." *North Carolina Historical Review* 72, no. 4 (1995): 387–415.

Deloria, Vine, Jr. *Custer Died for Your Sins.* New York: Macmillan, 1969.

Dixon, Bradley J. " 'His One Netev Ples': The Chowans and the Politics of Native Petitions in the Colonial South." *William and Mary Quarterly* 76, no. 1 (2019): 41–74.

Duncan, Barbara. *Cherokee Clothing in the 1700s.* Cherokee, NC: Museum of the Cherokee Indian Press, 2016.

Duncan, Barbara, and Brett Riggs. *Cherokee Heritage Trails Guidebook.* Chapel Hill: University of North Carolina Press, 2003.

Edwards-Ingram, Ywone. "Before 1979: African American Coachmen, Visibility, and Representation at Colonial Williamsburg." *Public Historian* 36, no. 1 (2014): 9–35.

Farrer, Claire F. *Thunder Rides and Black Horse: Mescalero Apaches and the Mythic Present.* Long Grove, IL: Waveland, 1996.

Gable, Eric, and Richard Handler. "Deep Dirt: Messing Up the Past at Colonial Williamsburg." *Social Analysis,* no. 34 (1993): 3–16.

Gallivan, Martin D. *James River Chiefdoms: The Rise of Social Inequality in the Chesapeake.* Lincoln: University of Nebraska Press, 2003.

———. *The Powhatan Landscape: An Archaeological History of the Algonquian Chesapeake.* Gainesville: University Press of Florida, 2016.

Gallivan, Martin D., and Danielle Moretti-Langholtz. "Civic Engagement at Werowocomoco: Reasserting Native Narratives from a Powhatan Place of Power." In *Archaeology as a Tool of Civic Engagement,* edited by Barbara J. Little and Paul A. Shackel, 47–66. Lantham, MD: AltaMira, 2007.

Gallivan, Martin D., and Danielle Moretti-Langholtz, and Buck Woodard. "Collaborative Archaeology and Strategic Essentialism: Native Empowerment in Tidewater Virginia." *Historical Archaeology* 45 (2011): 10–23.

Geist, Christopher D. "African-American History at Colonial Williamsburg." *Cultural Resource Management* 20, no. 2 (1997): 47–49.

Gilley, Brian Joseph. *A Longhouse Fragmented: Ohio Iroquois Autonomy in the Nineteenth Century.* Albany: State University of New York Press, 2014.

Gleach, Frederic. *Powhatan's World and Colonial Virginia: A Conflict of Cultures.* Lincoln: University of Nebraska Press, 1997.

Handler, Richard, and Eric Gable, *The New History in an Old Museum: Creating the Past at Colonial Williamsburg.* Durham, NC: Duke University Press, 1997.

Hazel, Forest. "Looking for Indian Town: The Dispersal of the Chowan Indian Tribe in Eastern North Carolina, 1780–1915." *North Carolina Archaeology* 63 (2014): 34–64.

———. "Occaneechi-Saponi Descendants in the North Carolina Piedmont: The Texas Community." *Southern Indian Studies* 40 (1991): 3–30.

Hobsbawm, Eric. *The Age of Capital, 1848–1875.* London: Weidenfeld and Nicolson, 1975.

———. *The Age of Empire, 1875–1914.* London: Weidenfeld and Nicolson, 1987.

———. *The Age of Revolution: Europe, 1789–1848.* London: Weidenfeld and Nicolson, 1962.

Howard University and John Milner Associates, Inc. *Research Design for Archaeological, Historical, and Bioanthropological Investigations of the African*

Burial Ground (Broadway Block) New York, NY. Washington, DC: Howard University, 1993.

Jackson, Jason Baird. "Ethnography and Ethnographers in Museum-Community Partnerships." *Practicing Anthropology* 22, no. 4 (2000): 29–32.

———. *Yuchi Folklore: Cultural Expression in a Southeastern Native American Community.* Norman: University of Oklahoma Press, 2012.

Karp, Ivan, and Steven D. Lavine, eds. *Exhibiting Cultures: The Poetics and Politics of Museum Display.* Washington, DC: Smithsonian Institution, 1991.

Kauanui, J. Kēhaulani, and Patrick Wolfe. "Settler Colonialism Then and Now." *Politica & Società*, no. 2 (2012): 235–58.

LaRoche, Cheryl J., and Michael L. Blakey. "Seizing Intellectual Power: The Dialogue at the New York African Burial Ground." *Historical Archaeology* 31 (1997): 84–106.

LeMaster, Michelle. "In the 'Scolding Houses': Indians and the Law in Eastern North Carolina, 1684–1760." *North Carolina Historical Review* 83, no. 2 (2006): 193–232.

Lerch, Patricia Barker. *Waccamaw Legacy: Contemporary Indians Fight for Survival.* Tuscaloosa: University of Alabama Press, 2004.

Lonetree, Amy. *Decolonizing Museums: Representing Native America in National and Tribal Museums.* Chapel Hill: University of North Carolina Press, 2012.

Lowery, Malinda Maynor. *Lumbee Indians in the Jim Crow South: Race, Identity, and the Making of a Nation.* Chapel Hill: University of North Carolina Press, 2010.

Malick, Terrence, dir. *The New World.* Hollywood, CA: New Line Cinema, 2005. DVD.

Mallios, Seth. *The Deadly Politics of Giving: Exchange and Violence at Ajacan, Roanoke and Jamestown.* Tuscaloosa: University of Alabama Press, 2006.

Merrell, James H. "Second Thoughts on Colonial Historians and American Indians." *William and Mary Quarterly* 69, no. 3 (2012): 451–512.

———. "Some Thoughts on Colonial Historians and American Indians." *William and Mary Quarterly* 46, no. 1 (1989): 94–119.

Mihesuah, Devon Abbott, and Angela Cavender Wilson, eds. *Indigenizing the Academy: Transforming Scholarship and Empowering Communities.* Lincoln: University of Nebraska Press, 2004.

Miller, Michael. "'400 Years Is Long Enough': Virginia's 'First Contact' Indian Tribes Demand Federal Recognition." *Washington Post*, May 26, 2017.

Moretti-Langholtz, Danielle, and Buck Woodard, eds. *Building the Brafferton: The Founding, Funding, and Legacy of America's Indian School.* Williamsburg, VA: Muscarelle Museum of Art, 2019.

Nabakov, Peter. *A Forest of Time: American Indian Ways of History.* Cambridge: Cambridge University Press, 2002.

Oakley, Christopher Arris. *Keeping the Circle: American Indian Identity in Eastern North Carolina, 1885–2004.* Lincoln: University of Nebraska Press, 2005.

Oberg, Michael Leroy. *The Head in Edward Nugent's Hand: Roanoke's Forgotten Indians*. Philadelphia: University of Pennsylvania Press, 2013.

Peers, Laura. *Playing Ourselves: Interpreting Native Histories at Historic Reconstructions*. London: Rowman and Littlefield, 2007.

Perdue, Theda, and Christopher Arris Oakley. *Native Carolinians: The Indians of North Carolina*. Rev. ed. Chapel Hill: University of North Carolina Press, 2010.

Phillips, Ruth B. "Disrupting Past Paradigms: The National Museum of the American Indian and the First Peoples Hall at the Canadian Museum of Civilization." *Public Historian* 28, no. 2 (2006): 75–80.

Potter, Stephen. *Commoners, Tribute, and Chiefs: The Development of Algonquian Culture and History in the Potomac Valley*. Charlottesville: University Press of Virginia, 1994.

Richardson, Marvin D. "Racial Choices: The Emergence of the Haliwa-Saponi Indian Tribe, 1835–1971." PhD diss., University of North Carolina at Chapel Hill, 2016.

Richter, Daniel. *Facing East from Indian Country: A Native History of Early America*. Cambridge, MA: Harvard University Press, 2001.

Rountree, Helen C. *Pocahontas's People: The Powhatan Indians of Virginia through Four Centuries*. Norman: University of Oklahoma Press, 1990.

———. "The Termination and Dispersal of the Nottoway Indians of Virginia." *Virginia Magazine of History and Biography* 95, no. 2 (1987): 193–214.

Rountree, Helen C., and E. Randolph Turner III. *Before and after Jamestown: Virginia's Powhatans and Their Predecessors*. Gainesville: University of Florida Press, 2002.

Saul, Gwendolyn, and Ruth Jolie. "Inspiration from Museum Collections: An Exhibit as a Case Study in Building Relationships between Museums and Indigenous Artists." *American Indian Quarterly* 42, no. 2 (2018): 246–70.

Shannon, Jennifer. "The Construction of Native Voice at the National Museum of the American Indian." In *Contesting Knowledge: Museums and Indigenous Perspectives*, edited by Susan Sleeper-Smith, 218–50. Lincoln: University of Nebraska Press, 2009.

Sider, Gerald. *Living Indian Histories: Lumbee and Tuscarora People in North Carolina*. Chapel Hill: University of North Carolina Press, 2003.

Sleeper-Smith, Susan, ed. *Contesting Knowledge: Museums and Indigenous Perspectives*. Lincoln: University of Nebraska Press, 2009.

Smithers, Gregory D., ed. *Indigenous Histories of the American South during the Long Nineteenth Century*. London: Routledge, 2018.

Snelgrove, Corey, and Rita Kaur Dhamoon, and Jeff Corntassel. "Unsettling Settler Colonialism: The Discourse and Politics of Settlers, and Solidarity with Indigenous Nations." *Decolonization* 3, no. 2 (2014): 1–32.

Spivey, Ashley Atkins. "Knowing the River, Working the Land, and Digging for Clay: Pamunkey Indian Subsistence Practices and the Market Economy, 1800–1900." PhD diss., William & Mary, 2017.

Starn, Orin. "Here Come the Anthros (Again): The Strange Marriage of Anthropology and Native America." *Cultural Anthropology* 26, no. 2 (2011): 179–204.

Strong, Pauline Turner. "Recent Ethnographic Research on North American Indigenous Peoples." *Annual Review of Anthropology* 34 (2005): 253–68.

Thornton, Russell, ed. *Studying Native America: Problems and Prospects.* Madison: University of Wisconsin Press, 1998.

Tuck, Eve, and K. Wayne Yang. "Decolonization Is Not a Metaphor." *Decolonization* 1, no. 1 (2012): 1–40.

US Congress, S1074 Senate Committee on Indian Affairs Testimony, October 30, 2013.

Wallace, Anthony F. C. *Tuscarora: A History.* Albany: State University of New York Press, 2012.

Warren, Stephen. *The Shawnee and Their Neighbors, 1795–1870.* Urbana: University of Illinois Press.

———. *The Worlds the Shawnees Made: Migration and Violence in Early America.* Chapel Hill: University of North Carolina Press, 2016.

Waugaman, Sandra, and Danielle Moretti-Langholtz. *We're Still Here: Contemporary Virginia Indians Tell Their Stories.* Richmond, VA: Palari, 2006.

White, Richard. "Indian Peoples and the Natural World: Asking the Right Questions." In *Rethinking American Indian History*, edited by Donald L. Fixico, 87–100. Albuquerque: University of New Mexico Press, 1998.

Williamson, Margaret Holmes. *Powhatan Lords of Life and Death: Command and Consent in Seventeenth-Century Virginia.* Lincoln: University of Nebraska Press, 2003.

Wolfinger, Kirk, and Lisa Quijano Wolfinger, dirs. "Pocahontas Revealed." *Nova*, season 34, episode 7. Boston: NOVA/WGBH Educational Foundation, 2007. Television.

Woodard, Buck. "An Alternative to Red Power: Political Alliance as Tribal Activism in Virginia." *Comparative American Studies* 17, no. 2 (2020): 142–66.

———. "Indian Land Sales and Allotment in Antebellum Virginia: Trustees, Tribal Agency, and the Nottoway Reservation." *American Nineteenth Century History* 17, no. 2 (2016): 161–80.

Woodard, Buck, Danielle Moretti-Langholtz, and Angela Daniel. "Werowocomoco: A Powhatan Place of Power." Poster session, annual meeting of the Society for Applied Anthropology, Vancouver, BC, March 2006.

Woodard, Buck, Danielle Moretti-Langholtz, and Stephanie Hasselbacher. *Sites of Significance in the Sappony Indian Settlement: High Plains Churches, Schools, and Christie General Store.* Richmond: Virginia Department of Historic Resource, 2017.

Woodard, Buck, Danielle Moretti-Langholtz, and Martha McCartney. *Heritage Properties of Indian Town: The Mattaponi Indian Baptist Church, School, and Homes of Chiefly Lineages.* Richmond: Virginia Department of Historic Resources, 2017.

Chapter 11

Repatriation as a Catalyst for Building Community-Engaged Curriculum

April K. Sievert and Jessie Ryker-Crawford

The Learning NAGPRA project, which addresses ethics specifically related to repatriation, was the first of its kind funded by the National Science Foundation program for Cultivating Cultures of Ethical STEM.[1] This project mindfully brought together Indigenous and non-Indigenous participants to research how practitioners in different fields and contexts learn and teach about repatriation and NAGPRA, and to collectively develop open access resources and curriculum. Information collected through surveys, interviews, a guided teaching study, and collaborative collegium meetings provided the means for developing new curriculum and approaches. Individual working groups addressed four different approaches to learning about repatriation—learning about worldviews, exploring the contexts that affect repatriation, how case studies can be used instructively, and what cultural resource management professionals need to know about NAGPRA. The Learning NAGPRA project demonstrates that sustained engagement among differently situated scholars from Indigenous and non-Native institutions can result in not only new approaches to pedagogy, but a better understanding of the scope of the restorative justice that repatriation brings.[2]

Originally conceived at Indiana University, the Learning NAGPRA project studies how and in what contexts repatriation ethics are taught and learned in order to explore the ways in which this training can be improved. From the perspective of a Midwestern research university, we were stuck with the question—What does successful, accessible, and pro-active training to manage collections and conduct repatriations even look like? For this, the long-standing curriculum in repatriation at the Institute of American Indian Arts in Santa Fe, a tribal-serving college,[3] provided a useful model.[4] In this paper we describe how meaningful consultation regarding repatriation inspired collaborative, NAGPRA-related work in and beyond the classroom.

Engaging with NAGPRA

Communities of engagement may take on different forms. Some emerge through a mutual desire to build interdisciplinary and engaged scholarship. Others develop through long-term relationships between individual schol-ars at universities or museums and the communities within which they work. Still others grow out of federal mandates to consult with descendant communities, for example, in identifying traditional cultural properties to comply with section 106 of the National Historic Preservation Act, or in working with collections and archaeological practice subject to the Native American Graves Protection and Repatriation Act (NAGPRA). Sonya Atalay provides a nuanced overview of degrees of cooperation and com-munity engagement in her book *Community-Based Archaeology*, in which she lays out research methods for participatory research in archaeology. She recognizes that mandated consultation sometimes plants the seeds of cooperation, but often falls short of true collaboration.[5]

Resources to guide participatory research have expanded, especially with the methodological advances outlined by Atalay. However, archaeol-ogists and biological anthropologists have been slower to develop partic-ipatory perspectives than scholars in fields less fraught with the tensions that surround repatriation, such as in history, law, or the arts. Even thirty years after the passage of NAGPRA, over 100,000 ancestral individuals remain in collections across the nation. One might ask why Native scholars would want to engage with institutions that still hold ancestral remains "on shelves," beyond gaining their ancestors' return? An entrenched research archaeology east of the Mississippi River continues to proceed largely without true consultation with federally recognized Native nations. This, we affirm, needs to change, and repatriation can provide one avenue for developing relationships that could turn toward other research.[6]

We use the term catalyst to indicate that repatriation may in some cases not merely incentivize action, but can also spark meaningful interaction beyond repatriation or into a larger sphere of endeavor that surrounds the repatriation process. Although engagement that begins in compliance with federal mandates can open doors, it can only do so if institutions recognize that consultation for repatriation cannot be perfunctory. Longer-term relationships with Native nations and Native scholars can create spaces for working collaboratively over and beyond repatriation. In contrast, perfunctory conversations with people who may or may not have legal standing does not constitute consultation. Under NAGPRA law, consultation is solely reserved for Alaska Native communities, descendant Hawaiian organizations, and federally recognized Native nations. In many cases, inadequate conversations often create deep distrust, and, in others, legal action and fines.[7]

Perhaps nowhere has the problem been as pervasive as in the Midwestern states that experienced the forced removal of Indigenous people. In 1846, when the United States forcibly removed the Miami from their Indiana homelands, they became the last Native nation removed from Ohio, Indiana, and Illinois. Institutions with large collections in states impacted by removal share a common characteristic: almost no contact with Native nations removed from their homelands. In these states, ancestral remains and funerary objects derived from archaeological excavation have not been subject to adequate consultation.

Large precontact populations in the region left huge sites and cemetery areas, leading to equally large collections of ancestral remains. Major infrastructure projects supported initially by the New Deal, and later by data recovery projects mandated by section 106 of the 1966 National Historic Preservation Act to address large-scale development projects (reservoir and highway construction, in particular) accounted for tens of thousands of exhumations in the eastern US between 1930 and 1990, when NAGPRA was signed into law. Interstate highways crossing through Illinois, Indiana, and Ohio cut through some of the most heavily populated areas of precontact times.[8]

When institutions holding archaeological collections prepared inventories to be submitted to National NAGPRA in 1995, as mandated by the law, they counted sets of human remains based on recorded data that was vague, or incomplete, at best—leaving questions as to the exact number of individuals or cultural affiliation. In most cases east of the Mississippi, archaeologists and curators classified precontact people as culturally unidentifiable (CUI) under the law. The implication of CUI designation meant that these remains and objects would not be subject to repatriation and no further work need be done. Modifications to the law in 2010, which detailed a process to return the CUI remains as well, changed that and forced institutions to address the task of repatriating *all* Native American ancestral remains. CUI designations for ancestors and objects sometimes resulted from a resistance to repatriation, and other times from a genuine belief that affiliating ancient people with contemporary nations is nearly impossible, based on a false assumption that certainty is required under the law.

The absence of federally recognized nations from their homelands has exacerbated the challenges of consultation. Removal has resulted in a huge backlog of repatriations, caused, in part, from institutions that did not get ahead of the process. The cost of real consultation and staffing for repatriation work hinders moving forward swiftly with compliance work unless institutions can be successful in receiving federal NAGPRA grants or agree to allot internal funding. Other factors include mistaking slow responses from tribes in the 1990s for lack of interest. Fear of starting a process that results in transferring collections, which in many cases had been held for over eighty years, may be another reason. In the most extreme cases, ancestral remains were deliberately shielded from repatriation. For example, in 2016, Thomas A. Munson, a former superintendent of the Effigy Mounds National Monument was sentenced for illegally removing remains of over forty individuals from the park in 1990 and hiding them in his garage until they were recovered in 2012. While funding shortages, a seemingly insurmountable task, and fear may be contributing factors, they are by no means excuses. It is small wonder that tribes descended from the ancient people of the Midwest became frustrated to the point of resorting to legal action.[9]

Unfortunately, inaction derived also from simply not knowing what to do, in spite of a substantial literature on repatriation and NAGPRA. Although archaeological ethics received more attention post–NAGPRA passage, much of the discussion was theoretical and hypothetical, not directly applied to the actual processes necessary for successful repatriation. For at least the first twenty years that NAGPRA was in effect, the distance between descendant tribes and academic anthropologists who worked with Indigenous materials from the Midwest extended far beyond the physical geography that separated the campuses and museums from tribal headquarters in Oklahoma and elsewhere. Consultation mandates are finally closing this gap.[10]

The classroom has become a space where researchers and representatives of federally recognized Native nations can come together. As university educators, it is incumbent on us, and our responsibility, to make sure that our students are equipped to understand how to comply with NAGPRA. Non-Native students also need to understand the perspectives of descendants dispossessed of not only land, but connections to the land through the removal of their ancestors' remains and funerary objects. Tribal students likewise need to understand how work with the institutions can move forward in an equitable fashion.

The Learning NAGPRA Project: A Dialogue

Here we present our perspectives as coauthors, but also turn to individual narratives to relay our personal positioning and identities as teachers in nontribal and tribal settings.

Sievert: When I accepted an offer to direct the Glenn A. Black Laboratory of Archaeology (GBL), the largest archaeological laboratory and repository in Indiana, little did I know just how very soon I would be engaging with federally recognized tribes—for the obvious reason—in consultation for repatriation. In 2013, I accepted the responsibility for over 1,400 ancestral individuals and thousands of funerary objects. Up to that time there had been no repatriations, and only one open repatriation claim was on file. Correspondence between the GBL, tribal NAGPRA coordinators, and Tribal Historic Preservation Officers (THPOs) had been primarily in response to inadvertent discoveries during archaeological fieldwork. Discovery of any human remains must be reported to Indiana's Division of Historic Preservation and Archaeology (DHPA) in compliance with state statute (Indiana Code 14-21-1-27), which governs burial grounds and their preservation and treatment on the state level.[11] However, the state law does not require archaeologists or repositories to notify individual tribes.

At the same time, faculty members at Indiana University (IU), who had been trying for years to gain the attention of university administrators on the issues of NAGPRA compliance got traction, and, by 2012, the administration was listening and convened a Human Remains Committee.

Indiana University administrators created and funded a NAGPRA office in 2013 as a central point from which to address claims, to coordinate efforts by four units across the campus, correct and complete inventories, conduct consultations, submit required notices, and handle repatriations. So, at essentially the same time that I got to GBL knowing quite a lot about teaching and archaeology but little of how to actually repatriate anything, IU hired a NAGPRA director, Dr. Jayne-Leigh Thomas, an osteologist who understood repatriation from working on such issues in Washington State. It was that conjunction that demonstrated how different an abstract understanding of NAGPRA is from a practical undertaking under the law. Eric Hemenway, speaking from his perspective as a tribal repatriation specialist, noted how the emotional impact of doing NAGPRA changes dramatically when one actually starts practicing NAGPRA compliance. In 2014, after a whirlwind tour of tribal headquarters in Oklahoma, it became clear to Jayne-Leigh Thomas and I, that IU had to move much more concertedly and demonstrably on compliance. We could only do this by establishing real relationships with tribal professionals, whose patience had worn thin, and who had little reason to trust us. Also clear to me was that I was poorly prepared for entering into the emotional and potentially contentious conversations that can arise.[12]

With this realization came the comprehension that future archaeologists, biological anthropologists, and curators were likely as green as I was in being able to assume the challenge of meaningful compliance with NAGPRA, in spite of teaching and thinking about ethics for over a decade. Even in 2014, many across the larger Midwestern research university network had unconsciously perpetuated a systemic ignorance of the legislation, and misperceptions about the scale to which Native communities had been dispossessed. Clearly, Midwestern universities with collections subject to NAGPRA were not only complying poorly, and thus subject to legal action, they were also not training future professionals sufficiently to fully understand the ethical contexts for NAGPRA, let alone the legal responsibility and actual process for repatriating ancestral remains and cultural objects.

University educators have two responsibilities. First, they must see that collections under their control are repatriated. Second, they must help other institutions do the same work by appropriately training their students. I decided upon two courses of action. Paramount was to guide 1,400 ancestors back to federally recognized tribes according to the law.

Second, I committed to addressing the educational vacuum surrounding the ethical implementation of NAGPRA.

Ryker-Crawford: Through teaching a number of courses on repatriation at a multitribal college, I am exceptionally aware both of the substantial interest that Native American museum studies students have in repatriation issues and of the horror stories that tribal communities have endured with past parochial archaeological undertakings. The Native communities with whom I work are correct in their assessment of archaeologists: they have disregarded or failed to look for the richness of history, culture, and philosophical lifeways that each sovereign Native nation has conscientiously held onto for millennia.

The general absence of consultation has led to incomplete archaeological hypotheses that could have been remedied through a more in-depth understanding of the living communities that are being studied. Skewed data and the publication of outright misinformation is the usual outcome. In Jim Enote's now widely circulated keynote presentation for the 2015 Association for Tribal Archives, Libraries, and Museums (ATALM) conference—titled "A Museum Collaboration Manifesto"—he eloquently communicates this reality arising from the simple fact that Native American people have rarely been included in the study of their own culture:

> After many years working within museology we continue to see items in collections disguised with mistaken and unsuitable interpretations. With so much error many items gain false significance and meaning by the hand of outdated standards and practice. It is strange enough that things are removed from their local setting and context, now they have been renamed and reframed in languages and contexts foreign to the place and people from which they were born.[13]

The libraries of this nation are littered with anthropological publications that hold a great amount of false interpretations of the archaeological data and disclose sacred and culturally sensitive materials. Dissertations written by doctoral students based upon inaccurate descriptions of tribal cultural objects continue to perpetuate bad science, and numerous archaeological publications circulate completely false information. These ongoing problems could have been ameliorated at any time through a collaborative approach to archaeology.

Despite these challenges, community-engaged methodologies hold great promise for both Native American communities and archaeological professionals. The study of humanity is no small matter, and we are at a place where new theoretical and methodological stances, such as those carried out through the Learning NAGPRA project, allow for an all-encompassing and drastic shift in how we work together on the matters of repatriation and the crafting of academic literature.

The Learning NAGPRA Project

In 2015, the Society for American Archaeology (SAA) distributed a survey to its members to gather data about opinions relating to NAGPRA and repatriation. The survey gathered demographic, educational, and occupational data and included questions meant to gauge attitudes in particular about the provisions for repatriating culturally unidentifiable remains.[14] Archaeologist Diane Gifford-Gonzalez, writing on behalf of the SAA's board of directors, had this to say about the survey results: "We have heard loud and clear . . . that we need to do a better job of educating North Americans about NAGPRA and what is involved in consultation and compliance."[15]

As educators who had have studied college-level teaching and learning epistemologies as well as archaeological ethics, we are aware that first and foremost we mentor students in becoming researchers, and that training for teaching and service often takes a back seat. As late as the early 2000s, Susan K. Bender, Pyburn, and Smith pointed out that the idea that archaeology is, in most cases, an *applied* science, was an afterthought in the training of graduate students. Twenty years ago, a workshop on "Teaching Archaeology in the 21st Century" produced principles of curricular reform that included the proviso that "curriculum should redress ideas about exclusivity of rights to interpret the past that archaeologists may have." We believe that NAGPRA should be forcing archaeologists to substantially rethink the field's claim on interpreting the past.[16]

More and more graduate students were born after the passage of NAGPRA, and most learn postcolonialist perspectives as undergraduates. One would think that students would be offered the opportunity to learn how to become repatriation-savvy archaeologists or curators. In fact, thirty years after the law's passage, there is no excuse for ignoring ethical, NAGPRA-related training. Younger scholars do not have the same feelings about repatriation that an older generation might. Indeed, the results of the SAA survey indicated much higher receptivity to repatriation among responders who identified themselves as students than among older practitioners.[17]

Ryker-Crawford: When IU and the Glenn A. Black Laboratory of Archaeology approached the IAIA museum studies department to work closely with them on the Learning NAGPRA project, it was with an air of elation that we wholeheartedly accepted. We have been teaching the topic of museum repatriation ethics to undergraduate Native American students since before NAGPRA was passed. Our first full "Introduction to Repatriation" course was launched in 1998, taught by the well-known academic of Native American art history and museological theorist Nancy M. Mithlo (Chiricahua Apache). In 2004, we added a second course, "Issues in Repatriation," to the museum studies curriculum. Students wanted both an introductory course that explained how Native American activism led to the passage of NAGPRA and an upper-level repatriation course that focused on case studies after the law's ratification. In 2008, we added a third repatriation course, on "Cultural Reclamation," which focuses upon international Indigenous activism on topics of intangible cultural repatriation movements—such as the appropriation of traditional plant knowledge (TPK) by large pharmaceutical corporations for financial profit and the return of control (with financial compensation) to originating Indigenous communities surrounding the knowledge systems, innovations, and practices of medicinal plant use.

We knew the importance of training our students in techniques of close and meaningful collaborative research. Many of our graduates return to their communities to work in tribal museums and cultural centers— some taking up the role of Tribal Historic Preservation Officer as well. What we were not sure of, though, was whether our ways of teaching collaborative research models would translate to a Big 10 university setting with a majority non-Native student population. The Learning NAGPRA project afforded both myself and my colleague in the IAIA museum studies program, Felipe J. Estudillo Colón (Laguna Pueblo), the opportunity to share the skills that we have learned both in the classroom and in the field. At Indiana University we had a space to offer knowledge sets that had been built through the interaction of Native American faculty and students from tribes across the nation.

Sievert: In some ways, IU was a natural place for the Learning NAGPRA project to develop. Researching how students were learning about NAGPRA and how they were preparing for a professional career in which repatriation was the norm seemed like a natural outgrowth of pedagogy work that a core faculty at IU had been doing for years. Methods adopted from the scholarship of teaching and learning could provide a pathway for addressing the poor NAGPRA awareness and understanding among our students. IU supports both curricular innovation and graduate student preparation under its Center for Innovative Teaching and Learning (CITL). For over ten years, I had taught a pedagogy course for anthropology graduate students to address the realities of teaching, something often omitted in graduate professional training (despite the fact that if they become college faculty, this is what they will be paid to do).

Among IU anthropologists in 2015, we had professors known for developing archaeological ethics and for promoting archaeology in the public interest (K. Anne Pyburn, a NAGPRA director passionate about moving IU out of the repatriation Dark Ages, Jayne-Leigh Thomas, and Brian Gilley, an Indigenous anthropologist who had reinvigorated the campus's First Nations Educational and Cultural Center.) We also had the developer of the Indiana University Collegium on Inquiry in Action, a project funded by the Teagle Foundation to improve graduate student preparation for teaching (Jennifer Meta Robinson), and an academic specialist in CITL who worked particularly with graduate students (Katherine Kearns). The Learning NAGPRA project developed with myself, Pyburn, Thomas, and Gilley as co-principal investigators for a two-stage project, with Robinson and Kearns as senior personnel. Although work on ethics and pedagogy was customary at IU, applying those principles to the problem of NAGPRA illiteracy would be another matter. Jessie Ryker-Crawford and Felipe Colón from IAIA joined the core project staff as primary consultants.

The project funded a postdoctoral scholar to act as project manager and coordinate the many moving parts of the project. We recruited Dr. Teresa Nichols, a cultural anthropologist with archaeological and ethics experience who studies heritage. She developed and distributed surveys of students and educators; conducted interviews with students, faculty, and museum professionals; organized and facilitated meetings; and analyzed information we gathered.[18]

The Collegium Model for Interaction

In 2008, IU's Jennifer Meta Robinson had received funding from the Teagle Foundation to bring faculty and graduate students from four departments together to study how graduate students could bring research methods to bear on their teaching effectiveness. This provided a chance for faculty to work with biology (science), anthropology (social science), and communication and culture (humanities) graduate students in a forum facilitated by scholars from the Learning Science Department in the School of Education. What became clear at the outset was that departmental attitudes and disciplinary cultures were not necessarily aligned. Students familiar with qualitative research and critical theory and those trained in scientific methodology with its quantitative foci and evolutionary theory were challenged with learning how to use new terminology to communicate effectively. Even such common terms as *research*, *study*, or *evaluation* are used and understood in different ways, for maximum miscommunication.[19] Working concertedly over three years with students from these disciplines affected enhanced understanding, better communication, and appreciation for breaking down disciplinary barriers. We thought that the lessons learned in the graduate student collegium might apply in crossing disciplinary and cultural differences among people from a wide variety of backgrounds and perspectives on repatriation.

The Learning NAGPRA project brought together both Indigenous and non-Native specialists in repatriation, cultural resource management, museums operation, and teaching. We hoped to convene a series of collegium meetings with invited participants from across the disciplines who could help us identify and address problems in training for repatriation. Each of three Learning NAGPRA collegium meetings, to be held annually, had approximately twenty individuals (including our project personnel) from among THPO and tribal heritage or NAGPRA experts, archaeologists (Indigenous and not), biological anthropologists, and museum and pedagogy specialists. Larry Zimmerman, from Indiana University-Purdue University at Indianapolis (IUPUI), not only has long championed public archaeology, but also has been on the forefront of work to educate on matters of ethics and cultural justice, and his input proved invaluable. In addition, his connection to teaching museum methods and working with the Eiteljorg Museum of American Indians and Western Art in Indianapolis helped us bridge the gap between IU's need to repatriate, and IAIA's long history of teaching Indigenous students about museums and repatriation. Each of the three collegia included four Indigenous and non-Native graduate students providing the opportunity to introduce twelve students to the problems being addressed. At the heart of Learning NAGPRA is the IAIA curriculum, developed by professors Ryker-Crawford and Colón, which is founded on Indigenous perspectives. Students learn from citizens of Native nations who have direct experiences with repatriation. Their perspectives bring to light the emotions, the historical trauma, of Native peoples whose ancestors' right to eternal rest have been violated.[20]

During the first collegium meeting, held in 2015, the large group cast about a bit for direction, brainstormed, and identified areas of deficiency in college curricula. Indiana University and IAIA faculty then took ideas generated about research data and curriculum needed to understand and address problems to a workshop at the Amerind Foundation in Arizona, in 2016. Over the next two years and two collegium meetings the project participants and consultants solidified into four working groups to develop curriculum designed to address specific needs: learning worldviews related to repatriation, learning contexts for the practice of NAGPRA-based repatriation, training for cultural resource managers aligned with professional education credentials for the Register of Professional Archaeologists (RPA), and case studies for wide usage. In addition, the project supported surveys of students and educators, a survey of the RPA membership, and over forty interviews of both students and professionals across the continent. It included a semester-long study of the effects of teaching NAGPRA interventions carried out in specific courses at both tribal-serving, and nontribal universities. Team members also studied how textbooks for archaeology and bioanthropology treat ethics and repatriation.

We held the third collegium meeting at IAIA in Santa Fe in August of 2017. This allowed the non-Native participants an opportunity to experience directly the approach that this institute takes toward handling and curation of Indigenous material culture, and to interact with some of the IAIA students. We hired four IAIA students to take notes for the four working groups, thereby increasing exposure to the Learning NAGPRA project to additional Indigenous students. The main project outcome is an open-access website, on which the curriculum and resources developed are presented.[21]

Reactions to Learning NAGPRA

Even before we actually began the work in 2015, and even as recently as 2018, the Learning NAGPRA project has been poorly received in some tribal circles. The critique emanated from the fact that IU's holdings subject to NAGPRA were massive, and repatriation had not progressed much in over twenty years. It may have looked as though our commitment to repatriation was less important than seeking a grant from the National Science Foundation (which has funded at least some of the removal of remains in the first place), in order to support a teaching study. In 2015, the National NAGPRA Review Committee heard public comment criticizing the grant that we received, and discussions arose on possible forms of action to be taken against Indiana University, though none surfaced in the months following. Our Native critics rightly doubted our credibility, because we had not already repatriated large numbers of remains. Later, in 2015, after we had held the first collegium meeting in Bloomington, Indiana, and developed a website that better explained the project and the participants, overt negative commentary began to diminish, but had not disappeared. Simply explaining that we could both repatriate, and address how to train future professionals, has been insufficient to quell critique, despite the fact that an about-face in Indiana University's directives toward compliance as well as different personnel in some repositories on IU's campus had taken place. The pushback was important, because it reinforced the need for better communication and inclusivity in any work purporting to improve compliance with NAGPRA. A history of poor consultation efforts under NAGPRA and inadequate communication about projects related to ancestral remains and elder objects by non-Native scholars may have left Native scholars and educators mostly in the dark.[22] We hoped the project itself would increase openness, foster the opportunities for comment, and expand the network of NAGPRA educators in communication.

The community created by Learning NAGPRA is extensive. For the Learning NAGPRA project, we convened a core group to construct curriculum, as well as a fluid group of additional participants both Indigenous and non-Native to test classroom interventions in tribal and nontribal colleges, review our curriculum development, contribute statements and perspectives to the curriculum we are developing, provide interviews, and participate as discussants in forums at conferences. Two organized public panels held at the Denver Museum of Nature and Science and Chicago Field Museum brought in specialists from those museums and from practitioners in the region. Six forums held at national conferences for the Society for American Archaeology, the American Anthropological Association, the American Association of Physical Anthropology, and the Association for Tribal Archives, Libraries, and Museums presented discussion about the project itself, or about issues in teaching and experiences that the conversations and research generated, including one developed

Indigenous and non-Indigenous students who had been a part of the project. The project created a community of scholars, including over seventy people, of which 30 percent were Indigenous or minority scholars. We did not have a hard time including additional faculty in the project, as it appears that there has been a pent-up need to address repatriation, and to make certain that qualified people are out there to take on the work of repatriation in the Midwest and beyond.

Conclusions

Basic improvements in NAGPRA training, particularly in the ethical practice of repatriation, is one step toward steering the archaeology ship in a more progressive direction in terms of repatriation east of the Mississippi. Research archaeology can and is changing. We argue that it must change. Part of this change stems from building better relationships with Native scholars who bring Indigenous knowledge, pedagogies, and means of assessing learning outcomes. Our survey of students indicates a high level of receptivity, and a recognized need for more training to handle repatriation. But not all Midwestern anthropologists and repository directors are moving in this direction at the same pace. For example, the 2018 meeting of the Midwest Archaeological Conference was disquieting in that in one session, a discussant praised recent excavations and called for more excavation, even though burials were being encountered. In another session, I (Sievert) privately queried a student about the disposition of a collection on which they had worked, and that student later sought me out for additional conversation because my question was upsetting. The student indicated uncertainty as to the repatriation status of the collection and realized that this was problematic. In informal conversations with students who participated in Learning NAGPRA, it became clear that students had been previously uncomfortable even talking about the issues and appreciated the chance to freely communicate.[23] Having students participate has paid off already, as two of the twelve graduate students we included in the project found positions to handle repatriation under NAGPRA for two large universities with hundreds of ancestors. Countless other students who attended panels and presentations have become more vocal about ethical issues related to racism and disrespect.

NAGPRA is human rights legislation that redresses the legacy of colonial attitudes at the root of archaeological practice as it developed in the nineteenth century. Returning materials to Native nations is not only ethical, it is federal law. Would we as anthropologists imagine disregarding any other human rights laws? And is the process of repatriating cultural items, without fully engaging with the people whose ancestors languish in repositories, enough? We argue that the answer is an emphatic no. Repatriation is just the beginning. A fuller realization of NAGPRA as human rights legislation requires mentoring both non-Indigenous students and Indigenous students. Learning NAGPRA is a step in this direction, loosening the reins of scientific research so that descendant communities can not only join but drive the work. In the era of BIPOC lives matter, NAGPRA provides one platform for which to addresses needed change.

Notes

1. National Science Foundation, "Cultivating Cultures for Ethical STEM (CCE STEM) Program Solicitation NSF 18-532," https://www.nsf.gov/pubs/2018/nsf18532/nsf18532.htm.

2. Sievert, April, Teresa Nichols, K. Anne Pyburn, Jayne-Leigh Thomas, "Learning NAGPRA and Teaching Archaeology," in *History and Approaches in Heritage Studies*, ed. Phyllis Messenger, Susan J. Bender, and Paul A. Shackel (Gainesville: University Press of Florida, 2019), 87–106.

3. The Institute of American Indian Arts, or IAIA, is a fully accredited undergraduate and graduate multitribal college. Established in 1962 by executive order under President John F. Kennedy, IAIA was originally established as an upper-level high school arts program geared specifically toward addressing the impoverishment of tribal reservations, offering art classes that would aid Native American students in making a living through their cultural art. In 1975, IAIA became a two-year college offering degrees in studio arts, creative writing, and museum studies. It was accredited in 1984 by the Higher Learning Commission and by the National Association of Schools of Art and Design (NASAD); in 1986 IAIA became one of the five congressionally chartered colleges in the nation, charged with the study, preservation, and dissemination of traditional and contemporary expressions of Native American language, literature, history, oral traditions, and the visual and performing arts. Today, IAIA offers two-year and four-year degrees in creative writing, Indigenous liberal studies, museum studies, cinematic arts, studio arts, and performance arts, and master's degrees in creative writing and studio arts; at the time of publishing, IAIA is finalizing a master's degree in cultural administration.

4. This project, Learning NAGPRA, was funded by two grants through the National Science Foundation Program: Cultivating Cultures of Ethical STEM

(CCE-STEM grants nos. 1449465 and 1540447, 2015–19) awarded to Indiana University, Bloomington.

5. Sonya Atalay, *Community-Based Archaeology: Research with, by, and for Local Communities* (Berkeley: University of California Press, 2012), 48.

6. Ibid., 46–51.

7. Chip Colwell-Chanthaphonh and T. J. Ferguson, eds., *Collaboration in Archaeological Practice: Engaging Descendant Communities* (Lanham, MD: AltaMira, 2008); Zoe E. Niessel, "Better Late than Never: The Effect of the Native American Graves Protection and Repatriation Act's 2010 Regulations," *Wake Forest Law Review* 46, no. 4 (2011): 837–65; Chris Sikich, "Hamilton County Parks Fined for Archaeological Digs into Native American Graves," *Indianapolis Star*, November 13, 2017, https://www.indystar.com/story/news/local/hamilton-county/2017/11/13/hamilton-county-parks-fined-archaeological-digs-into-native-american-graves/850253001/.

8. National Historic Preservation Act, 1966 (2000), §106, https://www.fema.gov/national-historic-preservation-act-1966-amended-2000.

9. National Park Service, https://www.nps.gov/orgs/1563/efmo-sentencing.htm.

10. Kathleen S. Fine-Dare, *Grave Injustice: The American Indian Repatriation Movement and NAGPRA* (Lincoln: University of Nebraska Press, 2002); Nina Swidler, Kurt E. Dongoske, Roger Anyon, and Alan S. Downer, eds., *Native Americans and Archaeologists: Stepping Stones for Common* (Lanham, MD: AltaMira, 1997); Karen D. Vitelli, *Archaeological ethics* (Walnut Creek, CA: AltaMira, 1996).

11. Indiana Code 14-21-1-27, https://law.justia.com/codes/indiana/2010/title14/ar21/ch1.html.

12. Eric Hemenway, "Trials and Tribulations in a Tribal NAGPRA Program," *Museum Anthropology* 33, no. 2 (2010): 172–79.

13. Jim Enote, "Museum Collaboration Manifesto," 2015, http://ashiwi-museum.org/collaborations/museum-collaboration-manifesto/.

14. Elise Alonzi, "SAA Repatriation Survey," *SAA Archaeological Record* 16, no. 4 (2016): 15–20.

15. Diane Gifford Gonzalez, 2016. "Member Survey: Repatriation and SAA's Relationship to NAGPRA," *SAA Archaeological Record* 16, no. 4 (2016): 14.

16. Susan J. Bender, K. Anne Pyburn, and George S. Smith, "Revising the Archaeology Curriculum to Meet the Demands of the 21st Century," in *Handbook of Curriculum Development*, ed. Limon E. Kattington (New York: Nova Science, 2010), 387–401.

17. Alonzi, "SAA Repatriation Survey."

18. For additional information about the impetus behind and context for the project see Sievert, Nichols, Pyburn, and Thomas, "Learning NAGPRA and Teaching Archaeology."

19. Jennifer M. Robinson et al., "Teaching on Purpose: A Collegium Community Model for Supporting Intentional Teaching," *Journal on Excellence in College Teaching* 26, no. 1 (2015): 81–110.

20. Ibid.; Larry J. Zimmerman, "Integral, Ancillary, or Incidental: Teaching Ideal or Real in Social Science Research Ethics?," *Teaching Ethics* 12, no. 2 (2012): 149–55.

21. Learning NAGPRA, "Learning NAGPRA: Resources for Teaching and Training," Indiana University, accessed February 4, 2021, https://lrnagpra.sitehost.iu.edu/home.php.

22. National NAGPRA Review Committee, "Minutes of the 55th Meeting of the Native American Graves Protection and Repatriation Committee," Amherst, MA. March 3–4, 2015.

23. Colwell-Chanthaphonh and Ferguson, *Collaboration in Archaeological Practice.*

Bibliography

Alonzi, Elise. "SAA Repatriation Survey." *SAA Archaeological Record* 16, no. 4 (2016): 15–20.

Atalay, Sonya. *Community-Based Archaeology: Research with, by, and for Local Communities.* Berkeley: University of California Press, 2012.

Bender, Susan J., K. Anne Pyburn, and George S. Smith. "Revising the Archaeology Curriculum to Meet the Demands of the 21st Century." In *Handbook of Curriculum Development*, edited by Limon E. Kattington, 387–401. New York: Nova Science, 2010.

Colwell-Chanthaphonh, Chip, and T. J. Ferguson, eds. *Collaboration in Archaeological Practice: Engaging Descendant Communities.* Lanham, MD: AltaMira, 2008.

Enote, Jim. "Museum Collaboration Manifesto." 2015. http://ashiwi-museum.org/collaborations/museum-collaboration-manifesto/.

Fine-Dare, Kathleen S. *Grave Injustice: The American Indian Repatriation Movement and NAGPRA.* Lincoln: University of Nebraska Press, 2002.

Gonzalez, Diane Gifford. "Member Survey: Repatriation and SAA's Relationship to NAGPRA," *SAA Archaeological Record* 16, no. 4 (2016): 14.

Hemenway, Eric. "Trials and Tribulations in a Tribal NAGPRA Program." *Museum Anthropology* 33, no. 2 (2010): 172–79.

Indiana Code 14-21-1-27. Accessed 5/25/2018. https://law.justia.com/codes/indiana/2010/title14/ar21/ch1.html.

Learning NAGPRA. "Learning NAGPRA: Resources for Teaching and Training." Indiana University. Accessed February 4, 2021. https://lrnagpra.sitehost.iu.edu/home.php.

National Historic Preservation Act, 1966 (2000), §106. https://www.fema.gov/national-historic-preservation-act-1966-amended-2000.

National NAGPRA Review Committee. "Minutes of the 55th Meeting of the Native American Graves Protection and Repatriation Committee." Amherst, MA. March 3–4, 2015.

National Park Service. Accessed 12/14/2018. https://www.nps.gov/orgs/1563/efmo-sentencing.htm.

National Science Foundation. "Cultivating Cultures for Ethical STEM (CCE STEM) Program Solicitation NSF 18-532." https://www.nsf.gov/pubs/2018/nsf18532/nsf18532.htm.

Niessel, Zoe E. "Better Late than Never: The Effect of the Native American Graves Protection and Repatriation Act's 2010 Regulations." *Wake Forest Law Review* 46, no. 4 (2011): 837–65.

Robinson, Jennifer M., Katherine Dowell Kearns, Melissa Gresalfi, April K. Sievert, and Tyler Booth Christensen. "Teaching on Purpose: A Collegium Community Model for Supporting Intentional Teaching." *Journal on Excellence in College Teaching* 26, no. 1 (2015): 81–110.

Sievert, April, Teresa Nichols, K. Anne Pyburn, and Jayne-Leigh Thomas. "Learning NAGPRA and Teaching Archaeology." In *History and Approaches in Heritage Studies*, edited by Phyllis Messenger, Susan J. Bender, and Paul A. Shackel, 87–106. Gainesville: University Press of Florida, 2019.

Sikich, Chris. "Hamilton County Parks Fined for Archaeological Digs into Native American Graves." *Indianapolis Star*, November 13, 2017. https://www.indystar.com/story/news/local/hamilton-county/2017/11/13/hamilton-county-parks-fined-archaeological-digs-into-native-american-graves/850253001/.

Swidler, Nina, Kurt E. Dongoske, Roger Anyon, and Alan S. Downer, eds. *Native Americans and Archaeologists: Stepping Stones to Common Ground.* Lanham, MD: AltaMira, 1997.

Vitelli, Karen D. *Archaeological Ethics.* Walnut Creek, CA: AltaMira, 1996.

Zimmerman, Larry J. "Integral, Ancillary, or Incidental: Teaching Ideal or Real in Social Science Research Ethics?" *Teaching Ethics* 12, no. 2 (2012): 149–55.

Chapter 12

The Collaboration Spectrum

Legendary Stories as Windows into Gendered Change in Stó:lō Understandings of Territoriality

Keith Thor Carlson, Naxaxalhts'i
(Albert "Sonny" McHalsie),
Colin Murray Osmond, and Tsandlia Van Ry

Introduction

When one of our Stó:lō families hosts a potlatch feast to transfer a hereditary name across generations we always hire a speaker from another family to conduct the work and to be the voice through which the family communicates its history. When a loved one passes away the people who conduct the funeral ceremony, and those who dig the grave, have to come from outside the family. It's also like this when we clean our cemeteries. We clear the brush and grass away as communities each year, but we can't clean our own family members' graves. That history is too close to us. It's too strong. We need someone else to be in between. . . . These traditions show that there is important work that we need our friends and allies to do with us and sometimes for us. We have history and we live and communicate that history every day through our ceremonies and our oral traditions. But there are times when it is appropriate to have someone you trust communicate aspects of that history to others on your behalf. Doing it this way allows us to humble ourselves, and it enables others to see that the historical interpretation has passed through another set of eyes and ears.

—Naxaxalhts'i[1]

Naxaxalhts'i (aka Albert "Sonny" McHalsie, historian and cultural advisor at the Stó:lō Research and Resource Management Centre, and coauthor on this chapter) points out that it has long been a sign of respectful discernment among the Coast Salish to acknowledge that while some types of work are best done by oneself, other tasks are better accomplished through partnering and collaboration. Indeed, the Stó:lō Coast Salish communities along the lower Fraser River watershed in southwestern British Columbia have a long history of collaborating on research projects with outsiders. Sometimes the research questions and activities are initiated by the community, who then invite a trusted researcher to participate. Other times a researcher comes with an idea and pitches it to the Stó:lō. On still other occasions the ideas emerge jointly from Stó:lō community members and outsider researchers who have been in sustained conversations. In this last scenario, the sort that this chapter aspires to promote and describe, the research questions ideally are *codesigned*, the research itself is *coexecuted*, the interpretation and analysis are *cocreated*, and then both parties participate in *cocommunicating* the results.

Research relationships, in this context, necessarily take the expression of partnerships. Research in one project inherently informs the next; conversations built around one research project inevitably sustain themselves in one form or another so as to help inspire and inform the content and the expression of subsequent research projects. This vision of community-engaged scholarship (CES) recognizes that each component of every research project and activity exists on a spectrum that adapts and adjusts across projects and within projects. That is to say, the degree to which the outside researcher and the community members cooperate and collaborate on each project (and indeed on each component of each project) varies depending upon a host of matters including the individual partners' passion, priorities, availability, capacity, expertise, and emotional investment. The guiding principle is to facilitate shared authority. Sharing authority realizes key objectives from both parties achieving a comfortable balance of labor and responsibility. This better ensures that both partners see and experience the benefits from their investment in the project.[2]

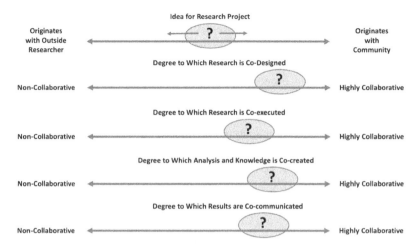

Figure 12.1. Spectrum of community-engaged scholarship collaborative activity.

Over the past half century, the Stó:lō communities have been able to increasingly and effectively convince researchers who want to work in their territory of the merits of the adage "Nothing about us without us." When the Stó:lō decide to partner with others (and it is important to note that for several decades now the Stó:lō have had sufficient in-house research capacity to go it alone on many research projects when they so desire) the collaborations are premised upon a set of principles that forefront the Stó:lō people's position as both carriers and definers of their own inherent rights. This is a position that recognizes the inseparability of Stó:lō people's rights from their lands and from interpretations of their history. A second and reciprocal expectation is that outside researchers commit to building and sustaining trusting and respectful relationships that are mutually enriching.[3]

The Stó:lō Research and Resource Management Centre (SRRMC) in Chilliwack operates a research registry program for the purpose of coordinating research projects involving its staff, so as to better protect Stó:lō history and culture. SSRMC approval of a project entitles researchers to access the vast oral and archival history records held in the Stó:lō archives—a repository to which accepted researchers are likewise expected to contribute once their research activities are complete. Importantly, SSRMC policies highlight their desire to "occupy the field." To protect Stó:lō history and culture, SSRMC staff make an ongoing effort to "engage in research and resource management activities [that include] interacting with a community of academic researchers and institutions."[4]

Experience since the 1960s has convinced the Stó:lō of the benefits of interaction and cooperation as means of achieving certain research goals and capacity building. Indeed, back in 1999, Chief Lester Ned of Sumas First Nation in his capacity as Yewal Siya:m (head chief of all the Stó:lō communities) was clear in speaking with Keith Carlson and Naxaxalhts'i (coauthors on this chapter who at the time were the staff historian and staff cultural advisor, respectively, at the Stó:lō office) that the most important part of all research activities was the integrity of the evidence and the analysis. "Tell us [the Stó:lō leadership and communities] what we need to know, not what we want to know," Chief Ned explained. This principal has remained at the forefront of Stó:lō research policies ever since; and it continues to guide the research collaborations of the authors of this chapter.

Chief Ned's directive speaks to Indigenous peoples' desire for high quality research and analysis that is conducted *with* and *for* the Indigenous communities that can pass peer review, withstand legal challenges, contribute to the advancement of scholarship, and ultimately stand the test of time. Too often in his experience, Chief Ned explained, well-meaning

Figure 12.2. Naxaxalhts'i (Albert "Sonny" McHalsie) pointing to a heritage feature.

scholars had allowed their compassion and sympathy for the Stó:lō people as victims of settler colonialism to color their research and shape their conclusion. Too often, in his opinion, researchers tried to anticipate the research outcomes that they thought Stó:lō people wanted to be told, and then shaped their analysis to meet those expectations. Rather than using the research and analysis process as an opportunity to expand understanding and potentially challenge preconceived notions of what was in Indigenous people's best interests, some non-Indigenous community-based researchers had followed a paternalistic methodology. Such action, regardless of how well intentioned, ultimately worked to reinforce stereotypes of Indigenous oral history as politically malleable and of Indigenous people's and their allies' use of archival and archaeological evidence as selective. The result was compromised scholarship that adversaries were able to discredit in court and in the forum of public opinion.

From the perspective of the authors of this chapter, however, the challenges facing Indigenous communities and their research partners go well beyond the need to ensure intellectual rigor and respectful collaboration. The bigger challenges are those associated with what we regard as the *conundrum of double permanence*: despite whatever it may have been that members of settler society or Indigenous people once thought about, or even wished for, regarding one another's future (or lack thereof) in North America, both Indigenous people and settlers are here to stay. It served American and Canadian settler interests to promote national narratives that portrayed Indigenous people as a doomed and vanishing race destined to be either eclipsed and replaced by a supposed superior British/American people, or assimilated and absorbed into the emerging hegemony of settler-colonial society.

Conceiving Indigenous people as a vanishing race with no future, it was easy for successive generations of settlers to compromise Indigenous treaty rights. Conceiving Indigenous people as vanishing enabled settlers to consider themselves as benevolent and kind when they set up Indian boarding and residential schools that were designed to physically separate Indigenous youth from their parents, and intellectually and spiritually separate Indigenous children from their culture. National narratives conveniently located Indigenous people as tragic, even noble, victims of circumstance (as opposed to victims of settler violence and ideology).[5]

Despite the diversity of Indigenous cultures found across the North American continent, in settler narratives all Indigenous people inevitably were divided into one of two groups—good Indians, who accepted the inevitability of their displacement as the owners, occupiers, and regulators of lands and resources, and bad Indians, who rejected the inevitability of settler hegemony and naively and tragically fought against the reservation and reserve systems that government imposed.[6]

From the perspective of non-Indigenous Canadians and Americas today, the conundrum of double permanence is that Indigenous people have indeed survived and, like non-Indigenous Canadian and American settler societies who regard themselves as having broken free from their earlier British colonial overlords, Indigenous people see themselves as rightfully having a future in the lands now called Canada and the United States. In Indigenous eyes, their own permanence is given meaning through articulations of cultural resilience, political resurgence, and economic reemergence.

The conundrum of double permanence is reflected in the way historians have traditionally relegated Indigenous people to only the introductory chapters of American and Canadian history textbooks, where they were assigned minor roles in the unfolding drama of American Manifest Destiny and Canadian Dominion. In these classic national narratives, Indigenous people were depicted as "a problem" that the settler state needed to solve—assimilation being the inevitable solution. To the extent that Indigenous people retained a presence in the later chapters of more recently composed versions of our national narratives, they shifted from being portrayed as "a problem" *for* settler colonial states, to becoming instead "people with problems" *within* settler colonial states. In these narratives, they are defined by problems such as poverty, unemployment, technological backwardness, and drug and alcohol addictions. The solution posited in these narratives was simple: assimilation. For Indigenous people themselves, however, assimilation has never been the solution. Rather, it has been, and remains, the problem.

The conundrum of double permanence is likewise reflected in the way these Canadian and American narratives have been framed. Settler time, as Mark Rifkin has recently explained, centers the nation-state so as to orientate pivotal events, periodizations, and chronologies in ways that are counter to, and subversive of, Indigenous temporal sovereignty.[7] Settler time reflects the fact that settler narratives inevitably depict the most important thing in Indigenous people's history as being settler society. Decolonized narratives require decolonized chronologies and a reframing of history so that, rather than Indigenous people being seen within American and Canadian histories, the United States and Canada are instead positioned within Shawnee, Myaamia, or Stó:lō histories, for example. Instead of Indigenous people being described as problems for settlers in the early chapters of nation state narratives and then people with problems in later chapters, decolonized narratives portray Canadian and American settler colonialism as profoundly disruptive forces in Indigenous histories where the final chapters remain to be written.

Indeed, the settler-colonial nation-state is a relatively recent phenomenon. Whether Canada and the United States will still exist in a recognizable form in two hundred years is an open question. Less likely is the possibility that in two hundred years there will not still be Stó:lō, Shawnee, and Miami Indigenous nations in recognizable forms. But, even if settler colonial states ultimately prove to be malleable and even transitory, settler permanence will remain a reality. The challenge is to work today to codesign and coconstruct systems that restore meaningful self-governance and control over significant lands and resources to Indigenous people in a manner that is simultaneously not compromising of the safety and prosperity of non-Indigenous settler people.

What Chief Ned was asking us to do, therefore, was to help lay the groundwork for a world where settlers were presented with historical evidence and interpretation revealing Indigenous resilience and permanence as both an ongoing reality and a future inevitability. He was not so much asking us to avoid being political, but to avoid being polemical; to ensure that our research was rigorous, to demonstrate strong connections between our evidence and our interpretation, and to work collaboratively to cocreate new knowledge that could be intelligible and meaningful to both Indigenous and settler communities. His words remind us to be aware that, like all other forms of humanistic and social scientific enquiry, community-engaged scholarship is inherently taking place within a political environment precisely because it seeks to help provide answers to urgent and pressing contemporary problems.

Mapping the Transformers' Travels: Gender, Colonialism, and Stó:lō Territoriality

In this chapter we highlight and reflect upon some of the ways that we negotiated collaboration and cooperation among ourselves and with various members of the Stó:lō community in our research project titled "Mapping the Transformers' Travels: Gender, Colonialism, and Coast Salish Territoriality."[8] In particular we examine the ways that each of us has worked to try give up certain individual privileges so as to share authority in ways that contributed to better meeting one another's needs.

One of the ways we have sought to share authority is through the way we present our ideas and reflections in this essay. Keith Carlson drafted most of the early sections and conclusion of this essay in consultation with, and with input from, the other authors. But, to provide opportunities for each of us to speak directly, we have created space for individual reflections in the latter sections of this essay.

We begin with a discussion of how the idea for the research project originated within the Stó:lō community, highlighting the way that informal conversations between friends can inspire original academic and intellectual enquiry. We then move to a discussion of our research methods and objectives. Finally, we describe some of our preliminary findings from a particular set of the historical records under examination.

Although our primary purpose is to highlight the spectrum of collaboration within research partnerships, we want to do so through a close examination of a particular case study. In particular, we will discuss findings from our efforts to test the hypothesis that nineteenth-century Canadian settler-colonial policies aimed at reshaping Coast Salish family structures (i.e., the banning of polygamy and arranged marriages coupled with pressuring Coast Salish families to adopt nuclear family housing and male-centered band governance) had unanticipated and largely overlooked effects on the way Coast Salish societies have come to understand and experience tribal territoriality today.

To accomplish this, we seek to determine the extent to which there had formerly been a gender balance in Coast Salish society wherein elite males emphasized tribal territorial exclusivity and elite females prioritized tribal territorial inclusivity so as to assess the degree to which settler colonialism caused this to become destabilized. Our research suggests that distinctly female Stó:lō perspectives on space had been largely eclipsed by colonial policies and attitudes that situated authority in the hands of men. Over time, colonial policy-makers equated Indigenous interest in resources with proximity to residence and not with regard to geographically dispersed social and economic networks associated with extended families.

Figure 12.3. Colin Osmond, Sonny McHalsie, and Keith Thor Carlson take a trip down the Fraser River to visit the site of one of the Stó:lō's "Transformer" sites.

Historical and Cultural Context

Although European, British, and American explorers and fur traders had been visiting Coast Salish territory for more than half a century, it was not until the arrival of significant agrarian and urban settlers in the 1860s (following the short-lived but dramatic Fraser River gold rush of 1858) that Stó:lō people experienced direct pressure to change the way they organized their families and related to their land and resources. Prior to settler colonialism, elite Coast Salish parents arranged marriages for their children with elite families from other settlements principally for the purposes of building peaceful relations and to secure access to food resources that were not either readily or reliably available within one's own territory.[9] Polygamy was the norm, and as a result residence among the elite tended to be patrilocal.[10] Brides almost always relocated to live in their husband's settlement, for it was an affront to a woman's cowives (*sxáye*) and her cowives' parents' families if a husband showed excessive favor to one spousal relationship over another. Interfamily relations would be strained if a husband tried to compel his wives to reside for any length of time (let alone permanently) in a favored cowife's parents' village.

In this system, women played vitally important roles in the diplomatic, political, and economic spheres that linked communities.[11] While, like men, their influence and responsibilities varied from person to person, from a structural perspective, women (and especially elite women from influential wealthy families) worked to ensure peaceful relations and the equitable sharing of resources across tribes and between families. But women were also more. Each woman also brought knowledge of her home community with her—ranging from information about resource locations and harvest timing to esoteric private knowledge relating to spirit helpers, spirited places, medicines, and cures. Importantly, each woman knew the sxwoxwiyá:m (legendary stories) carried by her parents and their families, and upon marriage she additionally learned the stories of her husband as well as those of her cowives. Her children grew up familiar with, and fluent in, the stories that gave meaning to each of their parents' tribal communities. Women additionally carried bonds of affection to their sisters who, under this system, were inevitably married into polygamous relationships themselves and living with cowives of their own in the settlements of their husbands.

Individually, a wife worked to ensure the health and strength of the relationship between her husband's parents and her own mother and father. Collectively, cowives shared authority and responsibility. They cooperated in harvesting, assisted one another during ceremonies, and, importantly, coraised their children—all of whom were siblings to one another. Indeed, every elite child had at least two names, one to be known by among their father's family, and one to be called by when among their mother's family. All elites thus essentially had dual citizenship and were additionally linked together through a geographically dispersed web of complex intercommunity social and economic connections.

Settler colonialism by definition has the goal of disassociating Indigenous people from one another and from their ancestral lands. It manifests itself through a host of oppressive systems and intertwined structures that together work to alienate Indigenous people from the traditions, mechanisms, and practices that their ancestors used to connect to, and manage, their lands and resources.

Settler colonialism unfolded among the Coast Salish in much the same way that it did elsewhere across the North American continent.

Stó:lō people were restricted to small tracts of land known as Indian reserves, and their actions outside of these reserves were systematically curtailed as settlers consolidated their control.[12] Stó:lō people were, on the one hand, denied the lands most suited to Western-style economic activity (1869) while, on the other hand, many of their land and aquatic resource-use activities (such as the commercial sale of salmon in 1886) were criminalized, as were their governance system (the anti-potlatch law of 1884) and their spirituality (the anti-"tamanawas" or winter dance law of 1884).[13] Their ability to participate in, and influence settler governance was likewise denied through legislation that linked Indian enfranchisement to the loss of status and Indigenous rights. Their children were compelled to attend residential schools, where they were separated from their families and inculcated through assimilationist curriculum.[14] And their ancient hierarchical system of collective rights and privileges were undermined as inferior to and incompatible with liberalism's idea of the ideal autonomous individual. Throughout, settler colonialism challenges Stó:lō social structures and notions of gender balance by promoting a patriarchal definition of familial and political authority and by privileging the idea of the nuclear family, grounded in a particular residence, as normative.[15]

Codesigning Research

This research project began in the Spring of 2011 when Keith, the senior author of this chapter, stopped by Myra Sam's house on the Th'ewá:lí (Soowahlie) First Nation for an impromptu visit. He and Myra's husband Wesley had been close friends. They had gotten to know one another two decades earlier while Keith was collaborating on two extensive oral history research projects, one examining the subject of traditional Coast Salish leadership and the other working with Stó:lō war veterans to lay the ground work for respecting and acknowledging the role of Stó:lō military personnel in the Canadian military. At the time Keith had been employed as the staff historical researcher for the Stó:lō Tribal Council office in Chilliwack British Columbia and Wesley was a respected elder known to carry knowledge from his grandfather, the renowned tribal historian Robert Joe. After Wesley's passing Keith remained in communication with Myra, despite having relocated to take up a faculty position at the University of Saskatchewan in 2001 (two provinces away). Over the coming years Keith visited Myra whenever he was in the Fraser Valley (where he sustained an active CES research program) and he would occasionally mail Myra packages of dried Labrador tea leaves that he picked in northern Saskatchewan to help substitute for those she could no long pick herself in the Fraser Valley due to urban expansion into her traditional harvesting area.

It was a cool wet day in early May when Keith arrived at Myra's house. Inside, Myra and her closest friend Marge Kelly were sitting at Myra's kitchen table drinking tea. The two widows held prominent positions as the Th'ewá:lí community's representatives on the intertribal Stó:lō Elder's Council.[16] When Keith arrived, Myra and Marge were discussing how it seemed to them that regardless of the family connections that linked people together across tribal divisions, the political leadership of the various Stó:lō First Nations seemed to struggle to find ways to cooperate with one another when it came to sharing access to, and the wealth derived from, natural resources such as forestry located within their traditional territories. As they talked, they cited several examples to support their view. They additionally noted that the majority of the elected and hereditary chiefs were male. Over several cups of tea, they explained that while they appreciated the importance and necessity of each chief working to protect the remaining natural resources within his particular community's tribal territory, they were disappointed over the chiefs' apparent reluctance to find ways to better share so as to ensure the economic and social health of all the Indigenous communities throughout the region.

Of course, an important context for the tensions Myra and Marge were describing among the chiefs was the way in which the weight of Canadian settler-colonial policies aimed at displacing Indigenous people from their lands and resources had fallen disproportionately heavy on the Indigenous people of this part of Canada's Pacific province. Industrial resource extraction, which had commenced with the 1858 Fraser River gold rush and the subsequent construction of a series of transportation and commodity corridors, the development of intensive agriculture and industrial forestry, mining, and hydroelectric dam construction, had turned the lower Fraser River watershed into one of the most densely populated, industrially impacted, and commercially influential regions in Canada. And more recent actions by the provincial government to transform vast tracts of Crown lands into provincial recreational parks for the enjoyment of greater Vancouver's ever-expanding population meant that there were fewer and fewer open lands remaining that the Stó:lō communities could access for hunting, gathering, and spiritual activities. Indeed, the contentious portion of the chief's meeting that Myra and Marge had attended involved the Stó:lō political leadership discussing the issue of identifying potential new treaty settlement lands from among the remaining Crown lands within Stó:lō territory. Such lands, if acquired through the BC treaty process, would acquire a status similar to Indian reserves in that they would be under exclusive Stó:lō control. Some Stó:lō tribes had almost no Crown land remaining within which to identify potential new treaty settlement lands, while others had more options. How would this inequity, a product of settler colonialism, be resolved?

But, as Myra pointed out, while both the quantity and quality of Crown lands that Stó:lō people were able to access and control had been greatly diminished by non-Indigenous industrial logging since the arrival of Xwelítems ("the hungry people"—non-Indigenous settlers), natural resources had in fact never been equitably distributed in Coast Salish territory. Indeed, hearing similar observations from elders of an earlier generation, the anthropologist Wayne Suttles argued that what distinguished the Coast Salish world was less the abundance of resources than the variation of their availability due to ecological diversity and seasonal fluctuations. Suttles argued that it was the complex system of social networks linking people from one ecological niche to another that facilitated the exchange of economic wealth across tribal lines. Linkages across the Coast Salish "cultural continuum" allowed for a shared regional prosperity.[17]

Myra and Marge observed that when it came to important tasks such as finding safe homes for "at risk" Indigenous children regardless of the tribe in which the children were registered, the social networks remained effective. In Myra and Marge's opinion, this was likely because the committees that oversaw the operations of child welfare services consisted primarily of Stó:lō women. These women, it seemed, thought and acted in terms of cooperation within and among extended families—identities that cut across tribal boundaries and First Nation band membership lists. Why, Marge and Myra wondered, did the largely male political leaders seem so consistently less inclined to cooperate when it came to ensuring equitable access to inequitably distributed economic resources? What was it, in other words, that made male leaders think in terms that seemed to emphasize tribal exclusivity, whereas female leaders tended to think in terms that accentuated intertribal cooperation and inclusivity?

Over the course of another couple of cups of tea Myra, Marge, and Keith wondered if perhaps this apparent disjuncture was part of a larger and more complex pattern with roots in deeply held cultural traditions. Keith suggested that perhaps it was alternatively, or additionally, a product of colonial-induced cultural change—that is, the adoption of colonial notions of masculinity that championed male authority in the political and resource management realms.[18] Further conversation sparked additional speculation wherein the three wondered if over the past century and a half there had been a gendered division in terms of the way Stó:lō people adjusted to forces promoting either cultural continuity or cultural change. In thinking of historical examples from within the oral traditions and in archival records with which Myra, Marge, and Keith were familiar, it appeared to the three that, when it came to political action, high status elite name-carrying Coast Salish men had often been expected to emphasize behavior designed to protect regional resources for the benefit of their home (local) community. Women, on the other hand, seemed to have more often been inclined to think broadly and regionally, and to have prioritized ways of facilitating sharing access to what they and others had.

Myra's and Marge's questions ultimately inspired Keith to engage in a series of supplementary conversations throughout the Stó:lō community. Keith first approached his long-time friend and research collaborator, Naxaxalhts'i (Sonny McHalsie)—the Stó:lō Nation's historian and cultural advisor (and coauthor on this chapter). Together they mulled over the comments Myra and Marge had made, and gradually the framework for a collaborative research project emerged.

Meanwhile, during a visit to the more northern Coast Salish community of Tla'amin, Keith had a conversation with Elder Mary George who likewise highlighted remarkably similar issues to those initially raised by Myra Sam and Marge Kelly. Subsequent encouraging conversations with Tla'amin treaty research coordinator Michelle Washington led to formal consultation with political leaders from the Tla'amin Nation. Naxaxalhts'i then joined Keith in traveling to Tla'amin, where the two outlined their idea for a formal research project and invited Tla'amin to become a partner. After further consultation, leaders from both the Stó:lō and Tla'amin communities provided letters endorsing a formal grant application. However, due to restricted space, in this chapter we will only be discussing our work within the Stó:lō community.

Naxaxalhts'i comes from a blended family. His mother was Stó:lō from the Chawathil First Nation (a member of the Tíyt [upriver] tribal community) in the Fraser Valley, and his father was Nlakapamux from the Boston Bar First Nation located in the Fraser Canyon. Naxaxalhts'i is a Nlakapamux ancestral name. His father was employed by the Canadian Pacific Railroad where transfers were common. As a result, Naxaxalhts'i's family relocated several times to settlements on both sides of the Stó:lō-Nlakapamux border. As a youth, Naxaxalhts'i had been fascinated with the oral stories describing the origins of tribal communities and the transformer narratives that explained how the world came to assume its current and permanent form. He grew up hearing such stories in both informal and ritual context from elders on both sides of his family.

As a young adult in the mid-1980s, Naxaxalhts'i secured employment first as an archaeological assistant and then later as a cultural researcher with the Stó:lō Tribal Council. In that capacity, he had the privilege of formally interviewing elders as part of his job. With each interview and conversation, it became clearer to Naxaxalhts'i that these ancient stories both connected his community to ancestral lands and likewise provided teaching and insights on how to live a good life that was consistent with his elders' experiences and teachings. It also became clear to him that many Stó:lō people of his generation were no longer familiar with these stories. Residential schools and a host of other colonial factors had worked to disconnect Stó:lō people from their ancestors' narratives.

For Naxaxalhts'i, this was distressing. Through his interviews with elders and his research work in the library and archives he had come to develop an ever-deeper appreciation for the importance of the distinct ways his Stó:lō ancestors understood their history—as distinct form a settler-colonial understanding. On several occasions in the early 1990s, Skwah First Nation elder Yamelot (Rosaleen George), for instance, had explained to both him and Keith that knowledge of history was directly tied to social status within Coast Salish society. In Yamelot's words, "To know your history is to be *smelá:lh*—that's 'worthy.' If you don't know your history (if you've lost it or forgotten it), well, then you are *s'téxem*—and that's 'worthless.' "[19] People without history, in the Stó:lō view, were not only potentially poor in terms of material wealth (i.e., they might not know where they had rights to fish salmon, to hunt game, or to trap, or to pick betties and tubers) but they were also potentially poor in spirit. Indeed, within Stó:lō cosmology, people who were disconnected from ancestor spirits were in danger of losing touch with who they were. Without knowledge of who and where their ancestors were they could not effectively communicate with their ancestors and so lacked the spiritual guidance and nurturing that Stó:lō people regarded as essential to gaining the knowledge and insights to live a healthy life.

Naxaxalhts'i had dedicated the vast majority of his research activities over the preceding decades to learning and communicating ancient *sxwoxwiyá:m* (myth-age legendary stories describing the origins of the world and how it came to assume its current and fixed form). His interviews with elders had especially imprinted on him the importance of legendary stories as windows through which he could better view and understand the world of his ancestors. Sxwoxwiyá:m not only taught lessons, Naxaxalhts'i determined; they additionally anchored people to the landscape—thereby securing the Stó:lõ's place in the world.

Independently and together, Keith and Naxaxalhts'i had been discussing and trying to better appreciate and understand legendary narratives for many years, but Myra's and Marge's discussion provided a slightly different perspective that sparked new lines of enquiry. Over the previous two decades, Naxaxalhts'i had begun to share certain legendary stories he had learned from elders past and present to other Stó:lõ people as well as to the wider non-Indigenous society through bus and boat tours of Stó:lõ territory where he pointed out sites associated with legendary stories.[20]

Naxaxalhts'i's tours became especially popular with members of non-Indigenous society who were active in trying to promote reconciliation between Indigenous and settler societies. Faculty from the several regional universities scheduled Naxaxalhts'i's bus tours as fieldtrips for their classes, as did federal and provincial government agencies (such as the Royal Canadian Mounted Police) who integrated them into their newly designed cultural sensitivity and awareness training programs. The tours were also in high demand among K–12 school teachers and their students. Through his sharing of sxwoxwiyá:m, Naxaxalhts'i assists settler Canadians hoping to see the landscape through a Stó:lõ cultural lens. He helps them appreciate geographical features not merely as geological formations but as animated storied places where X̲á:ls the transformer had inscribed the ancient history of the Stó:lõ people. Naxaxalhts'i was, in other words, helping make the culturally intangible visible. Myra and Marge's comments provided a new focus and a sense of urgency for Naxaxalhts'i in his work reviving and communicating sxwoxwiyá:m.

After sustaining their conversation about the implications of a gendered perspective within sxwoxwiyá:m over the course of many months, Keith and Naxaxalhts'i visited with other female Stó:lõ knowledge keepers to solicit their insights and perspectives. Among those with whom conversations were held were Mary Malloway of Yakweakwioose, Kasey Chapman of Seabird Island, and Chief Rhoda Peters of Chawathil, each of whom provided observations that echoed and reinforced things Myra and Marge had earlier articulated. Naxaxalhts'i and Keith additionally began to review audio files and fieldnotes that they had taken during earlier oral history interviews with now deceased female elders, including Matilda Gutierrez of Chawathil, Rosaleen George of Skwah, Edna Douglas of Cheam, and Edna Bobb of Seabird Island, looking for references to gendered perspectives on territoriality.

Guidance and collaboration were also sought from Naxaxalhts'i's colleagues who made up the professional research staff at the Stó:lō Research and Resource Management Centre. In particular Dave Schaepe, director and senior archaeologist of the SRRMC, was consulted and invited to provide his reflections and suggestions. Dave's experience as a senior member of the Stó:lō treaty negotiation team coupled with his earlier doctoral research, which examined intercommunity connections in the precontact era, provided him with deep insights.[21] He offered suggestions that helped to focus the project, and his insights into the key contemporary political challenges facing the Stó:lō communities reinforced for Naxaxalhts'i and Keith the importance of shaping the historical research project such that would contribute meaningfully to contemporary circumstances.

Following these consultations and conversations, Keith drafted a grant application for the Canadian Social Science and Humanities Research Council (SSHRC) in which Dave Schaepe was listed as a formal collaborator. After one failed attempt, the team resubmitted their grant and secured funding the following year.

Coexecuting Research

As mentioned, the overall project has two dimensions. The first is a social and cultural history of the gendered repercussions of colonial interference into Coast Salish family structures (in particular polygamy, communal multifamily housing, and arranged marriages). For reasons of space, that aspect of the project will not be directly discussed in any detail here. For the purposes of this essay we will only be focusing on one particular component of the gender shift in Stó:lō people's perspectives on territoriality—that revealed through measurable changes in the content of sxwōxwiyám describing the world's creation, tribal origins, and ancient transformations.[22]

Over the past 150 years various ethnographers have worked with Stó:lō knowledge keepers to record sxwōxwiyám. Keith and Naxaxalhts'i identified the archival repositories that contained historical recordings of sxwoxwiyá:m and then with grant funding we supported one of Keith's doctoral students, Colin Osmond, to serve as the senior student researcher for the project. Colin worked closely with Keith and Naxaxalhts'i to design an Excel spreadsheet that would be used for coding and data input for the project, with the goal of having the Excel later translated into an XML database. Colin also participated in community consultation sessions. In the second year of the grant, we hired several undergraduates as well as one high school student to work as summer research assistants. One, Jenna Casey, was a senior undergraduate history honours student at the University of Saskatchewan, where the previous summer she had been employed by Keith as a summer intern working on a community-engaged research project with a local Saskatchewan First Nation. A second, Amber Brauner, was also a University of Saskatchewan student with sophisticated German language skills. She was hired to translate the text of the sxwox-wiyá:m that the anthropologist Franz Boas had originally published in German in 1895.[23] To facilitate layered mentoring, these junior student researchers worked under Colin's direct supervision on transcription, coding, and data entry.

We next consulted with Wenona Victor, a Stó:lō faculty member at the University of the Fraser Valley, located in the heart of Stó:lō territory. She assisted us in identifying Tsandlia Van Ry, a Stó:lō undergraduate student at UFV who had strong research skills and a keen desire to learn more about her community's history. Tsandlia (a coauthor on this chapter) had lived until recently away from her tribal homeland. She indicated to us that she did not have a deep connection or familiarity with Stó:lō ancestral traditions, but that she was eager to become involved so as to learn. Dave Schaepe then made available physical space within the Stó:lō research office for Tsandlia to work.

Keith and Naxaxalhts'i reviewed the students' work, conducted their own parallel research, and communicated with Stó:lō knowledge keepers and political leaders to keep them abreast of developments and progress. In the second and third years of the project, with much of the information now entered into the database, Keith, Naxaxalhts'i, and Colin facilitated a series of community consultation sessions in the Stó:lō communities, where, with the undergraduate and high school research assistants participating, they presented the preliminary findings and invited people to assist in interpreting and analyzing the information. Through these sessions, they additionally sought out knowledge keepers and invited them to orally share their sxwoxwiyá:m stories so they could be included in the database (an open invite and ongoing process).

Throughout the project, Keith consulted with several Stó:lō educators in the K–12 system, as well as those from the Tla'amin community.[24] The research team worked with most closely with Rod Peters (Indigenous Education Coordinator for the Fraser Cascade School District) to identify opportunities for incorporating knowledge gathered from this project's research into high school class rooms.

Cocreating Knowledge

Our research and analysis on this project remain preliminary, but suggestive. It appears that our original research hypothesis had merit. At this stage, with research ongoing, we now have 190 versions of Stó:lō sxwoxwiyá:m in our database—and the number continues to grow. Due to space constraints, for the purposes of this chapter, we will focus on one particular corpus of sxwoxwyyá:m—those recorded by Franz Boas in 1890 in his interviews with the Stó:lō knowledge keepers.[25] For comparative analytical purposes, we provide some content and statistical comparison between these nineteenth-century recordings and those that were recorded with later generations of elders in the years between 1960 and 1990—the decades when Stó:lō people and allied local ethnographers and linguists were working diligently to document and record Stó:lō oral traditions.

In the summer of 1890, when Boas conducted his interviews with Stó:lō people, a growing number of Stó:lō elite were no longer participating in arranged marriage and living in polygamous family units. For the first time in Coast Salish memory, large numbers of young men and young women from elite families were forming monogamous marriage unions motivated by interpersonal love rather than joining in polygamous unions orchestrated by elders whose principal motivations were economic and diplomatic. It was also in this era that married couples moved out of communal longhouses and into Western-style nuclear family housing—typically small bungalows. And, of course, it was also in this era that many of the food gathering resources sites that earlier had been the focus of interfamily marriage diplomacy were now being alienated by settler commercial, agricultural, and urban developments. In this era as well, settler military and police forces imposed new systems of regulation onto Stó:lō community for the purpose of curtailing violent intercommunity relations. Indigenous raiding and warfare were criminalized and settler systems of police surveillance and judicial oversight imposed in their place—and in the process the complex Stó:lō system of peacemaking was undermined. The economic and political underpinnings of arranged polygamous marriages were, in other words, disrupted and challenged by a colonial system of land management and interpersonal regulation. Put another way, this began the process of disconnecting particular gendered aspects of Stó:lō culture from Stó:lō praxis.

And while settler colonialism was imposing these new controls over Indigenous lands and bodies it was simultaneously introducing new economics and technologies that, despite their role in furthering settler colonial agendas, Stó:lō people were selectively able to take advantage of and put to their own uses. Wage labor opportunities at the industrial salmon canneries, in the logging industry, on railroad construction, and on commercial farms, coupled with introduced technologies such as glass jar canning as a means to preserve meats, vegetables, and fruits, were making it possible for Stó:lō people to conceive of nuclear families as viable social and economic units. Likewise, the introduction of dry good stores where Stó:lō people could use the money they had accumulated through wage labor to purchase foods they had not themselves hunted, harvested, or preserved, worked to reinforce the sense of the nuclear family with a male patriarch as a viable stand-alone unit.

None of these pressures and changes should be taken to suggest that the extended family or the tribal grouping became unimportant to Stó:lō people during this era. Rather, changes brought about by settler colonialism worked to accentuate certain already existing aspects of Stó:lō society while simultaneously undermining others. It created a narrow, gendered, window of opportunity even as it closed the door on other avenues of traditional agency.

Meanwhile, middle-aged and elderly people from elite families at this time were still in, or had relatively fresh memories of having grown up in, marriages where polygamy among the elites was the norm, where extended families lived communally in large longhouses, and where marriages among the elite had been arranged through carefully orchestrated works of intercommunity diplomacy. The pressures of settler colonialism, in other words, were unevenly applied, while the agency behind Indigenous responses was inequitably distributed.

In collecting and indexing sxwōxwiyám, we were able to identify and quantify shifts in the content of the narratives. We do not claim that the recordings we have analyzed represent an exhaustive corpus of Stó:lō legendary stories, for certainly there were and are knowledge keepers out there who have had, and still carry, stories that have not been captured in text or audio recordings and made available through archives and libraries. This is as it should be. Moreover, the database is a living record. Additional copies of earlier recorded narratives continue to be drawn to our attention and then incorporated into the database. Nonetheless, the knowledge keepers who have guided us and collaborated on this project feel confident, as do we, that we have included in our database the vast majority of extant recorded sxwōxwiyám. The changes over time are revealing and suggestive of the relationship between colonialism, gender, and territoriality.

We are unable to determine from the notations Franz Boas made while transcribing Stó:lō legendary stories whether those stories that had slipped from the oral lexicon by the 1960s. As we noted earlier, Boas simply stated that the stories he recorded came principally from Chief George Chehalis, Chief Chehalis' wife, and "other Indians." However, it seems likely that these stories were originally told by female informants. The protagonists and other key characters in these early recordings of the stories were often women, and indeed many of the female characters were named. We hypothesize that as arranged polygamous marriage unions were replaced by self-directed monogamous marriages, those narratives featuring Stó:lō women that emphasized the connections between Coast Salish tribes appear to have been forgotten. What remained are narratives emphasizing male characters and the origins and identity of tribal communities. These stories, through their narrative structure and plots highlight tribal exclusivity as opposed to interconnectivity and inclusivity.

Franz Boas presented his German language rendering of Stó:lō sxwoxwiyá:m as twelve discrete narratives. It is unclear from Boas's published and unpublished works the extent to which these categorizations were his own or those provided by Stó:lo people. Both of the two initial sxwoxwiyá:m consist of the accounts of the Stó:lō transformer X̲á:ls. The first X̲á:ls story is divided into eighteen subnarratives (similar to chapters within a book) describing X̲á:ls's miraculous and awe-inspiring acts of transformation. Sometimes in these stories X̲á:ls is depicted as a collective (three brothers and a sister who were the children of Red-headed Woodpecker and Black

Bear) whereas on other occasions within the narrative Xá:ls is described as a single man (usually the youngest brother of the collective). To use the terminology of contemporary elders, these are the stories that explain how Xá:ls "made the world right" by fixing people, animals, plants, and other things into their permanent forms, and by correcting situations that he found inappropriate or undesirable. For instance, in one of the stories Xá:ls is described as having "found a man and a woman whose sex organs were on their foreheads. Then he slid them lower to the proper place. If he hadn't done that, the people would still be wearing their genitalia on their chests or foreheads." In total, the first Xá:ls story with its eighteen subsections depict the actions of twenty-six characters, of whom twenty-one are male and five are female. Of the eighteen subcomponents of the first Xá:ls story recorded by Boas, our database list only four as still circulating among knowledge keepers in the 1960–90 era.

The second of the Xá:ls stories that Boas presents is an account of the Transformer creating the founders of the various Stó:lō tribal communities. Boas titles this sxwoxwiyá:m "Tribal Legends from the Lower Fraser River." Within the story are the accounts of original genealogical founders of twelve of the Stó:lō tribes—for instance the Matsqui tribe's founder was a man transformed by Xá:ls into a beaver, and so Beaver is to this day regarded by the Matsqui as their first person. These tribal origin stories are site specific and serve to historicize the ontological anchors for contemporary tribal communities while demarcating their geographic extent. Twenty-one characters are mentioned in these accounts, of whom sixteen are male and five are female. These stories remain in circulation today and are often referenced by both elected and hereditary Stó:lō chiefs—indeed the list of tribal origin stories circulating today numbers twenty-five, suggesting that Boas's informants chose not to share all of the accounts with the ethnographer. However, what strikes us as different is that the subnarratives of the individual tribal communities' origins are today most often referred to in isolation of one another. That is to say, what elders presented to Boas in 1890 as a whole has become broken into parts and used to express tribal authority and ownership of specific tribal spaces; the larger collective story has been fragmented to allow for tribal exclusivity.

Third on Boas's lists are ten stand-alone sxwoxwiyá:m that for the most part seem to operate in isolation of one another in terms of their plots and narrative structures. They too sometimes tell of how the world came to take its current recognizable form through transformations, but, importantly, they do not reference Xá:ls. One story tells of a selfish boy who was abandoned by his family, but who eventually redeemed himself and was transformed into the North Star. Another details the adventures of Eagle, Woodpecker, and Woodpecker's wife—a woman whose vagina was lined with teeth. Still another discusses the origins of salmon and fire. There are a total of seventy-two male and thirty-three female characters in these twelve stories. Women play prominent roles in many of the narratives, and in three they are clearly the main character protagonists.

Our analysis suggests that, unlike the earlier Xá:ls stories, which were all linked together and depicted actions that seem to occur in chronologic order as Xá:ls passes through Stó:lō territory, these next ten stories are different. What makes them similar is that they lack both a sense of chronology and a notion of particular geographic place. For this reason, we had designated them "in-between stories." The in-between stories contain very few geographic references. The majority of these stories could occur anywhere in the lower Fraser River watershed, which in fact seems to be intentional with these sxwoxwiyá:m. Stories like these suggest that in-between stories were likely commonly known across multiple tribal and regional boundaries. From what we have been able to interpret, it does not seem to have been important to story tellers or listeners *where* the actions occurred. Rather what was important was *that* they occurred. Their significance and import, therefore, could be appreciated by all regardless of tribal affiliation. They highlight the ability of certain sxwoxwiyá:m to transcend spatial as well as social boundaries. Interestingly, our database reveals that none of the eighteen in-between stories recorded by Boas were still in circulation in the 1960–90 era. However, one in-between story that Boas did not record in the nineteenth century was recorded in the 1960–90 era—that of the generous man who was rewarded by Xá:ls by being transformed into a cedar tree so he could continue sharing with all of the Stó:lō people for all time. In this narrative there are no female characters.

The fourth and final group of sxwoxwiyá:m in Boas's collection consist of ten longer narratives that Boas listed separately from one another but that we have grouped together because of their shared theme of collaboration. Like the in-between stories, these ten had largely fallen from the Stó:lō lexicon by the 1960–90 era. These ten collaboration stories have plots that are much more complex than any of the earlier listed Xá:ls stories, tribal origin stories, or in-between stories. They also have more female characters who engage in a wider range of interpersonal relations than what is found in any of the earlier stories. Importantly, like the X̱á:ls stories, the collaboration stories also describe actions and occurrences that are anchored to characters and activities within a particular tribal community's geographical space, but what sets these stories apart is that the characters in the narrative travel and engage in activities that take place in other territories. That is to say, the characters in these stories are from particular places, and linked to those places, but they engage in actions that see them travel across tribal boundaries to visit named locations within the landscape of other neighboring regional tribes. Each story emphasizes either interpersonal, intertribal, or interspecies cooperation. Significantly, only two of these stories were still circulating and recorded during the 1960–90 era, and each of these later recordings contains much less detail than any of the versions recorded by Boas. Moreover, the female characters in these two later recordings have much diminished roles.

The above discussion is brief and only reflects one subset of the larger body of research we are conducting for this project, but we feel the results are illustrative. Over the past century and a half important shifts have taken place in the scope and focus of the sxwoxwiyá:m being shared within the Stó:lō communities. These changes in the content of legendary stories suggest shifts in the meaning that people, as tellers/speakers, have invested into sxwoxwiyá:m and that others, as listeners/hearers, have drawn from the stories. Importantly, for the purposes of helping to try and answer the question that Myra Sam and Marge Kelly originally asked, the shifts in the content of these stories reflect a diminished role for women within the corpus of Stó:lō foundational narratives. While the number of tribal origin stories circulating in the Stó:lō community was sustained (indeed more stories in this genre are being shared today than Boas originally recorded from his informants) the stories that emphasized cross-tribal and regional connections are far fewer in number and those that remain contain less detail. Further, those few remaining collaboration stories that remained in circulation in the 1960s–90 era had fragmented such that, with one exception, rather than representing stories of inter-tribal connectivity and extended-family inclusivity, they had been shortened in such a way that a listener might easily hear them as emphasizing tribal exclusivity.

Given the other sources and documents analyzed in the larger research project, it is clear that there is a correlation, if not causation, between the shift in story content and the onset and continuance of settler colonialism. Settler efforts at disconnecting Stó:lō people from their ancestral lands and at dividing interconnected families and multisettlement tribal communities into individual village-based "bands" delegitimize Indigenous political unity and undermine the traditional position of women as not only knowledge keepers and knowledge sharers, but as diplomatic, economic, and political forces. The narrative shift we have documented in sxwōxwiyám illustrate not only the political impacts but the social consequences of the creation of reserves, band registration lists, and patriarchal governance—all of which worked to undermine the complex female-underpinned system of supertribal connections and collaboration.

Partners' Perspectives

Naxaxalhts'i: There are three principal aspects of our culture that cover all the others. *Sxwoxwiyá:m* (our legendary stories), *sqwelqwel* (our more recent personal histories), and *shxweli* (the spirits of our ancestors that animate the current world). All things fit into these three categories. As each of us travels on our own personal journey of discovery, we can get the latter two on our own through our lived experience (sqwelqwel) and through prayer and ritual (shxweli). But our legendary sxwoxwiyá:m are lost if they are not shared and circulated. So, what makes this collaborative project so important is that it provides us with new tools for doing just that.

All these sxwoxwiyá:m stories are important to everybody. Making them accessible in new ways so that the written narratives can be there for all Stó:lō people to categorize and index is an exciting and powerful development. With this database we will have a single easy-to-access tool that we can turn to and ask, "Who's ancestors are sturgeon; whose ancestors are black bear?" At my office at the SRRMC, I always have people coming up to ask me about our origin and transformer stories. "Are there any references to climate change in sxwoxwiyá:m stories?" is a question that someone asked me just the other day. We'll I've never thought about that. Prior to us working on this project, I'd have to go and review print copies of sxwoxwiyá:m in our office library and archives. This index and database will make answering those kinds of questions easier. And I know that with the database we will be able to think of even more new questions to ask that would never have occurred to us before. It reminds me of the time a few years ago when Grand Chief Kat Pennier asked for a research project to be conducted to see if we could learn what the sxwoxwiyá:m teach us about environmental management and care. I worked with a student from the University of Saskatchewan to

320 | Carlson, Naxaxalhts'i, Osmond, and Van Ry

try and answer that question, but we had to spend a lot of time digging for information that now will be at our fingertips.

I've worked here for three decades now. Sxwoxwiyá:m have always been an important part of our research activities, but it was the repatriation of one of our stone ancestors from a museum in Seattle back to Stó:lō territory that really inspired research into these legends to begin in earnest. This showed that people really believed that the spirits are in these stones; they are not just stories about an artifact, they are sxwoxwiyá:m that show us our real history and our living ancestors. Communities are asking me, "Sonny, what is our sxwoxwioyam? Can you help us get them?" This database delves deep into sxwoxwiyá:m that have been lost.

The sxwoxwiyá:m are what define our rights and our title. They distinguish us as unique from other Canadians and from other Indigenous people. That's the main reason they are so important to us. Our Aboriginal rights and our UNDRIP (United Nations Declaration on the Rights of Indigenous Peoples) rights all make sense only in light of the sxwoxwiyá:m that tell us who we are by telling us what our ancestors did and how the transformers made our world. Sxwoxwiyá:m teach us the reality of shxweli (ancestor spirits) as real and powerful. As stories of the past, they explain how our ancestor spirits are active in the places that they frequented.[26]

Today we live in an era that some people call the "Indian Renaissance." We are bringing our culture back to life after a century and a half of settler colonialism in our territory. But so many aspects of our culture have been weakened and injured over the years that we need to be especially careful to bring things back in ways that protect their original integrity. Between 1884 and 1951, our potlatches and winter dances were illegal. Those were among the most important forums where we shared our sxwoxwiyá:m and tended our relationships with the spirits. So, for the sxwoxwiyá:m we are reviving today, integrity is key. We know that colonialism has slowly over the past seven generation eroded some of the content. This isn't simply a loss of culture, it's also dangerous in the sense that changing these stories will confuse and upset our ancestors. So, the original content of stories must be found, revived, and maintained in the form that our ancestors originally shared—that they will recognize when they hear them being spoken today.

These are not fairy tales that people can make up, or add to, or modify. They are our sacred founding stories. I know I struggle with some Stó:lō people who have said that they feel it is OK to make up new sxwoxwiyá:m or to modify and adapt existing sxwoxwiyá:m, or to take out parts of the stories that they don't feel comfortable with or to add things to the stories that make them feel more comfortable. We shouldn't do this. So, accessing the words of ancestors that have been ignored or lost is important. Bringing these forward and sharing them are strengthening our rights and title and our culture.

In terms of intercommunity conflicts and tensions, I know that today some tribes claim what other tribes consider to be their territories. Some people misuse sxwoxwiyá:m in this process because of the inaccurate way that settlers have sometimes attached the wrong Stó:lō name to certain geographical features. I could list other examples, but I don't want to do that here, because I don't want to accentuate these conflicts, and I don't want to outline other people's mistakes in case it confuses people and causes the errors to be repeated. But what I do know is that we want to give people the tools to start correcting these things on their own. The database will help with this. Some of this process will be disruptive for a time when the database first becomes accessible. But this knowledge is going to strengthen people and communities in the long run.

And we also know that this database will disrupt the way people talk about sxwoxwiyá:m going forward. Because in the past you didn't have a way to access sxwoxwiyá:m except through the voices of elders. Now with the database someone could look things up and what they find might not be what they want to find, because, with 150 years of colonialism, their memories of their elders' words may have been forgotten or maybe a bit jumbled.

And then there is the issue of violence, and, in particular, violent sex that appears in some of the ancient sxwoxwiyá:m. We need to think about how we want to share or not share these stories with the current generation, and especially with younger people. We know that the Stó:lō world 150 years ago was sometimes violent in ways that would not be acceptable today. We don't do slave raids anymore, and we don't approve of nonconsensual sex. With the passing of time, we don't know the exact way our ancestors used to explain or contextualize those sxwoxwiyá:m that had that sort of content, and so we don't want to just throw these stories out there for teachers and students to look at without that historical and cultural context. We know that Christian morality probably caused some of these stories to fall away over the years. We know that some societal changes associated with the arrival of settler society were not necessarily looked on as bad things. This is not to in anyway apologize for colonization, but, since colonization, we Stó:lō people have adapted. Some changes my ancestors resisted, and other changes they accepted or even embraced. What this tells me is that these sxwoxwiyá:m stories are not just things we need to relearn and memorize, they are things we need to think about and try to understand and interpret. I appreciate the opportunities that CES methodologies and long-term research partnerships with Keith have brought, as they mean that aspects of the processes of cultural revitalization, interpretation, and communication are collaborative—we each have intellectual tools, cultural insights, gifts, and perspectives that we share and that enrich one another.

Tsandlia van Ry: Ey Swayel Siyám Siáye, Tsandlia tel skwi:x, Tèlí tsel kwe Sq̓ewqeyl. (Hello respected leaders and friends. My name is Tsandlia. I am Stó:lō Ts'elxwéyeqw, and I am from Skowkale.) I was excited to join the research team, as it not only focuses on the implications of settler colonialism and Indigenous territoriality, but would also allow me to focus on how the sxwoxwiyá:m have shifted and changed by erasure and other colonial influences. As a Stó:lō woman, who grew up away from my traditional territory, I had limited opportunity to learn my culture and my history. This research project allowed me the opportunity to reengage with my culture and history, while also contributing meaningfully to a project for my community. CES allows us the opportunity to learn and research these topics directly with and from community members. As a student researcher, and a Stó:lō woman working with Stó:lō history, what appealed to me most was the opportunity to focus my participation within a framework that emphasized learning and researching through an Indigenous lens.

My primary role was to transcribe the sxwoxwiyá:m from multiple sources and enter them into a spreadsheet that indexed geographical references and people. Through transcription of the sxwoxwiyá:m, I worked to analyze the legendary narratives and observe any changes in content or form. As I began working through the sxwoxwiyá:m, I recognized a pattern emerging within the narrative as well as three prominent themes. A grand narrative could be seen in stories recorded in different times and places. I recognized themes that showed consistency in narratives and cultural continuity across territories, the importance of geography to identity, and also the significance of cultural knowledge to Indigenous health and well-being.

We know that colonization is a process that shapes people. It shapes Indigenous people's understanding of themselves, their feelings about other Indigenous peoples, and their emotional and psychological positioning in that dominant society.[27] As colonization shaped us Stó:lō people, it also shaped and changed the narratives that were being told by various elders from different communities. Even simply within the Ts'elxwéyeqw (Chilliwack) territory, elders tell similar variations of the same story. The historic processes and ongoing maintenance of colonization have continued to fragment—or worse, erase—these narratives. As someone who studies kinesiology and aspires to a career in the health field, I recognize that this disconnect impacts the health and well-being of communities and will have effects on Stó:lō ways of knowing for generations to come, as the transfer of oral history and culture is central to a community's cultural health.

As Stó:lō people, we commonly introduce ourselves by naming the mountain, the river, the tribal ancestor, the tribe, and the family, and through this we locate ourselves in a set identity that is framed geographically, politically, and genealogically.[28] Through my participation on this research project, I was better able to understand the importance of our sxwoxwiyá:m. In doing so, I am able to revitalize that knowledge through this community-based research. This knowledge comes directly from community members, past and present, which improves the cultural connection between generations. Through my work on this project, I developed an appreciation of the intimate effects of colonization and the ways that colonization has compromised our ability to continue as Indigenous people in ways that our ancestors would recognize.[29]

I have no doubt that Indigenous cultural knowledge and competency is directly related to Indigenous people's well-being. Cultural stress is a direct result of Canadian settler colonialism's ongoing efforts to erase Stó:lō control of our territory, and the effects can be seen directly through our analysis of the sxwoxwiyá:m.

Taiaiake Alfred has argued that Indigenous "people can't survive disconnected from the land; that the crisis of dependency we face, which is denied in psychological and spiritual terms in addition to economic terms, requires a restoration of a relationship, on spiritual, psychological and physical terms, between Indigenous people and their land."[30] My research on this project suggests that through colonialism we have been physically as well as narratively removed from our territory, and denied the ability to strengthen that relationship with the land. It is my hope and aspiration that through the database we are creating, Stó:lō people will be able to access narratives that for generations have been eclipsed by colonialism, and through this reconnection they will be able to strengthen that relationship through knowledge of the territory.

In my own journey as a Stó:lō woman who grew up outside of my ancestors' territory, geography has been crucial to cultural healing and reconnecting to my community. My role as a researcher on this project will help make the sxwoxwiyá:m more accessible to community members who will directly benefit from gaining a better understanding of how our ancestors understood their world, and their history.

Keith Carlson: It is not just that collaboration enables you to do better scholarship, it actually allows you to do new types of scholarship in ways that you could otherwise never do alone. This project examining sxwoxwiyá:m is enriched by the diversity of voices, perspectives, and experiences that have gone into shaping it. As an ethnohistorian it is rewarding to find ways to work in collaborative partnerships with communities to answer questions that they have asked so as to meet objectives that they have identified as meaningful. Not too many years ago the term people were using was "community-based research," but while that *may* have referred to engaged collaborative scholarship as we define it here, it too often only described work that non-Indigenous scholars conducted with Indigenous informants while being temporarily based in an Indigenous community. Indigenous people in this model were too often merely subjects and academic too often regarded themselves as the experts creating new knowledge. CES is something different.

The process of collaborating is as important as the outcomes of the collaboration. Each project like this inevitably contributes capacity to the next. In addition to whatever else it is, each project is an investment of emotional labor that reinforces and sustains the social foundation upon which the collaboration and partnership operates. My own CES scholarship simply would not be possible if my relationships with my Indigenous partners broke down. Equally important is the fact that my CES scholarship would simply not be as intellectually valuable to either myself, my partners, or the broader world if my relationships with my Indigenous partners were not sufficiently robust that they could accommodate and transcend occasional divergences in opinion and interpretation.

One thing that stands out for me in this project is the way that informal conversations with friends (Myra and Marge) could inspire original academic and intellectual inquiry involving a host of researchers and learners. Now that the project is well underway, it seems incredible that earlier scholars had not already examined key aspects of what are the core components of this research collaboration. But of course, that is also perfectly understandable. The questions emerged from within Coast Salish communities and through Coast Salish conversations that took place within a particular historical context. They are not things that emerged purely from intellectual curiosity, nor did they develop simply from within the academic historiography.

But that does not mean that they do not intersect and contribute to scholarly debates. Territoriality in the Coast Salish world had been a subject of local Indigenous debate, academic enquiry, and settler-colonial political consternation, for a long time. In the past I have sought to engage these conversations, perhaps most directly in my book *The Power of Place, the Problem of Time: Aboriginal Identity and Historical Consciousness in the Cauldron of Colonialism*, where I posited that gendered perspectives informed the waxing and waning of supertribal collective identity in the nineteenth century. In that study, I sought to determine whether sxwoxwiyá:m might reveal new insights into the strategies and tactics that nineteenth century Stó:lō people used when they engaged with colonial upheaval and displacement. To what extent, I wondered, did sxwoxwiyá:m provide Stó:lō people with accounts of how their ancestors dealt with ancient tragedy and challenge (i.e., intercommunity conflict, volcanic eruption, unexpected absence of salmon or game, etc.) in ways that might have served as precedents to guide their navigation of settler colonialism? In that earlier study I approached sxwoxwiyá:m as windows through which I sought to better understand Stó:lō historical consciousness as something sometimes separate and distinct from Stó:lō history.

In this current project, we are examining Coast Salish legendary stories in a manner that goes beyond the analysis of my earlier work. On this project, in addition to finding guidance in conversations with elders and knowledge keepers, I sought inspiration from the seminal scholarship into ethnopoetics pioneered by Dennis Tedlock and Del Hymes. Tedlock and Hymes have each encouraged us to embrace Indigenous ways of organizing knowledge and memory as an avenue to building a deeper appreciation of cultural history. Integral to this process is the inclusion of poetry, voice, song, ritual, and dance.[31] And to better accomplish this we have the benefit of not only classic works of Coast Salish anthropology by non-Indigenous scholars such as Franz Boas, Wayne Suttles, and, more recently, Bruce Miller, but also intellectual enquiry and analysis by Coast Salish scholars such as Michael Marker and Jo-Ann Archibald, who are advancing a dialogic methodological framework that provides Indigenous people and their outside research partners with a model to better ensure that their work serves decolonizing ends.[32] These perspectives enable us to more effectively look at the content of legendary sxwoxwiyá:m for what they might reveal about tribal inclusivity and tribal exclusivity with an eye to seeing how these stories have changed over time due to the colonial-induced changes to family structures (and thereby gender roles and gender perspectives) within Stó:lō Coast Salish society.

CES relationships are built upon a web of cultural expectations and social obligations that ultimately transcend the actions and the personalities of any one researcher. In her 1999 pathbreaking book *Decolonizing Methodologies: Research and Indigenous People*, Māori scholar Linda Tuhiwai Smith challenged Indigenous people to assert themselves and assume authority and authorship over research that involved and impacted them. She also pointed out ways in which non-Indigenous scholars could reimagine their scholarship to enable them to participate respectfully and supportively in the decolonizing agenda. Smith's book has been joined since then by other examples of Indigenous research practice. Indigenously driven research coupled with methodologies and analysis that emphasized partnerships and the cocreation of knowledge offer avenues for extricating history and anthropology from the legacy of colonial complicity.[33] Additionally, CES is necessarily situated within the context of settler colonialism.[34]

Just as transformation is central to the plot of every sxwoxwiyá:m legendary story so too should it be embraced in any CES research partnership. Legendary characters within sxwoxwiyá:m transform one another through their dialogue and interactions in ways that in turn are reflected in the transformations that occur within both Coast Salish storytellers and story listeners when sxwoxwiyá:m are shared between people and across generations. Outsider researchers and community members who are engaged in CES likewise dialogue, interact, and inevitably transform one another through their collaborative research activities. CES, therefore, necessarily embraces notions like hybridity in that it recognizes that not only is the research a product of the coming together of insider and outsider perspectives, but so too are the insider and the outsider themselves shaped and changed through the collaboration process. Collaboration necessitates reflection on the relationship, on one's partner(s), and on oneself. What is seen is inevitably less a mirror images than something new that emerges through interaction.

Projects like the one described in this chapter place emphasis on a methodology of sustained conversation where external scholars return to communities and engage in conversations with the same (and new) people on the same and similar subjects over the course of years—and often over the course of multiple research projects. Sustained conversations like the ones I engaged in with Myra, and continue to engage in with Naxaxalhts'i, are in fact webs of dialogue, for when we meet again a few months later to pick up our conversation we inevitably discover that each of us has been carrying that conversation to others within our networks of intellectual exchange. As Naxaxalhts'i continues to do today, prior to her passing Myra not infrequently told me that she had discussed aspects of our conversation with others during those times when I was away. She brought the insights of these conversations and subsequent ruminations to her sustained conversations with me. Likewise, when appropriate, I've shared aspects of my conversations with Myra and Naxaxalhts'i with trusted family, friends, and colleagues who I have encountered in between my visits with Stó:lō people. In this way, sustained conversations have the potential to become genuinely deep multifaceted conversations where ideas and interpretations are cocreated in webs of interaction across time. Sharing such as this is what makes CES so rewarding.

Colin Osmond: As a PhD candidate doing CES, I immediately recognized this project's potential and eagerly accepted the role as research coordinator when it was offered to me. I have been working with the Stó:lō and the Tla'amin communities for the past several years. I first began doing community-engaged work with Coast Salish communities as an undergrad at Simon Fraser University. As part of a jointly run Simon Fraser University / University of Saskatchewan Tla'amin field school, I was asked by the Tla'amin to research the history of their male elders working in the commercial logging industry. This project blossomed into a master's thesis supervised by Keith at the University of Saskatchewan, where I had the opportunity to expand my study to the Stó:lō—a Coast Salish group who had similar questions about their men working in the logging industry. My relationship with these Coast Salish communities spawned from questions raised by these communities, and I continue to seek community guidance and collaboration in my PhD research with the Tla'amin and Mi'kmaq communities.

When I started to work on this project, Keith and Naxaxalhts'i had already done plenty of leg work. I hit the ground running by helping draft, proofread, and edit the SSHRC grant for this project's major funding. Once the news was received that we had been granted funding, I quickly went to work designing student research plans and identifying potential students. Finding students at the University of Saskatchewan was greatly aided by the history department's unique initiative—the Community-Engaged History Collaboratorium, a facility that pairs top-level undergraduate students with community partners to work on a wide range of topics.[35] On a Tla'amin component of this project that space limitations does not allow us to consider in detail here, we also worked closely with Hegus Clint Williams, and Gail Blaney and Karina Peters (Tla'amin teachers in the local K–12 systems in Powell River) to identify Tla'amin high school students that we could hire to do data entry and research during the summer months.[36]

Once we had our research team in place, I worked closely with the team of student researchers (Tsandlia Van Ry, Drew Blaney, and Kirsten Paul) to create summer research internships. My PhD research continues to work with the Tla'amin community to better understand their relationship with wage labor, community identity, and family organization in the twentieth century, so having the opportunity to travel more frequently to Tla'amin territory to work on this project allowed me to spend much more time in the community. Keith and I had also worked out an arrangement that allowed me to conduct my own research alongside research and supervision for this project. This allowed me to travel and work in the community in ways that are simply impossible with average graduate student funding packages and coursework/RA obligations.

My work on this project also gave me the opportunity to represent this project at two different high-level academic conferences. We organized two panels in 2018 (the Native American and Indigenous Studies Association in Los Angeles and the Canadian Historical Association in Regina). These conferences allowed us to present our preliminary findings to a broader audience, and to share the successes and challenges we faced when conducting this type of CES. The neat thing about our panels was that they were not formed only by faculty and Indigenous leadership—75 percent of our panels were made up of graduate and undergraduate students. Further, two of the four presenters on our panels were Indigenous.

Such a balance is worth commenting on. In the still-too-prevalent occurrence of non-Indigenous scholars presenting *about* or *for* Indigenous people, this project aspired to create opportunities for us to present *with* our Indigenous partners. Indeed, this was identified as a priority in the original grant application and is directly linked to the commitments this project has made to build capacity in Coast Salish communities.

I highlight these elements of our project not to brag or toot our own horn. Rather, I do so in a way that is meant to show the multiple and varied ways that this project has sought to work with Indigenous people on a variety of levels. As a PhD student learning the ropes of CES, this project has provided me with a wealth of knowledge and experience in how to conceptualize, design, and execute a project that accomplishes the precarious balance between meeting rigorous academic guidelines and conducting research that is not only interesting and relevant to Indigenous people, but also is collaborative and inclusive of Indigenous voices and perspectives.

Conclusion

Clearly, settler colonialism has had profound and often unanticipated effects on Indigenous communities. We look forward to the completion of the collaborative CES research project outlined above so that we will be able to comment and report on our analysis and conclusions more fully. But what has become clear, and what we can say with certainty, is that the collaborative partnerships that have shaped this project have themselves provided us with lessons and insights that highlight the benefits of relationship building as well as serendipity. Together, these hold the potential for enhancing our own future CES activities.

One of the most distinctive, and perhaps most exciting, elements of this project are the layers of mentorship that occur between the various partners and participants at the different stages and phases of this community-engaged work. Indeed, the day that Myra and Marge discussed with Keith the original ideas for this project over cups of tea, they were mentoring Keith. Keith then worked closely with them to listen and learn more about the ways that colonialism interfered with age-old Coast Salish gender dynamics and territoriality before engaging other Salish knowledge keepers and graduate, undergraduate, and high school students to join us on this project. This process required most of the research team members to recognize their role as a mentee, while at the same time stepping up to be a mentor for other people on the research team. That is to say, Myra and Marge mentored Keith, Naxaxalhts'i and Keith mentored one another in different spheres, Keith mentored his graduate students, and the graduate students mentored the undergraduate students, who then mentored the high school students.

Who mentored and who was mentored was a fluid process that depended upon context. Codesigning the project required the various partners to assume at different times greater or lesser leadership roles than did the coexecution stage of the research, likewise with regard to the cocreation of knowledge and the co-communication of the results. Indigenous high school students and university undergraduate students, for instance, were being mentored in research methodologies by graduate students and faculty, but along with elders and knowledge keepers these youth also assumed leadership roles over outside academics and graduate students when it came to implementing and interpreting the subtleties of certain local Indigenous cultural protocols.

Moreover, while certain archival and ethnographic collections were identified as research priorities for the undergraduate and high school students, these researchers were encouraged to tackle sources within those collections in whatever order they felt would be most fulfilling to their own personal and academic interests. This served a dual purpose—researchers got to work on sources that they found interesting, but they also brought their unique personal, cultural, and familial insights and knowledge of these themes and topics to enrich development of the greater project.

Throughout the process, Keith and Naxaxalhts'i noticed that allowing students to focus in on certain areas brought new levels of analytical sophistication to the project. Indeed, Tsandlia's knowledge of, and interest in, Indigenous community health and well-being allowed her to see themes and trends within the larger project in ways that differed from, and enriched, those that Keith had originally anticipated.[37] Collectively, these webs of mentorship helped make this CES project more collaborative than traditional community-based research projects, and ultimately helped it to result in more well-rounded and balanced research and analysis.

The era of scholarly research where one white academic would travel to an Indigenous community, feverishly record stories for a short period of time, return to the university to engage in a lengthy period of reflection without community input, and eventually publish a peer-reviewed work of scholarship from which the benefits rarely returned to the community is thankfully over. We recognize, however, that our current work and the database we are constructing benefits from this earlier style of work, and we appreciate the energy of earlier scholars and the generosity of an earlier generation of Stó:lō knowledge keepers. In significant portion, our project is designed to help return these sxwoxwiyá:m in a new, exciting, and adaptive way that contributes to genuine capacity building in Coast Salish communities. This project not only recognizes, but fully embraces, that hybridity occurs at every level of our scholarship. All research partners necessarily transform one another and in turn are transformed by one another throughout a collaborative research project. For those of us who had the opportunity to participate in this project, advantages and benefits derived from collaborating across the cultural divide hopefully made that gap a little smaller.

Notes

1. Albert "Sonny" McHalsie, prologue to *Towards a New Ethnohistory: Community-engaged Scholarship among the People of the River* (Winnipeg: University of Manitoba Press, 2018), x.

2. Maria Mayan has reached similar conclusions. She argues that within community-based participatory research there should be no "one leader." Rather, emerging best practices recognize that research relationships should be designed to be collaborative efforts to reach broad benefits, and having a single person claiming leadership of the entire project can drastically skew results and sour relations between institutions and communities. See Maria Mayan, Sanchia Lo, Merin Oleschuk, Ana Laura Pauchulo, and Daley Laing, "Leadership in Community-Based Participatory Research: Individual to Collective," *Engaged Scholar Journal* 2, no. 2 (2016): 11–24.

3. Cree scholar Shawn Wilson has described such research expectations as the "Three Rs" of Indigenous research methodology: respect, reciprocity, and relationality—in which "respect is more than just saying please and thank you, and reciprocity is more than giving a gift." Embedded within these principles, Wilson argues, is an obligation upon outside researchers to engage in a "deep listening and hearing with more than the ears," and to attempt to develop a "reflective, non-judgmental consideration of what is being seen and heard," as well as "an awareness and connection between logic of mind and the feelings of the heart." Wilson, *Research Is Ceremony: Indigenous Research Methods* (Black Point, NS: Fernwood, 2008), 86, 59.

4. Stó:lō Research and Resource Management Centre, "Rights and Title," accessed March 18, 2018, http://www.srrmcentre.com/rightstitle.

5. A seminal and still inspiring work on this subject is Brian Dippie, *The Vanishing American: White Attitudes and U.S. Indian Policy* (Middletown, CT: Wesleyan University Press, 1985).

6. Thomas King, *The Inconvenient Indian: A Curious Account of Native People in North America* (Minneapolis: University of Minnesota Press, 2018).

7. Mark Rifkin, *Beyond Settler Time: Temporal Sovereignty and Indigenous Self-Determination* (Durham, NC: Duke University Press, 2017).

8. We are grateful to the Social Sciences and Humanities Council for funding this research through one of their Insight Grants, 2016–20.

9. Wayne Suttles, *Coast Salish Essays* (Vancouver: Talonbooks, 1987), esp. ch. 3, "Affinal Ties, Subsistence, and Prestige among the Coast Salish."

10. Wilson Duff, *The Upper Stalo Indians of the Fraser Valley, British Columbia* (Victoria: British Columbia Provincial Museum, 1952), 79, 83.

11. Duff, *The Upper Stalo*, 92–93, 95–96.

12. Keith Thor Carlson, *The Power of Place, the Problem of Time: Aboriginal Identity and Historical Consciousness in the Cauldron of Colonialism* (Toronto: University of Toronto Press, 2010), ch. 8, "Reservations for the Queen's Birthday Celebrations, 1864–1876."

13. Carlson, *The Power of Place*, ch. 6, "Identity in the Emerging Colonial Order." See also Keith Thor Carlson, "Innovation, Tradition, Colonialism, and Aboriginal Fishing Conflicts in the Lower Fraser Canyon," in *New Histories for Old: Changing Perspectives on Canada's Native Past*, ed. Ted Binnema and Susan Neylan (Vancouver: University of British Columbia Press, 2007), 145–74.

14. Carlson, *The Power of Place*, esp. ch. 7, "Identity in the Face of Missionaries and the Anti-Potlatch Law."

15. Keith Thor Carlson, "Familial Cohesion and Colonial Atomization: Governance and Authority in a Coast Salish Community," *Native Studies Review* 19, no. 2 (2010): 1–42.

16. Th'ewá:lí being one of the more than two dozen First Nations from more than a dozen tribes that make up the larger Stó:lō community along the lower Fraser River watershed. The intercommunity elders' council is called Lalem Ye Stó:lō Siyolexwa (House of Respected Elders).

17. "Variation in Habitat and Culture on the Northwest Coast" and "Coping with Abundance: Subsistence on the Northwest Coast," both of which are reproduced in Suttles, *Coast Salish Essays*.

18. See Scott L. Morgensen, "Cutting to the Roots of Colonial Masculinity," in *Indigenous Men and Masculinities: Legacies, Identities, Regeneration*, ed. Robert Alexander Innes and Kim Anderson (Winnipeg: University of Manitoba Press, 2015), 38–61; Leah Sneider, "Complementary Relationships: A Review of Indigenous Gender Studies," in *Indigenous Men and Masculinities: Legacies, Identities, Regeneration*, ed. Robert Alexander Innes and Kim Anderson (Winnipeg: University of Manitoba Press, 2015), 62–79; Colin Osmond, "Giant Trees, Iron Men: Masculinity and Colonialism in Coast Salish Loggers' Identity" (MA thesis, University of Saskatchewan, 2016).

19. Rosaleen George, in conversation with Keith Carlson, May 1995.

20. Naxaxalhts'i's tours are now known as Bad Rock Tours. See http://www.srrmcentre.com/cie.

21. David M. Schaepe, "Pre-colonial Sto:lo-Coast Salish Community Organization: An Archaeological Study" (PhD diss., University of British Columbia, 2009).

22. Meanwhile, media coverage of contentious intertribal disputes between Coast Salish communities reinforced for Keith and Naxaxalhts'i the potential

broader value and immediate applicability of their line of enquiry. Intertribal tensions that were manifesting as court battles, legal injunctions, and interpersonal hostilities along the Fraser River had been capturing headlines in the mainstream press of late and would continue to do so into the coming years. The highly publicized disputes between the Duwamish and Muckleshoot near Seattle, the Yale and Stó:lō in the Fraser River Canyon, and the Musqueam, Squamish, and Tsleil-Waututh in the vicinity of Vancouver, were among the most visible of these contestations.

23. An edited translation of Boas's *Indianische Sagen* had been published in the 1990s by Dorothy Kennedy and Randy Bouchard, but we wanted to be able to confirm portions of the translation and then to reproduce the entire document for teachers and others to use as an open access file, and so it was decided to create our own translation.

24. There Hegus (Chief) Clint Williams among others encouraged us to try and identify opportunities within the project for local First Nations students to be involved in meaningful ways that would help build academic capacities and cultural competencies within the upcoming generation. In particular, we worked with Gail Blaney, Karina Peters, and Drew Blaney to create curriculum for incorporating knowledge gathered from this project's research into high school classrooms. These lesson plans included preliminary maps of select sxwoxwiyá:m and codesigned memory mapping exercises that helped teach students how to think spatially and creatively about Indigenous knowledge and legendary stories. We also regularly updated the teachers and educators on the project progress and sought their advice on what pedagogical outcomes would be most useful to their needs. One of the highlights of this research process was when Drew Blaney worked with Karina Peters and Tla'amin students to compose a song to accompany a Tla'amin legendary story that Keith had found buried and unindexed in the Powell River archives, but that otherwise appeared to have dropped from the Tla'amin lexicon.

25. Boas explains that "most of the following legends were told to me by George Chehalis and his wife." Unfortunately we do not know which narratives were shared by George Chehalis, which were shared by his wife, and which were shared by other Stó:lō people whom Boas met while conducting interviews at the hop yards in 1890. In personal letters to his family, Boas complained that, while George Chehalis was a "gem" with nearly unparalleled knowledge of legendary narratives, he was frustrated by Ms. Chehalis's efforts at redirecting conversations to the more recent history of colonialism. Unfortunately, little of her voice has survived in the ethnographic record. Recently Margaret Bruchac has similarly discussed how Boas and his male informants actively diminished the role that Indigenous women played in the ethnologies he and his principally male informants collected. See Margaret Bruchac, *Savage Kin: Indigenous Informants and American Anthropologists* (Tucson: University of Arizona Press, 2018).

26. United Nations Declaration on the Rights of Indigenous, 2007, https://www.un.org/development/desa/indigenouspeoples/declaration-on-the-rights-of-in-digenous-peoples.html.

27. Taiaiake Alfred, "Cultural Strength: Restoring the Place of Indigenous Knowledge in Practice and Policy," *Australian Aboriginal Studies*, no. 1 (2015): 3–11.

28. Linda Tuhiwai Smith, "Culture Matters in the Knowledge Economy," in *Interrogating Development: Insights from the Margins*, ed. Frederique Apffel-Mar-glin, Sanjay Kumar, and Arvind Mishra (New Delhi: Oxford University Press, 2010), 217–33.

29. Alfred, "Cultural Strength."

30. Ibid.

31. Dennis Tedlock, *The Spoken Word and the Work of Interpretation* (Phil-adelphia: University of Pennsylvania Press, 1983); Dell H. Hymes, *Now I Know Only So Far: Essays in Ethnopoetics* (Lincoln: University of Nebraska Press, 2003).

32. Jo-ann Archibald, *Indigenous Storywork: Educating the Heart, Mind, Body, and Spirit* (Vancouver: University of British Columbia Press, 2008), 59–82; "An Indigenous Storywork Methodology," in *Handbook of the Arts in Qualitative Research*, ed. J. Gary Knowles and Ardra L. Cole (Thousand Oaks, CA: Sage, 2008), 371–84.

33. Linda Tuhiwai Smith, *Decolonizing Methodologies: Research and Indig-enous People* (London: Zed Books, 1999). More recently, Smith has continued to engage in conversations over Indigenous research methods in her article "Cul-ture Matters in the Knowledge Economy." See also Margaret Kovach, *Indigenous Methodologies: Characteristics, Conversations, and Contexts* (Toronto: University of Toronto Press, 2009); Wilson, *Research Is Ceremony*; Archibald, "An Indigenous Storywork Methodology"; *Indigenous Storywork*.

34. Patrick Wolfe, *Settler Colonialism and the Transformation of Anthropology: The Politics and Poetics of an Ethnographic Event* (New York: Cassell, 1999). More recently, in *Settler Colonialism*, Lorenzo Varacini has provided settler-colonial studies with a theoretical framework. Lorenzo Varacini, *Settler Colonialism: A Theoretical Overview* (New York: Palgrave Macmillan, 2010). More recently still, Adam Barker has provided an overview of the current state of settler colonialism studies. Adam Barker, "Locating Settler Colonialism," *Journal of Colonialism and Colonial History* 13, no. 3 (2012), https://doi.org/10.1353/cch.2012.0035.

35. Colin Osmond, "The Collaboratorium—University of Saskatchewan Launches Initiative in Community-Engaged History," *Active History*, July 26, 2016, http://activehistory.ca/2016/07/the-collaboratorium-university-of-saskatchewan-launches-initiative-in-community-engaged-history/.

36. To help identify these students, I worked with Karina Peters and Gail Blaney to develop lesson plans that tasked students with reading and transcribing legendary stories. Students were then asked to plot the spatial elements of the story using basic mapping tools. This gave students the opportunity to create

visual representations of the textual elements of the legendary stories, teaching them to think spatially about oral traditions that often only exist in written text, not on the physical landscape. Teaching students that these stories took place in physical places in the Coast Salish world helps them to better appreciate the vast landscapes that their ancestors lived, worked, and traveled upon before the invention of Indian reserves in the colonial period.

37. Similarly, Drew Blaney's passion for and experience in revitalizing Tla'amin language, songs, and dances led him during research on a different part of our research project to analyze a specific set of Tla'amin legendary stories recorded by in the 1970s. Drew's knowledge of ʔayʔaɟuθəm (the Tla'amin's language) enabled him to add these legends to the database but also aided him in other research taking place in the Tla'amin community. Kirsten Paul, the granddaughter of Elsie Paul, the eminent Tla'amin elder and author of *Written as I Remember It: Teachings (ʔəms taʔaw) from the Life of a Sliammon Elder*, was able to use her family knowledge when reviewing Tla'amin legends that both added a layer of complexity to our project and also fed into her high school education and her post–high school plans.

Bibliography

Alfred, Taiaiake. "Cultural Strength: Restoring the Place of Indigenous Knowledge in Practice and Policy." *Australian Aboriginal Studies*, no. 1 (2015): 3–11.

Archibald, Jo-ann. *Indigenous Storywork: Educating the Heart, Mind, Body, and Spirit*. Vancouver: University of British Columbia Press, 2008.

———. "An Indigenous Storywork Methodology." In *Handbook of the Arts in Qualitative Research*, edited by J. Gary Knowles and Ardra L. Cole, 371–84. Thousand Oaks, CA: Sage, 2008.

Barker, Adam. "Locating Settler Colonialism." *Journal of Colonialism and Colonial History* 13, no. 3 (2012). https://doi.org/10.1353/cch.2012.0035.

Bruchac, Margaret. *Savage Kin: Indigenous Informants and American Anthropologists*. Tucson: University of Arizona Press, 2018.

Carlson, Keith Thor. "Familial Cohesion and Colonial Atomization: Governance and Authority in a Coast Salish Community." *Native Studies Review* 19, no. 2 (2010): 1–42.

———. "Innovation, Tradition, Colonialism, and Aboriginal Fishing Conflicts in the Lower Fraser Canyon." In *New Histories for Old: Changing Perspectives on Canada's Native Past*, edited by Ted Binnema and Susan Neylan, 145–74. Vancouver: University of British Columbia Press, 2007.

———. *The Power of Place, the Problem of Time: Aboriginal Identity and Historical Consciousness in the Cauldron of Colonialism*. Toronto: University of Toronto Press, 2010.

Dippie, Brian. *The Vanishing American: White Attitudes and U.S. Indian Policy.* Middletown, CT: Wesleyan University Press, 1985.

Duff, Wilson. *The Upper Stalo Indians of the Fraser Valley, British Columbia.* Victoria: British Columbia Provincial Museum, 1952.

Hymes, Dell H. *Now I Know Only So Far: Essays in Ethnopoetics.* Lincoln: University of Nebraska Press, 2003.

King, Thomas. *The Inconvenient Indian: A Curious Account of Native People in North America.* Minneapolis: University of Minnesota Press, 2018.

Kovach, Margaret. *Indigenous Methodologies: Characteristics, Conversations, and Contexts.* Toronto: University of Toronto Press, 2009.

Mayan, Maria, Sanchia Lo, Merin Oleschuk, Anna Paucholo, and Daley Laing. "Leadership in Community-Based Participatory Research: Individual to Collective." *Engaged Scholar Journal* 2, no. 2 (2016): 11–24.

McHalsie, Albert "Sonny." Prologue to *Towards a New Ethnohistory: Community-Engaged Scholarship among the People of the River*, edited by Keith Thor Carlson, John Sutton Lutz, David M. Schaepe, and Naxaxalhts'i (Albert "Sonny" McHalsie). Winnipeg: University of Manitoba Press, 2018.

Morgensen, Scott L. "Cutting to the Roots of Colonial Masculinity." In *Indigenous Men and Masculinities: Legacies, Identities, Regeneration*, edited by Robert Alexander Innes and Kim Anderson, 38–61. Winnipeg: University of Manitoba Press, 2015.

Osmond, Colin. "The Collaboratorium—University of Saskatchewan Launches Initiative in Community-Engaged History." *Active History*, July 26, 2016. http://activehistory.ca/2016/07/the-collaboratorium-university-of-saskatchewan-launches-initiative-in-community-engaged-history/.

———. "Giant Trees, Iron Men: Masculinity and Colonialism in Coast Salish Loggers' Identity." MA thesis, University of Saskatchewan, 2016.

Rifkin, Mark. *Beyond Settler Time: Temporal Sovereignty and Indigenous Self-Determination.* Durham, NC: Duke University Press, 2017.

Schaepe, David M. "Pre-colonial Sto:lo-Coast Salish Community Organization: An Archaeological Study." PhD diss., University of British Columbia, 2009.

Smith, Linda Tuhhiwai. "Culture Matters in the Knowledge Economy." In *Interrogating Development: Insights from the Margins*, edited by Frederique Apffel-Marglin, Sanjay Kumar, and Arvind Mishra, 217–33. New Delhi: Oxford University Press, 2010.

———. *Decolonizing Methodologies: Research and Indigenous People.* London: Zed Books, 1999.

Sneider, Leah. "Complementary Relationships: A Review of Indigenous Gender Studies," in *Indigenous Men and Masculinities: Legacies, Identities, Regeneration*, edited by Robert Alexander Innes and Kim Anderson, 62–79. Winnipeg: University of Manitoba Press, 2015.

Stó:lō Resource and Research Management Centre. "Cultural Interpretation and Events." Accessed February 7, 2021. http://www.srrmcentre.com/cie.

———. "Rights and Title." Accessed March 18, 2018. http://www.srrmcentre.com/rightstitle.

Suttles, Wayne. *Coast Salish Essays*. Vancouver: Talonbooks, 1987.

Tedlock, Dennis. *The Spoken Word and the Work of Interpretation*. Philadelphia: University of Pennsylvania Press, 1983.

United Nations Declaration on the Rights of Indigenous Peoples, 2007. https://www.un.org/development/desa/indigenouspeoples/declaration-on-the-rights-of-indigenous-peoples.html.

Varacini, Lorenzo. *Settler Colonialism: A Theoretical Overview*. New York: Palgrave Macmillan, 2010.

Wilson, Shawn. *Research Is Ceremony: Indigenous Research Methods*. Black Point, NS: Fernwood, 2008.

Wolfe, Patrick. *Settler Colonialism and the Transformation of Anthropology: The Politics and Poetics of an Ethnographic Event*. New York: Cassell, 1999.

Afterword

Where Do We Go from Here?

JACKI THOMPSON RAND

Recently, I met online with members of a tribal cultural preservation division at their invitation to discuss a project about which I had no prior knowledge. The director inquired if I would share my "guidelines" for community engagement with Indigenous people that they could adopt for their use in the community. Community members had expressed reluctance to share family stories, photographs, and personal experiences, all of which are critical to the success of the project. The director shared that she had hired a trusted community member as an interlocutor for the working group to foster cooperation, but progress was slow. The ironies and implications stacked up in my historian's mind as I formulated the answer to, at first blush, a reasonable question. Although I had numerous suggestions to offer, I had no "guidelines" to share. Like the community engaged work discussed in these pages, my own work is built on relationships, trust, and respect as opposed to an extractive approach in which the studied have no personal stake or voice. As others have said, community priorities, collaboratively defined methods, and goals that serve more than the academic partners' priorities reflect a set of values around knowledge preservation and production that, for now, we discuss as something apart from conventional academic research or as an intervention in positivism.

In a way, this volume represents guidelines for where we as research-ers go from here. If read from cover to cover, researchers, students, and public historians, Native and non-Native alike, imagine ethical guidelines. Their creative approaches to sources, methods, and Indigenous voices advance both academic and Indigenous knowledges. Oral history, archival collections, government documents, material culture, archeological studies, all of which are familiar to most scholars, are found here. Their interventions are not concerned with sources or approaches used in academic work per se. Rather, they seek to illuminate the orientation of the scholar and citizen researcher in community engaged research, work that values multiple priorities, Indigenous knowledge and goals, agreed upon protocols, and stipulated boundaries. CES methodologies require letting go of power that academics have assumed and displayed when conducting research *on* American Indians.

Academic institutions present obstacles to community-engaged research, and they often fail to recognize and compensate researchers for this work. Community-engaged scholars in the humanities, social sciences, and arts are often disadvantaged in numerous ways and will continue to be so without changes to the academic environment. Traditional academics, conventional departments, and those who defend the archaic standards of academic institutions continue to police community-engaged scholars. In addition to the conventional approach to a review of a scholar's work, there are other difficulties—obtaining funding is a challenge, lack of similarly minded colleagues creates isolation, and the pace of our work raises questions. As Benjamin Barnes and Stephen Warren modeled in producing this volume, we will have to do the work ourselves. Scholars and citizen scholars who have spent significant portions of their careers in community-engaged research have shared their experiences and invaluable lessons for others who might undertake this work, rigorously, grounded in ethics, and without investment in academic power as it is conventionally configured. The gathering of this work into one volume is critically important for up-and-coming graduate students and junior faculty who now have numerous authoritative sources they may cite to reinforce their own claims as rigorous scholars in academic environments that would question the legitimacy of their work.

Community-engaged scholarship is driven as much by the needs and agendas of Native nations and communities as by the venerable academic question. One of the most devastating outcomes of colonialism, in the past and ongoing, is the loss of knowledge that occurred as a result of removals, boarding schools, codes of Indian offenses, parceling of land, and Christianization. The US assimilation project was all encompassing. Nevertheless, Native peoples persisted. By the end of the nineteenth century, it became increasingly clear that colonizers had failed to completely destroy the Native population of the United States. US policy-makers crafted legislation, made bureaucratic interventions, and used the courts to rededicate themselves to what historian Patrick Wolfe called the "logic of elimination." Deprivation, disease, US troops, settler violence, and Indian removal had already devastated the Indigenous population by the last quarter of the nineteenth century. These changes ushered in a sea change in federal-American Indian relations.[1]

Natives had been territorially confined according to treaty stipulations. Congregated in isolation, made reliant on government rations, under watch of the US army and the local Indian agent, Native nations and communities were left without recourse when strangers like Richard Pratt arrived and swept their children off to federally supported boarding schools. Many were lost to disease. The US divided Indian-held lands into individual parcels, redefined remaining lands as "surplus," and required the Native nations and their citizens to sell it back to the United States far below market value. Individualized landholding was a disaster and resulted in the loss of millions of acres of land. Meanwhile the Code of Indian Offenses, as written by the Bureau of Indian Affairs, criminalized cultural practices that were then prosecuted in tribal courts whose judges were selected by the bureau. By the end of the nineteenth century, a quarter of a million Native people remained in what is now the US mainland. Those survivors lost many loved ones and community members and much more—knowledges that made their way of life possible. Those losses were devastating to the people who witnessed the last quarter of the nineteenth century.

Readers might ask, "What is left to know after such devastation?" As the work in this volume shows, the Indigenous persisted. Granular analyses of tribal histories, cultures, languages, and practices are the evidence of this persistence. Even in the late nineteenth century, Native women continued to bead using traditional methods and men shifted their energies to the arts. Language found a place to shelter in those activities even as young ones were being carried off to boarding schools. Communities saved seeds, lineages, and stories during the height of the BIA's power over them. Natives used Bible translations to relearn what had been lost. By the 1930s, Native art students at Bacone College, working under the direction of Dick West, were using anthropological notes as part of their training.[2]

Treaties and maps helped to maintain knowledge of Indigenous spaces from which nations had been separated. Museums filled with material culture lost to collectors during the era of assimilation inspired the revival of lost designs and methods, language recovery, and other knowledges. Throughout the twentieth century, Indigenous scholars, activists, artists, and poets pushed aside dominant ideas of vanishing Indians and embraced a fragmented heritage with renewed intentions to preserve, recover, and recreate the ancestors' legacies. It is in that context that the wondrous recovery of the Miami language, discussed here for the first time, occurred, proving that language death can be thwarted. This does not romanticize the struggles of Native peoples, nor does it predict a happy ending. Rather, community-engaged work occurs and becomes meaningful in the context of our ancestors' efforts to survive amid grave hardships.[3]

The work of community-engaged scholarship is about pursuing social justice in a land ravaged by violence over centuries. For Indigenous people, tribal sovereignty and self-determination are at the center of the social justice project. Scholars can play a part in strengthening tribal sovereignty through knowledge recovery and production. We can also do more by building infrastructure within our institutions that rest on recognition of Native nations, tribal sovereignty, and, particularly in the case of land-grant universities, an obligation to repay a debt. Recognition of faculty work in community-engaged scholarship is critical; integrating the values that guide community-engaged scholarship into universities, as well as museums, libraries, and archives, is a social justice imperative. Land acknowledgments are an insufficient stand-in for resources, dedicated space, and lasting relationships with Native nations.

This infrastructural fantasy of mine is not simply to advance the careers of professors, but the education of Indigenous graduate students. Native young people who go off to college frequently imagine themselves turning a degree into a means to help their people. For a long list of reasons, these dreams are frequently thwarted. Work in community-engaged scholarship is a means by which young scholars can build a bridge into the kind of work they can only faintly perceive. In this way, training Indigenous students reinforces tribal sovereignty and self-determination. In the context of this volume, Benjamin Barnes and Stephen Warren's undertaking points us in the direction of another intervention—building capacity within our institutions to dedicate resources to American Indian relations in which the standards of community-engaged research are embedded, which would be welcome in Indian Country.

Where are the guidelines for this structural intervention? Perhaps this is the work that we have to do ourselves, as Ben and Steve did. Their approach involved facilitating conversations, over time, the results of which are in our hands. Those conversations would center on building a case for an Office of Indian Affairs within the university world. We can say with confidence that there is an existing need. We are not the only scholars working on projects involving Native peoples in the US. Such work is not confined to the arts, humanities, and social sciences. Most scholars starting out to work on a project in Indian Country have little to no experience about first steps, what to take into consideration, and how to proceed. They do not understand the history of white scholar expectations of self-governed communities with limited resources in terms of time, funding, energy to be rediscovered by academics. Such an office would be a resource for scholars in any field who, left to their own devices, will not know the burden they pose to an unsuspecting Indigenous government. More than a service provider, the imagined Office of Indian Affairs would help to facilitate conversation, provide institutional access, and work directly with Native nations about how the institution represent their needs and concerns to others within. How can we begin to articulate this vision based on these needs? That requires a conversation.

There are perils to institutionalizing Indigenous-university relations within the corporate structures, values, and practices that have set into the academy—cynicism, exploitation, resistance, and even opportunism and competition among interested parties. I have written about my experiences at the National Museum of the American Indian (NMAI) elsewhere and repeat it here to illustrate the possibilities of creating opportunities for greater access to Native nations and peoples despite the pitfalls. As the sole Indigenous person on the Smithsonian secretary's planning committee at the NMAI, I conceptualized and planned community consultations in Indian Country throughout the United States. I designed these consultations to empower community members, elders, and educators to inform the architectural program of the collection facility at Suitland, Maryland, and for the Mall Museum. Most significantly, those richly collaborative consultations set the direction for creating protocols for the care and management of Indigenous collections as well as the management of community access to collections. As the early consultations coincided with the creation of NAGPRA legislation, they also became a crucial avenue for tribes to weigh in on those talks with Smithsonian management. At the time, community consultations of this kind were almost unheard of in the museum establishment. My intervention succeeded in counteracting the insulated decision-making dynamics that I observed within the NMAI project. Indigenous constituents entered into what had been insider conversations.

The consultations had a flawed premise, which I only came to see in hindsight. Each collaboratively planned and executed meeting aimed to follow the museum director and board of trustees' mandate to facilitate the creation of "a museum different" "by American Indians," not "for American Indians."[4]

In retrospect, the meetings I organized between NMAI planners and Indigenous community attendees followed a deeply flawed model of engagement. The Smithsonian agenda was the first, indeed the only, priority. We approached the attendees as consultants, hence "NMAI community consultations," from whom we sought feedback to the proposed projects—a storage facility in Maryland and a museum on the National Mall. Our question was, "What do you think about what we want to do?" This approach was not new. Other federal representatives had approached Native communities with the same question in other contexts of arguably far more historical significance. One example of this approach is the Indian Reorganization Act, conceptualized by John Collier as a means to reverse allotment, reconsolidate Native lands, and enhance tribal governance through the adoption of constitutions by Native nations that were modeled after the United States. Collier did not invite American Indian leaders to share their priorities, which were significant questions about the impact on historic treaties, for example. His proposal, although presented as beneficial to tribes, was less concerned with their priorities and more with the US vision of tribal government. The only thing that mattered was whether tribes voted up or down on Collier's Indian New Deal. This approach is repeated in the academy. Researchers set out to convince Indigenous community members, and now tribal councils, to participate or sign off on projects that have already left the station.[5]

NMAI conversations with American Indian community members represented an opportunity for Smithsonian planners to gain insights about how they perceived the museum, how they envisioned the museum, how the museum might care for ill-gotten collections. The essential aim was to achieve a legitimate standard of authenticity. Native citizens' first priority—tribal sovereignty and self-determination—had no place on the agenda, even though at that moment it was uppermost in their minds. Consultations in 1989 and 1990 quickly bogged down as Native leaders seized the agenda and turned the conversation to the long-standing, painful issues of cultural patrimony and repatriation. As a result, we made little progress toward planning for the collections facility during the first year. Rather, Native invitees used the two-day meetings to address Smithsonian representatives about human remains, funerary objects, and sacred objects held in the institution's collections and to make clear their demands for repatriation of the materials to the tribes. Account after account spilled forth about the atrocities committed against Indigenous gravesites, thefts of material culture, and Smithsonian refusals to answer the questions of tribal governments about remains and objects held in the collections. Caught off guard, the Smithsonian representatives faced unexpected pressure to respond effectively to these queries and concerns. Simultaneously, the language for the future Native American Graves Protection and Repatriation Act (NAGPRA) was being hammered out on Capitol Hill. It was not until NAGPRA was passed in November 1990, a year and a half after the first gathering, that the consultations turned to the Smithsonian planners' museum-centered agenda.

In hindsight, I interpret the substance of those early meetings as acts of Indigenous resistance to a presumptuous consultation process that centered on the planners' priorities over that of the "consultants." Smithsonian planners, including myself, mistakenly ignored the elephant in the room—the fate of human remains and culturally significant items taken from them in the traumatizing chaos of colonialism—to chat about how to construct an "authentic" American Indian museum on the National Mall. In comparison to the return of human remains, the museum was of less concern to the Native peoples, who well understood how the remains came to lie in the capital city. During the nineteenth century, US soldiers removed American Indian cadavers from battlefields and transported them to Washington, DC, where they were stored at the US Army Medical Corps Museum before they were moved to the Smithsonian after the turn of the century. Numbering in the thousands, identified and unidentified human remains were stored in boxes in the museum's collections. Self-made Smithsonian archeologists dug through tribal cemeteries and carted away the remains of community members. Historically, the Smithsonian ignored or denied tribal petitions to obtain the remains for ceremonial internment. For decades, officials denied communities' requests for the return of human remains on the basis of a scientific research imperative embedded in the mission to support "the increase and diffusion of knowledge." In looking back, I can see that the significance of the Native attendees' disregard for the agenda in terms of the politics of repatriation was something more complex than "radically cool" Native noncompliance, as I thought at the time. The premise of the meetings was based in the uncritical goal to extract useful information and opinion to create the Museum Different. In the end, Native participants flipped the script and focused the meetings on their own priorities, fully displaying their desire for justice and tribal sovereignty.[6]

Like the repatriation-related debates of the 1980s and 1990s, the current debate about the place of community-engaged scholarship in academia features dynamics of power and distrust. Non-Native doubters worry about diminished academic standards and the comparability of CES to "serious scholarship." They worry that practitioners of community-engaged scholarship will abandon methodological conventions, analytical frameworks, and reverence for archival sources. Archaeologists, both in the academy and in museums, have expressed their fear of "giving back" human remains, sacred and funerary objects, and cultural patrimony. Natives could not be trusted with items outside of museum and university collection walls. But, thirty years after the passage of the NAGPRA, it is clear that persistent non-Native concerns about Native nations' and their ability to safeguard archival materials, human remains, and associated funerary objects were unfounded.

Community-engaged scholarship, ideally, is based on trust and respect, collaboration, cooperation, and shared goals. In doing so, community-engaged work does not reproduce the academic canon and its conventions. Community-engaged scholarship is rigorous, disciplined, and research-based. Its practitioners institute change that matters to Indigenous peoples, and sometimes integrate themselves into academia. In contrast to symbolic land acknowledgments, for example, community-engaged scholars challenge the academy to work with American Indian communities as equal partners, to respect Indigenous governments as sovereign, to acknowledge Indigenous ways of thinking, and to cease the erasure of the Indigenous presence in the land on which they stand. In the years ahead, as community-engaged methodologies take hold, the guidelines for this quietly radical project will have to be worked out.

Notes

1. Patrick Wolfe, "Settler Colonialism and the Elimination of the Native," *Journal of Genocide Research* 8, no. 4 (2006): 387–409; Robert N. Clinton, "Redress-

ing the Legacy of Conquest: A Vision Quest for a Decolonized Federal Indian Law," *Arkansas Law Review* 46 (1993): 77–159.

2. Lisa K. Neuman, "Painting Culture: Art and Ethnography at a School for Native Americans," *Ethnology* 45, no. 3 (2006): 173–192.

3. The term "language death" is not one that the Miami people and the Myaamia Center choose to use, but rather they refer to this the state of extreme morbidity of Indigenous languages as being dormant, or even as of the language sleeping.

4. Edward Rothstein, "Museum With an American Indian Voice," *New York Times*, September 21, 2004.

5. Floyd A. O'Neil, "The Indian New Deal: An Overview," in *Indian Self Rule: First-Hand Accounts of Indian-White Relations from Roosevelt to Reagan*, ed. Kenneth R. Philp (Logan: Utah State University Press, 1995).

6. Andrew Gulliford, "Bones of Contention: The Repatriation of Native American Human Remains," *Public Historian* 18, no. 4 (1996): 119–43; Devon A. Mihesuah, introduction" to special issue "Repatriation: and Interdisciplinary Dialogue," *American Indian Quarterly* 20, no. 2 (1996): 153–64.

Bibliography

Clinton, Robert N. "Redressing the Legacy of Conquest: A Vision Quest for a Decolonized Federal Indian Law." *Arkansas Law Review* 46 (1993): 77–159.

Gulliford, Andrew. "Bones of Contention: The Repatriation of Native American Human Remains." *Public Historian* 18, no. 4 (1996): 119–43.

Mihesuah, Devon A. Introduction to special issue "Repatriation: An Interdisciplinary Dialogue." *American Indian Quarterly*, 20, no. 2 (1996): 153–64.

Neuman, Lisa K. "Painting Culture: Art and Ethnography at a School for Native Americans." *Ethnology* 45, no. 3 (2006): 173–92.

O'Neil, Floyd A. "The Indian New Deal: an Overview." In *Indian Self Rule: First-Hand Accounts of Indian-White Relations from Roosevelt to Reagan*, edited by Kenneth R. Philp. Logan: Utah State University Press, 1995.

Rothstein, Edward. "Museum With an American Indian Voice." *New York Times*, September 21, 2004.

Wolfe, Patrick. "Settler Colonialism and the Elimination of the Native." *Journal of Genocide Research* 8, no. 4 (2006): 387–409.

Contributors

Daryl Baldwin (Miami Tribe of Oklahoma) is acting director of the Cultural Ecology Office and executive director at the Myaamia Center, Miami University, Oxford, Ohio.

Benjamin J. Barnes is chief of the Shawnee Tribe.

John. P. Bowes is a professor in the Department of History, Philosophy, and Religious Studies and interim dean of the College of Letters, Arts, and Social Sciences, Eastern Kentucky University, Richmond.

Bobbe Burke is Miami Tribe relations coordinator emerita at the Myaamia Center, Miami University, Oxford, Ohio.

Keith Thor Carlson is a professor in the Department of History and Tier One Canada Research Chair in Indigenous and Community-Engaged History at the University of the Fraser Valley, Burnaby, British Columbia.

Marti Chaatsmith (Comanche and Choctaw) is associate director of the Newark Earthworks Center, Newark, Ohio.

Sandra L. Garner is the inaugural Chief Floyd Leonard Faculty Fellow at the Myaamia Center, Miami University, Oxford, Ohio.

Brian Hosmer is a professor and department head in the Department of History, Oklahoma State University, Stillwater.

George Ironstrack (Miami Tribe of Oklahoma) is director of the Education Office and assistant director at the Myaamia Center, Miami University, Oxford, Ohio.

Christine Ballengee Morris is a professor in the Department of Arts Administration, Education, and Policy, Ohio State University, Columbus, Ohio.

G. Susan Mosley-Howard is professor and dean emerita at Miami University, Oxford, Ohio.

Naxaxalhts'i (Albert "Sonny" McHalsie) (Stó:lō) is a cultural advisor/historian at the Stó:lō Research and Resource Management Centre, Chilliwack, British Columbia, and has received an honorary LLD from the University of Victoria, Victoria, British Columbia.

Colin Osmond is a Social Sciences and Humanities Research Council postdoctoral fellow at Mount Saint Vincent University, Halifax, Nova Scotia.

Jacki Thompson Rand (Choctaw) is an associate professor in American Indian Studies in the College of Liberal Arts and Sciences, and associate vice-chancellor for Native affairs at the University of Illinois Urbana-Champaign.

Tsandlia Van Ry (Stó:lō) is an undergraduate student at University of the Fraser Valley, Burnaby, British Columbia.

Jessie Ryker-Crawford (White Earth Anishinaabe) is an associate professor in Museum Studies, Institute of American Indian Arts, Santa Fe, New Mexico.

Haley Shea (Miami Tribe of Oklahoma) is a research associate at the Myaamia Center and a visiting assistant professor in the Department of Educational Psychology, Miami University, Oxford, Ohio.

Cameron Shriver is a research associate at the Myaamia Center and a visiting assistant professor in the Department of History, Miami University, Oxford, Ohio.

April K. Sievert is director of the Glenn A. Black Laboratory of Archaeology and a senior lecturer in the Department of Anthropology, Indiana University, Bloomington.

Glenna J. Wallace is chief of the Eastern Shawnee Tribe of Oklahoma.

Stephen Warren is chair of the Department of American Studies and program coordinator for Native American and Indigenous Studies at the University of Iowa, Iowa City.

Buck Woodard is a professorial lecturer in the Department of Anthropology, American University, Washington, DC.

Index

Note: Pages in *italics* refer to illustrative matter.

CPSIA information can be obtained
at www.ICGtesting.com
Printed in the USA
BVHW081857090223
658229BV00003B/42

9 781438 489940